Contents

Body Shame

Physical appearance plays a powerful role in social relationships. Those who feel shame regarding the way they look, and who think others view their appearance negatively, can therefore be vulnerable to impoverished social relationships and a range of psychological difficulties. However, there are few books which look specifically at the many permutations of body shame and their differing treatments.

In this book, researchers and therapists from a wide range of different disciplines explore the role of shame in various physical and psychological disorders, and provide practical advice on management and treatment. Chapters are organised to address issues of conceptualisation, assessment and treatment, on topics such as:

- Definitional controversies
- Biopsychosocial and evolutionary origins of body shame
- Effects on adjustments of maturation and ageing process
- Specific forms of disfigurement
- The role of body shame in depression, eating disorders and body dysmorphic disorder.

Body Shame gives the reader insight into the nature and mechanisms of shame, how it can focus on the body, how it can underlie a variety of psychological difficulties, and how to intervene to help resolve it. This book will be invaluable for practitioners from different disciplines working with people who have problems centred on their physical appearance and/or functions, and clinicians working with various mental health problems.

Paul Gilbert is Professor of Clinical Psychology at the Mental Health Research Unit at Kingsway Hospital, University of Derby and Derbyshire Mental Health Services Trust. He is author of *Depression, The Evolution of Powerlessness*, Psychology Press, 1992 and the co-editor of *Genes on the Couch*, Brunner-Routledge, 2000.

Jeremy Miles is Lecturer in Biostatistics at the Department of Health Sciences, University of York.

Body Shame

Conceptualisation, Research and Treatment

Edited by Paul Gilbert and Jeremy Miles

 **Brunner-Routledge**
Taylor & Francis Group

HOVE AND NEW YORK

First published 2002 by Brunner-Routledge
27 Church Road, Hove, East Sussex BN3 2FA

Simultaneously published in the USA and Canada
by Brunner-Routledge
29 West 35th Street, New York, NY 10001

Brunner-Routledge is an imprint of the Taylor & Francis Group

Typeset in Times by RefineCatch Limited, Bungay, Suffolk
Printed and bound in Great Britain by
TJ International Ltd, Padstow, Cornwall

British Library Cataloguing in Publication Data
A catalogue record for this book is available from the British Library

Library of Congress Cataloging-in-Publication Data
Body shame : conceptualisation, research, and treatment / edited by
Paul Gilbert and Jeremy Miles.
    p. cm.
    ISBN 1-58391-165-0 (hbk)—ISBN 1-58391-166-9 (pbk.)
      1. Body image disturbance. 2. Shame. I. Gilbert, Paul,
    1942– . II. Miles, Jeremy, 1968–
   RC569.5.B65 B63 2002
   616.85′2—dc21   2002071246

ISBN 1-58391-165-0 (hbk)
ISBN 1-58391-166-9 (pbk)

Contributors

Bernice Andrews is a Reader in Psychology at Royal Holloway University of London. Over the past 10 years she has researched and published extensively on issues of shame in general and body shame in particular.

Anthony Carr is currently Head of Clinical Psychology at the University of Plymouth. He has maintained a clinical role in terminal care and cancer care for many years and his interest in body image arose from the problems faced by many cancer patients, where the illness and/or its treatment had profoundly affected their appearance. Altered appearance presents yet another difficulty with which many patients have to cope and Tony's work with the plastic surgeons in Plymouth is aimed at improving these patients' quality of life.

Alex Clarke is a Consultant Psychologist in plastic and reconstructive surgery at the Royal Free Hospital, London. She has acted as a consultant to the organisation 'Changing Faces' and has a particular interest in the psychological aspects of reconstructive surgery.

Geraldine Coughlan is a Chartered Clinical Psychologist interested in psychological management of long-term medical conditions. She is currently working in pain management at the National Hospital for Neurology and Neurosurgery, London.

W. Ray Crozier, PhD, is Reader in Psychology in the School of Social Sciences, Cardiff University. His research interests are in shyness, including its relationship to shame and embarrassment, and blushing, particularly its role in social interactions.

Ann-Sophie Ekströmer is an Art Therapist and Cognitive Psychotherapist working at the Astrid Lindgren's Children's Hospital, Stockholm, Sweden. She works with children with different somatic diseases and teaches in art therapy education. She is also a ceramist.

Paul Gilbert is Professor of Psychology at the University of Derby and Director of the Mental Health Research Unit, Kingsway Hospital. He has a long interest in working with mood disorders and shame and has recently been developing the compassionate mind cognitive based intervention for shame-related disorders.

Stefanie C. Gilbert, PhD, is Assistant Professor of Psychology at Howard University in Washington, DC and a licensed Clinical Psychologist in Maryland. She is President of the Washington Society for the Study of Eating Disorders and Obesity and a member of the Governance Board for the Graduate Certificate Program in Women's Studies at Howard University.

Merryn Gott is a Lecturer in Social Gerontology working at the Sheffield Institute for Studies on Ageing, University of Sheffield. Her principle research interests include sexuality, sexual health and ageing, and 'end of life' care for older people.

Stephen Kellett is both an Occupational Psychologist and Clinical Psychologist working with people with chronic and enduring mental health problems in Barnsley CPS NHS Trust. His main psychodermatological research interest at present is the anti-acne drug Roaccutane and its effect on mental and physical health.

Gerry Kent is a Clinical Psychologist working in the Department of Psychology, University of Sheffield. His research interests involve a variety of topics within health psychology, but particularly psychological aspects of disfigurement.

Gabrielle Lodnert is a Clinical Psychologist at the Centre of Cognitive and Sex Psychotherapy, Stockholm, Sweden. She works with different types of sexual disorders, mostly in couple therapies. She is currently writing a project on 'Psychological Reactions to Prostate Cancer – with Special Consideration to Sexual Functioning'.

Kevin J. McKee is a Chartered Psychologist and is Lecturer in Social Gerontology in the Sheffield Institute for Studies on Ageing. He has developed a programme of research on the well-being of frail older people, supported by grants from the UK Economic and Social Research Council, the Engineering and Physical Sciences Research Council, and the NHS R&D Policy Research Programme. He has authored over 40 publications and is Editor of the *Social Psychological Review*.

Jeremy Miles, PhD, is a Lecturer in the Department of Health Sciences at the University of York. He conducts research on the psychological impact of chronic disease, and has a particular interest in methodological issues relating to this area.

Andrew R. Thompson is a Clinical Psychologist in the NHS in Barnsley, Yorkshire, UK, and a Clinical Lecturer in the Clinical Psychology Unit,

University of Sheffield, UK. He specialises in the treatment of adult mental health problems and has various research interests within this field.

J. Kevin Thompson, PhD, is a Professor of Psychology at the University of South Florida in Tampa, Florida. His research interests are body image disturbances and eating disorders. He has edited, authored or co-authored four books on these topics.

David Veale is an Honorary Senior Lecturer in Psychiatry at the Royal Free Hospital and University College Medical School, London and a Consultant Psychiatrist at the Priory Hospital North London. His special interest is in cognitive behaviour therapy for obsessive compulsive and body dysmorphic disorders.

Acknowledgements

Ideas often grow from conversations. We are indebted to Dr James MacDonald who set up the first national Shame Interest Group in the UK. This group was designed to create opportunities for informal presentations and discussion on shame, and stimulated many of us. James ran it from Warwick University before it moved to Derby in 1998. This group now meets once or twice a year and many have contributed to our ideas for this book. We are very grateful to them.

One of us (J.M.) would also like to thank Dr Patrick McGhee, of the University of Central Lancashire, for introducing me to the area of psoriasis research, and the Psoriasis Association of Great Britain, which funded my initial research into the area. Also special thanks to my wife, Susanne Hempel, who continues, against her better judgement, to support me in this and other endeavours.

P.G. would like to especially thank Dr B. Andrews, Dr D. Lee, Dr S. Kellett, Dr A. Thompson and Dr K. Goss for their support and sharing of various ideas. Also apologies to Jean for the early morning absences, and thanks for the TLC that heals all shame.

Preface

The last ten years have seen a rapid growth of interest in the concept of shame. It has become a rich area for research into self-conscious emotion, has stimulated explorations into early development, the dynamics of social relationships, and its role in psychopathology. Although our bodies can be a focus of shame, the shame literature itself has not focused specifically on the issue of bodily appearance and function. Rather, shame is often seen as a generalised negative affect and judgement about a global sense of self. However, shame can be focused on specific abilities, appearance and functions and hence it seemed to us that focusing on a targeted aspect of shame, that is shame of one's body, could be of value to both clinicians and researchers. Indeed, this book grew out of a discussion between Paul Gilbert, whose focus has been primarily on shame and its relationship to mood disorders, and Jeremy Miles, who has focused on body image disorders, especially those with psoriasis. Through our discussions we realised that the 'body image disorder' and 'shame' literature were two fairly separate literatures, so we thought it would be very useful to explore to see if they could be linked and concepts from one could cross-fertilise concepts in the other.

We are delighted to say that the authors to this volume have addressed this aim admirably. Here then are a number of chapters seeking to weave together our understanding about the development of body and body schema in relationship to shame.

The book is organised into three parts. Part I, Chapters 1–5, contains the following. The opening chapter offers a wide-ranging overview of the concepts of shame and how shame needs to be contextualised within a biopsychosocial model. What is shaming depends partly on social contexts and cultural rules but there are also evolutionary algorithms underpinning the acceptable from the less acceptable. The chapter also explores themes of body shame's relationship to psychopathology and interventions. In Chapter 2 Stephanie Gilbert and Kevin Thompson explore how the experiences of our bodies changing, as we grow and become sexually active, affect our sense of self. They explore in detail how concepts of body shame can be used to understand certain aspects of vulnerability to disorders and in particular eating disorders. In Chapter 3 Kevin McKee and Merryn Gott explore the other end of the age spectrum, that is how ageing individuals can develop a sense of shame about the failings and disabilities of their bodies. Shame in relationship to the changing functions and abilities associated with ageing is a very neglected area and these authors offer fascinating insights. In Chapter 4 Anthony Carr explores the issues of measurement in body shame by drawing on the more developed psychometric area of body image disturbance. He notes the distinctions between body shame and body image disturbance, but also how body image disturbance has been linked with a number of disorders, such as body dysmorphic disorder. He offers interesting insights into the different areas of research and measurement techniques in body image disturbance and shame and how cross-fertilisation may enrich both. In Chapter 5 Gerry Kent and Andrew Thompson offer an important overview about the role of shame in disfigurement. Disfigurement would seem to be a core theme for body shame, and their explorations for treatment and intervention will be very valuable to clinicians.

Part II is called 'Body shame and disfigurement'. This section has chapters focusing on specific kinds of appearance and functional related disorders. In Chapter 6 Jeremy Miles explores the relationship of shame to psoriasis. He pays particular attention to the linkage between stress, shame and psoriasis. In Chapter 7 Stephen Kellett explores acne. This is a stressful condition that usually has an early onset in adolescence, and can have a significant impact on adolescent psychosocial development. Early identification of those who will have serious psychological difficulties as a result of acne and appropriate help are therefore called for. In Chapter 8 Geraldine Coughlan and Alex Clarke explore that shame can be associated with burn disfigurements. Burns are clearly an acquired disfigurement, e.g., as a result of accidents. They also explore the important work of societies such as Changing Faces, which helps people adjust to these disfigurements. In Chapter 9 Ann-Sophie Ekströmer explores the experience of children who have bowel disorders. These children can become very sensitive to rejection and develop all kinds of coping behaviours for this disorder. Finally, Gabrielle Lodnert explores how men with prostate cancer, particularly those who lose their sexual ability, can have a heightened sense of shame. This can have a major effect on the intimacy of their relationships, especially if associated with intimacy withdrawal.

Part III, called 'Body shame and psychological disorders', looks at how body shame can be involved in more generalised disorders. In Chapter 11 Ray Crozier explores the relationship between blushing, shame and social anxiety. He makes clear the distinctions between shame and embarrassment and explores the way in which blushing can give different signals to an audience. In Chapter 12 Kenneth Goss and Paul Gilbert explore body shame in relationship to eating disorders. They provide both a functional analysis and evolutionary model for eating disorders and look at the way in which some aspects of eating disorders, such as food restraint, can be seen as a pride compensation for shame. In Chapter 13 Bernice Andrews explores the important work that she and others have done on the experience of shame of one's body following on from sexual abuse in childhood. She shows how the early onset of body shame, related to abuse, is associated with chronic depression in women. She also shows how it is possible to have an intense sense of shame about one's body, not as a result of a disfigurement, but as a result of how others have treated it. In Chapter 14 David Veale explores shame in relationship to body dysmorphic disorders. Mild forms of these difficulties are common in many forms of body shame in so far as they involve checking and careful camouflage. Severe forms are far less common but are extremely disabling and in the extreme can be associated with suicide. He explores the growing awareness of this complex problem and the development of interventions.

Many authors note some kind of distinction between concern or fear of what others think abut the self (external shame) and what one thinks and feels about one's self (internal shame). There is also some consensus that the degree of disfigurement or disability is often a poor indicator of psychological adjustment and shame. Much depends on the personal meanings people give their difficulties. Hence, the psychological dimension of many of the disorders discussed here are central to adjustment and quality of life. We hope that in the long term increasing awareness of body shame issues will be reflected in appropriate psychological services. So we hope that this selection of chapters and themes will stimulate interest in body shame both as a phenomena in itself and also its relationship to other psychopathologies and therapy.

Paul Gilbert and Jeremy Miles
November 2001

Part I

Introduction

Chapter 1

Body shame

A biopsychosocial conceptualisation and overview, with treatment implications

Paul Gilbert

Introduction

Shame has recently received increasing theory and research attention, as both a personal experience (to feel ashamed: Tangney & Fischer, 1995; Gilbert & Andrews, 1998) and an interpersonal process, via acts of stigmatising and shaming (Crisp, 2001; Jacoby, 1994). The experience of shame can be focused on many characteristics of the self, such as feeling ashamed of emotions (e.g., one's anxiety, anger or sexual feelings); behaviours (e.g., things one has done in the past); perceived personality traits (e.g., laziness or carelessness) or even states of mind (e.g., mental illness). When people experience their physical bodies as in some way unattractive, undesirable and a source of a 'shamed self' they are at risk of psychological distress and disorders (Thompson & Kent, 2001). Such experiences are sometimes referred to as body image disturbances (e.g., Carr, Chapter 4, this volume; Cash & Grant, 1996). However, the concept of 'body shame' directs attention to negative experiences of both appearance and *functions* of the body, which can involve various sensory modalities (e.g., smell, and touch as well as vision or image, Ekströmer, Chapter 9, this volume). Moreover, by focusing on shame we can distinguish stigma, internal and external shame, and humiliation, and consider body shame in the context of developing self-awareness competencies that unfold in social and cultural contexts. Hence, this book brings together authors from different backgrounds to address the nature of 'body shame', and its relationship to psychopathology and treatment. As 'body shame' is a relatively new concept that can link different literatures, the opening sections of this chapter offer an overview of current approaches to shame. We note the complexity of our self-conscious emotions and their relationship to primary emotions. An evolutionary and biopsychosocial framework is outlined that offers the possibility of integrating physiological, psychological and socio-cultural processes and interactions. In the latter sections the relationship of shame to psychopathology is explored with a consideration of some key elements in psychological interventions.

The nature of shame

Emotions such as rage/anger, fear/anxiety, sadness/despair and joy/happiness are often considered as primary or basic emotions (Panskepp, 1998) and are the main components of our negative and positive affect systems (Clark, 2000). We share these emotions with many other animals, they can be elicited by simple threats and losses, and we know something of their evolutionary history (Nesse, 1998) and neurophysiology (Panskepp, 1998). Emotions such as shame, embarrassment, pride and guilt are sometimes referred to as secondary, higher-order or self-conscious emotions (Lewis, 1995; Tangney, 1995). These emotions are less shared (if at all) with other animals, are relatively new on the evolutionary stage and we know much less about their neurophysiology (although see Schore, 2001). Self-conscious emotions develop later than primary emotions and are dependent on various, unfolding competencies (Lewis, 1992; Tangney & Fischer, 1995; Zahn-Waxler, 2000). These competencies begin to unfold from around two years of age and include: an ability to recognise self as an object for others, theory of mind (able to make judgements about what others are thinking), awareness of the contingencies for approval and disapproval, and competencies for role-taking and understanding social rules. It is these self-conscious competencies that blend with primary emotions that give rise to self-conscious emotions of shame, pride and guilt. Thus, a threat to the self as a social agent (e.g., shame) can recruit negative primary emotions (e.g., anxiety, anger, disgust) and reduce positive emotions in various ways. Hence, as we will note below, some people will respond to a threat to the self (e.g., criticism or rejection) with anger while others will show more anxiety and submissive behaviour. In other words, self-conscious emotions operate through, and are shaped by, our competencies for a sense/construction of self as a social agent.

There are, in fact, a number of different conceptualisations and debates on what actually constitutes a shame experience. For example, there is debate on whether shame can occur in babies, before the development of self-conscious competencies (Barrett, 1995; Gilbert, 1998a). Tangney (1995) argued that shame experiences are primarily ones of 'emotion', and although there are events that are more likely to elicit shame than others Tangney makes clear that shame comes from the self-relevant meanings given to the event rather than the type of event; a principle central to cognitive formulations of emotion.

The way self-conscious emotions, such as shame, blend primary emotions is complex and still not well understood. For example, shame commonly involves anxiety but is also different from it. For example, one patient related an incident where she had felt intense shame; her boyfriend telling her he had found out that she had had an abortion some years before, and was now unsure if he wanted to continue the relationship with 'a person who could do that kind of thing'. She said, 'I just felt this panic, and inner sense of deflation like something was going out of me. Everything in me just stopped and I couldn't say anything. I wanted to die then – just not be there. I never want to feel like that again . . . This [her abortion] is going to haunt me for the rest of my life.' Later, she acknowledged another set of thoughts and feelings about her boyfriend and disappointment in him; that he could not be more under-standing and accepting – if he really loved her.

In some cultures (e.g., Japan) social anxiety and shame have always been closely linked (Takahashi, 1989). However, although Gilbert, Pehl and Allan, (1994) and Gilbert (1998a) argued that there is a huge overlap between the processes involved in shame and social anxiety, these two literatures have largely ignored each other, despite evidence for their current measures being very highly correlated (Gilbert, Pehl & Allan, 1994; Gilbert, 2000a). Using the aforementioned example we can also note the sense of dejection or defla-tion that people experiencing shame can speak of. Indeed, some believe that a sudden decrement in positive affect is central to shame (e.g., Nathanson, 1994).

Hence, one way to see shame is as a multifaceted experience that has various aspects and components. These include:

1. *A social or external cognitive component*: Shame affects are often elicited in social contexts and are associated with automatic thoughts that others see the self as inferior, bad, inadequate and flawed; that is, others are looking down on the self with a condemning or contemptuous view. This is linked to stigma consciousness and is explored in more detail below.
2. *An internal self-evaluative component*: For many theorists shame involves a global negative self-evaluation as bad, inadequate and flawed (Fischer & Tangney, 1995). Shame is thus commonly associated with negative automatic thoughts about the self. Indeed, many self-critical and self-attacking thoughts (e.g., I am useless, worthless, ugly, no good, a bad person, a failure) are in essence self-devaluations and internally shaming thoughts. This will be explored in more detail below.
3. *An emotional component*: The emotions and feelings recruited in shame are various but include anxiety, anger and disgust in the self and self-contempt. Some people talk of a type of inner deflation (as the lady above did) or dejection, although there is little research on this aspect. Tomkins (1981, 1987), Kaufman (1989) and Nathanson (1994) argued that shame is an affect associated with the interruption and sudden loss of positive affect. Although positive affect is inhibited or reduced in shame (Tangney, 1995), it is unclear if this can be seen as the basis of shame since most other negative affects (e.g., anxiety and sadness) also involve changes in positive affect (Gilbert, 1998a). Shame affect is often seen as the opposite of pride (Mascolo & Fischer, 1995); that is, shame is related to diminishment and loss, but has also been linked to dignity (Gilbert, 1998a) and in anthropological writings, to (dis)honour

(Lindisfarne, 1998). Kaufman (1989) and Nathanson (1994) both develop Tomkins' idea that shame often binds (or fuses with) other primary emotions such as anxiety, anger or disgust, giving different textures to how shame is experienced.

4. *A behavioural component*: Shame is often associated with specific defensive behaviours such as a strong urge to 'not be seen,' avoid exposure, to hide, and/or run away (Lewis, 1992; Tangney, 1995). Eye gaze is commonly averted and the individual may feel behaviourally inhibited. These responses have been linked to a rapid onset of submissive defensive behaviours (Gilbert & McGuire, 1998; Keltner & Harker, 1998). However, when anger is the emotion elicited in shaming encounters, the desire to retaliate or gain revenge against the one who is 'exposing' the self (as inferior, weak or bad) can be high, although may be inhibited or expressed (Retzinger, 1991). When there is a focus on the 'other as bad' for the shaming this has been referred to as humiliation. Again, we explore this in more detail below.

5. *A physiological component*: Shame is clearly related to a stress response although the exact nature of it is unclear. In some cases it may involve heightened parasympathetic activity (see Schore, 1994, 1998). As noted above, although we know something of the neurophysiology of primary emotions, such as anger, anxiety and disgust (Panskepp, 1998), we know much less about the neurophysiology of shame.

So, shame is a complex set of feelings, cognitions and actions, tendencies whose exact complexion can vary from person to person. It is an experience that is self-focused however, dependent on the competencies to construct self as a social agent and thus is called a self-conscious emotion (Fischer & Tangney, 1995). Like other emotions (e.g., anxiety, anger or disgust) there may be fast, affect-based, limbic-centred processing systems that point to a complexity of the cognition–emotion interaction (Panskepp, 1998). Also, like other emotions, while some people seem able to tolerate shame feelings (at least to some degree) without acting out defensive behaviours (e.g., hiding or concealing), others find them intolerable and will go to great lengths to avoid both the situations eliciting them and the feelings themselves.

Competing to be attractive

One way of helping to explore the complexity of shame and highlight the reasons why shame should not be reduced to (say) social anxiety, even when it is one of its more common components, is to suggest that negative emotions are often reactions to threats. Different threats are associated with different emotions, for example, jealousy, sadness, anger and anxiety (Nesse, 1998). This leads to the question of what are the threats that our capacity for shame evolved to cope with? Scheff and Retzinger (see Retzinger 1991, 1998) have argued that shame is related to threats and disruptions to social bonds. Framed in a slightly different way, Gilbert (1997, 1998a) suggested that shame is an affective-defensive response to the threat of, or actual experience of, social rejection or devaluation (loss of status) because one is (or has become) *unattractive* as a social agent.

Conceptualised this way turns a spotlight on to questions of why humans are so sensitive to how 'attractive' (and not just physically) they are to others. This, in turn, is linked to questions of the distal processes that may have led to the evolution of self-conscious competencies (e.g., theory of mind). Part of the answer may be related to the evolution of behavioural strategies that function to enable animals to develop social roles and interactional patterns for example, to form sexual and alliance relationships (Gilbert & McGuire, 1998). For example, for many species, from fish to humans, a central social strategy (serving reproductive fitness) is to attract others (via various displays and signals) and engage them in certain types of roles and relationships. For sexual behaviour one can think of the various colourings, plumages, size and scent displays that are used to attract mates. For millions of years the power of attraction as a social strategy has shaped the evolution of minds and brains. Indeed, for millions of years humans have competed to be seen as attractive to others because those who were so regarded had better access to social resources (support from others, allies and sexual partners) that enhanced their fitness. Those regarded as unattractive and rejected, ostracised or 'demoted' will have suffered in the competition for such resources. Consequently, over millions of years various mental mechanisms may have evolved to track and attend to such threats and respond to them with various defensive behaviours (Gilbert, 1997, 2001a). As relationships became more central to a range of inclusive fitness outcomes, it can be suggested that one of the evolutionary pressures that gave rise to our various competencies that unfold from two years onwards (such as our ability to recognise self as an object for others, theory of mind, awareness of the contingencies for approval and disapproval, and competencies for role-taking and understanding social rules) was the importance of eliciting (manipulating) positive responses (care, support and acceptance) from others.

There is little doubt that from the cradle to the grave humans are highly dependent on the help and support they receive from others. Indeed, in many types of relationships (e.g., between infants and parents, friends and lovers), signals of acceptance and being valued are physiologically regulating and impact on stress hormones and various neurotransmitters that are linked to positive affect (Cacioppo et al., 2000; Schore, 1994, 2001). In order to participate and engage others in mutually beneficial social roles one must be included and valued (Baumeister & Leary, 1995). However, as Tooby and Cosmides (1996) suggest, engaging successfully in many forms of social relationship, such as eliciting parental investment, developing supportive peer relationships, and attracting desirable mates, there is an underlying competition. This is because investing in relationships is not cost free. Hence, people will invest their time and energy in those with whom they can form beneficial relationships; relationships that are in some way useful to their own interests, whereas associating with those who are seen as unattractive in some way can be detrimental to self-interests. Clearly, in general then, we want to be someone others will invest in rather than reject.

However, there are both cultural and evolutionary reasons to make selections between people and reject some in favour of others. For example, Kurzban and Leary (2001) suggest that stigmatisation and ostracism are part of the process by which individuals decide whom to associate and cooperate with and whom to exclude, reject and avoid. Moreover, the domains over which exclusion are most powerful represented those that are evolutionary meaningful. Hence, stigmatisation is closely linked to signals of disease and physical deformity to avoid contamination, and poor (in group) cooperators and out-group members.

Social attractiveness

Concerns with body image, passing exams, sporting ability, demonstrating our wit or intelligence are all examples where we recognise that our *acceptability*, *rank and status* among our peers and group, and to potential sexual partners (our worth to them) depends on being recognised as having some value and we are approved of, desired and chosen by them. We are impression managers (Leary, 1995) and impression management strategies offer potentially fascinating insights into shame and shame avoidance. Importantly, however, as Leary (1995) makes clear, impression management can follow two different strategies; damage limitation or status and reputation enhancement. As noted below, damage limitation strategies in social presentation have much overlap with shame-avoidant strategies.

On the whole, humans often try to create advantageous roles *by trying to stimulate positive feelings* in the minds of others about the self (e.g., to be approved of and chosen); we want potential lovers to have desirous feelings for us, friends to find us interesting and engaging, colleagues to find us good cooperators and authority to see our talents as useful and desirable. Santor and Walker (1999) have shown that having qualities that one thinks others will value are especially related to self-esteem. This is more so than having qualities that one (only) values oneself. Leary et al. (1995) suggested that self-esteem is a form of internal tracking of one's attractiveness to others and a sense of belonging. In other words, it is what one thinks others will value about the self that is often key to self-esteem and confidence.

The essence of the argument is therefore that humans have evolved high level motivations to compete to be liked, approved of and valued (Barkow, 1989) and avoid stigmatisation (Kurzban & Leary, 2001). In order to do this, humans try to stimulate the positive emotions of others (i.e., to stimulate desires in a potential lover, or liking in a potential friend, or be seen as a valued resource). This is not to say that aggressive strategies to get what one wants or defend oneself are redundant strategies. Indeed, they are used throughout the animal and human world. However, aggression, for the most part, is designed to elicit fear in its target, not positive affect and desire. Aggression runs the risk of injury, and of others taking flight thus losing the potential for sexual engagement or alliance-building. We can depict these two alternative (but not mutually exclusive) strategies for social interactions in Table 1.1.

To have a 'feel for' one's attractiveness to others, one has to track not only how others react to the self, and what one's current support network or alliances are, but also the qualities that a group gives high attractiveness ratings to (e.g., intelligence, forms of beauty, being a rock musician or poet, tenderness, toughness or bravery). This recruits social comparison (Gilbert, Price & Allan, 1995), abilities to track and evaluate what one thinks others think about the self (opinion and personal reputation tracking; Gilbert, 1997) and mimicry (Abrams, 1996). Individual members of a group will (usually) try to conform to the standards that increase rather than decrease their social attractiveness. This is not to say that people necessarily compete for high rank or dominance (though some will do of course) but that it is the avoidance of *unwanted* inferiority and rejection that is at stake. Shame then can appear when we sense that we are failing to elicit positive affects in others, and instead are stimulating their anger, anxiety or contempt. As such we are vulnerable either to attacks and rejection or disengagement that damage our social opportunities to develop advantageous relationships. *These, then, are the threats that shame evolved to cope with.* Fischer and Tangney (1995) suggest that: 'With shame, a person wishes to be judged positively in a given situation but instead is judged negatively (by self or other) for some action or characteristic, especially something that signals a deep-seated flaw' (p.7).

In this context shame can be seen as not so much as the distance from the ideal self or falling short of standards as often thought, but closeness to the

Table 1.1 Strategies for gaining and maintaining rank-status

Strategy	Aggression	Attractiveness
Tactics used	Coercive	Showing talent
	Threatening	Show competence
	Authoritarian	Affiliative
Outcome desired	To be obeyed	To be valued
	To be reckoned with	To be chosen
	To be submitted to	To be freely given to
Purpose of strategy	To inhibit others	To inspire, attract others
	To stimulate fear	To stimulate positive affect

Source: From Gilbert and McGuire (1998).

'undesired self' (Ogilive, 1987); that is, one is a person vulnerable to rejection, ostracism; an object for derision. Exploring the idea that shame was about failure to live up to ideals and using qualitative methods Lindsay-Hartz, de Rivera and Mascolo (1995) found that:

> To our surprise we found that most of the participants rejected this formulation. Rather, when ashamed, participants talked about being who they did *not* want to be. That is, they experienced themselves as embodying an anti-ideal, rather than simply not being who they wanted to be. The participants said things like. 'I am fat and ugly,' not 'I failed to be pretty;' or 'I am bad and evil,' not 'I am not as good as I want to be.' This difference in emphasis is not simply semantic. Participants insisted that the distinction was important . . . (p.277).

Based on a review of the evidence and current theory Gilbert (1998a) suggested that it is the:

> . . . inner experience of self as an unattractive social agent, under pressure to limit possible damage to self via escape or appeasement, that captures shame most closely. It does not matter if one is rendered unattractive by one's own or other people's actions; what matters is the sense of personal unattractiveness – being in the social world as an undesired self; a self one does not wish to be. Shame is an involuntary response to an awareness that one has lost status and is devalued (p.22).

As noted then, whereas we may hope to elicit positive feelings (e.g., liking and desires to associate with the self) in the mind of others, when we feel shame there is a belief that we have (or will) stimulated negative feelings (contempt, ridicule, disgust or disinterest) in the minds of others, and as a consequence, this will lead them to either not wish to form useful relationships with us, to disengage, actively reject the self or even attack the self. When shame is internalised individuals may have similar evaluations to parts of themselves; that is, certain aspects of the self activate feelings of self-directed anger, contempt or hatred rather than feelings of acceptance and pleasure. In body shame this would be reflected in ideas such as 'I hate, or am disgusted by, my body (e.g., psoriasis or disfigurements).

Defensive system processing, defensive behaviours and shame

We have seen then that signals from others, which are interpreted as 'loss of attractiveness,' and/or self-evaluations of loss of attractiveness, can be major threats because they may block our ability to engage with others in useful social relationships. Behaviourally speaking there is a loss of hoped-for social rewards, and as such may well operate through brain systems for detecting and responding to loss of rewards (Gray, 1987). Elsewhere, it was argued that there are two central psychobiological organising systems for information processing: *the defence and safeness systems* (Gilbert, 1989, 1993, 2001a). Threats are processed through an evolved defence system. Peoples' defensive systems will be affected by individual differences in genes, ongoing physiological states, previous learning and current contexts. Thus, for some people, defensive affects and behaviours may be more easily triggered, more intense and of longer duration than for others.

Some threats and fears have an innate component; for example, infant separation from mother, early onset fear of strangers, snakes, heights and possibly fear of ostracism. Such will be built into the defence system, as well as conditioned fears that are acquired and elaborated later. The defence system influences attention (primes for early detection), controls arousal and selects a response(s) from a menu of evolved responses to threats (see Table 1.2). Defence emotions (e.g., fear, anxiety, anger and disgust) and behaviours (e.g., fight, flight) are designed to be engaged rapidly because in the past, speed and being 'better safe than sorry' was often more adaptive than spending time to make accurate judgements (Gilbert, 1998b). A possible menu of basic defensive behaviours is given in Table 1.2.

Another automatic response in social encounters is the blush (see Crozier, Chapter 11, this volume). The defensive behaviours outlined in Table 1.2 are all fairly old in evolutionary terms, designed for rapid responding, are mostly

Table 1.2 Some types of common defensive behaviours

Specific defence	Function
Defensive fight	Protection, deterrent
Escape	To put distance between self and threat. Movement away reduces defensive arousal
Help-seeking	To elicit protection and support from another. Movement towards other acts as reassurance
Submitting	To inhibit one's own threat eliciting behaviour (e.g., challenging others) and deactivate actual or possible aggression from another
Hiding	Seeking cover to avoid being seen
Camouflage	Concealing the self. Includes concealing inner feelings
Cut off	Breaking contact with aversive arousal eliciting cues, e.g., covering one's eyes, turning away
Demobilisation (short term)	Freeze-faint to reduce activity in threatening environment
Demobilisation (long term)	Depressed mood, anhedonia fatigue Disengagement from and demobilisation within high-threat or low-resource environments

Source: From Gilbert (2001a).

coordinated via processes in the limbic system (Le Doux, 1998; Panskepp, 1998) and (in humans) various cortical processes that regulate limbic system functioning (Schore, 1994, 2001). Evolution is a very conservative process and on the whole will use and adapt what already exists to fit new functions (Buss, 1999). This being the case, there is no reason to believe that a threat to a social bond or to one's ability to attract others is going to use completely new or different types of defences, but more likely will use (and modify) those already available in the system. Hence, just as self-conscious emotions are blends of primary emotions (positive and negative affect) orchestrated by self-conscious competencies (e.g., theory of mind abilities), so shame-based behaviours are blends of earlier types of defence. Thus, basic defensive behaviours (fight, flight, submit) are the bedrock for shame but are orchestrated by those self-conscious competencies that start to develop in a child from two years onwards.

Attention and threats

Attention mechanisms and arousal control systems involved in social threats are highly complex (see Heinrichs & Hofmann (2001) for an excellent review of attentional processes in social anxiety). We clearly need to know much more about attentional mechanisms in shame and the social anxiety literature offers useful methods to study these (Heinrichs & Hofmann, 2001). Although evaluations underpin emotions, they can be made rapidly, automatically and outside conscious control, and this includes self-relevant evaluations (Koole, Dijksterhuis & van Knippenberg, 2001). People can feel threatened and start responding *before* they can consciously articulate what they feel threatened about. In a number of fascinating experiments on priming, Baldwin and his colleagues found that if people are shown rapidly masked pictures of approving or disapproving faces (i.e., people did not know they had seen a face) these will affect their self-evaluations. Being shown disapproving faces produces more negative self-evaluation than approving ones. Moreover, these effects are conditionable (see Baldwin & Fergusson, 2001 for a review).

This creates an intriguing notion that self-conscious affects can be triggered before becoming conscious of the relevant meanings. Indeed, some believe (e.g., see Retzinger, 1991) that shame can be bypassed in that shame, as such, does not actually become fully conscious and some people may only experience their defensive emotions (e.g., anger) and not shame and anxiety associated with rejection or negative self-evaluation. Another intriguing finding is that once an affect is activated, it can influence subsequent processing. In other words, if one's immediate response to a threat is anger then not only will the anger come with various action tendencies but also with dispositions for information processing that affects subsequent processing. Lerner and Keltner (2001) call this *appraisal tendency*; appraisals that are guided by the aroused affect. These findings fit the idea of basic defence and safeness processing systems that can organise response dispositions below the level of consciousness (see also McNally, 2001 for a fascinating discussion of such issues). Over the next few years such findings will help to shape our understanding of shame-based experiences.

Safeness

Although shame is about feeling threatened, a few comments should also be made about safeness. As noted elsewhere (e.g., Gilbert, 1993, 2001b) cognitions, behaviours and affects are often related to a balance in these (threat-defence and safeness) organising systems. For some time it has been suggested that children acquire a sense of safeness with others via their experiences of attachment (e.g., see Liotti, 2000). Indeed, love and care operate through the approach and safeness system (Gilbert, 1993). Those with poor early attachments will have more experiences of being stressed/threatened (e.g., by separations, abuse, criticism or neglect) or fear in the parent (Liotti, 2000) and tend to suffer various psychobiological patterns of activation that shift the balance to threat system processing (see Schore 1994, 2001) and damage limitation. Moreover, poor early attachments can incline people to feel easily threatened by interpersonal conflicts and possible rejection (Sloman, 2000; Liotti, 2000). Cloitre and Shear (1995) have explored the concept of defence and safeness processing in relation to attachment theory and social anxiety, noting how socially anxious people often overuse defenceness system processing at the expense of safeness, or looking on others as friends and allies. Lodnert (Chapter 10, this volume) explores shame of sexual problems in the context of attachment history.

There is another aspect here, however. This is that the more safe people feel with those around them (the more they feel supported and cared for), the easier it may be to explore, process and integrate potentially shameful events (e.g., making mistakes, failing or disfigurements). Perhaps this is because they have learnt that even if they do behave 'badly', others around them will forgive them quickly and reconciliation is possible, a relationship rupture is not catastrophic; or they feel loved regardless of how they look. Experiencing safeness and acceptance (a non-shaming, and an understanding, warm environment) may also be key to the ability to explore the painful and shameful in the therapeutic context (see below).

Submissive behaviour and shame

So safeness is important but for now we will stay with shame as threat-based. What is interesting is that social threats can recruit any of those behaviours (either singly or in combination) as outlined in Table 1.2. This is what complicates shame and why shame cannot be reduced to social anxiety. Social anxiety is an outcome of a social threat, defined in terms of an affective behavioural response (Gilbert, 2001b; Gilbert & Trower, 2001). However, a shame response, routed in the threat of being an unattractive social agent (loss of positive social rewards), could be one of anxiety or anger or demobilisation (felt as inner deflation, dejection and possibly linked to a parasympathetic response and loss of positive affect). On the whole, though, the pattern of *behaviours* noted in shame are submissive, associated with desires to conceal the self, hide, escape, avoid eye gaze and inhibition of confident display behaviour and outputs (Gilbert & McGuire, 1998; Keltner & Harker, 1998). Subordinates can, of course, feel angry and act aggressively and so the anger in shame should be distinguished from that of humiliation (discussed later).

Summary

One way to see shame is as routed in (failures of) our evolved strategies (and efforts) to be attractive and engage others in relationships that are beneficial to reproductive interests (attracting friends, lovers and helpful authorities). Shame is a defensive response or pattern of responses to threats and losses of social attractiveness. Social threats and lost bonds, such as loss through the death of a loved one, will produce changes in positive affect (and may increase anger) but not shame, as it carries no information of our relative attractiveness as a social agent (a reason why shame cannot be reduced to disruption of social bonds alone, or reductions in positive affect alone). Threats to our social attractiveness, however, are the issue in shame, and the response to such a threat or event can be rapid and recruit fast-acting limbic-centred processes and responses as depicted in Table 1.2; the most common being those of subordinate defensive behaviours (e.g., flight and submissiveness).

Coping and defensive behaviour

There are, of course, major complexities in connecting the rapidly triggered limbic-centred defensive affects and behaviours with human coping behaviours; not least because coping behaviours can be planned and rehearsed (rather than automatic) and enacted in advance or as preventive measures. To date, the linkages between basic defensive behaviours (e.g., fight, flight, submit) and human coping styles have been poorly formulated. There have, however, been numerous studies of coping behaviour that we cannot review here (e.g., Larazus, 1994) except to say that coping can be focused on the problem (problem-focused) or one's emotional state (emotion-focused coping). Coping with risks to one's self-presentation are many and at times highly sophisticated (Leary, 1995). What is interesting, however, is that when social attractiveness is at issue, people will have to try to manage both the things they feel ashamed about (e.g., body appearance) and their emotions and automatic defensive behaviours (see Crozier, Chapter 11, this volume, for discussion of the management of blushing). Expressing too much anxiety or too much anger could be more shaming and damage self-identity and social reputation (Gilbert, 2001a). Whether one acts out anger to being shamed or not may depend on the perceived risks (Lerner & Keltner, 2001), one's cultural background (Cohen, 2001; Cohen, Vandello & Rantilla, 1998) and the status/power relationship between people (Allan & Gilbert, 2002). Help-seeking, for coping with shame, may also be inhibited for fear of further shame (MacDonald, 1998). Instead, people may try to cope with these powerful emotions (fear and anger) with a host of emotion-focused coping efforts such as using alcohol, avoidance, denial or disassociation.

Clark and Wells' (1995; Clark, 2001) model of social anxiety highlights the role of defensive coping behaviours and damage limitation (or what they call safety behaviours) in potentially shaming situations (being seen as inept, boring or unattractive). In their model, symptoms of anxiety are believed to create a negative image in the eyes of the other, in part because of perceived bodily appearances and functioning (e.g., eye-gaze avoidance, poor speech flow, trembling hands, sweating, blushing). The fear of creating negative impressions activates further anxiety (and more symptoms), which we would see as an automatic defence. This then elicits patterns of defensive or damage limitation (safety) behaviours. Such behaviours may include controlled and automatic efforts at concealment and social withdrawal or avoidance or more submissiveness. These behaviours, especially efforts at concealment, may maintain the fear and do not modify negative beliefs. Moreover, people can feel ashamed of their need for, or use of, these behaviours, including alcohol use (see Gilbert, 2001b for a further discussion).

In essence, people can be mindful of how their automatic reactions and coping efforts themselves impact on others. For example, David who had scars from previous acne would get anxious in new, potentially sexual situations and worry about how a woman might view his face. However, as his anxiety built he would also worry as to how he could conceal his anxiety and not (also) be seen as socially inept. Jon, on the other hand, who had a car accident scar, would get angry if people drew attention to it, but then would get anxious in case others saw him as too touchy and aggressive, and he hated the way this scar 'had made him aggressive'. There is then an interaction between a threat of being unattractive, our immediate automatic defensives and our coping behaviours. As in most aspects in this area, more research is needed on these linkages.

There are also a host of coping styles that affect both specific and non-specific aspects of coping. For example, Veale (Chapter 14, this volume) discusses body shame related to an excessive focus on, and checking of, appearance even in the absence of any obvious body disfigurement. In some types of body shame, checking appearance can become excessive, although not reach the extent of a disorder (Carr, Chapter 4, this volume).

There are a range of coping styles that can be related to body (and other) shame issues. For example, some people who feel vulnerable to rejection by others can develop submissive and appeasing *styles* of social relating. These individuals may go out of their way to put the needs of others first (people pleasers) in order to be liked and accepted. For example, Mary, who thought she was physically unattractive and 'always battling with her weight', felt that if she compensated by always being nice to others they would like her. She made many allowances for the poor behaviour of her husband because she felt grateful to him that he had married her, and that if he left her she would never find anyone else. To fully understand body shame then, we need to understand both automatic defences and the coping styles people develop as ways of coping in everyday relating, including the development of attachment bonds and friendships. It should also be noted that pride can be a compensation for shame. For example, those who have feelings of shame in their bodies can turn excessive control over their bodies into sources of pride and positive control (see Goss & Gilbert, Chapter 12, this volume).

Rumination

Finally, we should note an important post-event aspect of shame – that of rumination. Beck, Emery and Greenburg (1985) suggested that in social anxiety the key emotions occur before or during a social encounter, whereas shame is marked by rumination after encounters. Ongoing work in our department, exploring the relationship of rumination to shame, suggests that rumination could play a major role in linking shame to other problems such as depression. Using self-report measures of shame and rumination with students suggested a possible interaction between shame and rumination in relation to depression. This is early days in this research and we have not distinguished between angry-vengeful, fearful and self-attacking rumination. Many therapists and researchers have suggested that rumination and 'dwelling' can act to maintain stress arousal and hence may have major impacts on the physiological substrates of stress (e.g., cortisol) mood and the activation of negative self-schema (Gilbert, 2000d).

The external and internal evaluations of shame

So far we have noted that the need to be seen as attractive is an evolved need (for attracting others and building beneficial relationships), that a perceived loss of attractiveness can be a threat (e.g., of rejection) and that such threats can elicit basic defensive behaviours (e.g., fight, flight, submit) that are built into the shame response. We have also noted a number of complexities in the degree of conscious awareness people have in regard to threat processing. However, we have glossed over some crucial complexities in the *evaluations* that underpin shame. In essence these come down to evaluations and feelings that are focused on 'self as seen and judged by others', or 'self as object', and 'self as judged by self'. These evaluations are dependent on the emergence of certain competencies (e.g., theory of mind) that arise from about two years of age (Zahn-Waxler, 2000). Thompson & Kent (2001) refer to this as 'self from the outside' and 'self from the inside'. Similar distinctions have been made in social anxiety (Hofmann & Barlow, 2001). In fact, the interactions between 'what I think others think about me' and 'what I think about me given what I think others think about me' have been understood to be central to social behaviour for a considerable time (Retzinger, 1991). For example, Scheff (1988) notes that Cooley at the turn of the last century argued that:

> . . . Many people of balanced mind and congenial activity scarcely know that they care about what others think of them, and will deny, perhaps with indignation, that such care is an important factor in what they are and do. But this is illusion. If failure or disgrace arrives, if one suddenly finds that the faces of men show coldness and contempt instead of the kindness and deference that he is used to, he will perceive from shock, the fear, the sense of being outcast and helpless, that he was living in the minds of others without knowing it, just as we daily walk the solid ground without thinking of how it bears us up (as quoted by Scheff, 1988, p.398).

Cooley coined the term the 'looking-glass self' to refer to the way we judge and feel about ourselves according to how we think others judge and feel about us. The looking-glass self has three cognitive aspects:

> The imagination of our appearance to the other person; the imagination of his judgement of that appearance; and some sort of self-feeling, such as pride or mortification (as quoted by Scheff, 1988, p.398).

Such considerations have given rise to the study of what Baldwin called relational schemas – that is representations of self as seen through the eyes of others and how these influence self-evaluations (see Baldwin & Fergusson, 2001).

External shame, stigma, fear of negative evaluation and social anxiety

As much social behaviour is about attempts to control social interactions (to maximise benefits and minimise harms), it is our ability to have models of ourselves as we 'exist in the minds of others' that is often key to human social interaction. We need to know if we are attractive to others or not (Gilbert, 2001b; Gilbert & Trower, 2001). This links with our evolved abilities for 'theory of mind'; that is to be able to understand what might be in the minds of others; what others are thinking about us (Gilbert, 2001b). Hence, we can experience ourselves (and of course our bodies) as 'an object for others'; that is, as social beings who are judged and evaluated, and we have feelings according to how we think others judge our abilities and bodies (Lewis, 1992). Indeed, a blast of shame feelings may be triggered by self-consciousness elicited at the moment one is aware that the other can 'see' (part of) the self; that is, one becomes conscious of oneself as an object in the mind of the other and the feelings one has generated in the mind of the other (e.g., contempt, disgust, disdain).

Shame is thus commonly linked to the fear of exposure that will result in some form of social diminishment, devaluation or rejection (Lewis, 1992). The classic statement of 'I don't want you to see me this way or like this' captures the feelings that lie behind much social avoidance, although it is also linked to feelings of dignity and loss of dignity (Gilbert, 1998a). I have called this aspect *external shame* to refer to a class of feelings (such as anxiety and sadness) associated with things one thinks *others* see as bad, weak, inadequate or disgusting in the self and could, would or have resulted in rejection, attacks or losing attractiveness in the eyes of others (Gilbert, 1997, 1998a, 1998b). A similar but different concept has been called *stigma consciousness* (Pinel, 1999). This relates to experiences of being seen as having stigmatised traits and/or of acting in a way that locates one as belonging to stigmatised group (e.g., the mad, bad, ugly or ill). Jacoby (1994) distinguished between actual experiences of being stigmatised (enacted stigma) and the anticipation of stigma or felt stigma. There is little doubt that people with disfigurements or body shame problems often have both and can recall events and scenes of being stigmatised (Kent & Keohane, 2001). They may be acutely sensitive and aware of people looking at them and of observers distancing themselves from them. However, from her study of epilepsy, Jacoby (1994) suggests that felt stigma may be a more powerful predictor of psychological adjustment than actual or enacted stigma.

The constellation of primary emotions that can be part of external shame or stigma consciousness is complex. For example, as noted above, fear and anxiety are only two (of a number of possible) responses to such stigma or being seen as unattractive. To be viewed with fear (e.g., as a source of contamination, if one has a skin disease), contempt or disdain, one might become angry and focus on the injustice of such judgements, or one might believe one can easily overcome such stigma, or one has many other attractive attributes to compensate, or one might use defensive exclusion and denial and not attend to such information. Goffman (1968) recognised that to carry stigmatisable traits did not automatically lead to self-devaluation, and there is good evidence for this view (Crocker & Major, 1989). Camp, Finlay and Lyons (2002) have reviewed data on the link between stigmatisation and self-esteem and also provide qualitative data showing that these linkages are complex. People have a host of ways of protecting self-esteem even if they carry stigmatised traits or labels (e.g., a mental illness or disfigurement).

On a more positive side, even though some people can recognise they are at risk of severe social sanction (e.g., for certain sexual behaviours or appearances), they are prepared to fight against such stereotypes and explore ways to cope with social rejection (see Coughlan & Clarke, Chapter 8, this volume). We can also think of the history of the shaming of women who have fought for the right to vote, or for contraception, or sexual freedom at the turn of the century (and still goes on in various cultures), or those fighting for homosexual rights. For some people *not* to stand up against unfair stigmatisation can be a source of personal shame.

Nonetheless, even though people might not self-devalue if they feel rejected (or rejectable) for having certain attributes (Camp, Finlay & Lyons, 2002), the fear of rejection and distress to rejection can be intense and lead to a host of defensive and concealment behaviours (Thompson & Kent, 2001). Such distress and defensive behaviours have often been seen as crucial to the experience of shame, and historically the 'self as object' has been core to the concept of shame (Gilbert, 1998a). Indeed, Wilson (1987) notes that in some traditions shame *only* operates at the level of how 'self exists for the other,' be this in imagination, in memory or in actuality.

Of course, it might be argued that the feelings of distress (anxiety, low mood) and the defensive behaviours of external shame (e.g., concealment) or felt stigma are not 'real shame' and that the real feelings of shame must involve some self-devaluation. This is problematic for a number of reasons. Firstly, shame is a socially contextualised experience. Secondly, fear and anxiety are common outcomes to the experience that others (will) look down on the self (stigma, external shame). This has been called *fear of negative evaluation* (Leary & Kowalski, 1995) and is regarded as central to the adjustment reactions for many who have concerns about their bodies (Thompson & Kent, 2001). To argue that the distress and anxiety these individuals can feel is not related to shame's constellation of affects, associated as they are with evaluations of self as a social agent, fear, anger and hiding and avoidance behaviours, unless accompanied by self-devaluation, would seem odd.

It is also clear that the defensive behaviours to being observed are crucial to how people cope with stigma. For example, Smart and Wegner (1999) manipulated the concealing and non-concealing of an eating disorder. When engaged in interactions, people attempting to conceal 'the disorder' had more anxiety and more intrusive negative thoughts than non-concealers. Major and Gramzow (1999) explored concealment and fear of stigma for an abortion. Concealers had greater distress, made more efforts at thought suppression but had more intrusive thoughts. Those with disfigurements, who use concealment and avoidant strategies, tend to have more anxiety, loss of valued roles and fear of developing intimate relationships (Kent & Thompson, Chapter 5, this volume).

Whether or not people self-devalue or self-blame, it is clear that being the object of the negative evaluation of others can be distressing and produce a host of defensive behaviours (Camp, Finlay & Lyons, 2002). Moreover, it would seem that it is when there is a risk of exposure that shame affects come to the fore (Lewis, 1992). People may come to terms with their own disfigurements or disabilities and feel relatively relaxed in the privacy of their own space, but it is the actual or felt reaction of others that can be most distressing. Nonetheless, the relationships between experiences of rejection (Leary, 2001), the breaking of social bonds, (Retzinger, 1991), stigma and feeling demoted in the eyes of others, with internal shame and self-esteem, are hot topics for debate and research.

Internal shame

When shame affects are constellated around self-(de)evaluation and feeling textures of being personally bad, undesirable, weak, inadequate or disgusting to oneself, this can be referred to as *internal* shame (Gilbert, 1998a). This is the shame that relates to cognitive notions of *negative self-schema* (Beck et al., 1979). Rational emotive behaviour therapist, Albert Ellis (1977), has argued that it is the global rating of the self for personal failings, limitations or attributes that produce serious emotional distress. Hence, in rational emotive behavioural therapy and cognitive therapy, people are encouraged to not globally rate the self (Gilbert, 2000b). Although Ellis does not use the term 'internal shame' to refer to the tendency to globally rate and 'damn' the self, it can be seen this way.

Internal or internalised shame (like external shame or felt stigma) is far from a new concept. Kaufman (1989) discusses how shame can be internalised and represented in forms of scenes and scripts; memories of feelings of being shamed (see also Nathanson, 1994). We are most vulnerable to internalising shame when our social needs for love, affiliation, belonging and status are thwarted. In other words, it is being shamed by those we most depend on to mirror and affirm a sense of attractiveness (being a valued person) that carries most risk of being internalised. Derived from Tomkins' theory of shame, Cook (1996) developed a scale called *the internalised shame scale* which, in essence, is a measure of negative self-evaluation. McKinley's (1999) concept of objectified body consciousness distinguishes surveillance (self as one thinks one appears to others) from shame – the internalisation of negative views about the self (i.e., I am what others see me to be). Hence, all we are really attempting to do here is draw attention to the need to separate out the different foci around which shame affects constellate.

There are important clinical reasons for making these distinctions (self as object to others, and self as object to oneself) clear. For example, I have worked with people who have very high external shame, are deeply distressed by rejection from others, fear negative evaluation and criticism and have a variety of anxiety disorders. They are rejection sensitive (Leary, 2001; Goss & Gilbert, Chapter 12, this volume). Most therapists will have heard some heart-rending stories of rejection and social put-down of their patients (see Kent & Keohane, 2001 for examples). Many authors to this volume draw attention to the sense of social awkwardness, the intense distress and the social hiding, concealing and avoidance behaviours those with disfiguring conditions can experience. However, they may like themselves as people and not see their inner selves as bad or flawed. There is not global self-devaluation (Camp et al., 2002). Moreover, in the context of a reassuring therapeutic relationship (or trusted friends and family), they are able to feel relatively safe. Furthermore, if shown certain social skills to manage their disorders and the social domain, they may make good adjustments (e.g., see Coughlan & Clarke, Chapter 8, this volume).

On the other hand, there are some people who have heightened internalised shame and may even hate themselves. These individuals feel very internally persecuted, find it difficult to trust a therapist and will often dismiss the reassuring efforts of a therapist. In the extreme, they may have beliefs such as 'I am bad at the core of me', or 'if you knew the real me you would not like me'. There is therefore a very clear, testable hypothesis – that the more shame is internalised (focuses on self-devaluation) the more difficult it is to treat, that specific interventions may be necessary to address internalised shame – and these differ from those of external (self as object) forms of shame or stigma consciousness (see Veale, Chapter 14, this volume, for further examples).

Internalisation

There is much we do not yet understand about the internalisation of shame and the way negative emotions are directed at the self. However, the capacity to internalise shame probably begins early in life as children learn how their behaviours and characteristics are judged and reacted to by others (e.g., parents and peers); that is, they learn what feelings they stimulate in others (e.g., approval and disapproval; Barrett, 1995; Lewis, 1992; Stipek, 1995). This links to a now sizeable literature on how early relationships between children and their carers shape relational schemas (Baldwin & Fergusson, 2001) and basic brain architectures and psychobiological processes (Schore, 2001). It remains unclear exactly at what time the interactions between the infant and carer begin to build the sense of self as loved and lovable, desired and desirable, but there seems to be numerous processes involved that change with age. In the first months of life, infants are highly attentive and responsive to the face of a parent and attuned to positive smiling faces (and other accepting behaviours) of the mother. Children clearly gain pleasure from the smiles directed at them from their mothers; i.e., mothers taking pleasure in the 'being' of their infants (Schore, 1998). Children of depressed mothers, where such positive interactions may be lowered, can have long-lasting emotional and cognitive problems (Murray & Cooper, 1997). Infants who are disfigured or unattractive in some way may also be at a disadvantage in terms of elicit-ing positive affect in a carer (Etcoff, 1999). Such examples indicate the crucial role the 'other' plays in the emotional development of the child and a sense of a desirable self (Schore, 2001).

However, as noted above, although infants can show defensive reactions (such as changes in body posture, eye-gaze avoidance, cut-off and distress) to miss-attuned behaviours (e.g., the mother presents a blank face to an infant's facial expression; Schore, 1998) there is debate as to whether this is shame or better viewed as basic defensive reactions that will later become the basis for shame (Barrett, 1995). Much depends on whether one sees shame as depend-ent on the competencies for objective self-awareness that emerge around two years of age (Zahn-Waxler, 2000). Nonetheless, as the child develops these competencies, numerous interactions occur (with parents, siblings and peers) such that the child learns they are a positive attractive 'object' to the other (their social attraction strategies work well) or one who elicits anger, con-tempt or rejection. Such emotional experiences become the source for self-referencing and self-schema and are thus internalised representations of self (Baldwin & Fergusson, 2001). They will also recruit patterns of defensive responses (e.g., fight, flight, submission). These defences themselves can become a source for internal shame. For example, Sally who was physically abused by her father, would feel automatically fearful and act submissively in his presence. Later in life any conflict with a man could trigger these auto-matic defences (anxiety and submissive inhibition) but this reaction was itself seen by her as evidence of a weak 'pathetic' self. Helping her understand the evolved function and adaptiveness of her early fearful submission and that the label of a 'weak self' was a later elaboration on her reactions, helped her to de-shame her reactions and begin to explore ways of coping with a good deal of conditioned anxiety. Note that in this example the affective experience and automatic triggering of her defensive style (fearful submission to father) pre-existed any cognitive elaboration. But we need to know much more about the process of internalisation and how some children can appear more robust than others to resist internalisation and the development of negative self-schema. This will probably involve better understanding of the interaction between temperament and social contexts (Gilbert & Miles, 2000a). Indeed, this integrative work is beginning to emerge in the social anxiety literature (see the excellent Crozier & Alden (2001) edited text).

The internalising process continues throughout life. For example, Lash-brook (2000) has shown that the avoidance of ridicule and shame are power-ful reasons why adolescents conform to peer group pressure. Although not conceptualised as a shame issue, Kelman and Hamilton (1989) explored the way people can be induced to engage in highly immoral acts (e.g., soldiers committing a massacre) and internalise the reasons for doing so, to avoid both cognitive dissonance and social rejection and ridicule. Indeed, probably the fear of stigma and rejection is one of the most powerful forces behind compliance and obedience. Kelman and Hamilton (1989) also offer a fascinating discussion of the differences in the processes of internalisation of *rules, roles and values*. They also raise important questions about what it is that leads people to think others have *the legitimacy* to judge them in the way they do or request them to behave in certain ways (adopt certain rules and roles). Undoubtedly, while some people have public presentations that give the appearance of obedience, they may not internalise these rules or values in private (see Scott, 1990). Presumably, for people to internalise stigma (be internally ashamed) they must see 'the other' as having, if not the right, then the skill or power, to judge them so. To the best of my knowledge there has been no research in either the social anxiety literature or shame literature on this aspect (although see Alden, 2001). However, the moment a person refuses to accept the legitimacy of the 'judger or rejecter' then they are also refusing to internalise (Camp et al., 2002).

This leads to a testable hypothesis that the more people see 'the (rejecting) other' as a legitimate judge of them, or as having some power over them, the more they may internalise and agree with negative judgements others may make about them. But note that legitimacy is something that *must be given to the other*, and one can also refuse to give it. Hence, another set of research questions are: What factors influence this giving of power, this giving of legitimacy, to others to judge the self? Is it related to our dependency on them; some development of the sense of self as may come from (loving or neglectful) early attachment relationships; the way we learn obedience in childhood; temperament, or social contexts? And how do we internalise the values of our group such that some women, for example, do judge themselves by the standards set by the media? This is no small issue because one way of helping people deal with internalised shame is to help them re-evaluate the legitimacy of the other to be a judge of them. Bergner (1987) explored various therapeutic ways for doing this.

Another issue in regard to internalisation is how changing characteristics of the self (e.g., changing body shapes or acquiring a disfigurement) interact with pre-existing self-schema (see Gilbert & Thompson, Chapter 2, this volume). Lee, Scragg and Turner (2001) have pointed out that in post-traumatic stress disorder shame can arise from two sources. A traumatic event may confirm underlying negative beliefs about the self or disconfirm positive beliefs. In the case of body shame the arrival of acne (e.g., Kellett, Chapter 7, this volume) or a disfigurement may significantly shatter a person's positive self-schema if physical attractiveness had been central to their self-esteem. Alternatively, a person who believed they were not that attractive in the first place may, with the onset of a disfiguring condition, have a negative self-schema confirmed and exacerbated with an intensification of shame.

Humiliation

Another reaction to feeling 'looked down on' or stigmatised is humiliation. In most texts, shame and humiliation have been bracketed together – they are seen as identical. Gilbert (1997, 1998a), however, argued that while there are many overlapping features (the core feature to both being attacks on relative social status, standing, power and/or attractiveness), the cognitions in humiliation differ from those of internal shame. Humiliation involves external attributions ('it is the other who is bad for rejecting or attacking the self') while for internal shame there is internal attribution (e.g., feeling to blame in some way for the rejection/attack). Shame responses tend to be ones of flight (escape avoidance) and submissive defensive reactions, or damage limitation, whereas humiliation represents a more aggressive defence (counter-attacking) of one's social standing (Gilbert, 2001a). These distinctions have of course been made many times before. In object relations theory, for example, they are seen as the schizoid-paranoid (bad world) and depressive (bad self) positions, respectively (Gilbert, 1992).

So, humiliation is what can be done to you but you may not agree with (do not legitimise) the judgement of the one humiliating you. Consider torture: we don't talk of the shame of torture but humiliation. In humiliation the other is bad whereas in shame it is the self who is bad. Moreover, the desires of torturers are not usually to shame people but to humiliate them and these are clearly quite different desires. Miller (1988) writes:

> There are important phenomenological differences between shame and humiliation that relate the states to distinct self and other interactions and to distinct levels of self-definition. Humiliation implies an activity occurring between oneself and another person. 'Humiliated' has a double meaning. It is a state or status, a feeling about where the self is positioned in relation to others; but it is also an interpersonal interaction. Someone has *done something* to the person. More especially humiliation involves being put into a lowly, debased, and powerless position by someone who has, at that moment greater power than oneself. Humiliation often involves rage over one's position, but not always. It may also involve shame over one's position or depression. But the key to humiliation is not the secondary reflections upon the significance of one's state (i.e., it is enraging; it is shameful) but the direct experience of feeling put into that state by another person with more power . . .
>
> In contrast to humiliation, shame involves primarily a reflection upon the self by the self . . . Ashamed persons are looking at themselves and judging themselves to be inferior, inadequate or pathetic (pp.44–45).

Klein (1991) argued that '*people believe they deserve their shame; they do not believe they deserve their humiliation*' (p.117, italics in the original). While both shame and humiliation focus on harm to the self, humiliation may be a less self-conscious and self-focused experience than shame. Humiliation involves: (1) a focus on the other as bad rather than the self; (2) external rather than internal attributions for harmful events; (3) a sense of injustice and unfairness; (4) and a burning desire for revenge. Indeed, vengeance (Frijda, 1994) and (in)justice (Solomon, 1994) seem so intimately linked to humiliation that it is difficult to imagine it without them.

However, shame and humiliation share a complex relationship. For example, Tangney, et al., (1996) differentiated between constructive and destructive responses to anger and found that shame was significantly associated with destructive anger (e.g., vengeful rumination or interpersonal withdrawal) that may lead to the continuation of interpersonal conflict. However, in our own work with students (n = 155; Gilbert & Miles, 2000b), using a direct measure of self-other blame for being criticised or put down by others, we found that: (1) self-blame for criticism was only weakly inversely correlated with blaming others for criticism (r = −0.16); (2) self-blame was significantly correlated with external shame, fear of negative evaluation, feelings of shame and depression, whereas blaming others was not; indeed, blaming others was weakly but significantly inversely correlated with shame feelings (r = −0.20); (3) both self-blame and blaming others were significantly associated with anger at being criticised; and (4) using a social comparison scale, self-blame was significantly associated with feeling relatively inferior to others, while blaming others was significantly associated with feeling relatively superior. In a principle component analysis, we found that self-blame loaded heavily on a general factor that included shame, depression, fear of negative evaluation and feeling inferior, while other-blame loaded negatively on this factor. What was unexpected was that a measure of anger and hostility, which includes a tendency to be verbally and physically aggressive, dropped out as a separate factor. Blaming others did not load on this factor. While such findings support possible distinctions between humiliation and shame, clearly more research (including possible gender differences) is required to better understand this complex relationship.

Summary

The above section has drawn attention to a number of overlapping but separable concepts. These are stigma and stigma consciousness, and external shame. Both pertain to experiences of how one thinks others judge and feel about the self. It is possible to be very sensitive to such judgements but not necessarily feel internal shame. One could feel humiliation, for example, especially if one did not identify with the values of the stigmatiser. Internal shame, however, relates to the internal organisation of self-evaluations and feelings.

The biopsychosocial contexts for body shame

So far we have explored the nature of shame and the way it can act as a filter through which people can come to experience themselves. In this section we now begin to focus in on the body. To start with, it is important to contextualise body shame in its social context because what becomes shaming and shameful is routed in social and interpersonal interactions as played out between shamed and shamer. Indeed, the evolved origins of self-conscious affects and competencies were to help us be socially responsive, both within our intimate relationships and wider social groups. Thus, the interactions between shamed and shamer are not encapsulated interactions of only two (or a few) actors but such interactions themselves are often contextualised in wider social and cultural meaning systems that value certain attributes and devalue others (Cohen, 2001). Hence, shamer–shamed interactions are themselves emergent from complex, dynamic, historical-social interactions that operate at a variety of levels.

Shame is not only a personal, distressing-affective experience but it penetrates into the subtlest levels of our being, including our physiology. Not only can shame and stigma be major stressors, with all the cascade of physiological effects of stress, but our bodies and brains can be shaped over time by being shamed and rejected (Schore, 2001). From this physiological shaping come amplified dispositions to be sensitive and responsive to potential shame. To do justice to the complexity and multilayered nature of shame, we need a biopsychosocial approach; one that pays due regard to the interactions between processes. These models are available although rarely used. One of my favourites is the ethological model of Hinde (1989, 1992). He developed a multi-process model of interactions and levels for outlining various complex biopsychosocial interactions (shown in Figure 1.1). Included are: *cultural values and economic opportunities; styles of family interactions; key social relationships; personal evaluations of self and others; biological state and target organ functioning*.

This model outlines the complex interactions between an individual's biological state, the nature of the relationships they seek, the type of relationships they elicit and form, and how all these are embedded in socially scripted or prescribed sets of (acceptable) behaviours and values. These scripts influence the attributes for (personally) gaining or losing value in the eyes of others (honour, pride, acceptance and shame, Gilbert, 1995). They also provide the guidance for stigmatising others. For example, in one group, refusing to engage in fighting may be seen as promoting peace or self-restraint and is valued, while in another it is seen as a mark of cowardice and is shameful (Cohen, 2001; Overing, 1989). The theme of the socially prescribed characteristics of bodies, be it for gender-related body shapes, skin textures or body functions are addressed by the authors in this volume.

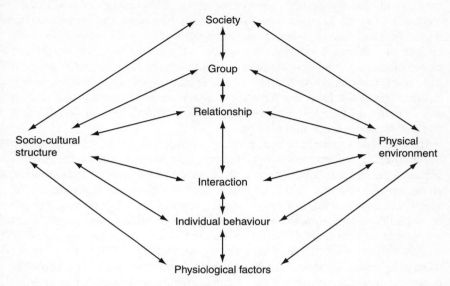

Figure 1.1 Hinde's (1992) ethological model of bipsychosocial interactions, with kind permission from Hinde

The body

Not only is the body that part of us that is immediately observable to others, it is also connected to a complexity of self-conscious experiences. It has been noted that while we may think of ourselves as individual minds or personalities, our existence can only take place in an embodied self (e.g., see Friedman & Moon, 1997). And our body often operates outside our control; it grows, ages, changes in its functions, can become sick and disabled, and will eventually decay and die. Becoming sick can be a source of shame as we encounter a need for care; to allow our body fluids and products to be cleaned or tested by others, to lose control over functions, abilities or mind; and here the attitudes of those around who will care for us matter greatly (Lazare, 1987). And how we got sick (e.g., HIV or smoking-induced lung cancer) can be source of stigma too. We may come to hate our bodies and what goes on in them or tune into them as a source of understanding of the self; to work with rather than against our bodies (Friedman & Moon, 1997).

Consider also that there are various neurological conditions where people do not recognise their own bodies or body parts, and can even experience different body parts as having a will of their own, as in alien hand syndrome, for example (Feinberg, 2001). Moreover, some people can feel that some of their limbs are so alien to them, they seek to have them amputated while others will seek medical intervention to change their bodies because they feel they are of the 'wrong sex'. Hence, the sense of ownership of one's body, identification with it, control over one's bodily functions and looks, and the degree to which the experiences of a personal body is imbibed with interest, neglect or pleasure or disdain is complex. There is still much we do not understand about the development of body schema, its neurophysiological substrates and linkage to a sense of self (Feinberg, 2001; Panskepp, 1998). Nonetheless, one's body can be experienced as an aspect of self that defines one in a certain way (e.g., male–female, able–disabled, beautiful–ugly) that one can work on, shape and change.

In recent years there have been a variety of different theoretical approaches to the study of the body. Sociological approaches have focused on the body as socially constructed, subject to socially varying views of what is acceptable, attractive and desirable and what is not. Such concerns are almost as old as humans themselves. For example, it is unclear when humans first began to use body paints and adornments as signals of group belonging, sexual enhancers and status or role definers (e.g., hunter or fighter) but these are certainly ancient behaviours noted in many cultures. As Shilling (1993) notes, with the increasing means to shape, clothe, decorate or alter the body, the body has become *a project*, a vehicle for social engagement that is attended to in order to send certain signals about the self and secure desirable social relationships.

One of these signals is body smells that can be a focus for body shame (Ekstromer, Chapter 9, this volume) and even reach delusional proportions (Veale, Chapter 14, this volume). However, in the last hundred years, with the industrial manufacture of soap, there has been a proliferation in the West of concern with hygiene and smell. This is marked by views such as 'cleanliness is next to Godliness'. In a fascinating article on the billions of pounds' industry in the selling of soaps and perfumes, Bunting (2001) argues that: 'Soap's triumph is the ultimate demonstration of how consumer capitalism, with its tools of persuasion and seduction can permanently alter the whole gamut of human behaviour, from public conventions to the most private, intimate moments with our own bodies' (p.40). In order to sell products, manufacturers have brought about an increased focus on the need to control natural body functions and smells and a heightened sensitivity to smell, disgust and hygiene. The use of smell and cleanliness to attract or repel has been part of advertising for some time. As Bunting notes, manufacturers have targeted people's insecurities of social acceptability. Camay, in the 1920s, warned women that: 'Every woman is in a beauty contest every day of her life'. This sentiment can be seen in many body-focused domains as product sellers have cajoled and seduced people into buying products to enhance their attractiveness, as well as emphasising the need for hygiene – and the unhygienic as objects of disdain and disgust. Such social changes impact on people's experiences of their own bodies and their functions and hence body shame sensitivities. We also now know that some exposure to bacteria (dirt) is useful to aid in the development of children's immune systems – we can become overly clean!

Social values, be they created by group identities or product selling, shape both our social and personal judgements of 'the ideal or acceptable body' as it pertains to certain categories related to gender, age and sexual advertising. From a feminist perspective, McKinley (1999) developed the concept of *obectified body consciousness*, part of which is derived from awareness that social audiences construct views on what is the ideal/acceptable body for women and how women feel pressured to adopt these values (if they are to be attractive to others) when it comes to how they feel about, treat and shape their own bodies. As noted above, this pressure is partly related to the fact that humans are highly evolved and motivated to conform, try to fit in and copy behaviours that appear associated with higher (rather than lower) status (Abrams, 1996; Cohen, 2001).

Evolutionists (Buss, 1999; Etcoff, 1999) have directed attention to the fact that bodies are also adverts for genes. If males are attracted to young, clear-skinned women, with particular hip-to-waist ratios, it is partly because investing in such women and siring offspring with them has served male reproductive interests over the long term. And males have long sought to control the sexual behaviour of females with (in humans) various forms of institutionalised control. Growing up in such cultures, where sexual attractiveness can be located in body shapes and forms, women's self-esteem has been traditionally more linked to body attractiveness than men's and there are both evolutionary and social reasons for this (Gilbert & Thompson, Chapter 2, this volume; Wade & Cooper, 1999). However, a recent newspaper report (Shabi, 2001) claims that increasing numbers of men are suffering from 'the tyranny of objectification' and body scrutiny, resulting in preoccupation with body size and shape. The obsessional drive to be muscular and avoid being seen as 'small and puny' has given rise to a new disorder labelled 'bigorexia' or 'machismo nervosa' (see also Goss & Gilbert, Chapter 12, this volume).

Bodies can become 'adverts' that stimulate feelings in others. As such the body, or aspect of it, can become a source of pleasure for both self and other, something to display and utilise for good effect, or a liability, something that can be a source of rejection, to be covered or hidden. Importantly, of course, 'bodies' are not fixed but undergo constant changes with ageing. The experiences of changing body shapes, functions and abilities are contextualised in social relationships where such changes are given both personal and social meaning. McKinley (1999) found that objectified body consciousness changes with age with older women (mothers) compared with younger women (daughters) being less focused on how their body appears to others and body shame. Gilbert and Thompson (Chapter 2, this volume) explore the changing experiences of one's body during late childhood and adolescence and its relationship to potential shame, while McKee and Gott (Chapter 3, this volume) explore how the experience of bodily changes in later life, and how increased vulnerability to 'falls' and sexual loss, can impinge on body shame.

Allied to evolved algorithms for body aesthetics (e.g., skin texture and body proportionality, smell and the competition/conflicts between male and female sexual strategies), the power of culture to shape body aesthetics should not be underestimated. Note, for example, the changes in the 'ideal shape' of Western women in the last few hundred years and how it has become progressively 'thinner' quite recently (Etcoff, 1999; McKinley, 1999). We can but ponder the role of recent media and computer-enhanced images of physical beauty of young women, to be held up as status models, and the efforts to copy them and have 'body self-esteem'. From an evolutionary point of view, the more competition intensifies as more competitors enter the market, and as the potential value of doing well increases, the more values and behaviours can get pushed to extremes (Gilbert, 1989; Goss & Gilbert, Chapter 12, this volume).

The body of the child

It is not only our own bodies that we subject to 'shaping' but also our children's. Parental attitudes and behaviours to their children's appearance can have an enormous impact on what children are subjected to and how they learn about what is acceptable and unacceptable in their appearance or bodily functions (including sexuality). This can be much more than simply clothing them, attending to their cleanliness, hairstyles, giving them pierced ears or coping with disfigurements. So powerful is body shaping, to avoid being different, that in some cultures parents disfigure a child to fit a norm. For example, in some African tribes the lips are extended with the use of small (and enlarging) discs placed in the lips. Perhaps originally introduced to make them less attractive to slave traders, it has become part of their group identity. Just over a hundred years ago the *Koskimo-kwakitutl*, a native American tribe of the Pacific Coast, wrapped their babies' heads in sugar cloth to elongate and deform them as a mark of belonging to the tribe and of status (Feest, 2000, p.285). In most cultures, deformed feet would not be regarded as attractive and yet for nearly a thousand years in China foot-binding and deforming the feet were used (tragically) to enhance the attractiveness of their daughters, despite the desperate pain this caused. Jung Chang (1992), in her popular book *Wild Swans*, recounts the experiences of her grandmother, capturing the role of stigma and shame avoidance in these practices.

> In those days, when a woman was married, the first thing the bridegroom's family did was to examine her feet. Large feet, meaning normal feet, were considered to bring shame on the husband's house hold. The mother-in-law would lift the hem of the bride's long skirt, and if the feet were more than four inches long, she would throw down the skirt in a demonstrative gesture of contempt and stalk off, leaving the bride to the critical gaze of the wedding guests, who would stare at her feet and

insultingly mutter their disdain. Sometimes the mother would take pity on her daughter and remove the binding cloth; but when the child grew up and had to endure the contempt of her husband's family and the disapproval of society, she would blame her mother for having been too weak (p.31–32).

We could also draw attention to the millions of women who have their genitals mutilated in various forms of female circumcision, and the family stigma/shame and dishonour that is seen to exist if this is not done (Hicks, 1996). There is little doubt then that cultural shame-based body shaping and control has much to answer for. Bodies, no less than values, abilities and behaviour are thus subject to cultural shaping (Abrams, 1996). If Chairman Mao can be thanked for one thing it would be for ending foot-binding even though it was probably because women with deformed feet were no use as soldiers. Sadly, if those with bound feet could not then work in the fields they were stigmatised. Such historical events testify to the rapid change in what is and is not shaming that can sweep through a culture in certain circumstances when the status norm changes.

Failure of parents to attend to their children's appearance can also cause distress. For example, one of our patients, who was bright and won a place at a local grammar school, recalled much shame because, as coming from the poor side of town, his parents could not afford the school uniform and he was often easily identified as 'poor'. He always felt out of place and hated his success at going to this school. Feelings of not 'fitting in' and 'looking different' from others is a common experience in shame and young children can be dependent on parents to help them 'fit in' by 'looking after' their appearance. On the other hand, some parents compete to have their children 'look nice', entering them for pageants and so forth – the appearance of the child reflects on the parent. In regard to functions, Gilbert and Thompson (Chapter 2, this volume) note that the onset of menarche can be a difficult time, and mothers can help their daughters learn how to manage these bodily processes and avoid shame or mothers, due to their shame of menstruation, may pass on shame to their daughters. In some cultures, aspects of sexuality and menstruation can be associated with disgust and women are expected to distance themselves at these times (Gregor, 1990).

Also, of course, family environments can provide loving and accepting experiences for their children and their bodies or shaming ones. Not only may children be subject to unkind and shaming interactions (being labelled as ugly, awkward, looking stupid) but the way parents touch their children's bodies, caress them or offer physical contact and affection can affect the development of body schema. Touch is known to have many physiological regulators that are stress-reducing (Field, 2000). There is little research on the experience of physical affection and later problems with body shame proneness, but one suspects that 'feeling comfortable with one's body' may relate to these experiences, although there may be temperamental differences in how children seek out and respond to physical affection. Clearly, for children with disfiguring conditions, parental behaviours, including those of giving physical affection, may be important in helping them come to terms with a disfigurement.

Andrews (Chapter 13, this volume) explores yet another domain of body shame arising from how others have acted on and towards a child's body. This is the linkage between body shame and sexual abuse. Her research has shown that even in the absence of physical disfigurements, abused women can develop intense body shame, which is related to chronic depression. Body violations such as abuse and rape can be seen as another route by which people come to experience their own bodies as objects of disdain and disgust. The experience of violations goes with the experience of 'being spoiled, damaged, ruined'. In this sense, abuse can be experienced like an (inner) disfigurement – of something that was good being made ugly and bad. Body shame then can be an important experience even for those with no obvious appearance difficulties. (See Lewis, 1998, for a discussion of the link between stigma and shame in sexual abuse.)

The face

What constitutes an attractive face has been subject to much research especially in terms of its proportionality (e.g., eye-to-eye distance, nose length) and facial recognition (Young & Bruce, 1998). Face shapes carry markers of underlying physiological processes linked to reproductive outcomes, such as the levels of testosterone (which in men shape jaw and cheek bone shape) and oestrogens (which in women shape facial bone architecture and lips fullness). The face, perhaps more than any other body area, is thus the focus for what Shilling (1993) calls *the project*, attended to with make-up, shaving, cosmetic surgery and so forth, with individuals (and the media) altering facial appearance to fall in line with what is deemed socially desirable. The face is not only the body area always visible (apart for say use of the veil in certain cultures), it is also a source of social signalling and communication via its multitude of muscles serving expressions. Facial expressions signal emotions and emotional dispositions, with happy and kind facial expressions being more attractive than angry or sad ones. Although eye gaze can have different meanings in different contexts, Larsen and Shackelford (1996) found sex differences in personality associated with eye gaze. Audiences judged eye-gaze-avoidant men and women differently, but in general eye-gaze avoidance is judged as indicating unattractiveness, low confidence, untrustworthiness and even low intelligence.

Facial appearances elicit different responses in others. For example, the face of 'the baby' elicits protective and caring behaviours in others. What constitutes an 'attractive' face is related to the relative portions of the face

(Etcoff, 1999; Young & Bruce, 1998). Be it in babies or adults attractive faces are looked at more, while ugliness is turned away from. The (evolved) rules that govern the aesthetics of a face are relatively culturally invariant, with no cultures finding highly disproportionate faces or poor skin quality attractive, though there are also cultural differences (Young & Bruce, 1998). Nonetheless, Etcoff (1999) notes that fashions and cosmetic use change over time. 'The enormous creased eyelids seen on Greta Garbo and other stars of the 1930s are rarely seen today. The favoured skin colours are no longer the palest shades' (p.146). Although facial scarring is today generally regarded as undesirable, in the eighteenth century, some males would deliberately scar their faces because it was associated with duelling and hence depicting bravery.

Appearance and function

Body (and facial) shame is thus related to an unwanted physical appearance. A number of authors to this volume focus on the appearance domains of body shame. Included are shame related to acne (Kellett, Chapter 7, this volume), psoriasis (Miles, Chapter 6, this volume), blushing (Crozier, Chapter 11, this volume), burns (Coughlan & Clarke, Chapter 8, this volume) and body dysmorphic disorder (Veale, Chapter 14, this volume). What all these authors point out is that the actual degree of disfigurement is only weakly associated with adjustment reactions and it is the personal meanings of any disfigurement that is important (Thompson & Kent, 2001).

However, as noted at the beginning of this chapter, body functions are also subject to shame. These themes are discussed by Ekströmer (Chapter 9, this volume) looking at bowel-related disorders and in regard to sexual functions by Gilbert and Thompson (Chapter 2, this volume), McKee and Gott (Chapter 3, this volume) and Lodnert (Chapter 10, this volume). The relation of shame to eating and vomiting and laxative use are discussed by Goss and Gilbert (Chapter 12, this volume).

A biopsychosocial model for body shame

Given the outline above, we are now in a position to offer a biopsychosocial model for body shame (see Figure 1.2). This part is focused more on the psychosocial aspects and is short on the 'bio' for which I hope readers will forgive me.

Social and cultural contexts

Within a biopsychosocial model the experience of one's body, and the sense of pride, contentment or shame of it, is derived from a complex set of interacting social processes and value systems that inform individuals about what is attractive and acceptable. These can be guided by underlying evolved

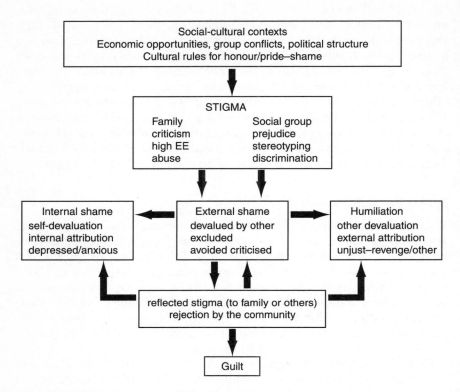

Figure 1.2 A biopsychosocial model for (body) shame

algorithms on body aesthetics (e.g., on skin textures, facial proportions and body shapes) but there are also cultural variations, some of which can be extreme (e.g., foot-binding). Bodies can also be marked, decorated, shaped and clothed according to rules governing group identity and appearance. Also body colour, shape and size are always conceptualised in a social domain, giving rise to complex self-identities (e.g., see the fascinating discussion of feelings of stigma and identity in people of mixed ethnic parents, where people can feel their identity 'is spoiled' by being too white; Storrs, 1999). In some cultures deformities can be seen as the result of karma – bad behaviour in a previous life and be felt as a stigma. In some cultures and historical periods, larger women rather than thin ones were regarded as beautiful. Cultural contexts are then the threads from which shame and stigma are woven.

Who controls whom?

If cultural rules and values are so key to shame and stigma then how do such arise? Well, of course, there may be many reasons for stigmatising others, such as stigmatising those who are diseased to avoid contamination or who are in some way dangerous, or those who do not pull their weight (Kurzban & Leary, 2001). Recently Rozin et al. (1999) have investigated a fascinating theory that suggests that different types of violation can produce different types of emotions in observers. For example, violation of rights could elicit anger; violations of authority/obedience could elicit contempt, whereas losing control over one's body and desires could elicit disgust. This points to different types of stigma being related to different types of emotions in stigmatisers. However, here we would like to explore another aspect and suggest that one of the key domains for the social orchestration of shame and stigma is control. Thus we can ask: who is trying to control who by using stigma and shame as the vehicle of control?

As we have seen, stigmatising, devaluing and rejecting are threats, and can be used to coerce others. Hence, the cultural dynamics of stigma and shame require insights into how groups coalesce around certain values and in whose interests these values operate. For example, evolutionary psychology can inform us about underlying conflicts between the sexual strategies (e.g., for males to seek to control female sexuality, Buss, 1999) and how these show up in cultural rules. For example, male control over female sexuality is noted in many species and Wilson and Daly (1992) suggest that 'women as property' remain a core mindset of men:

> . . . whose operation can be discerned from numerous phenomena which are culturally diverse in their details but monotonously alike in the abstract. These phenomena include socially recognised marriage, the concept of adultery as a property violation, the valuation of female chastity (and virginity), the equation of the protection of women with protection from sexual contact, and the special potency of infidelity as a provocation for violence (p.291, brackets added).

Control of female sexuality (and the female body) has been institutionalised in social and religious forms for hundreds of years and more, with all kinds of justification, often involving the shaming/stigmatising of female sexuality and appearance. However, there is little awareness by the actors that unconscious algorithms, hammered out over millions of years, are perhaps guiding them. These themes even show up in so-called love songs with their themes of jealous possession and threat!

Failure to control that which one is seen to own (and hence control) can result in stigma. Hence, as Lindisfarne (1998) notes, shame and honour are not only socially defined but attention should be given to those who have the power to define them and *benefit from them*. She points out that in many cultures, male honour and shame can be related to control of a woman's sexuality and her body. Males can lose honour and be shamed by failure to control women in their network. There can even be an acceptance of honour-killing of wives or daughters who break the rules (e.g., who commit adultery).

Seeing 'the other' as 'property' with entitlements of ownership and control (including over the body) can also be a mindset for how parents see and treat their children. Many societies take it as given that parents 'own' and can (and should) control their children (they are their property). Not only does this bestow entitlements to indoctrinate them in whatever religion they like, or their own cultural values, but as noted above, to deform them to fit the cultural norm. Britain is even resisting European recommendations that parents should give up the right to be free to smack (hit) their children (Leach, 2002). To de-stigmatise and de-shame the violations of a child's body by hitting or deforming (e.g., foot-binding), parents form beliefs that they are doing these things 'for the child's own good'.

Ownership and control over others is also related to status and rank. For example, there are numerous examples where leaders and emperors of various cultures have seen their subjects (or those conquered in war) as 'property,' giving them legitimacy to treat them as slaves, to offer them as a sacrifice to the Gods, punish them how they wished, exert control over their lives and/or try to manipulate their values to fit their own self-interests. The mindset of treating 'others as objects', to be used for one's own self-interests, or as property with entailments of control, to indoctrinate and to shape as we want, is a far more common relational schema that we care to admit, and in my view reaches far beyond the sexual strategies outlined by Wilson and Daly (1992). Be this as it may, types of shame and stigma are related to these power (ownership) dynamics between shamer and shamed.

Self-control

The concept of ownership also applies to our own bodies; that is, a body is believed to 'belong' to a person; they 'own it' and as such they should take control over it. To lose body control (e.g., of one's functions) can appear deeply shaming. A key component of social anxiety is that one has lost control over one's anxiety. In other forms of mental illness one has lost control over one's own mind. In some forms of stigma of (say) the obese, stigma is not just about appearance but the implication that one has lost control over one's eating (impulses). Social values give very clear instructions into what desires, emotions and body functions one should control and failure to do so is shaming – 'control yourself – pull yourself together – make yourself respectable'!

Rebellion

Although there can be evolved dispositions for certain relationship patterns, these require social contexts to embed themselves. In regard to male control of female sexuality, or parents beating their children, there is nothing inevitable (or desirable) about it. Indeed, civil law and civil liberties (at their best) are designed to inhibit such exploitation (control of one over another) and stigmatisation. Nor should we assume all are passive victims to the values imposed on them, and the power of resistance is as important to understand as the power of control (Scott, 1990). Thus, we return to the fact that people can and do resist possible stigma and we need more research in this area. Thus, in the case of body shape (e.g., thinness) while some will take pride in their ability to meet a cultural norm or high standard and out-compete others, other women will resist such cultural stereotypes. Yet for others control over one's body (e.g., as in anorexia) can itself be an act of resistance, and striving for a self-identity one can be proud of (see Goss & Gilbert, Chapter 12, this volume).

Stigma, shame and humiliation

To sum up so far, it can be seen that cultural rules (which may be underpinned by various evolved algorithms and economic systems – for example, making profits from soap selling or the fashion industry) set the background for what others stigmatise and express prejudice and discrimination. Being 'big' if one is a Sumo wrestler is likely to be given prestige rather than be stigmatised. Concern with one's facial appearance may be increased in societies that highly value facial appearances (e.g., via advertising products) and media display of numerous 'difficult to achieve' models. Families will also be influenced in their shaming and stigmatising of each other and their children by cultural rules. As noted above, body cleanliness is very culturally influenced and so children can be criticised for not 'keeping clean' or 'being dirty'. In some cultures a woman's sexual behaviour (and body) comes under the control of the family. Severe sanctions may be given to breaking the rules (e.g., dress codes in religious groups) or engaging in certain behaviours (e.g., sex outside of marriage). The understanding of body shame, and the relationships between stigma, external shame, internal shame and humiliation therefore needs to be socially contextualised in this textured world of values and meanings. Moreover, how these reflect the conflicts between male and female sexual strategies and group dynamics require further research.

Reflected shame/stigma

Reflected stigma is the stigma that befalls a person, family or group as the result of other people's stigmatisable behaviour. There are two aspects to this. Firstly as noted above, are the ways families attempt to alter/shape the bodies of their children (e.g., genital mutilation, foot-binding or presenting the child as clean and tidy, or attractive). Failure to do this (i.e., the child is seen as not matching up to the cultural values of the group) can result in external shame and stigma of the family. The child is very much a potential object for reflected shame and stigma. If children break the rules or values of the group then stigma falls on those seen to have control over them (e.g., the parents). In a different way, Lewis (1998) discusses reflected shame in siblings of children with learning difficulties. Those feeling reflected shame may internalise it (i.e., there is something bad/flawed about us for having a child like this), or feel humiliated (how dare others see us this way). Also, as noted above, is patriarchal control of sexuality, where shame can fall on men because of failures to control 'their women'. Indeed, families may reject (interestingly often called dis-*owning*) their own kin for violations of social and family codes (e.g., daughters becoming pregnant, sons becoming homosexual or criminal) because of the stigma it can bring to the family or reflect on them. Such kin become the outcasts – the black sheep of the family.

The second source of reflected shame therefore concerns the shame/stigma that falls on others as a result of one's own stigmatisable traits or behaviours. For example, in our research with southern Asian women, they have impressed on us the importance of family *izzat* (family honour) and that from an early age girls are impressed that they must not do anything to damage it. To bring shame and stigma to the family can bring personal shame and guilt. Guilt is related to processes outlined by Zahn-Waxler (2000) and relates to capacities for empathy and feelings about having harmed others (see also O'Connor, 2000). It tends to be associated with desires for reparation (rather than concealment) and sadness. To offer an example of reflected body shame, consider a patient of mine who we will call Jane. She had severe psoriasis from the age of nine. She felt that her family were 'deeply embarrassed and shamed' by her appearance and would at times refuse to take her out because of the way she looked. Jane felt deeply angry and humiliated by her family's attitudes to her psoriasis and this anger was a key focus for her therapy. However, her family's behaviour towards her, especially at times of psoriasis flare-ups, also compounded her own internalised shame. At times she acknowledged that she let her psoriasis get out of control (would not self-care) both as a form of self-punishment and disgust, but also as a way of getting back at others. Such anger, and getting back at others by using a condition, has been poorly researched. Another patient who had been sexually abused was told by her mother that she should never reveal this for it would bring shame to her (the mother) and family. Indeed, one of the reasons children's claims of abuse are dismissed is because this reflects so badly on those supposed to protect them, that the persons (e.g., parents) cannot tolerate their own shame of complicity or failure. This is a terrible predicament for the abused person, because to reveal something like sexual abuse can feel like a betrayal of the family, and as damaging the family – and betrayal is associated with both shame and guilt.

Overview

The above model seeks to give an overview of the multiple layers by which shame and stigma can be analysed and researched. Shame is clearly an experience that arises in an individual – in their field of consciousness of the self. Yet to explore shame and stigma only from the inside is to impoverish the concepts. As we open up shame and stigma to wider analysis, we see just how entangled it is with all aspects of us as a social species. Not only do we need to explore what evolved strategies are ticking away in the background of relationships (e.g., control over female sexuality), but we need to understand better the way social values develop and spread through populations and get internalised.

Pyschopathology and body shame

As there are already some excellent reviews on the linkage of body shame (or body image disturbance) to psychopathology and therapy (e.g., Cash & Grant, 1996; Thompson & Kent, 2001), and because many of the authors of this volume address these issues in their own areas, only a few subsidiary thoughts will be noted here.

Firstly, body shame can be linked to a range of psychopathologies including eating disorders, social anxiety and mood disorders. There is also good evidence that those with disfigurements are at a high risk of disorders (especially social phobia) that require attention (Newell & Marks, 2000; Thompson & Kent, 2001). Mood can impact on body image as both a consequence and cause, for example, as someone becomes depressed they may become more negative in their experiences and perceptions of their body. Pre-existing mood or anxiety disorders (or vulnerability to them) can influence body evaluations and also adjustment to a disfiguring or disabling condition, or to changes in one's body with ageing.

Secondly, as many authors to this volume note, crucial to the linkages between body appearances, unattractiveness, disfigurements and functions, with shame and with psychopathology, is the finding that it is not (just) the objective degree of unattractiveness, disfigurement or dysfunction but the social and psychological meanings given to them that is crucial; that is, to the degree to which any undesirable physical characteristics impact on key social goals (e.g., for forming relationships) and self-esteem (Kellett & Gilbert 2001; Kent & Keohane, 2001). Diener, Wolsic and Fujita (1995) found that in students subjective well-being was only weakly associated with physical attractiveness and that other factors such as personality (e.g., neuroticism), or the extent to which physical attractiveness was central to self-esteem, may interact with any linkage between physical attractiveness and subjective well-being. However, presumably their participants were all relatively 'normal'-looking individuals and we cannot say that this would be the same for those with disfiguring conditions.

Thirdly, the physiological mediators of stress (such as changes in cortisol) can impact on the physical mediators of some disorders (e.g., acne, psoriasis and bowel disease; Kellett & Gilbert, 2001). Hence, helping people cope with stress, be this shame-based or from other sources, can be key to helping people self-manage their condition.

Fourthly, there is now much evidence from animal and human research that negative social interactions, associated with hostility and/or rejection, impact on stress hormones and a host of neurotransmitters such as serotonin and dopamine (Cacioppo et al., 2000; Gilbert, 2001b, 2001c; Schore 2001). Thus, there are likely to be complex interactions between the stress of the experience of stigma, body shame, how people cope with it and how others around them react to their coping. This is a theme of special importance to children with bowel diseases (Ekströmer, Chapter 9, this volume) or sexual dysfunctions (Lodnert, Chapter 10, this volume) where family dynamics are often central. Indeed, the support or criticism of intimates over body shape, disfigurements or loss of abilities (e.g., loss of sexual interest, be this from shame of sex or depression) can relieve or add to a sense of an unattractive self.

Fifthly, we have suggested that the relative balance of external and internal shame will impact on psychopathology and its treatment (Kaufman, 1989; Veale, Chapter 14, this volume). Internal shame involves a particular constellation of negative thoughts and feelings about oneself, often associated with affect memories and scenes (Kaufman, 1989). This links with a growing research literature on the nature of self-criticism and self-attacking. Self-dislike and self-attacking are known to be highly predictive of psychopathology. For example, Zuroff, Koestner and Powers (1994) found that the degree of self-criticism in childhood is a predictor of later adjustment. Gilbert and Clark (submitted) found that there may be at least two forms of distinguishable self-criticism. One focuses on avoidance of mistakes and desires for self-improvement; the other is a form of self-contempt and hatred leading to desires to get rid of, remove or destroy, the hated aspect of the self. The latter seems more highly associated with psychopathology.

Finally, we should note that further research in this area requires both good clinical and objective assessment. In his chapter, Carr (Chapter 4, this volume) offers an important overview of assessment issues and measures. Andrews (2002) has developed a new shame scale that measures body shame as one of its aspects.

Psychotherapy

Shame can affect people's preparedness to come forward for help. When they do come forward, as for most psychological interventions, the therapeutic relationship can affect people's preparedness to engage, to be honest and to feel encouraged to undertake the steps necessary for change (Safran &

Muran, 2000). Many forms of therapy involve *bonds, tasks and goals* (Gilbert, 2000b). While most approaches, be they psychodynamic or cognitive-behavioural, agree on the salient role of (safe) therapy bonds/relationships, they see them in different ways (e.g., attachment versus collaborative/cooperative). However, different people may need different types of relationship to 'feel safe' and we should not assume that one type fits all. MacDonald (1998) and McDonald and Morley (2001) have discussed the issue of revealing 'the shameful' in therapy and the way therapy contexts need to create sufficient safeness for a person to feel able to explore and engage. An empathic awareness of, and sensitivity to, the distress of body shame is obviously important. However, people can feel heightened shame in medical encounters especially when speaking of or showing the affected areas or functions (Lazare, 1987) and the therapeutic relationship can itself be experienced as activating shame. A 'poor bond' can lead to early disengagement.

There has been some discussion of problems of shame in therapy (e.g., Anastasopoulos, 1997; Gilbert, 1998c; Osherson & Krugman, 1990;) and how it affects the focus of a therapy (shame can be hidden and denied) and how shame can be a problem in the therapist as well as the patient (Retzinger, 1998). However, there has been little research on the special qualities of the therapeutic relationship for people with body shame. Shame (in both client and therapist) can be a special problem especially if clients are very withdrawn or use aggressive defences.

As noted above, the therapeutic relationship with individuals whose shame is primarily external, and focuses on the fear of the reactions of social audiences, is likely to be different than with those whose shame is highly internalised. Moreover, internalisers probably are more vulnerable to a range of psychological disorders, including depression, substance abuse, and eating disorders. Indeed, Cook (1996) shows high levels of internal shame (as measured by negative self-evaluation) for all these disorders.

Formulation

The first stage of psychological intervention is focused on formulation. Here the therapist may need to ascertain a range of areas depending on the case:

1 the nature of the presenting difficulty and typical symptoms, ascertaining the possibility of depression, anxiety, eating or other disorders;
2 whether the problem is of chronic or acute onset;
3 historical factors such as experiences of being stigmatised, quality of attachment relationships (e.g., neglect or abuse);
4 the social context in which difficulties arise, for example, the style of the family, peer and work interactions;
5 the key beliefs a person has about their disfigurement, disability or

dysfunction. These will focus on beliefs about the reactions of others, and also self-evaluation. Cognitive therapists will assess people's typical automatic thoughts;

6 the typical emotions that are generated in shame situations (e.g., anger vs. anxiety) and their linkage to automatic thoughts;
7 the typical defensive, safety and coping behaviours (e.g., social avoidance, submissive inhibition) and how these impact on adjustment and social engagement.

There are many measures for assessing psychopathology and increasing measures for assessing body and appearance problems (see Carr, Chapter 4, this volume; Carr, Harris & James, 2000). These can be used both clinically and for research.

Interventions

Interventions are the *tasks and goals* of therapy and different therapeutic approaches have different tasks and goals (Gilbert, 2000b). *Behaviour therapy* – stresses the importance of understanding the elicitors of emotions and a functional analysis of coping behaviour; what is its purpose – why does the person act this way? (See Goss & Gilbert, Chapter 12, this volume.) It pays particular attention to the nature of defensive, damage limitation or safety behaviours (e.g., avoidance). Are these currently or previously functionally useful? Another key aim is to aid exposure to the 'feared and avoided' so that people learn how to tolerate and cope with distressing emotions (e.g., anxiety) and the situations that elicit them. Overcoming distress by exposure (rather than avoidance) is key to older forms of therapy such as Buddhist approaches. A key component in working with social anxiety (and shame) is reducing dysfunctional safety behaviours (Clark, 2001; Wells, 1998) by practising alternative behaviours and coping with anxiety. As Coughlan and Clarke (Chapter 8, this volume) outline, people can feel safer and in control when they know how to act – hence the value of skills training. And, finally, adaptive behaviours will increase when they are associated with rewards and successful outcomes.

Cognitive therapy (CT)

CT focuses on thoughts, interpretations and meanings (Beck et al., 1979; Beck, Emery & Greenberg, 1985; Clark, 2001). There is the use of guided discovery, inference chains and generating alternatives to stress-increasing thoughts. People are taught how to monitor their thoughts and feelings and identify key self-other schema.

There have been comparatively few randomised controlled trials for shame, let alone body shame disorders. However, Cash and Grant (1996) provide an excellent overview of studies using primarily cognitive behavioural therapy for body image disturbances with some promising findings. Many authors to this volume also explore various interventions and strategies for working with types of body shame. There seems to be a number of core features that may help people.

1 The therapist may discuss openly the nature of 'shame' and use the term shame, or felt stigma with people to have a shared language for engagement. Because shame can recruit powerful emotions that can involve inhibition of thoughts and being unable to express oneself, or sudden rushes of anger, Gilbert (2000b) suggested discussion on the nature of shame, what it is and how it works (one can be ashamed of shamed inhibited response, such as not being able to speak about one's feelings and appearing stupid). Explaining shame can give people a language for their feelings. Anecdotally, some patients have found this very helpful.

2 People's core beliefs and styles of thinking can be explored using cognitive therapy techniques such as Socratic types of questioning, for example, 'what would that mean for you'? or 'what would you conclude from that'? (Beck, Emery & Greenberg, 1985; Gilbert 2000b). These help to reveal people's key concerns. There are a large array of cognitive-behavioural interventions, as noted above (Beck, Emery & Greenberg, 1985). These may include learning the relationship between thinking and feeling and self-monitoring in certain contexts, for example, 'This person looks awkward in my presence, therefore I'm going to be rejected by this person.' In cognitive approaches these are often portrayed in a circular form such that the person gains insight into how their thinking affects their feelings and behaviours and how their behaviours can worsen the problems (Clark, 2001; Kellett, Chapter 7, this volume).

3 The therapeutic relationship can enable people to express their distress and feel understood. As the relationship develops various negative thoughts can be worked with and alternative ideas explored. For example, to the thought: 'This person looks awkward in my presence, therefore I'm going to be rejected by this person' could become 'This person is not sure what to say, feels awkward, but if I help them to feel less awkward they may well have an interest in me as a person.' Coughlan and Clarke (Chapter 8, this volume) explore this aspect in detail.

4 The social anxiety literature depicts a large range of techniques for helping with social anxiety (e.g., Clark, 2001; Wells, 1998) and these can be adapted for working with body shame. Of special importance is addressing people's (often) maladaptive coping, especially the tendency to use various defensive behaviours (e.g., fight, flight), and what some cognitive therapists call safety behaviours, such as avoidance and concealment. Wells (1998) also has discussed attentional control and meta-cognitions as a focus for intervention (see also Crozier, Chapter 11, this volume). To

date these approaches have not been systematically applied to body shame but look good candidates for being helpful.

5 Because people can be ashamed of their shame responses (e.g., feel ashamed that one cannot look up, or has to hide, or flies into a rage), it can be very helpful to focus on the *positive* and protective *functions* of a person's shame defences. For example, anger can be seen as a way of defending oneself against hurt by staying strong – it gives one courage. Or avoidance can be seen as the best way people could (at the time) think of to protect themselves from further harm/rejection. Time spent *valuing* the defensive behaviours and considering their useful (as well as not so useful) functions can de-shame them and help to build the therapeutic alliance. People may have various thoughts that they are stupid and bad (or may appear such) for acting in the way they do. Therapists can explore these and help to re-evaluate them.

6 Encouraging the use of support groups of other sufferers can be very useful for some people, especially if the disorder is relatively rare. Again, one suspects that those with intense internalised shame, or where there are unaddressed other issues (e.g., abuse) may struggle in these contexts. Some people may simply refuse to come to groups.

7 Helping the person develop various coping options and skills for dealing with negative reactions from others is very helpful for some individuals (Coughlan & Clarke, Chapter 8, this volume).

8 Addressing relationship problems and dysfunctional family dynamics can be important for some individuals.

Self attacking and compassionate mind

There are many ways of helping people with internalised shame (e.g., Bergner, 1987; Kaufman, 1989). For some individuals therapy may need to work on underlying depression and anxiety (Gilbert, 2000b). Recently, it has been suggested that where there is significant self-directed hostility, challenging these cognitions and feelings may be helped by teaching a 'compassionate mind' approach. Here the person learns to challenge their negative thoughts by practising generating a compassionate and warm affect in the challenge itself (Gilbert, 2000c, 2000d). For example, a person may have the belief that 'others will reject me because of the way I look. Therefore I can't make friends.' Alternative thoughts might be generated by asking the person: 'What would you say to a friend who has a similar difficulty?' This helps to focus the person on both evidence against a negative belief and also what is likely to be helpful and supportive at times of difficulty. Hence, an alternative set of thoughts might be: 'It may be difficult for others to at first see past my disfigurement or disability, but if I make an effort to relate to them there are many other qualities to relating. I may have more difficulty in starting relationships, but friendships are based on liking a person, trust and kindness.

Because others may have difficulty relating to my disfigurement or disability, this does not make me a worthless or unlovable person.'

In compassionate mind work, the person might first learn to be empathic to their own distress (e.g., it is sad and distressing that I have this difficulty) and space is given to grieving, if this is appropriate. Some people bypass their sadness and focus on anger or have thoughts like: 'I am stupid/weak to let this upset me; I should be stronger' or 'I should not worry so much about what others think of me.' Being sensitive to grief and the actual or possible losses that a disfigurement or disablement can bring can be key to a process of coming to terms with it. Secondly, there is a focus on the feelings of warmth and compassion, when thinking about alternative thoughts. For example, people may use imagery of compassionate people and how they might look or sound. Once this affect is elicited (to some degree), they then go over their 'alternative coping thoughts' in their mind trying to generate as much compassion and warmth as possible. The therapist may say, 'Let's go through these alternative thoughts again but as you read them through try to imagine hearing them in your mind as if a compassionate part of you were speaking them.' Or the therapist may say, 'I'd like you to imagine the voice of someone who is very understanding of the distress you feel and they are speaking warmly and compassionately to you to encourage and support you.' The idea here is to get a warm *emotional tone* in the alternative thoughts. This can be practised a number of times in the therapy. Sometimes a person may use mental imagery of 'a kind and compassionate person' speaking to them with understanding and encouragement. The idea is to directly undermine *the affect* of the self-attacking. In a way it is like trying to generate an alternative incompatible affect, not unlike teaching people relaxation as a counter-affect for anxiety. Warmth can be a counter of hostility.

To date there is no clear evidence that this gives any additional advantage over evidence-based challenges and behavioural change. However, having developed this approach with self-critical depressed people, a number of them have suggested that this was a key aspect for them in beginning to believe in their alternative thoughts and generate internal feelings of being supported. Lee (personal communication) used compassionate imagery with a severely burnt lady. The lady had done reasonably well with cognitive interventions; however, adding compassionate imagery produced a further shift towards greater self-acceptance and liking, which had a major impact on her confidence and mood. It should be noted, however, that some people find compassionate mind work very difficult for they may have had little experience of others being 'kind' to them and can at times feel overwhelmed with sadness from which they cut off. Some people (with very dysfunctional backgrounds) find that they cannot generate compassionate feelings or imagery, and a good deal of time can be spent working with developing inner compassion (Gilbert, 2000d). Such people often require longer-term therapies.

Conclusion

This chapter has argued that all humans have a basic evolved need to belong and to be accepted in their intimate relationships and wider social groups (Baumeister & Leary, 1995); and thus seek to be attractive in the eyes of others. Hence, there is a basic sensitivity to, and often fear of, 'demotions' and 'put-downs' (being an undesirable, unattractive self) that could lead to exclusion, bullying, ostracism and loss of support acceptance. There are some domains (e.g., for disease and disability) that may be evolutionary important for shame and stigma (Kurzban & Leary, 2001). This being the case, all social relationships including dyads, small groups through to cultures can use stigma-shaming as a means of social control, coercion and social cohesion. Nonetheless, the specifics of the 'shameful' vary from group to group, for example, foot-binding, sexual behaviour, dress codes, physical appearance, control over oneself. For example, in some cultures, homosexuality is accepted and endorsed whereas in others parents may even beat up and reject their own children if they are seen to have such interests. To understand cultural variations in the focus of shame, it is first necessary to illuminate and understand the *common* human psychology and psychological processes behind cultural variations. We have also noted that stigma shame and prestige systems act like social glue that empower some (the unholders) and disempowers others (the value/rule-breakers or those who do not 'come up to standard').

This chapter has deliberately taken a broad, biopsychosocial overview of shame and body shame to avoid creating yet another subdivision within psychology. By offering such an overview, we can link into some of the complexities emerging in the shame literature and how shame can be central to body appearance and functional disturbances. The social allocations of status and attractiveness to specific physical traits, be they guided by evolved algorithms and/or social discourses, are key mechanisms by which we learn the social rules/values for attractiveness acceptance and stigma, and attempt to copy the behaviour and appearances of others who have high or acceptable status and thus be valued and accepted ourselves. We noted that there is a competitive dynamic behind this (e.g., Gilbert, 1989; Tooby & Cosmides, 1996) that recruits into people's self-appraisals, competencies such as social comparison, recognition of self as a social object for others and theory of mind. The products of these self-conscious competencies (e.g., beliefs that one is inferior to others, or that others have negative feelings, such as contempt or disdain, for the self) are the bedrock for shame. However, severe distress, focused on one's body, is not simply about not having the physical appearance one would like, or those deemed attractive by one's group. It is seeing oneself as possessing unattractive qualities that increases the risk of psychopathology.

There are then important reasons for understanding body image disturbances and body self-esteem as rooted in processes related to shame.

The most obvious are that there is a growing literature on shame that links together internal experiences and self-perceptions, social interactions and relationships, vulnerabilities to psychopathology and psychotherapeutic interventions that are targeted at shame. The authors to this volume address these issues and each add to our understanding of the complexities of body shame and the ways we may help people overcome it.

References

Abrams, D. (1996) Social identity, self as structure and self as process. In W.P. Robinson (ed.) *Social Groups and Identities: Developing the Legacy of Henri Tajfel* (pp.143–162). Oxford: Butterworth-Heinemann.

Alden, L.E. (2001) Interpersonal perspectives on social anxiety. In W.R. Crozier & L.E. Alden (eds) *International Handbook of Social Anxiety: Concepts, Research and Interventions to the Self and Shyness* (pp.381–404). Chichester: John Wiley & Sons.

Allan, S. & Gilbert, P. (2002) Anger and anger expression in relation to perceptions of social rank, entrapment and depressive symptoms. *Personality and Individual Differences*, 32, 551–565.

Anastasopoulos, D. (1997) Shame in psychotherapy with adolescents. *Journal of Child Psychotherapy*, 23, 103–123.

Andrew, B., Qian, M. & Valentine, J.D. (2002) Predicting depressive symptoms with a new measure of shame: The experience scale. *British Journal of Clinical Psychology*, 41, 29–42.

Baldwin, M.W. & Fergusson, P. (2001) Relational schemas: The activation of interpersonal knowledge structures in social anxiety. In W.R. Crozier & L.E. Alden (eds) *International Handbook of Social Anxiety: Concepts, Research and Interventions to the Self and Shyness* (pp.235–257). Chichester: John Wiley & Sons.

Barkow, J.H. (1989) *Darwin, Sex and Status: Biological Approaches to Mind and Culture*. Toronto: University of Toronto Press.

Barrett, K.C. (1995) A functionalist approach to shame and guilt. In J.P. Tangney & K.W. Fischer (eds) *Self-conscious Emotions: The Psychology of Shame, Guilt, Embarrassment and Pride* (pp.25–63). New York: Guilford Press.

Baumeister, R.F. & Leary, M.R. (1995) The need to belong: Desire for interpersonal attachments as a fundamental human motivation. *Psychological Bulletin*, 117, 497–529.

Beck, A.T., Emery, G. & Greenberg, R.L. (1985) Anxiety Disorders and Phobias: A Cognitive Approach. New York: Basic Books.

Beck, A.T., Rush, A.J., Shaw, B.F. & Emery, G. (1979) *Cognitive Therapy of Depression*. New York: John Wiley & Sons.

Bergner, R.M. (1987) Undoing degradation. *Psychotherapy*, 24, 25–30.

Bunting, M. (2001) Clean up. *The Guardian Weekend*, 6 October, 40–48.

Buss, D.M. (1999) *Evolutionary Psychology: The New Science of Mind*. Boston, MA: Allyn and Bacon.

Cacioppo, J.T., Berston, G.G., Sheridan, J.F. & McClintock, M.K. (2000) Multilevel integrative analysis of human behavior: Social neuroscience and the complementing nature of social and biological approaches. *Psychological Bulletin*, 126, 829–843.

Camp, D.L., Finlay, W.M.L. & Lyons, E. (2002) Is low self-esteem an inevitable consequence of stigma? An example from women with chronic mental health problems. *Social Science and Medicine*, 55, 823–834.

Carr, T., Harris, D. & James, C. (2000) The Derriford appearance sacle (DAS-59): A new scale to measure individual responses to living with problems of appearance. *British Journal of Health Psychology*, 5, 201–215.

Cash, T.F. & Grant, J.R. (1996) Cognitive behavioral treatment of body-image disturbances. In V. Vanen & M. Hersen (eds) *Sourcebook of Psychological Manuals for Adult Disorders* (pp.567–614). New York: Plenum Press.

Chang, J. (1992) *Wild Swans: Three Daughters in China*. London: Flamingo.

Clark, D.M. (2001) A cognitive perspective on social phobia. In W.R. Crozier & L.E. Alden (eds) *International Handbook of Social Anxiety: Concepts, Research and Interventions to the Self and Shyness* (pp.405–430). Chichester: John Wiley & Sons.

Clark, D.M. & Wells, A. (1995) A cognitive model of social phobia. In R.G. Heimberg., M.R. Liebowitz., D.A. Hope & R.R. Schneier (eds) *Social Phobia: Diagnosis, Assessment and Treatment* (pp.69–93). New York: Guilford Press.

Clark, L.A. (2000) Mood, personality, and personality disorders. In R.J. Davidson (ed.) *Anxiety, Depression and Emotion* (pp.171–200). New York: Oxford University Press.

Cloitre, M. & Shear, M.K. (1995) Psychodynamic perspectives. In M.B Stein (ed.) *Social Phobia: Clinical and Research Perspectives*. Washington, DC: American Psychiatric Press.

Cohen, D. (2001) Cultural variation: Considerations and implications. *Psychological Bulletin*, 127, 451–471.

Cohen, D., Vandello, J. & Rantilla, A.K. (1998) The sacred and the social: Cultures of honor and violence. In P. Gilbert & B. Andrews (eds) *Shame: Interpersonal Behavior, Psychopathology and Culture* (pp.261–282). New York: Oxford University Press.

Cook, D.R. (1996) Empirical studies of shame and guilt: The internalized shame scale. In D.L. Nathanson (ed.) *Knowing Feeling: Affect, Script and Psychotherapy* (pp.132–165). New York: Norton.

Crisp, A (2001) The tendency to stigmatise. *British Journal of Psychiatry*, 178, 197–199.

Crocker, J. & Major, B. (1989) Social stigma and self-esteem: The self-protective qualities of stigma. *Psychological Review*, 96, 608–630.

Crozier, W.R. & Alden, L.E. (2001) (eds) *International Handbook of Social Anxiety: Concepts Research and Interventions Relating to the Self and Shyness*. Chichester: John Wiley & Sons.

Diener, E., Wolsic, B. & Fujita, F. (1995) Physical attractiveness and subjective well being. *Personality and Social Psychology*, 69, 120–129.

Ellis, A. (1977) Psychotherapy and the value of a human being. In A. Ellis & R. Grieger (eds) *Handbook of Rational Emotive Therapy*. New York: Springer.

Etcoff, N. (1999) *Survival of the Prettiest: The Science of Beauty*. New York: Doubleday.

Feest, C.F. (2000) *The Culture of Native North American Indians*. Cologne: Koneman.

Feinberg, T.E. (2001) *Altered Egos: How the Brain Creates the Self*. New York: Oxford University Press.

Field, T. (2000) *Touch Therapy*. New York: Churchill Livingstone.

Fischer, K.W. & Tangney, J.P. (1995) Self-conscious emotions and the affect revolution: Framework and overview. In J.P. Tangney & K.W. Fischer (eds) *Self-conscious Emotions: The Psychology of Shame, Guilt, Embarrassment and Pride* (pp.3–22). New York: Guilford Press.

Friedman, L. & Moon, S. (1997) (eds) *Being Bodies: Buddhist Women on the Paradox of Embodiment*. Boston, MA: Shambhala Press.

Frijda, H.H. (1994) The lex Talionis: On vengeance. In S.H.M. Van Goozen., N.E. Van de Poll & J.A. Sergeant (eds) *Emotions: Essays on Emotion Theory* (pp.263–289). Hillsdale, NJ: Lawrence Erlbaum Associates Inc.

Gilbert, P. (1989) *Human Nature and Suffering*. Hove, UK: Lawrence Erlbaum Ltd.

Gilbert, P. (1992) *Depression: The Evolution of Powerlessness*. Hove, UK: Lawrence Erlbaum Associates Ltd and New York: Guilford Press.

Gilbert, P. (1993) Defence and safety: Their function in social behaviour and psychopathology. *British Journal of Clinical Psychology*, 32, 131–154.

Gilbert, P. (1995) Biopsychosocial approaches and evolutionary theory as aids to integration in clinical psychology and psychotherapy. *Clinical Psychology and Psychotherapy*, 2, 135–156.

Gilbert, P. (1997) The evolution of social attractiveness and its role in shame, humiliation, guilt and therapy. *British Journal of Medical Psychology*, 70, 113–147.

Gilbert, P. (1998a) What is shame? Some core issues and controversies. In P. Gilbert & B. Andrews (eds) *Shame: Interpersonal Behavior, Psychopathology and Culture* (pp.3–38). New York: Oxford University Press.

Gilbert, P. (1998b) The evolved basis and adaptive functions of cognitive distortions. *British Journal of Medical Psychology*, 71, 447–463.

Gilbert, P. (1998c) Shame and humiliation in the treatment of complex cases. In N. Tarrier, G. Haddock & A. Wells (eds) *Treating Complex Cases: The Cognitive Behavioural Therapy Approach*. Chichester: John Wiley & Sons.

Gilbert, P. (2000a) The relationship of shame, social anxiety and depression: The role of the evaluation of social rank. *Clinical Psychology and Psychotherapy*, 7, 174–189.

Gilbert, P. (2000b) *Counselling for Depression: A Cognitive-interpersonal Approach* (second edition). London: Sage.

Gilbert, P. (2000c) Social mentalities: Internal 'social' conflicts and the role of inner warmth and compassion in cognitive therapy. In P. Gilbert & K.G. Bailey (eds) *Genes on the Couch: Explorations in Evolutionary Psychotherapy* (pp.118–150). Hove: Brunner-Routledge.

Gilbert, P. (2000d) *Overcoming Depression: A Self-help Guide using Cognitive Behavioral Techniques* (revised edition). London: Robinsons-Constable and New York: Oxford University Press.

Gilbert, P. (2001a) Evolutionary approaches to psychopathology: The role of natural defences. *Australian and New Zealand Journal of Psychiatry*, 35, 17–27.

Gilbert, P. (2001b) Evolution, stress and depression. *Stress: The International Journal of the Biology of Stress*, 4, 121–135.

Gilbert, P. (2001c) Evolution and social anxiety: The role of social competition and social hierarchies. In F. Schnieder (eds) *Social Anxiety: Psychiatric Clinics of North America*, 24, 723–751.

Gilbert, P. & Andrews B. (1998) (eds) *Shame: Interpersonal Behaviour, Psychopathology and Culture*. New York: Oxford University Press.

Gilbert, P. & Clark, M. (submitted) Forms and functions of self-criticism and self-attacking: An exploration of differences.

Gilbert, P. & McGuire, M. (1998) Shame, social roles and status: The psychobiological continuum from monkey to human. In P. Gilbert & B. Andrews (eds) *Shame: Interpersonal Behavior, Psychopathology and Culture* (pp.99–125). New York: Oxford University Press.

Gilbert, P. & Miles J.N.V. (2000a) Evolution, genes, development and psychopathology. *Clinical Psychology and Psychotherapy*, 7, 246–255.

Gilbert, P. & Miles J.N.V. (2000b) Sensitivity to put down: Its relationship to perceptions of shame, social anxiety, depression anger and self-other blame. *Personality and Individual Differences*, 29, 757–774.

Gilbert, P., Pehl, J. & Allan, S. (1994) The phenomenology of shame and guilt: An empirical investigation. *British Journal of Medical Psychology*, 67, 23–36.

Gilbert, P., Price, J.S. & Allan, S. (1995) Social comparison, social attractiveness and evolution: How might they be related? *New Ideas In Psychology*, 13, 149–165.

Gilbert, P. & Trower, P. (2001) Evolution and process in social anxiety. In W.R. Crozier & L.E. Alden (eds) *International Handbook of Social Anxiety: Concepts, Research and Interventions to the Self and Shyness* (pp.259–280). Chichester: John Wiley & Sons.

Goffman, E. (1968) *Stigma: Notes on the Management of a Spoiled Identity*. London: Penguin Books.

Gray, J.A. (1987) *The Psychology of Fear and Stress* (second edition). Cambridge: Cambridge University Press.

Gregor, T. (1990) Male domination and sexual coercion. In J.W. Stigler, R.A. Shweder & G. Herdt (eds) *Cultural Psychology: Essays in Comparative Human Development* (pp.477–495). Cambridge: Cambridge University Press.

Heinrichs, N. & Hofmann, S.G. (2001) Information processing in social phobia: A critical review. *Clinical Psychology Review*, 21, 751–770.

Hicks, S.K. (1996) *Infibulation: Female Mutilation in Islamic Northeastern Africa*. New Brunswick: Transaction.

Hinde, R.A. (1989) Relations between levels of complexity in behavioral sciences. *Journal of Nervous and Mental Disease*, 177, 655–667.

Hinde, R.A. (1992) Developmental psychology in the context of other behavioral sciences. *Developmental Psychology*, 28, 1018–1029.

Hofmann, S.G. & Barlow, D.H. (2001) Social phobia (social anxiety disorder). In D.H. Barlow (eds) *Anxiety and its Disorders: The Nature and Treatment of Anxiety and Panic*. New York: Guilford Press.

Jacoby, A. (1994) Felt verses enacted stigma: A concept revisited. *Social Science and Medicine*, 38, 269–274.

Kaufman, G. (1989) *The Psychology of Shame*. New York: Springer.

Kellett, S. & Gilbert, P. (2001) Acne: A biopsychosocial and evolutionary perspective with a focus on shame. *British Journal of Health Psychology*, 6, 1–24.

Kelman, H.C. & Hamilton, V.L. (1989) *Crimes of Obedience*. New Haven: Yale University Press.

Keltner, D. & Harker, L.A. (1998) The forms and functions of the nonverbal signal of shame. In P. Gilbert & B. Andrews (eds) *Shame: Interpersonal Behavior, Psychopathology and Culture* (pp.78–98). New York: Oxford University Press.

Kent, G. & Keohane, S. (2001) Social anxiety and disfigurement: The moderating effects of fear of negative evaluation. *Journal of Clinical Psychology*, 40, 23–34.

Klein, D.C. (1991) The humiliation dynamic: An overview. *The Journal of Primary Prevention*, 12, 93–121.

Koole, S.L., Dijksterhuis, A. & van Knipperberg, A. (2001) What's in a name: Implicit self-esteem and the automatic self. *Journal of Personality and Social Psychology*, 80, 669–685.

Kurzban, R. & Leary, M. (2001) Evolutionary origins of stigmatisation: The functions of social exclusion. *Psychological Bulletin*, 127, 187–208.

Larsen R.J. & Shackelford T.K. (1996) Gaze avoidance: Personality and social judgments of people who avoid direct face-to-face contact. *Personality and Individual Differences*, 21, 907–917.

Lashbrook, J.T. (2000) Fitting in: Exploring the emotional dimension of adolescent peer pressure. *Adolescence*, 35, 747–757.

Lazare, A. (1987) Shame and humiliation in the medical encounter. *Archives of Internal Medicine*, 147, 1653–1658.

Lazarus, R.S. (1994) *Coping and the Self-management of Emotion*. New York: Oxford University Press.

Leach, P. (2002) You can't beat psychological input. *The Psychologist*, 15, 8–9.

Leary, M.R. (1995) *Self-presentation: Impression Management and Interpersonal Behavior*. Madison, WI: Brown & Benchmark's.

Leary, M.R. (2001) (ed) *Interpersonal Rejection*. New York: Oxford University Press.

Leary, M.R. & Kowalski, R.M. (1995) *Social Anxiety*. New York: Guilford Press.

Leary, M.R., Tambor, E.S., Terdal, S.K. & Downs, D.L. (1995) Self-esteem as an interpersonal monitor: The sociometer hypothesis. *Journal of Personality and Social Psychology*, 68, 519–530.

Le Doux, J. (1998) *The Emotional Brain*. London: Weidenfeld & Nicolson.

Lee, D.A., Scragg, P. & Turner, S. (2001) The role of shame and guilt in traumatic events: A clinical model of shame based PTSD. *British Journal of Medical Psychology*, 74, 451–466.

Lerner, J.S. & Keltner, D. (2001) Fear, anger and risk. *Journal of Personality and Social Psychology*, 81, 146–159.

Lewis, M. (1992) *Shame: The Exposed Self*. New York: The Free Press.

Lewis, M. (1995) Self-conscious emotions. *American Scientist*, 83, 68–78.

Lewis, M. (1998) Shame and stigma. In P. Gilbert & B. Andrews (eds) *Shame: Interpersonal Behaviour, Psychopathology and Culture* (pp.126–140). New York: Oxford University Press.

Lindisfarne, N. (1998) Gender, shame, and culture: An anthropological perspective. In P. Gilbert & B. Andrews (eds) *Shame: Interpersonal Behavior, Psychopathology and Culture* (pp.246–260). New York: Oxford University Press.

Lindsay-Hartz, J., de Rivera, J. & Mascolo, M.F. (1995) Differentiating guilt and shame and their effects on motivations. In J.P. Tangney & K.W. Fischer (eds) *Self-conscious emotions: The Psychology of Shame, Guilt, Embarrassment and Pride* (pp.274–300). New York: Guilford.

Liotti, G. (2000) Disorganised attachment, models of borderline states and evolutionary psychotherapy. In P. Gilbert & B. Bailey (eds) *Genes on the Couch: Explorations in Evolutionary Psychotherapy* (pp.232–256). Hove: Brunner-Routledge.

MacDonald, J. (1998) Disclosing shame. In P. Gilbert & B. Andrews (eds) *Shame: Interpersonal Behavior, Psychopathology and Culture* (pp.141–160). New York: Oxford University Press.

MacDonald, J. & Morley, I. (2001) Shame and non-disclosure: A study of the emotional isolation of people referred for psychotherapy. *British Journal of Medical Psychology*, 74, 1–21.

Major, B. & Gramzow, R.H. (1999) Abortion as stigma: Cognitive and emotional implications of concealment. *Journal of Personality and Social Psychology*, 77, 735–745.

Mascolo, M.F. & Fischer, K.W. (1995) Developmental transformations in appraisals of pride, shame and guilt. In J.P. Tangney & K.W. Fischer (eds) *Self-conscious Emotions: The Psychology of Shame, Guilt, Embarrassment and Pride* (pp.64–113). New York: Guilford Press.

McKinley, N.M. (1999) Women and objectified body consciousness: Mothers' and daughters' body experience in cultural, developmental and familial context. *Developmental Psychology*, 35, 760–769.

McNally, R.J. (2001) On the scientific status of cognitive appraisal models of anxiety disorders. *Behaviour Research and Therapy*, 39, 513–521.

Miller, S.B. (1988) Humiliation and shame: comparing two affect states as indicators of narcissistic stress. *Bulletin of the Menninger Clinic*, 52, 40–51.

Murray, L. & Cooper, P.J. (1997) *Postpartum depression and child development*. New York: Guilford Press.

Nathanson, D.L. (1994) *Shame and Pride: Affect Sex and the Birth of the Self*. New York: Norton Paperbacks.

Nesse, R. (1998) Emotional disorders in evolutionary perspective. *British Journal of Medical Psychology*, 71, 397–416.

Newell, R. & Marks, I. (2000) Phobic nature of social difficulty in facially disfigured people. *British Journal of Psychiatry*, 176, 177–181.

O'Connor, L.E. (2000) Pathogenic beliefs and guilt in human evolution: Implication for psychotherapy. In P. Gilbert & K.G. Bailey (eds) *Genes on the Couch: Explorations in Evolutionary Psychotherapy* (pp.276–303). Hove: Brunner-Routledge.

Ogilive, D.M. (1987) The undesired self: A neglected variable in personality research. *Journal of Personality and Social Psychology*, 52, 379–388.

Osherson, S. & Krugman, S. (1990) Men, shame, and psychotherapy. *Psychotherapy*, 27, 327–339.

Overing, J. (1989) Styles of manhood: An Amazonian contrast in tranquillity and violence. In S. Howell & R. Wills (eds) *Societies at Peace. Anthropological Perspectives* (pp.19–99). London: New York.

Panskepp, J. (1998) *Affective Neuroscience*. New York: Oxford University Press.

Pinel E.C. (1999) Stigma consciousness: The psychological legacy of social stereotypes. *Journal of Personality and Social Psychology*, 76, 114–128.

Retzinger, S. (1991) *Violent Emotions: Shame and Rage in Marital Quarrels*. New York: Sage.

Retzinger, S. (1998) Shame in the therapeutic relationship. In P. Gilbert & B. Andrews (eds) *Shame: Interpersonal Behavior, Psychopathology and Culture* (pp.206–222). New York: Oxford University Press.

Rozin, P., Lowery, L., Imada, S. & Haidt, J. (1999) The CAD triad hypothesis: A mapping between three moral emotions (contempt, anger, disgust) and three moral codes (community, anatomy, divinity). *Journal of Personality and Social Psychology*, 76, 574–586.

Safran, J.D. & Muran, J.C. (2000) *Negotiating the Therapeutic Alliance: A Relational Treatment Guide*. New York: Guilford Press.

Santor, D. & Walker, J. (1999) Garnering the interests of others: Mediating the effects among physical attractiveness, self-worth and dominance. *British Journal of Social Psychology*, 38, 461–477.

Scheff, T.J. (1988) Shame and conformity: The deference-emotion system. *American Review of Sociology*, 53, 395–406.

Schore, A.N. (1994) *Affect Regulation and the Origin of the Self: The Neurobiology of Emotional Development*. Hillsdale, NJ: Lawrence Erlbaum Associates Inc.

Schore, A.N. (1998) Early shame experiences and infant brain development. In P. Gilbert & B. Andrews (eds) *Shame: Interpersonal Behavior, Psychopathology and Culture* (pp.57–77). New York: Oxford University Press.

Schore, A.N. (2001) The effects of early relational trauma on right brain development, affect regulation, and infant mental health. *Infant Mental Health Journal*, 22, 201–269.

Scott, J.C. (1990) *Domination and the Arts of Resistance*. New Haven, CT: Yale University Press.

Shabi, R. (2001) Muscle mania. *The Guardian Weekend*, 21 July, 19–26.

Shilling, C. (1993) *The Body and Social Theory*. London: Sage.

Sloman, L. (2000) The syndrome of rejection sensitivity. In P. Gilbert & B. Bailey (eds) *Genes on the Couch: Explorations in Evolutionary Psychotherapy* (pp.257–275). Hove: Brunner-Routledge.

Smart, L. & Wegner, D.M. (1999) Covering up what can't be seen: Concealable stigma and mental control. *Journal of Personality and Social Psychology*, 77, 474–486.

Solomon, R.C. (1994) Sympathy and vengeance: The role of the emotions in justice. In S.H.M. van Goozen, N.E. van de Poll & J.A. Sergeant (eds) *Emotions: Essays on Emotion Theory* (pp.291–311). Hillsdale, NJ: Lawrence Erlbaum Associates Inc.

Stipek, D. (1995) The development of pride and shame in toddlers. In J.P Tangney & K.W. Fischer (eds) *Self-conscious Emotions: The Psychology of Shame, Guilt, Embarrassment and Pride* (pp.237–252). New York: Guilford Press.

Storrs, D. (1999) Whiteness as stigma: Essentialist identity work by mixed-race women. *Symbolic Interaction*, 22, 187–121.

Takahashi, T. (1989) Social phobia syndrome in Japan. *Comprehensive Psychiatry*, 30, 45–51.

Tangney, J.P. (1995) Shame and guilt in interpersonal relationships. In J.P. Tangney & K.W. Fischer (eds) *Self-conscious Emotions: The Psychology of Shame, Guilt, Embarrassment and Pride* (pp.114–139). New York: Guilford Press.

Tangney, J.P. & Fischer, K.W. (1995) (eds) *Self-conscious Emotions: The Psychology of Shame, Guilt, Embarrassment and Pride*. New York: Guilford Press.

Tangney, J.P., Wagner, P.E., Barlow, D.H., Marschall, D.E. & Gramzow, R. (1996) Relation of shame and guilt to constructive versus destructive responses to anger across the lifespan. *Journal of Personality and Social Psychology*, 70, 797–809.

Thompson, A. & Kent, G. (2001) Adjusting to disfigurement: Processes involved in dealing with being visibly different. *Clinical Psychology Review*, 21, 663–682.

Tomkins, S.S. (1981) The quest for primary motives: Biography and autobiography. *Journal of Personality and Social Psychology*, 41, 306–329.

Tomkins, S.S. (1987) Shame. In D.L. Nathanson (ed.) *The Many Faces of Shame* (pp.133–161). New York: Guilford Press.

Tooby, J. & Cosmides, L. (1996) Friendship formation and the bankers paradox: Other pathways to the evolution of adaptations for altruism. *Proceedings of the British Academy*, 88, 19–143.

Wade, T.J. & Cooper, M. (1999) Sex differences in the links between attractiveness, self-esteem and the body. *Personality and Individual Differences*, 27, 1047–1056.

Wells, A. (1998) Cognitive therapy for social phobia. In N. Tarrier, A. Wells & G. Haddock (eds) *Treating Complex Cases: The Cognitive Behavioural Approach* (pp.1–26). Chichester: John Wiley & Sons.

Wilson, E. (1987) Shame and the other: Reflections on the theme of shame in French psychoanalysis. In D.L. Nathanson (ed.) *The Many Faces of Shame* (pp.162–193). New York: Guilford Press.

Wilson, M. & Daly, M. (1992) The man who mistook his wife for a chattel. In J.H. Barkow, L. Cosmides & J. Tooby (eds) *The Adapted Mind: Evolutionary Psychology and the Generation of Culture* (pp.289–322). New York: Oxford University Press.

Young, A. & Bruce, V. (1998) Pictures at an exhibition: The science of the face. *The Psychologist*, 11, 120–125.

Zahn-Waxler, C. (2000) The development of empathy, guilt and internalization of distress: Implications for gender differences in internalising and externalizing problems. In R.J. Davidson (ed.) *Anxiety, Depression and Emotion* (pp.222–265). New York: Oxford University Press.

Zuroff, D.C., Koestner, R. & Powers, T.A. (1994). Self-criticism at age 12: A longitudinal study of adjustment. *Cognitive Therapy and Research*, 18, 367–385.

Chapter 2

Body shame in childhood and adolescence

Relations to general psychological functioning and eating disorders

Stefanie C. Gilbert and J. Kevin Thompson

Introduction

This chapter reviews the research to date that has examined body dissatisfaction and shame in normal and clinical samples and explores the environmental and dispositional variables that may contribute to body shame in children and adolescents. This discussion is divided into three areas: bodily shame related to assuming an adult female body; body shame associated with the onset of menarche and menstruation; and body shame related to childhood sexual abuse. This is followed by a discussion of the contributions of each of these factors to the development and maintenance of eating disorders in children and adolescents. We conclude with suggestions for future research in the area of childhood and adolescent body shame.

As reviewed by Gilbert (Chapter 1, this volume), the concept of 'body shame' is relatively new to the psychological literature, although the concepts of body image disturbance and body self-esteem are not new. One of the reasons for seeing these processes as related to shame is because much has now been written about the more general phenomenon of shame (Gilbert, 1989, 1998a, 2000; Kaufman, 1989; Lewis, 1992; Nathanson, 1994; Tangney & Fischer, 1995). Nonetheless, body shame has been explored by McKinley (1998, 1999) who coined the term 'objectified body consciousness', which has three components: *surveillance* – related to viewing one's body as an outside observer; *body shame* – related to internalized beliefs and self-evaluations derived from how far one's body varies from social depictions of the ideal or acceptable body; and *control beliefs* – related to how much control one feels one has over one's body. According to McKinley (1998, 1999), the experience of bodily shame involves a state of self-consciousness and embarrassment evoked when individuals view their body shape or appearance as falling short of society's representation of the ideal male or female.

As noted by Gilbert (Chapter 1, this volume), similar distinctions have been acknowledged in the literature on shame. He notes that external shame, or stigma consciousness, relates to thoughts and feelings about the self as a social object, and the expectations and experiences of acceptance or rejection by others. Internal shame, however, is rooted in how one experiences and views the self; one's own self-evaluations and affect distortion (e.g., self-devaluation or self-contempt).

The roots of body shame, like other forms of shame, are thought to be in early life shaming experiences, generally starting around two or three years of age (Lewis, 1993, 1995; Stipek, 1995), although some have suggested that shame can be experienced in the first months of life (Nathanson, 1994; Schore, 1994). Developmental theories implicate parental criticisms and put-downs, as well as rejection by peers, as contributing to anxiety and fear of negative evaluation and beliefs that others see the self as unattractive. When the reasons for social rejection are internalized, children judge the source of the rejection as in 'themselves,' become disappointed or distressed by the aspects of the body that elicit rejection and may develop very negative views about the self (e.g., I am unattractive, ugly). Internalization must be associated with negative affects such as self-disgust and self-contempt. As Gilbert notes, however, internalization is not inevitable, and while some children (and adults) can be greatly distressed by carrying physical attributes that will lead others to reject them, they may not develop the self-dislike or self-loathing that can be seen when shame is highly internalized.

Early life experiences of *being shamed*, however, are clearly risk factors for developing a sense of one's self as flawed, inadequate and undesirable (Gilbert, 1998a, 1998b; Lewis, 1987; Nathanson, 1994), which greatly increases vulnerability to various forms of psychopathology (Gilbert & Gerlsma, 1999; Kaufman, 1989; Tangney & Fischer, 1995), including depression (Andrews, 1995, 1998), alcoholism (Brown, 1991), social anxiety (Gilbert, 2000, 2001), and narcissism (Kingston, 1987; Wurmser, 1987).

Body shame and the adult female shape

Given these preliminary comments on body shame and the extraordinary subtlety and interdependence between the external world and the inner world, it is interesting to note the now well-documented fact that the majority of American women are unhappy with their bodies (for a review, see Thompson, 1996). Body dissatisfaction has become so widespread among women that it is now considered the norm (Rodin, Silberstein & Striegel-Moore, 1984; Thompson et al., 1999). Body shame may be less common, as it involves the more severe shaming perception that one has attributes (in this case, body shape, proportions, size or disfigurement) that others will find unattractive and be a cause for rejection or attack (Gilbert, 1998a, 2000; Kaufman, 1989; Tangney & Fischer, 1995). But where body dissatisfaction ends and body shame begins is unclear, and surveys have found that most women are actively trying to lose weight in an effort to alter their body shape (Polivy & Herman, 1987; Thompson & Sargent, 2000). Some of these women undoubtedly have issues of body shame. The power of cultural values to affect people's experience and satisfaction with their bodies is evidenced by the fact that the age at which body dissatisfaction first surfaces has decreased throughout the last decade or so, with girls as young as five expressing body dissatisfaction and concern about their weight (Davison, Markey & Birch, 2000; Thompson & Smolak, 2001).

Gender differences in body dissatisfaction emerge as early as eight or ten years of age (Cusumano & Thompson, 2001), with about half of adolescent girls reporting displeasure with their appearance (Cash, Ancis & Strachan, 1997). In general, while boys experience an increase in satisfaction with their appearance during adolescence, girls during the same period experience a decrease in appearance satisfaction (Hoare & Cosgrove, 1998; Rosenblum & Lewis, 1999).

Weight increases result in further distinctions between the sexes. In the teen years, being overweight is associated with lower body-esteem, but only for girls; among boys, overweight is associated with higher levels of body-esteem (Stradmeijer et al., 2000). A limited number of studies that have examined racial differences in body satisfaction among adolescents suggest that black adolescent girls tend to be more satisfied with their bodies than their white counterparts and less concerned with losing weight (Parnell et al., 1996; Serdulla et al., 1993; Striegel-Moore et al., 2000).

One explanation for pervasive female body dissatisfaction is that the American societal ideal of female beauty is so excessively thin as to be unattainable by most women who live in the society (Hsu, 1989; Thompson et al., 1999; Wolf, 1991). From a public health standpoint, it is so unrealistically low that pursuing and achieving it can interfere with developmental milestones such as puberty, pregnancy or menopause that involve increased stores of body fat (Rodin, Silberstein & Striegel-Moore, 1984).

Fashion magazines, television advertisements and shows, and motion pictures promote the American cultural 'glorification of thinness' (Gilbert & Thompson, 1996) by equating it with attractiveness, happiness and success, while at the same time linking fatness with such negative connotations as laziness, ugliness and failure (Rothblum, 1994). As a result, many girls and women who cannot achieve these standards may experience shame and 'a pervasive sense of personal inadequacy' (Bartky, 1990), and may adopt a cognitive and behavioral tendency to objectify their own bodies. Notwithstanding supportive parents or friends, many girls or adolescents may be unable to ignore images of ultra-thin models gracing billboards, magazine covers, television and film screens.

Since the feminine cultural ideal of a thin or 'waif-like' appearance is inconsistent with the development of curves and body fat inherent in puberty, it is not surprising that, among adolescent girls, body dissatisfaction is associated with early maturation (Attie & Brooks-Gunn, 1989; Graber & Brooks-Gunn, 1998; Odea & Abraham, 1999). In contrast, among boys, body dissatisfaction is associated with late maturation (Mussen & Jones, 1957,

1958; Petersen, 1985), perhaps because the masculine ideal is tall and muscular.

Because attractiveness continues to be an essential component of the female gender role, girls and young women may come to view their bodies as objects that exist solely for others' viewing and pleasure, a process referred to as self-objectification (Frederickson et al., 1998). The media may contribute to this dynamic by utilizing women's bodies to sell consumer products in commercial print and and television advertisements by linking products with images of sex, beauty and the female form.

According to objectification theory (Frederickson & Roberts, 1997), our culture socializes girls and women to evaluate their bodies as if they were outside observers (Frederickson et al., 1998), to focus on their physical appearance and how others may view it. The resulting 'objectified body consciousness' (OBC) (McKinley, 1995) is linked with shame and anxiety about body shape and appearance (Lyders, 1999), impaired cognitive abilities (Frederickson et al., 1998), diminished self-esteem (McKinley & Hyde, 1996) and disordered eating behaviors (Noll, 1997). Researchers investigating objectification theory have found that women exhibit higher levels of body 'surveillance', body shame, and body dissatisfaction than do men and that women's greater body consciousness appears to mediate the relationship between gender and body esteem (McKinley, 1998). Moreover, young Western girls grow up in a culture riddled with the 'latest diets', with the implicit message that body size can be altered by dietary restrictions (i.e., it is controllable; not to diet is itself shameful, indicating lack of concern or will power, laziness or greed).

These interactional dynamics begin at an early age. In childhood, girls are given a wealth of information about the importance of physical attractiveness in achieving social success. Beginning in grade school, children respond to girls, more so than boys, based on their physical attractiveness. Smith (1985), for example, found that attractive girls are more likely to be helped, patted and praised by their peers, while less attractive girls receive few of these positive responses. Less attractive girls are more likely than their attractive peers to be hit, pushed and kicked. No such relationships were found for boys. Such early life experiences communicate the message to girls that how they look will determine how their peers treat them.

Research indicates that children who are treated poorly due to their physical appearance may be more vulnerable to developing body dissatisfaction and shame. For example, perceptions of weight-related pressures from peers have been associated with increased frequency and severity of weight control behaviors in middle and elementary school girls (Shisslak et al., 1998). Approximately 75% of elementary school girls report experiencing sexual harassment incidents with peers that increased focus on their bodies or appearance, such as having boys stare at them, flip up their skirts or make comments about their appearance (Murnen & Smolak, 2000). Boys reported similar levels of sexual harassment incidents. However, a significant relationship between the frequency of these experiences and body esteem existed only for girls. Girls were more likely than boys to expect victims of sexual harassment to be scared. Those girls who expected this outcome had lower levels of body esteem than those who were uncertain of how victims would feel. Smolak and Levine (2001) suggest that girls who react to harassment with fear may have more negative attitudes towards their bodies.

Importantly, evidence suggests that, for girls, appearance-related feedback may lead to internalization of information not only about appearance but also about self-worth (Davison & Birch, 2001). For girls, but not for boys, a strong, positive association exists between body image and self-esteem (Lerner, Orlos & Knapp, 1976; Kwa, 1994; Joiner & Kashubeck, 1996; Knox, Funk, Elliott & Bush, 1998). Body satisfaction accounts for an even greater amount of global self-esteem among girls who suffer from eating disorders or depression (Joiner, Schmidt & Wonderlich, 1997). It is possible that girls who develop eating disorders or mood disorders may thus be especially vulnerable to negative environmental feedback regarding their appearance.

In this light, a history of appearance-related criticism or teasing from peers is associated with body dissatisfaction, eating disturbance and general psychological difficulties (Brown, Cash & Lewis, 1989; Cattarin & Thompson, 1994; Friedman & Brownell, 1995; Grilo et al., 1994; Heinberg, Wood, & Thompson, 1995; Thompson et al., 1991; Thompson & Heinberg, 1993). Teasing is associated with similar negative outcomes, particularly body image disturbance, in obese individuals (Thompson et al., 1995). However, overweight status alone is not predictive of body dissatisfaction in girls or young women. Rather, teasing comments appear to mediate the relationship between weight status and the development of body dissatisfaction (Cattarin & Thompson, 1994). Teasing comments can be internalized as thoughts and feelings about the self that, in turn, may lead to diminished self-esteem and impaired psychological functioning (Friedman & Brownell, 1995).

The relationship between teasing comments and body shame has not been systematically examined; however, the theoretical basis for such a relationship is clear. Chronic and severe appearance-related teasing communicates to the teasing victim that her peer group finds her physically unattractive and inferior, a cognition which has been theoretically linked to the phenomenological experience of shame (Gilbert, 1998a, 1998b, 2000). Shame displays in response to negative peer evaluation and subsequent negative self-evaluation may include a lack of confidence, eye-gaze avoidance, and a desire to go into hiding or disappear (Darwin, 1872/1965; Gilbert, 1989, 2000; Keltner & Harker, 1998; Lewis, 1992; Tangney et al., 1996).

The determination of one's low standing in the appearance domain can trigger a view of the self as undesirably inferior to others, unattractive, and an outsider, referred to by Gilbert (1992, 2000) as 'involuntary subordinate self-perception'. Involuntary subordinate self-perception has been associated with social anxiety, shame, and depressive disorders (Allan & Gilbert, 1997; Gilbert & Allan, 1998; Gilbert, 1992, 2000). Because of the strong association between body image and self-esteem in girls (Joiner & Kashubeck, 1996; Knox et al., 1998; Kwa, 1994; Lerner, Orlos & Knapp, 1976), appearance-related teasing may be interpreted as an overall rejection of the teasing victim. Teasing of this type may thus elicit involuntary subordinate self-perception, shame, and body shame and may predispose individuals to anxiety and mood disorders.

Negative commentary regarding appearance can originate not only from peers, but from family members, as well. In this regard, parental criticism and shaming have been associated with vulnerability to subsequent psychopathology (Gilbert & Gerlsma, 1999; Gilbert, Allan & Goss, 1996). In the area of body image, parental criticism of a child's appearance or weight has been linked with subsequent weight concern and dieting efforts (Shisslak et al., 1998; Thompson & Sargent, 2000). Parents can also pass on a legacy of body shame, body dissatisfaction and eating pathology to their children by modeling unhealthy eating attitudes and behaviors and self-deprecating messages about the female form. In this light, a mother's dissatisfaction with her body predicts the emergence of eating disturbances in her children (Stice, Agras & Hammer, 1999), and mothers' weight concerns are positively associated with higher weight concerns among girls (Davison, Markey & Birch, 2000).

It is unclear from the current research whether the relationship between mothers' body dissatisfaction and daughters' body dissatisfaction is mediated by observant modeling, mothers' verbal criticism of daughters' appearance and/or weight, or perhaps some other variable. Mothers who are unhappy with their bodies and engage in compulsive dieting or exercise rituals may unwittingly serve as models for their children, who then may adopt similar stances towards their own bodies. Alternatively, mothers who have a negative body image may interfere with their children's eating habits and offer greater admonitions than other mothers regarding eating and the potential hazards of getting fat. This, in turn, may lead daughters of such mothers to have greater weight concerns and body dissatisfaction than other children, regardless of their weight. In either manner, shame may mediate the relationship between maternal body dissatisfaction and children's body dissatisfaction and disordered eating behaviors.

Parental criticism of appearance is not only associated with daughter's weight and eating concerns but also to daughter's self-esteem. For instance, parental concern about a child's overweight status is associated with decrements in the child's perceptions of her own abilities, and higher maternal concern is associated with lower perceived physical and cognitive ability (Davison & Birch, 2001). Among female college and graduate students, parental put-downs and other verbal shaming have been associated with shame proneness and the adoption of low self-evaluations (Gilbert, Allan & Goss, 1996).

In summary, girls in our society are being reared in a culture that has deemed a normal weight female adult body to be unattractive. It is thus not surprising that many girls may seek ways to postpone or avoid their physical initiation into female adulthood. In this society, normal female adolescent development that involves accumulation of body fat is often associated with embarrassment and shame. Future research on the development of body dissatisfaction and disordered eating in adolescence would benefit from inclusion of shame measures to elucidate this dynamic. Research on parental criticism and peer teasing could benefit from the inclusion of assessments of both body dissatisfaction and bodily shame to determine the relative contributions of each of these to the etiology of eating disturbance and general psychological difficulties. Finally, further research is needed to clarify the distinction between body dissatisfaction and body shame in normal and clinical samples.

Menarche, menstruation and body shame

Adolescence is a time of dramatic bodily and emotional changes. For girls, the pubertal physical changes of breast development, accumulation of body fat in the stomach and hips, growth of pubic hair and onset of menstruation represent critical inputs to the formation of the adolescent's body image and sense of self (Attie & Brooks-Gunn, 1989). As these bodily changes occur, girls receive and process feedback from their environments that, in turn, helps shape the image and accompanying feelings they have about their bodies (Daniluk, 1998).

When feedback is primarily positive, the increasing responsibilities of young adulthood may be accompanied by a growing sense of confidence and emotional well-being. However, when the majority of environmental feedback regarding physical changes is negative, the experience of adolescence may be a difficult one, fraught with anxiety about these changes and shame about one's appearance as compared to the societal ideal (McKinley, 1998, 1999).

Perhaps more than any other physical change of adolescence, menarche shapes a young woman's view of herself, her body and her sexuality. The culture's attitudes towards the ideal female form will obviously impact adolescent females' reactions to menarche inasmuch as it constitutes the physical initiation into womanhood. Some cultures view this pivotal life event as symbolizing strength and maturity, while others have characterized menstruation as defilement, a threat or a curse. Advertisements in teen magazines tend to depict menstruation as a hygienic crisis or an embarrassing burden (Havens & Swenson, 1988; Merskin, 1999). These depictions can have a profound effect on a young woman's view of her menstrual cycle and the bodily changes that accompany it (Koff & Rierdan, 1995). When menstruation is associated with fear and repulsion, feelings of shame not only about one's body but also about one's sexual potential can be linked with this important event. Girls tend to discuss the onset of menstruation with their mothers rather than their fathers due to a fear of embarrassing their fathers and themselves (Brooks-Gunn & Ruble, 1983; Golub, 1992; Yalom, Estler & Brewster, 1982).

Studies examining female adolescents' attitudes and feelings towards menarche have produced conflicting findings. The majority of research suggests that adolescent girls' understanding of this event tends to be clouded by feelings of embarrassment, discomfort, shame, anxiety and ambivalence about growing up (for a review, see Daniluk, 1998). However, other research indicates that girls have mixed feelings (Koff & Rierdan, 1995; Moore, 1995) or even positive reactions to achieving menarche (Williams, 1983), including a sense of admiration for the female body and little shame or embarrassment (Amann-Gainotti, 1994). Clearly, given all of the conflicting findings in the literature on this topic, it may be that there are unidentified individual, familial and environmental variables that play important roles in influencing adolescent reactions to menstruation and menarche.

One critical factor in predicting reactions to the onset of menarche is the timing of the event. Specifically, menarche tends to be associated with negative affect and self-beliefs if it occurs substantially earlier or later than average. Most adolescents want to 'fit in' with their peer group and avoid behavioral statements of individuality (Harris, 1995) that might elicit negative emotions such as shame (Lashbrook, 2000). This suggests the possibility that some adolescent females who experience early signs of physical maturation may utilize drastic dieting or eating disordered behaviors in an attempt to keep weight down and thereby delay menarche to be more in line with that of their peers.

Studies examining the short and long-term effects of early and late maturation on psychological well-being have found mixed results. Early maturation in girls (11 years of age or younger) has been associated with lower self-esteem and poorer body image (Gallant & Derry, 1995; Graber & Brooks-Gunn, 1998; O'Dea & Abraham, 1999; Thompson, 1990), although some studies have found insufficient evidence of an association between the two variables (Ackard & Peterson, 2001; Stormer & Thompson, 1996; Thompson, 1992). In a recent retrospective study by Ackard and Peterson (2001), girls who entered puberty at an earlier age scored higher on measures of asceticism, drive for thinness, impulse regulation and social insecurity, and endorsed a thinner ideal body figure than those who entered puberty at an older age. Stice, Presnell and Bearman (2001) also recently found that early menarche was associated with elevated depression and substance abuse. Early maturation has also been associated with a tendency to engage in sexual intercourse earlier than later maturing girls (Gallant & Derry, 1995; Stattin & Magnusson, 1990), although there is some evidence that early maturation may merely exacerbate pre-existing childhood behavioral problems (Caspi & Moffitt, 1991). Female adolescents may treat their earlier maturing peers as outsiders (Ge, Conger & Elder, 1996; Graber et al., 1997), contributing to the difficulties faced by girls experiencing early menarche. Late maturing girls may experience anxiety about lagging behind their peers on this critical milestone, but seem to show an advantage over their peers in academic achievement (Dubas, Graber & Peterson, 1991) and in body satisfaction once puberty occurs (Simmons & Blyth, 1987).

The inconsistencies in this area suggest that certain variables, such as body shame, may mediate the relationship between early and late development and psychological well-being. For example, teasing related to early maturation may elicit body shame and predispose young women to a tendency towards excessive social comparison and/or internalization of societal standards of appearance (Stormer & Thompson, 1996). Research in this area would be enhanced by inclusion of shame and body shame measures to examine the precise foci of shame-related cognitions and affects related to this critical physical milestone.

Childhood sexual abuse and body shame

Body shame has been associated with traumatic bodily experiences, such as sexual abuse (Andrews, 1995, 1997, Chapter 13, this volume). Because sexual abuse clearly locates the abused in a highly subordinate position, it is not surprising that abused individuals can grow up feeling little more than objects for others, vulnerable to the power of others and may adopt involuntary submissive defenses (see Gilbert, Chapter 1, this volume). Part of this defensive structure is a basic self-to-other orientation that involves shame-related behaviors (such as social avoidance and inhibition of confident engagement), and self-perceptions (such as inferior, subordinate self-perceptions). For the abused, adopting subordinated roles (with high shame sensitivity), even though it may increase risk of depression and anxiety, may be one of the few ways the individual has of trying to create some degree of safety or damage limitation (just like any harassed subordinate in a social group; Gilbert & McGuire, 1998). It is known, for example, that shame displays are related to subordinate defensive behaviors, and that in the normal course of events shame and social anxiety displays can limit potential aggression from others (Gilbert & McGuire, 1998; Keltner & Harker, 1998). However, as Gilbert (Chapter 1, this volume) notes in the case of 'Sally,' these defensive behaviors may themselves become a source for further shame. Moreover, sexual abuse may elicit feelings of self-disgust, and 'self as violated, spoiled and damaged'. Self-disgust may be a primary affect of some forms of shame (Power & Dalgleish, 1997).

Research by Andrews (1995, 1997) suggests that there is a significant relationship between childhood abuse and bodily shame that cannot be accounted for by body dissatisfaction; body shame originating in abuse appears to be a subjective response that is quite distinct from body dissatisfaction. In a community sample of 101 women who had been followed for eight years, Andrews (1995) found that bodily shame, but not childhood abuse, was related to chronic or recurrent depression in abused women.

Childhood sexual and physical abuse constitute risk factors for the development of psychopathology (Rorty & Yager, 1993), including eating disorders (Neumark-Sztainer et al., 2000). Given the physical and emotional impact of childhood physical and sexual abuse, both shame and body shame are potential mediators of this dynamic (Andrews, Chapter 13, this volume). These may operate to instill in the victim a self-view as devalued and inferior relative to others, a self-perception that has been related to depression, social anxiety and other forms of psychopathology (Gilbert, 1989, 1992, 2000, 2001). Although a great deal of research on abuse has focused on shame, while ignoring the more specific construct of body shame (Eakin, 1995; Wolfgang, 1999) examinations of both measures will be important to future research in order to determine the distinct contribution of each.

Body shame, sexual abuse and eating disorders

Research in a variety of areas suggests that body shame may play a role in the development of body dissatisfaction and eating pathology (Goss & Gilbert, Chapter 12, this volume). Researchers have long noted deficits in self-esteem and body self-esteem (Mintz & Betz, 1988) and increased social physique anxiety (Frederick & Morrison, 1998; Reel & Gill, 1996) among individuals with eating disorder symptomatology, and, more generally, an association between lower levels of self-esteem and dieting behaviors (Liebman et al., 2001).

As noted above, research has linked disordered eating with childhood sexual and physical abuse (Dansky et al., 1997; Garfinkel et al., 1995; Neumark-Sztainer et al., 2000; Wonderlich et al., 2001; Wonderlich et al., 1996). Sexual abuse may serve as a risk factor for the development of eating pathology, even after controlling for the quality of family functioning (Neumark-Sztainer et al., 2000; Thompson et al., 2001), especially when high levels of psychiatric comorbidity are present (Wonderlich et al., 1997).

In a study of 9943 Connecticut public school students, Neumark-Sztainer et al. (2000) found that sexual and physical abuse were similarly related to disordered eating among both boys and girls. For boys, however, the association between sexual abuse and disordered eating was significantly stronger than that between physical abuse and disordered eating. Boys in her sample who had experienced sexual abuse were at greater risk for disordered eating than girls who had experienced sexual abuse. As the authors point out, these findings suggest the possibility of different etiological pathways for the development of eating disorders in boys and girls.

Other research has examined potential factors that may act as mediators in the association of childhood sexual abuse and disordered eating. In a recent study, Wonderlich et al. (2001) found that behavioral impulsivity and drug use were mediators between a history of childhood sexual abuse and body dissatisfaction, purging and restrictive eating. These relationships were sustained even in the absence of other variables such as depression, self-concept, perfectionism and self-perceptions. The authors suggest that eating disturbances in victims of sexual abuse may not begin with deficits in self-esteem or body image concerns but rather with impulsive and drug-using behaviors.

Among women who suffer from eating disorders, shame has also been related to the disordered eating behaviors themselves. In a study of Australian women with a wide range of disordered eating symptoms, shame associated with eating behavior was the strongest predictor of severity of eating disorder symptomology, with body shame and guilt about eating behavior also constituting effective predictors (Burney & Irwin, 2000).

Women who have bulimia nervosa or anorexia nervosa tend to report interpersonal difficulties (Evans & Wertheim, 1998; Fairburn et al., 1990; Grissett & Norvell, 1992; Norman & Herzog, 1986; Tobin et al., 1991; Yager et al., 1987) including a lack of self-confidence in social situations, social anxiety and a preoccupation with self-presentation (Bulik et al., 1991; Gross & Rosen, 1988; Hewitt, Flett & Ediger, 1995; McCauley, Mintz & Glenn, 1988; Striegel-Moore, Silberstein & Rodin, 1993). Bulik et al. (1991) found that women with eating disorders experience social fears that parallel the criteria for certain anxiety disorders and that these fears are not limited to those related to eating and drinking in public. It may thus be that the body shame and anxiety about eating, typically associated with eating pathology, may actually be part of a more generalized tendency to experience anxiety and shame in social situations (Bulik et al., 1991). Body dissatisfaction and disordered eating have both been linked with a tendency to compare one's body with others (Thompson et al., 1999). Social comparisons leading to negative self-evaluations can also be an important component of shame (Gilbert, 1998a).

In a two-phase study examining this dynamic, Striegel-Moore, Silberstein and Rodin (1993) found that bulimic women and non-bulimic women who scored high on a measure of eating pathology exhibited increased public self-consciousness and social anxiety relative to normal control subjects. Eating pathology was positively associated with a tendency to view one's self as a 'phony' or an 'imposter' in social situations.

Self-objectification, a process described earlier in this chapter, has been associated with both body shame and eating pathology (Noll, 1997). Two studies conducted by Noll (1997) provide preliminary evidence that body shame may mediate the relationship between self-objectification and disordered eating. Undergraduate women who scored higher on self-objectification reported greater body shame and disordered eating symptoms. In addition, body shame predicted the amount of candy that research participants would consume following a manipulation designed to increase body focus.

Finally, a recent study evaluated the potential role of shame as a mediator between sexual abuse and bulimic eating disturbance. Murray and Waller (in press) examined sexual abuse, including intrafamilial abuse, in a non-clinical sample of college women. Using regression analyses to test for the mediational role of shame, they found that shame partially mediated the relationship between overall sexual abuse and eating disturbance, but fully mediated the connection between intrafamilial abuse and bulimic symptomatology. These findings highlight not only the critical role of shame, but also the need to consider different dimensions of sexual abuse in testing models. Certainly, more research of this nature, especially with younger aged women, is indicated.

Conclusion

As Gilbert (Chapter 1, this volume) notes, there are important reasons for understanding body image disturbances and body self-esteem as rooted in processes related to shame. In this chapter, we have reviewed a wide-ranging body of evidence suggesting the close connections among body shame, body dissatisfaction, eating disturbance and psychological functioning. A variety of factors, such as teasing, media influences and self-objectification were found to influence these variables, either directly or via a mediational means. Operating perhaps independently of these social and relationship variables are also those of traumatic violations in the form of abuse. To date there is no data that allow us to say if there are different types of body shame relating to different sources (e.g., excessive teasing by peers versus abuse) or if it is a difference of degree, and currently there are few measures that may aid such investigations. However, although body shame is still in its infancy, as both a concept and research focus, we suspect it will not be long before researchers will begin to formulate and test the possibility of there being different types of body shame. For example, when (and under what conditions) does body shame spread to the whole self system such that people can see very little that is good and attractive about them, and when does it stay located in a specific domain?

Unfortunately, to date, there still exists little research with younger samples, particularly females in early adolescence. The extant findings reviewed herein, along with relevant data from older samples, however, do suggest that body shame in childhood and adolescence may have profound effects on one's body image, eating behaviors and overall psychological functioning. Clearly, additional work needs to be done in this important area. Researchers should especially consider the benefits of prospective work and analytic strategies that allow for testing of mediational models (i.e., path analysis and covariance structure modeling techniques).

References

Ackard, D.M. & Peterson, C.B. (2001) Association between puberty and disordered eating, body image, and other psychological variables. *International Journal of Eating Disorders*, 29, 187–194.

Allan, S. & Gilbert, P. (1997) Submissive behaviour and psychopathology. *British Journal of Clinical Psychology*, 36, 467–488.

Amann-Gainotti, M. (1994) Adolescent girls' internal body image. *International Journal of Adolescent Medicine and Health*, 7, 73–86.

Andrews, B. (1995) Bodily shame as a mediator between abusive experiences and depression. *Journal of Abnormal Psychology*, 104, 277–285.

Andrews, B. (1997) Bodily shame in relation to abuse in childhood and bulimia: A preliminary investigation. *British Journal of Clinical Psychology*, 36, 41–49.

Andrews, B. (1998) Shame and childhood sexual abuse. In P. Gilbert & B. Andrews (eds) *Shame: Interpersonal Behavior, Psychopathology and Culture* (pp.176–190). New York: Oxford University Press.

Attie, I. & Brooks-Gunn, J. (1989) The development of eating problems in adolescent girls: A longitudinal study. *Developmental Psychology*, 25, 70–79.

Bartky, S.L. (1990) *Femininity and Domination: Studies in the Phenomenology of Oppression*. New York: Routledge.

Brooks-Gunn, J. & Ruble, D.N. (1983) The psychological significance of secondary sexual characteristics in nine- to eleven-year-old girls. *Child Development*, 59, 1061–1069.

Brown, H. (1991) Shame and relapse issues with the chemically dependent client. *Alcoholism Treatment Quarterly*, 8, 77–82.

Brown, T.A., Cash, T.F. & Lewis, R.J. (1989) Body-image disturbances in adolescent female binge-purgers: A brief report of the reports of a national survey in the USA. *Journal of Child Psychology and Psychiatry*, 30, 605–613.

Bulik, C.M., Beidel, D.C., Duchman, E. & Weltzin, T.E. (1991) An analysis of social anxiety in anorexic, bulimic, social phobic, and control women. *Journal of Psychopathology and Behavioral Assessment*, 13, 199–211.

Burney, J. & Irwin, H.J. (2000) Shame and guilt in women with eating-disorder symptomology. *Journal of Clinical Psychology*, 56, 51–56.

Cash, T.F., Ancis, J.R. & Strachan, M.D. (1997) Gender attitudes, feminist identity, and body images among college women. *Sex Roles*, 36, 443–447.

Caspi, A. & Moffitt, T.E. (1991) Individual differences are accentuated during periods of social change: The sample case of girls at puberty. *Journal of Personality and Social Psychology*, 61, 157–168.

Cattarin, J. & Thompson, J.K. (1994) A three-year longitudinal study of body image and eating disturbance in adolescent females. *Eating Disorders: The Journal of Prevention and Treatment*, 2, 114–125.

Cusumano, D.L. & Thompson, J.K. (2001) Media influence and body image in 8–11 year old boys and girls: A preliminary report on the Multidimensional Media Influence Scale. *International Journal of Eating Disorders*, 29, 37–44.

Daniluk, J.C. (1998) Adolescence: Biological and Psychological Development. In J.C. Daniluk (ed.) *Women's Sexuality Across the Life Span*. New York: Guilford Press.

Dansky, B.S., Brewerton, T.D., Kilpatrick, D.G. & O'Neill, P.M. (1997) Rape PTSD and bulimia in a US sample of women. *International Journal of Eating Disorders*, 21, 213–228.

Darwin, C. (1965) *The Expression of Emotion in Man and Animals*. Chicago: University of Chicago Press. (Original work published 1872.)

Davison, K.K. & Birch, L.L. (2001) Weight status, parent reaction and self-concept in five-year-old girls. *Pediatrics*, 107, 46–53.

Davison, K.K., Markey, C.N. & Birch, L.L. (2000) Etiology of body dissatisfaction and weight concerns among 5-year-old girls. *Appetite*, 35, 143–151.

Dubas, J., Graber, J. & Peterson, A. (1991) The effects of pubertal development on achievement during adolescence. *American Journal of Education*, 99, 444–460.

Eakin, E.P. (1995) The relationship of internalized shame and adult adjustment in women with incest histories. *Dissertation Abstracts International: Section B: The Sciences and Engineering*, 56, 2861.

Evans, L. & Wertheim, E.H. (1998) Intimacy patterns and relationship satisfaction of women with eating problems and the mediating effects of depression, trait anxiety and social anxiety. *Journal of Psychosomatic Research*, 44, 355–365.

Fairburn, C.G., Jones, R., Peveler, R.C., Carr, S.J., Solomon, R.A., O'Connor, M.E., Burton, J. & Hope, R.A. (1990) Three psychological treatments for bulimia nervosa: A comparative trial. *Archives of General Psychiatry*, 48, 463–469.

Frederick, C.M. & Morrison, C.S. (1998) A mediational model of social physique anxiety and eating disordered behaviors. *Perceptual and Motor Skills*, 86, 139–145.

Frederickson, B.L. & Roberts, T. (1997). Objectification theory: Toward understanding women's lived experiences and mental health risks. *Psychology of Women Quarterly*, 21, 173–206.

Frederickson, B.L., Roberts, T.A., Noll, S.M., Quinn, D.M. & Twenge, J.M. (1998) That swimsuit becomes you: Sex differences in self-objectification, restrained eating, and math performance. *Journal of Personality and Social Psychology*, 75, 269–284.

Friedman, M.A. & Brownell, K.D. (1995). Psychological correlates of obesity: Moving to the next research generation. *Psychological Bulletin*, 117, 3–20.

Gallant, S.J. & Derry, P.S. (1995) Menarche, menstruation, and menopause: Psychosocial research and future directions. In A.L. Stanton & S.J. Gallant (eds) *The Psychology of Women's Health* (pp.199–259). Washington, DC: American Psychological Association.

Garfinkel, P.E., Lin, E., Goering, P., Spegg, C., Goldbloom, D.S., Kennedy, S., Kaplan, A.S. & Woodside, D.B. (1995) Bulimia nervosa in a Canadian community sample: Prevalence and comparison of subgroups. *American Journal of Psychiatry*, 152, 1052–1058.

Ge, X., Conger, R.D. & Elder, G.H., Jr. (1996) Coming of age too early: Pubertal influences on girls' vulnerability to psychological distress. *Child Development*, 67 (6), 3386–3400.

Gilbert, P. (1989). *Human Nature and Suffering*. Hove, UK: Lawrence Erlbaum Associates Ltd and New York: Guilford Press.

Gilbert, P. (1992) *Depression: The Evolution of Powerlessness*. Hove, UK: Lawrence Erlbaum Associates Ltd and New York: Guilford Press.

Gilbert, P. (1998a) What is shame? Some core issues and controversies. In P. Gilbert & B. Andrews (eds) *Shame: Interpersonal Behavior, Psychopathology and Culture* (pp.3–38). New York: Oxford University Press.

Gilbert, P. (1998b) Shame and humiliation in the treatment of complex cases. In N. Tarrier, A. Wells & G. Haddock (eds) *Treating Complex Cases: The Cognitive Behavioural Therapy Approach* (pp.241–271). Chichester: John Wiley & Sons.

Gilbert, P. (2000) The relationship of shame, social anxiety and depression: The role of the evaluation of social rank. *Clinical Psychology and Psychotherapy*, 7, 174–189.

Gilbert, P. (2001) Evolution and social anxiety: The role of attraction, social competition and social hierarchies. In F. Schnieder (ed) *Social Anxiety: Psychiatric Clinics of North America*, 24, 723–751.

Gilbert, P. & Allan, S. (1998) The role of defeat and entrapment (arrested flight) in depression: An exploration of an evolutionary view. *Psychological Medicine*, 28, 584–597.

Gilbert, P., Allan, S. & Goss (1996) Parental representations, shame, interpersonal problems, and vulnerability to psychopathology. *Clinical Psychology and Psychotherapy*, 3, 23–34.

Gilbert, P. & Gerlsma, C. (1999) Recall of shame and favouritism in relation to psychopathology. *Journal of Clinical Psychology*, 38, 357–373.

Gilbert, P. & McGuire, M. (1998) Shame, social roles and status: The psychobiological continuum from monkey to human (pp.99–125). In P. Gilbert & B. Andrews (eds) *Shame: Interpersonal Behavior, Psychopathology and Culture*. New York: Oxford University Press.

Gilbert, S. & Thompson, J.K. (1996) Feminist explanations of the development of eating disorders: Common themes, research findings, and methodological issues. *Clinical Psychology: Science and Practice*, 3, 183–202.

Golub, S. (1992) *Periods: From Menarche to Menopause*. Newbury Park, CA: Sage.

Graber, J.A. & Brooks-Gunn, J. (1998) Puberty. In E.A. Blechman & K.D. Brownell (eds) *Behavioral Medicine and Women: A Comprehensive Handbook* (pp.51–58). New York: Guilford Press.

Graber, J.A., Lewinsohn, P.M., Seeley, J.R. & Brooks-Gunn, J. (1997) Is psychopathology associated with the timing of pubertal development? *Journal of the American Academy of Child and Adolescent Psychiatry*, 36 (12), 1768–1776.

Grilo, C.M., Wilfley, D.E., Brownell, K.D. & Rodin, J. (1994) Teasing, body image, and self-esteem in a clinical sample of obese women. *Addictive Behaviors*, 19, 443–450.

Grissett, N.I. & Norvell, N.K. (1992) Perceived social support, social skills, and quality of relationships in bulimic women. *Journal of Consulting and Clinical Psychology*, 60, 293–299.

Harris, J.R. (1995) Where is the child's environment? A group socialization theory of development. *Psychological Review*, 102, 458–489.

Havens, B. & Swenson, I. (1988) Imagery associated with menstruation in advertising targeted to adolescent women. *Adolescence*, 23, 91–97.

Heinberg, L.J., Wood, K. & Thompson, J.K. (1995) Body image. In V.I. Rickert (ed.) *Adolescent Nutrition: Assessment and Management* (pp.136–156). New York: Chapman and Hall.

Hewitt, P.L., Flett, G.L. & Ediger, E. (1995) Perfectionism traits and perfectionistic self-presentation in eating disorder attitudes, characteristics, and symptoms. *International Journal of Eating Disorders*, 18, 317–326.

Hoare, P. & Cosgrove, L. (1998) Eating habits, body-esteem and self-esteem in Scottish children and adolescents. *Journal of Psychosomatic Research*, 45, 425–431.

Hsu, L.K. (1989) The gender gap in eating disorders: Why are the eating disorders more common among women? *Clinical Psychology Review*, 9, 393–407.

Joiner, G.W. & Kashubeck, S. (1996) Acculturation, body image, self-esteem and eating-disorder symptomatology in adolescent Mexican American women. *Psychology of Women Quarterly*, 20, 419–435.

Joiner, T.E., Schmidt, N.B. & Wonderlich, S.A. (1997) Global self-esteem as contingent on body satisfaction among patients with bulimia nervosa: Lack of diagnostic specificity? *International Journal of Eating Disorders*, 21, 67–76.

Kaufman, G. (1989) *The Psychology of Shame*. New York: Springer.

Keltner, D. & Harker, L.A. (1998) The forms and functions of the nonverbal signal of shame. In P. Gilbert & B. Andrews (eds) *Shame: Interpersonal Behavior, Psychopathology and Culture* (pp.78–98). New York: Oxford University Press.

Kingston, W. (1987) The shame of narcissism. In D.L. Nathanson (ed.) *The Many Faces of Shame* (pp.214–245). New York: Guilford Press.

Knox, M., Funk, J., Elliott, R. & Bush, E.G. (1998) Adolescent possible selves and their relationship to global self-esteem. *Sex Roles*, 39, 61–80.

Koff, E. & Rierdan, J. (1995) Early adolescent girls' understanding of menstruation. *Women and Health*, 22, 1–19.

Kwa, L. (1994) Adolescent females' perceptions of competence: What is defined as healthy and achieving. In J. Gallivan, S.D. Crozier & V.M. Lalande (eds) *Women, Girls, and Achievement* (pp.121–132). North York, Ontario: Captus University Publications.

Lashbrook, J.T. (2000) Fitting in: Exploring the emotional dimension of adolescent peer pressure. *Adolescence*, 35, 747–757.

Lerner, R.M., Orlos, J.R. & Knapp, J. (1976) Physical attractiveness, physical effectiveness and self-concept in adolescents. *Adolescence*, 11, 313–326.

Lewis, M. (1987) Introduction: Shame, the 'sleeper' in psychopathology. In H.B. Lewis (ed.) *The Role of Shame in Symptom Formation* (pp.1–28). Hillsdale, NJ: Lawrence Erlbaum Associates Inc.

Lewis, M. (1992) *Shame: The Exposed Self*. New York: Free Press.

Lewis, M. (1993) The emergence of human emotions. In M. Lewis & J.M. Haviland (eds) *Handbook of Emotions* (pp.223–235). New York: Guilford Press.

Lewis, M. (1995) Self-conscious emotions. *American Scientist*, 83, 68–78.

Liebman, M., Cameron, B.A., Carson, D.K., Brown, D.M. & Meyer, S.S. (2001) Dietary fat reduction behaviors in college students: Relationship to dieting status, gender and key psychosocial variables. *Appetite*, 36, 51–56.

Lyders, G.C. (1999) Body image and attitudes toward eating: The influence of objectified body consciousness and variations by gender and sexual orientation. *Dissertation Abstracts International: Section B: The Sciences and Engineering*, 60, 1861.

McCauley, M., Mintz, L. & Glenn, A.A. (1988) Body image, self-esteem, and depression-proneness: Closing the gender gap. *Sex Roles*, 18, 381–391.

McKinley, N.M. (1995) Women and objectified body consciousness: A feminist psychological analysis. *Dissertation Abstracts International*, 56, 05B (University Microfilms No. 9527111).

McKinley, N.M. (1998) Gender differences in undergraduates' body esteem: The mediating effect of objectified body consciousness and actual/ideal weight discrepancy. *Sex Roles*, 39, 113–119.

McKinley, N.M. (1999) Women and objectified body consciousness: Mothers' and daughters' body experience in cultural, developmental, and familial context. *Developmental Psychology*, 33, 760–769.

McKinley, N.M. & Hyde, J.S. (1996) The objectified body consciousness scale: Development and validation. *Psychology of Women Quarterly*, 20, 181–215.

Merskin, D. (1999) Adolescence, advertising, and the ideology of menstruation. *Sex Roles*, 40, 941–957.

Mintz, L.B. & Betz, N.E. (1988) Prevalence and correlates of eating disordered behaviors among undergraduate women. *Journal of Counseling Psychology*, 35, 463–471.

Moore, S.M. (1995) Girls' understanding and social constructions of menarche. *Journal of Adolescence*, 18, 87–104.

Murnen, S.K. & Smolak, L. (2000) The experience of sexual harassment among grade-school students: Early socialization of female subordination? *Sex Roles*, 43, 1–17.

Murray, C. & Waller, G. (in press) Reported sexual abuse and bulimic psychopathology among non-clinical women: The mediating role of shame. *International Journal of Eating Disorders*.

Mussen, P. & Jones, M.C. (1957) Self-conceptions, motivations, and interpersonal attitudes of late- and early-maturing boys. *Child Development*, 28, 243–256.

Mussen, P. & Jones, M.C. (1958) The behavior-inferred motivations of late- and early-maturing boys. *Child Development*, 29, 61–67.

Nathanson, D.L. (1994) *Shame and Pride: Affect Sex and the Birth of the Self*. New York: Norton Paperbacks.

Neumark-Sztainer, D., Story, M., Hannan, P.J., Beuhring, T. & Resnick, M.D. (2000) Disordered eating among adolescents: Associations with sexual/physical abuse and other familial/psychosocial factors. *International Journal of Eating Disorders*, 28, 249–258.

Noll, S.M. (1997) The relationship between sexual objectification and disordered eating: Correlational and experimental tests of body shame as a mediator. *Dissertation Abstracts International: Section B: The Sciences and Engineering*, 57, 5926.

Norman, D.K. & Herzog, D.B. (1986) A 3-year outcome study of normal-weight bulimia: Assessment of psycho-social functioning and eating attitudes. *Psychiatric Research*, 19, 199–205.

O'Dea, J.A. & Abraham, S. (1999) Association between self-concept and body weight, gender, and pubertal development among male and female adolescents. *Adolescence*, 34, 69–79.

Parnell, K., Sargent, R., Thompson, S.H., Duhe, S.F., Valois, R.F. & Kemper, R.C. (1996) Black and white adolescent females' perceptions of ideal body size. *Journal of School Health*, 66, 112–118.

Petersen, A. (1985) Pubertal development as a cause of disturbance: Myths, realities, and unanswered questions. *Genetic, Social and General Psychology Monographs*, 111, 205–232.

Polivy, J. & Herman, C.P. (1987) Diagnosis and treatment of normal eating. *Journal of Consulting and Clinical Psychology*, 55, 635–644.

Power, M. & Dalgleish, T. (1997) *Cognition and Emotions: From Order to Disorder*. Hove: Psychology Press.

Reel, J.J. & Gill, D.L. (1996) Psychosocial factors related to eating disorders among high school and college female cheerleaders. *Sport Psychologist*, 10, 195–206.

Rodin, J., Silberstein, L. & Striegel-Moore, R. (1984) Women and weight: A normative discontent. *Nebraska Symposium on Motivation*, 32, 267–307.

Rorty, M. & Yager, J. (1993) Speculations on the role of childhood abuse in the development of eating disorders among women. *Eating Disorders: The Journal of Treatment and Prevention*, 1, 199–210.

Rosenblum, G.D. & Lewis, M. (1999) The relations among body image, physical attractiveness, and body mass in adolescence. *Child Development*, 70, 50–64.

Rothblum, E.D. (1994) "I'll die for the revolution but don't ask me not to diet": Feminism and the continuing stigmatization of obesity. In P. Fallon, M.A. Katzman & S.C. Wooley (eds) *Feminist Perspectives on Eating Disorders* (pp.17–52). New York: Guilford Press.

Schore, A.N. (1994) *Affect Regulation and the Origin of the Self: The Neurobiology of Emotional Development*. Hillsdale, NJ: Lawrence Erlbaum Associates Inc.

Serdula, M.K., Collins, M.E., Williamson, D.F., Anda, R.F., Pamuk, E. & Byers, T.E. (1993) Weight control practices of U.S. adolescents and adults. *Annals of Internal Medicine*, 199, 667–671.

Shisslak, C.M., Crago, M., McKnight, K.M., Estes, L.S., Gray, N. and Parnaby, O.G. (1988) Potential risk factors associated with weight control behaviors in elementary and middle school girls. *Journal of Psychosomatic Research*, 44, 301–313.

Simmons, R.G. & Blyth, D.A. (1987) *Moving into Adolescence: The Impact of Pubertal Change and School Context*. Hawthorne, NY: Aldine de Gruyter.

Smith, G.J. (1985) Facial and full-length ratings of attractiveness related to the social interactions of young children. *Sex Roles*, 12, 287–293.

Smolak, L. & Levine, M.P. (2001) Body image in children. In J.K. Thompson & L. Smolak (eds) *Body Image, Eating Disorders, and Obesity in Youth: Assessment, Prevention, and Treatment* (pp.41–66). Washington, DC: American Psychological Association.

Stattin, H. & Magnusson, D. (1990) *Paths Through Life (Vol. 2) Pubertal Maturation in Female Development*. Hillsdale, NJ: Lawrence Erlbaum Associates Inc.

Stice, E., Agras, W.S. & Hammer, L.D. (1999). Risk factors for the emergence of childhood eating disturbances: A five year prospective study. *International Journal of Eating Disorders*, 25, 375–387.

Stice, E., Presnell, K. & Bearman, S.K. (2001) Relation of early menarche to depression, eating disorders, substance abuse and comorbid psychopathology among adolescent girls. *Developmental Psychology*, 37, 1–12.

Stipek, D. (1995). The development of pride and shame in toddlers. In J.P. Tangney & K.W. Fischer (eds) *Self-conscious emotions: The Psychology of Shame, Guilt, Embarrassment and Pride* (pp.237–252). New York: Guilford Press.

Stormer, S.M. & Thompson, J.K. (1996) Explanations of body image disturbance: A test of maturational status, negative verbal commentary, social comparison, and sociocultural hypotheses. *International Journal of Eating Disorders*, 19, 193–202.

Stradmeijer, J., Bosch, J., Koops, W. & Seidell, J. (2000) Family functioning and psychosocial adjustment in overweight youngsters. *International Journal of Eating Disorders*, 27, 110–114.

Striegel-Moore, R., Schreiber, G.B., Lo, A., Crawford, P., Obarzanek, E. & Rodin, J. (2000) Eating disorders symptoms in a cohort of 11 to 16-year-old black and white girls: The NHLBI Growth and Health Study. *International Journal of Eating Disorders*, 27, 49–66.

Striegel-Moore, R.H., Silbereisen, L.R. & Rodin, J. (1993) The social self in bulimia nervosa: Public self-consciousness, social anxiety, and perceived fraudulence. *Journal of Abnormal Psychology*, 102, 297–303.

Tangney, J.P. & Fischer, K.W. (eds) (1995) *Self-conscious Emotions: The Psychology of Shame, Guilt, Embarrassment, and Pride*. New York: Guilford Press.

Tangney, J.P., Miller, R.S., Flicker, L. & Barlow, D.H. (1996) Are shame, guilt, and embarrassment distinct emotions? *Journal of Personality and Social Psychology*, 70, 1256–1269.

Thompson, J.K. (ed.) (1990) *Body Image Disturbance: Assessment and Treatment*. New York: Pergamon Press.

Thompson, J.K. (1992) Body image: Extent of disturbance, associated features, theoretical models, assessment methodologies, intervention strategies, and a proposal for a *DSM–IV* diagnostic category – Body Image Disorder. In M. Hersen, R.M. Eisler & P.M. Miller (eds) *Progress in Behaviour Modification* (vol. 28, pp.3–54). Sycamore, IL: Sycamore Publishing.

Thompson, J.K. (ed.) (1996) *Body Image, Eating Disorders and Obesity: An Integrative Guide for Assessment and Treatment*. Washington, DC: American Psychological Association.

Thompson, J.K., Coovert, M., Richards, K., Johnson, S. & Cattarin, J. (1995) Development of body image, eating disturbance and general psychological functioning in female adolescents: Covariance structure modeling and longitudinal investigations. *International Journal of Eating Disorders*, 18, 221–236.

Thompson, J.K., Fabian, L.J., Moulton, D.O., Dunn, M.E. & Altabe, M.N. (1991) Development and validation of the Physical Appearance Related Teasing Scale (PARTS). *Journal of Personality Assessment*, 56, 513–521.

Thompson, J.K. & Heinberg, L.J. (1993) Preliminary test of two hypotheses of body image disturbance. *International Journal of Eating Disorders*, 14, 59–63.

Thompson, J.K., Heinberg, L.J., Altabe, M., & Tantleff-Dunn, S. (1999) *Exacting Beauty: Theory, Assessment and treatment of Body Image Disturbance*. Washington, DC: American Psychological Association.

Thompson, J. K. & Smolak, L. (2001) (eds) *Body Image, Eating Disorders, and Obesity in Youth: Assessment, Prevention, and Treatment*. Washington, DC: American Psychological Association.

Thompson, K.M., Wonderlich, S., Crosby, R.D. & Mitchell, J.E. (2001) Sexual violence and eight control techniques among adolescent girls. *International Journal of Eating Disorders*, 29, 166–176.

Thompson, S.H. & Sargent, R.G. (2000) Black and white women's weight-related attitudes and parental criticism of their childhood appearance. *Women and Health*, 30, 77–92.

Tobin, D., Johnson, C., Steinberg, S., Staats, M. & Enright, A.B. (1991) Multifactorial assessment of bulimia nervosa. *Journal of Abnormal Psychology*, 100, 14–21.

Williams, L.R. (1983) Beliefs and attitudes of young girls regarding menstruation. In S. Golub (ed.) *Menarche* (pp.139–148). Lexington, MA: Lexington Books.

Wolf, N. (1991) *The Beauty Myth*. New York: William Morrow.

Wolfgang, L.E (1999) Relationship between childhood sexual abuse in women, internalized shame, and attachments to peers, mother, and father. *Dissertation Abstracts International: Section B: The Sciences and Engineering*, 59, 4494.

Wonderlich, S.A., Brewerton, T.D., Jocic, Z., Dansky, B. & Abbott, D.W. (1997) Relationship of childhood sexual abuse and eating disorders. *Journal of The Academy of Child and Adolescent Psychiatry*, 36, 1107–1115.

Wonderlich, S., Crosby, R., Mitchell, J., Thompson, K., Redlin, J., Demuth, G. & Smyth, J. (2001) Pathways mediating sexual abuse and eating disturbance in children. *International Journal of Eating Disorders*, 29, 270–279.

Wurmser, L. (1987) Shame: The veiled companion of narcissism. In D.L. Nathanson (ed.) *The Many Faces of Shame* (pp.64–92). New York: Guilford Press.

Yager, J., Landsverk, J. & Edelstein, C.K. (1987) A 20-month follow-up study of 628 women with eating disorders, I: Course and severity. *American Journal of Psychiatry*, 144, 1172–1177.

Yalom, M., Estler, S. & Brewster, W. (1982) Changes in female sexuality: A study of mother/daughter communication and generational differences. *Psychology of Women Quarterly*, 7, 141–154.

Chapter 3

Shame and the ageing body

Kevin J. McKee and Merryn Gott

Introduction

Within Western societies, nearly everybody appears to hold negative stereotypes of ageing and older people. Common stereotypes of old age are that most older people are confused, resigned to decline, tired, slow and dependent (Unsworth, McKee & Mulligan, 2001). Such stereotypes both delimit and channel people's thoughts about, and responses to, older people. Researchers themselves are not immune to the blinkering effect of stereotypes, and therefore it is unsurprising that the dominant research paradigms operating in geriatrics and gerontology seek to chart the map of decline in later life, and classify older people in terms of the problems that they face. Older people are manifested in the literature through their 'functional impairment' or 'functional performance', their level of 'dependency' or their general 'frailty' (Jarrett et al., 1995; Rockwood et al., 1999; Woodhouse et al., 1988).

It is partly due to the fact that old age is associated with poor physical health that later life ageing carries negative connotations, and why many individuals resist the label of aged (Slater, 1995). Interestingly, there is no consistent evidence that people get more dissatisfied with their body as they age. Indeed, some studies have shown the reverse – that older people report greater body satisfaction than young people (e.g., Reboussin et al., 2000; Öberg & Tornstam, 1999). Research does suggest, however, that an older person's body satisfaction is more related to body function than body appearance, and that body function is strongly related to well-being (Reboussin et al., 2000).

It is when the older person's body no longer functions as desired that the issue of shame might become pertinent. The role of shame in the meaning older people give to, and take from, their own bodily change and decline, is a matter for conjecture, since little direct research has been performed in this context. Nevertheless, the function that is argued for the emotion of shame is potentially implicated in the psychological processes that occur when an older person considers their bodily decline. As Gilbert (1998) points out, most shame theorists see shame as associated with particular types of appraisals. These can be either 'self as object' and exposed to the scrutiny of others (external shame) and/or internal shame, related to the inner experience of oneself as 'seen and judged through one's own eyes'. Mascolo and Fischer (1995) suggest that shame is generated by appraisal of having failed to live up to personal and others' standards of worth. However, Gilbert (see Chapter 1, this volume) makes a case that it is not so much distance from the ideal self but closeness to the 'undesired self' (Ogilvie, 1987) that is crucial to many shame experiences. In shame what matters is the sense of personal unattractiveness – being in the social world as an undesired self, a self one does not wish to be. An experience of shame occurs as an involuntary response to awareness that one has lost status and is devalued as an object to others, and this can meld into a sense of one's own identity as, for example, flawed, worthless, unattractive (Gilbert, 1998).

Ageing then involves a transformation in how one experiences oneself as an object to others (related to various cultural stereotypes), and a transformation in the internal experience of changing abilities and capacities. Old age, as an identity, is something that people resist and perceive negatively, even older people themselves (Netz & Ben-Sira, 1993). The transformation of individuals from people who consider themselves young and valued, to people who see themselves as frail and disabled, is surely a move from a desired state to an undesired state. As a respondent in a study by Fournier and Fine (1990) expresses, 'Getting "old" means getting weaker. When you get old, you hate to have people see you in a weakened condition. It depresses you' (p.340).

This chapter looks at two forms of bodily changes that have an incrementally greater chance of occurring with advancing age: injury as a result of a fall, and a failure of sexual functioning. Both events, it will be argued, can involve transformations to the individual's self-identity that can be lasting and resistant to intervention, and in which the emotion of shame may play a vital role.

Falls

Psychological factors in recovery from falls in older people

Falling is the sixth leading cause of death in older people (Tinetti, 1990). Community-based studies report that around one-third of older people fall at least once a year (Ryynänen et al., 1991), with injury from fall by far the greatest cause of hospitalisation of older people (Cryer, Davidson & Styles, 1993). In the short-term recovery period, decreased activity is reported in approximately 40% of fallers (King & Tinetti, 1995). In the longer term, only half of the patients experiencing a hip fracture as a result of a fall regain pre-event levels of mobility, and only 33%–50% regain pre-event independence levels (Jelicic, Kempen & van Eijk, 1996). Thus, fallers represent a population in which activity can be severely compromised long after the fall event.

Studies have shown that a patient's general health condition, cognitive functioning, age and the presence of co-morbidity influence the recovery process after a hip fracture as a result of a fall, as do general and technical complications related to surgery (Jelicic, Kempen & van Eijk, 1996). Even when the above-mentioned biomedical factors are accounted for, however, considerable variation in recovery remains. The possible effect that psychosocial factors may have on an individual's recovery after a fall has received relatively scant attention. The primary focus here is on cognitions, and specifically the influence of attributional style on recovery.

It has been demonstrated that over 70% of patients make attributions concerning the cause of their illness (Turnquist, Harvey & Anderson, 1988). A fall can be defined as an unexpected loss of control that results in a negative outcome. Whether or not the incident is attributed to an internal or external locus of causality may influence the rehabilitation success of the individual involved. Weinberg and Strain (1995), investigating the attributions made about falling by older people in the community, found that the strongest predictor of attribution made was self-rated health, with better self-rated health being associated with attributing the fall to external factors, and poorer self-rated health being related to internal attributions. Such a finding is in contrast with much of the work on attributions and health, where an internal causal attribution for a health problem is more often than not an indicator of improved chances of recovery. Just as individuals might perceive a past event to be internally or externally causal, they might hold generalised expectancies of whether future events are internally or externally controlled. Perceptions of control, whether the construct measured is locus of control (Rotter, 1966), perceived behavioural control (Ajzen, 1991) or self-efficacy (Bandura, 1977), have all been implicated in recovery from disabling events (e.g., Fisher & Johnston, 1996; Kaplan, Atkins & Reinsch, 1984; Lorig et al., 1989; Partridge & Johnston, 1989).

A recent study (McKee, Orbell & Radley, 1999) looked at the psychological predictors of perceived recovery in a group of older people hospitalised as a result of a fall. A convenience sample of 40 older people (over 65 years of age) were recruited. Data collection was carried out via a questionnaire-based interview, containing items tapping the domains of demographics, fall details, psychological impact of the fall, history of falls, pre-fall activity, general health, beliefs about the cause of the fall and expectations of recovery. Approximately two months after their initial assessment, participants were sent a postal questionnaire, assessing their well-being and perceived recovered activity. Analysis indicated that, controlling for health status and fall severity, beliefs regarding the cause of the fall, and whether it could have been prevented, contributed a significant proportion of explained variance in recovered activity. Indeed, causal beliefs contributed 11% of unique variance, and beliefs regarding whether the fall was preventable a further 16%. Despite limitations, the study's findings indicated the importance of control cognitions and causal attributions in explaining activity after a fall.

A second study (McKee, Orbell & Morgan, in press) sought to improve on the design of the previous study, and to focus on the importance of attributional issues in recovery from falls. Once again, a group of older people who had been hospitalised as a result of a fall were interviewed while in hospital, and interviewed two months later, following discharge. In this study, only fallers who sustained a proximal femoral fracture were recruited to the study, and a total of 82 were interviewed in hospital with 57 interviewed two months later following discharge. Part of the interview involved an assessment of the 'attributional style' of the participants. Abramson et al.'s (1989) concept of attributional style proposes that depressive reactions to negative life events are more likely to occur, be more intense, and last longer, when the events are attributed to stable (unchangeable over time) and global (affecting many areas of life) causes. Of the participants, 20.7% had such a 'hopelessness' explanatory style with regard to their fall event. That is, 17 of the participants attributed their fall to a stable, global, and internal cause.[1]

Hopelessness explanatory style was found to moderate the relationship between pre-fall activity problems and functional limitation post-fall, with the relationship significantly stronger for individuals with hopelessness explanatory style than for individuals without. When participants with a hopelessness explanatory style were compared to those without, there was no difference in the level of pre-fall activity problems, but participants with hopelessness explanatory style had worse functional recovery (see Figure 3.1). One interpretation is that the individual with hopelessness explanatory style is less easily influenced by rehabilitative interventions that might restore functional performance, due to their perception that the fall event was due to unmodifiable, irreversible factors. The study also indicated that those individuals who worried more about further falls after discharge were significantly more likely, two months later, to have fallen again. In addition, worry about further falls was significantly associated with a hopelessness explanatory style.

This study indicates that the way in which an older person frames the cause of their fall will have implications for their recovery from that event. Evidence for the involvement of identity in recovery comes, however, from a study by Yardley (in press). Yardley carried out a postal survey of fear of falling and activity restriction in a community sample of older people ($N = 224$). Part of the survey was a questionnaire on the consequences of falling, containing items derived from focus groups with older people. Yardley expected the items to be underpinned by a single dimension, but to her surprise when the items were subjected to factor analysis, two factors emerged. The items on one factor tapped issues relating to the physical damage caused by a fall, while the items loading on the other factor addressed issues relating to the

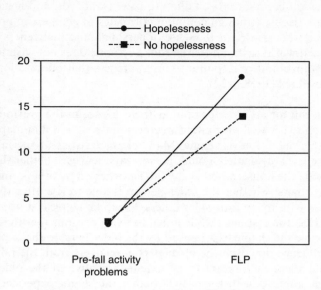

Figure 3.1 Moderation of the relationship between pre-fall activity problems and functional limitation post-fall (FLP) by hopelessness explanatory style for falls

damage done to a person's identity caused by a fall. While high scores on both factors predicted activity restriction when the same sample were surveyed six months later, the greater proportion of variance in activity restriction was predicted by the participants' scores on the damage to identity factor. Thus, the implication is that older people would rather restrict their activity than suffer the psychological damage they see arising from a fall.

Falls, shame, and interventions

Kingston (2000) criticises the medical model approach to falls, and seeks to understand the older person's response to a fall by reference to social models. In particular, he reflects on the relevance of two models: Glaser and Straus' (1971) notion of a 'status passage', whereby an individual may move from one status position in society to another; and Charmaz' (1987) construct of 'preferred identities'. Linking these models, Kingston argues that for many older people, a fall marks a transition to a lower status and a damaged identity, at the expense of a preferred, valued identity. Kingston also reflects on the idea of fall-as-metaphor, suggesting that the plunge into sin and loss of innocence that accompanies a 'fall from grace' carries some resonance for the older person who experiences a fall.

Gilbert has argued that:

[. . .] self-blame, self-consciousness, failing to meet standards, and negative social comparisons, although common correlates of shame, are not
central to it. [. . .] what matters is the sense of personal unattractiveness –
being in the social world as an undesired self, a self one does not wish to
be. Shame is an involuntary response to an awareness that one has lost
status and is devalued (1998, p.22).

The experience of a fall for an older person, as the evidence in the previous
section suggests, might very well precipitate an emotional reaction that maps
very closely onto this definition of shame. Many characteristics of the fall
might impact on the level of shame an older person experiences: whether the
fall is inside or outside the house; whether the fall is witnessed by others, and
the nature of those others; whether the older person is able to rise after the
fall, or, as is the case with many frail older fallers, has to lie helpless waiting
for assistance to arrive. Interestingly, while it is intuitively obvious that these
factors might influence the shame experienced by the older person, these are
factors that also influence how well the older person recovers from the fall.
While it is true that these factors are to an extent indicative of the older
person's frailty, it is interesting to speculate whether the shame experience
might not mediate the relationship between these characteristics of a fall and
later recovery.

Most work with older people post-fall reflects the dominance of the medical model, in that the work is carried out by geriatricians, nurses, physio-
therapists and occupational therapists. Psychological input is negligible. If
damaged identity and shame experienced is, as argued above, highly influen-
tial on the recovery of older people after a fall, then some psychological
input is essential. In particular, understanding the older person's construc-
tion of the cause of the event may be crucial. Within some health authorities, older people hospitalised after a fall are provided with information
leaflets that try to 'desensationalise' the experience – painting a fall as a
fairly common event that does not reflect negatively on the victim, and
which need not occur again if preventative action is taken. This intuitive
attempt to 'play down' the seriousness of the event may actually modify the
older person's attribution of causality, leading to a reduction in the numbers
of older people who 'catastrophize' the event (Peterson et al., 1998). Without proper evaluation, however, this is just conjecture, and there are
undoubtedly many older people who continue to respond to a fall with a
hopelessness explanatory style, despite the provision of information leaflets.
Such older people might benefit from cognitive behavioural therapy to help
them reframe the event as something that is not caused by internal, stable
and global factors. Indeed, in cases where the negative psychological
response to a fall is serious, there may be grounds for treating the fear of
falling that arises as a form of post-traumatic stress disorder, and developing
an intervention on that basis.

Sexual functioning

Sexuality and ageing

As already discussed, bodily changes experienced by older people must be examined within the context of an 'old age (which) symbolizes individual failure' (Gilleard & Higgs, 2000). Within this paradigm, where physical weakness is interpreted as bodily betrayal, all physical 'failings' interpreted as by-products of old age can damage self-esteem and elicit shame responses. However, the centrality of sexuality to personhood and identity can result in particular shame responses to sexual dysfunction attributed to ageing. Indeed, sexual 'failure' in later life can cause significant psychological distress, especially when considered within the context of societal attitudes towards ageing, and ageing sexuality in particular.

Although this discussion will concentrate upon the specific example of erectile dysfunction and is therefore male-focused, it is important to remember that older women may also experience comparable changes in sexual functioning and concomitant challenges to identity and self-esteem in later life. The effects of ageing upon female sexuality are still being debated (see for example, Gullette, 1997; Gannon, 1999), although it is recognised that for some older women physiological changes in sexual functioning associated with ageing (for example, decreased vaginal lubrication), as well as contemporary constructions of the youthful sexual ideal, may result in older women feeling that they are 'losing' their sexuality and femininity (Vincent et al., 2000). Indeed, the social pressures discussed below that may lead ageing to challenge male sexual identity could be even more keenly felt by women, as femininity is considered to be more compromised by social ageing than masculinity (Gilleard & Higgs, 2000).

Erectile dysfunction (ED) is a condition that is most prevalent amongst older men. Indeed, it has been estimated that a man aged 70 is three times more likely to have complete ED than a man aged 40 years (Glossman Petrischor & Bartsch, 1999) and studies to date indicate that between 20% and 52% of older men have experienced ED within the past year (Simons and Carey, 2001). Reasons for this increased prevalence of ED in later life include age-related physiological changes in sexual functioning and an increase in health conditions that can cause ED (for example, diabetes and cardiovascular disease). Moreover, older people are also 'disproportionately high' consumers of prescription medications, including those drugs that can result in impotence, such as antihypertensives (Schiavi, 1999).

The role of psychological factors in triggering ED among older men has received less attention. However, it has been suggested that age-related physiological changes in sexual functioning render individuals 'more vulnerable, sexually, to psychosocial stresses' (Schiavi, 1999, p.198). Moreover, for many older people the incidence of such stresses may also rise in later life as, for example, bereavement and health-related concerns become more common.

Prior to considering the nature of shame responses to ED, it is important to consider the wider situation conditioning responses to sexual dysfunction in later life. Indeed, responses to ED at an individual level must be examined within the context of attitudes towards ageing sexuality in general. We live in a society where norms that 'define and proscribe who may have sex with whom, when and how' (Foucault, 1978) deny the sexuality of older people. The stereotype of the 'asexual' older person is so pervasive within contemporary society that it channels responses to ageing sexuality on a number of levels. Little research is done on this issue, for example, partly because sexuality and sexual health are not perceived to be important to older people. Moreover, many health care professionals neither include sexual assessments in routine medical histories taken from older people, nor discuss the impact of newly diagnosed conditions on the sexual functioning of their older patients (Kellet, 1989). At an individual level, this neglect of later life sexuality can lead older people to feel that their own sexual feelings may be inappropriate, or even disgusting (Drench & Losee, 1996).

These feelings are likely to be further compounded by the belief held by many older people that they do not 'live up to' societal standards of attractiveness. Indeed, older people rarely fit contemporary notions of attractive, sexual beings and the few individuals that do 'have succeeded' in looking younger than their chronological age. The 'gerontophobic messages' that bombard us daily: 'how to stay young, how to get older without signs of ageing, how to stop the clock and so on' (Öberg & Tornstram 1999, p.629) underline the message that the ageing body is not sexy. This is likely to further damage self-esteem in later life which, as Tangney and Miller (1996) argue, can be a precursor to the development of shame responses.

These background factors create a situation where the experience of loss of sexual desire or ability can ignite feelings of both grief (of that which was previously enjoyed, potentially as a valued part of a relationship) and shame. To date, however, understanding the shame responses to ED and other changes in sexual functioning in both men and women is hampered by a lack of research. Indeed, although there has been increasing attention paid to the impact of ED on overall quality of life (for example, Litwin, Nied & Dhanani 1998), research to date has not specifically focused upon shame as a component of psychological responses to age-related changes in sexual functioning.

However, it is clear that ED can have long-lasting psychological implications both for the individual sufferer, as well as potentially for their sexual partner. Morgentaler claims that 'men with erectile dysfunction may experience loss of self-esteem, diminished sense of manliness, reduced assertiveness, depression, and even suicidal ideation' (1999, p.1715). Evidence of the distressing nature of ED can be found in research identifying disproportionately high levels of psychological distress associated with sexual dysfunction (Eysenck, 1971; Fagan et al., 1988), including symptoms of depression (Derogatis, Meyer & King, 1981), although the extent to which such symptoms precede the onset of ED remains unclear.

Intuitively, it would be expected that ED may not only impact upon the individual experiencing the condition, but also their sexual partner(s) and the overall quality of the relationship. Indeed, this supposition is supported by data identifying that couples who are unhappy with their sexual relationship report both poorer psychological well-being and poorer perceived quality of marriage (Edwards & Booth, 1994). However, again it is difficult to identify the direction of the relationship between sexual satisfaction and relationship satisfaction.

Sexuality, shame and interventions

The medical model has emerged as the dominant paradigm for the treatment of ED (Winton, 2000), especially in the case of older men where ED is attributed to ageing. As Schiavi (1999, p.8) notes:

> The social construction of aging as a medical problem has fostered the attribution of sexual difficulties to biological causes, neglecting psychosocial contributors to sexual well-being and satisfaction.

Furthermore, the tendency by clinicians to assume a physiological basis to later life ED in the first instance may be compounded by the attitude of the individual sufferer. Older men often attribute a physical causation to changes in sexual (dys)functioning and may, indeed, be resistant to receiving a psychological intervention (Schiavi, 1999). This has been explained in terms of the perceived difficulties that older people have in discussing sexual health issues, although empirical evidence indicates that the extent to which this hypothesis holds true in contemporary society is a matter of conjecture (Gott & Hinchliff, in press) and the role of clinician attitudes in recommending referrals of this nature to their older patients warrants further investigation.

Indeed, there is evidence that psychological interventions do have the potential to improve, and even reverse, ED if acceptable to the individual patient. Therapies used in this situation include cognitive behavioural therapy, which may help older men reframe their experience of ED and reconsider the negative self-appraisals they may attach to failure in sexual functioning (Beck, 1988). Such interventions may also help individuals develop more adaptive coping strategies to ED, for example by adopting 'accommodative coping' styles, which involve adjusting preferences and expectations in response to situational constraints, as opposed to 'assimilative coping' where the, potentially unrealistic, aim would be to modify these constraints (Brandtstadter & Renner, 1990).

However, little attention has been paid to the role of shame as a likely component of psychological reactions to ED, despite the implications of addressing feelings of shame in therapeutic settings if experienced following this type of sexual dysfunction. Indeed, when looking specifically at such reactions in relation to cognitions or beliefs about the self, it is apparent that ED is very likely to correspond to definitions of the shame response which posit that shame is experienced when the individual feels 'inferior, flawed, and inadequate' in the eyes of others (Gilbert, 1998). Indeed, such negative self-evaluations must be viewed in relation to the centrality of sexuality to masculine identity and personhood (Pridal, 2001). This is exemplified by the dual meanings attached to potency, which is not only defined in terms of sexual functioning, but also as 'inherent powerfulness or capacity' and authority (*Oxford English Dictionary*, 1989). Therefore, impotence is likely to strike at the heart of masculine constructions of the self, invoking feelings of powerlessness, of being incapable and essentially unmasculine. This proximity to the 'undesired self' (Ogilvie, 1987), the unmanly self, the impotent self and potentially, as discussed below, the aged self, creates ideal conditions for shame responses to occur.

This devaluation of the self may further be compounded by anticipatory fear of rejection by a sexual partner. Indeed, in this situation, where the damage to self is likely to interrupt positive affect for both the individual and their sexual partner, the 'external shame' (Gilbert; see Chapter 1, this volume) induced by the experience of ED is likely to be considerable. Sexual 'failure', therefore, is highly likely to lead to negative self-evaluation (Lewis, 1992) as feelings of being unattractive and worthless in ones own eyes, as well as in the eyes of a significant other, are internalised. In addition, the partner of an individual with ED may also experience similar feelings of being devalued and unattractive if they 'share the blame' for the episode of ED. This underlines the importance of including sexual partners in psychological interventions, if appropriate and desired by both parties.

Another intervention that may improve coping for some older people with ED may be the provision of educational materials detailing potential changes in sexual functioning that accompany 'normal ageing' (Schiavi, 1999). Indeed, Steinke (1994) has posited a relationship between knowledge and attitudes about sexuality and sexual health for older people, with inadequate knowledge of ageing sexuality leading to the internalisation of previously discussed stereotypes of the 'asexual older person' and a cessation of sexual activity. The role that shame plays in older people's attitudes towards their own sexuality has already been discussed and it may be that the provision of information may impact positively upon these shame responses. However, again, this remains unclear at the present time.

Conclusion

Poor health is so bound up in the social representation of ageing that similar symptoms presented by people of different ages will be interpreted differently. A sharp pain in the chest of a 25-year-old may be considered the result of indigestion or muscle strain. A pain in the chest of a 70-year-old is more likely to be interpreted as the signal of a myocardial infarction. A person of 30 falling over may be thought clumsy or drunk. A fall in a 70-year-old is more likely to be attributed to frailty. These 'attributional biases' occur in the mind of the observer, but very importantly they also occur in the mind of the observed.

Williamson and Fried (1996) found that 31% of a sample of 230 community-dwelling older people cited old age as the cause of difficulty in one or more tasks of daily living, with 20% of the sample citing old age as the cause in two or more tasks. Perceiving old age as a cause of physical disability might have serious psychological consequences. 'Old age' meets the criteria of a cause that is stable and global, thus fulfilling the requirements of a cause that, if selected, would be consistent with a hopelessness explanatory style (Abramson et al., 1989).

Here we have a potential catalyst for the transition between the Third Age and the Fourth Age (Laslett, 1991), that is, from a successfully ageing person to someone who is unsuccessful in dealing with the challenges of age. This transition has been referred to as the Body Drop (McKee, 1998), defined as a failure of the body which, when combined with an attribution of the cause of the failure to stable and global factors, such as ageing, leads to a reduction in functioning that endures, in some cases even after the restoration of the body. This change endures, it is argued, because the Body Drop transition is fundamentally a transition in self-identity, through which individuals come to think themselves no longer as people who are in an endless 'middle-youth' (Featherstone & Hepworth, 1991), but as people who are old. As Goffman (1963) has pointed out, management of the body is central to a person's virtual identity, the ability to construct a version of the self that is preferred rather than stigmatising. As a person ages, one might expect the maintenance of the contradiction between a 'subjective sense of inner youthfulness and an exterior process of biological ageing' (Turner, 1995, p.258), to create more psychological demands. When a major failure of the body occurs, the psychological reserves of the person may be presented with a challenge that cannot, finally, be met. The result is a sudden assimilation of the young 'inner' self by the old, malfunctioning external self.

Whether shame may function as a core mediating emotion of the Body Drop transition is an intriguing question. An argument may be made for humiliation to be more central to the Body Drop experience. But Klein (1991) argues that the essential distinction between shame and humiliation is that people believe they deserve their shame, they do not believe they deserve their humiliation. When it comes to issues of health and the body, Western culture is increasingly locked within the cult of individual responsibility, driven by a victim-blaming mentality (Ryan, 1971). It seems likely, therefore, that such deeply transforming events as a serious fall or erectile dysfunction could be seen as having a cause located within the self. Whatever form of self-blame occurs, shame will surely be a predominant accompanying emotion.

Note

1 This study used the more restrictive, earlier definition of hopelessness explanatory style, which requires that, in addition to a causative factor being stable and global, it is also internal to the individual, rather than subject to external influence (Abramson, Matalsky & Alloy, 1989).

References

Abramson, L.Y., Matalsky, G.I. & Alloy, L.B. (1989) Hopelessness depression: A theory-based subtype of depression. *Psychological Review*, 96, 358–372.

Ajzen, I. (1991) The theory of planned behaviour. *Organizational Behaviour and Human Decision Processes*, 50, 179–211.

Bandura, A. (1977) Self-efficacy theory: Toward a unifying theory of behavioural change. *Psychological Review*, 84, 191–215.

Beck, A.T. (1988) *Love is Never Enough*. New York: Harper Perennial.

Brandtstadter, J. & Renner, G. (1990) Tenacious goal pursuit and flexible goal adjustment: Explication and age-related analysis of assimilative and accommodative strategies of coping. *Psychology of Aging*, 5, 58–67.

Charmaz, K. (1987) Struggling for a self: Identity levels of the chronically ill. *Research in the Sociology of Health Care*, 6, 283–321.

Cryer, C., Davidson, L. & Styles, C. (1993) *Injury Epidemiology in the South East: Identifying Priorities for Action*. London: South Thames Regional Health Authority.

Derogatis, L.R., Meyer, J.K. & King, K.M. (1981) Sexual behavior and marital intimacy in Alzheimer's couples: A family theory perspective. *Sexuality and Disability*, 13, 239–254.

Drench M. & Losee R. (1996) Sexuality and sexual capacities of elderly people. *Rehabilitation Nursing*, 21, 118–123.

Edwards, J.N. & Booth, A. (1994) Sexuality, marriage and well-being: The middle years. In A.S. Rossi (ed.) *Sexuality Across the Life Course* (pp.233–259). Chicago, IL: University of Chicago Press.

Eysenck, H.J. (1971) Personality and sexual adjustment. *British Journal of Psychiatry*, 118, 593–608.

Fagan, P.J., Schmidt, C.W. Jr., Wise T. & Derogatis, L.R. (1988) Sexual dysfunction and dual psychiatric diagnosis. *Comparative Psychiatry*, 14, 245–252.

Featherstone, M. & Hepworth, M. (1991) The mask of ageing and the post-modern life course. In M. Featherstone, M. Hepworth & B.S. Turner (eds) *The Body: Social Process and Cultural Theory* (pp.371–389). London: Sage.

Fisher, K. & Johnstone, M. (1996) Experimental manipulation of perceived control and its effect on disability. *Psychology and Health*, 11, 657–669.

Foucault, M. (1978) *The History of Sexuality Volume I: An Introduction*. New York: Pantheon.

Fournier, S. & Fine, G. (1990) Jumping grannies: Exercise as a buffer against becoming 'old'. *Play and Culture*, 3, 337–342.

Gannon, L.R. (1999) *Women and Aging: Transcending the Myths*. London and New York: Routledge.

Gilbert, P. (1998) What is shame? Some core issues and controversies. In P. Gilbert and B. Andrews (eds) *Shame: Interpersonal Behaviour, Psychopathology and Culture* (pp.3–38). New York: Oxford University Press.

Gilleard, C. & Higgs, P. (2000) *Cultures of Ageing: Self, Citizen and the Body*. Harlow: Prentice Hall.

Glaser, B.G. & Straus, A.L. (1971) *Status Passage*. London: Routledge & Kegan Paul.

Glossman, H., Petrischor, G. & Bartsch, G. (1999) Molecular mechanisms of the effects of sildenafil (VIAGRA). *Experimental Gerontology*, 34 (3), 305–318.

Goffman, E. (1963) *Stigma: Notes on the Management of Spoiled Identity*. Englewood Cliffs, NJ: Prentice Hall.

Gott, C.M. & Hinchliff (in press) How important is sex in later life? The views of older people. *Social Science and Medicine*.

Gott, C.M., Rogstad, K.E., Riley, V. & Ahmed-Jusuf, I. (1999) Delay in symptom presentation among a sample of older GUM clinic attenders. *International Journal of STD and AIDS*, 10, 43–46.

Gullette, M.M. (1997) *Declining to Decline: Cultural Combat and the Politics of the Midlife*. Charlottesville, VA: University Press of Virginia.

Jarrett, P.G., Rockwood, K., Carver, D., Stolee, P. & Cosway, S. (1995) Illness presentation in elderly patients. *Archives of Internal Medicine*, 155, 1060–1064.

Jelicic, M., Kempen, G.I.J.M. & van Eijk, L.M. (1996) Do psychosocial factors affect recovery from hip fracture in the elderly? A review of the literature. *Journal of Rehabilitation Sciences*, 9, 77–81.

Kaplan, R.M., Atkins, C.J. & Reinsch, S. (1984) Specific efficacy expectations mediate exercise compliance in patients with COPD. *Health Psychology*, 3, 223–242.

Kellet, J. (1989) Sex and the elderly. *British Medical Journal*, 299, 934.

King, M.B. & Tinetti, M.E. (1995) Falls in community-dwelling older persons. *Journal of the American Geriatrics Society*, 43, 1146–1154.

Kingston, P. (2000) Falls in later life: Status passage and preferred identities as a new orientation, *Health*, 4, 216–233.

Klein, D.C. (1991) The humiliation dynamic: An overview. *The Journal of Primacy Prevention*, 12, 93–121.

Laslett, P. (1991) *A Fresh Map of Life: The Emergence of the Third Age*. Cambridge, MA: Harvard University Press.

Lewis, M. (1992) *Shame: The Exposed Self*. New York: The Free Press.

Litwin, M.S., Nied, R.J. & Dhanani, N. (1998) Health-related quality of life in men with erectile dysfunction. *Journal of General Internal Medicine*, 13, 159–166.

Lorig, K., Chastain, R.L., Ung, E., Shoor, S. & Holman, H.R. (1989) Development and evaluation of a scale to measure perceived self-efficacy in people with arthritus. *Arthritus and Rheumatism*, 32, 77–44.

Mascolo, M.F. & Fischer, K.W. (1995) Developmental transformations in appraisals of pride, shame and guilt. In J.P. Tangney and K.W. Fischer (eds) *Self-conscious Emotions: The Psychopathology of Shame, Guilt, Embarrassment and Pride* (pp.64–113). New York: Guilford Press.

McKee, K.J. (1998) The Body Drop: A framework for understanding recovery from falls in older people. *Generations Review*, 8, 11–12.

McKee, K.J., Orbell, S. & Morgan, K. (in press) Psychological factors in recovery from falls. *Proceedings of the British Psychological Society*.

McKee, K.J., Orbell, S. & Radley, K. (1999) Predicting perceived recovered activity in older people after a fall. *Disability and Rehabilitation*, 21, 555–562.

Morgentaler, A. (1999) Male impotence. *The Lancet*, 354 (9191), 1713–1718.

Netz, Y. & Ben-Sira, D. (1993) Attitudes of young people, adults, and older adults from three generation families toward the concepts 'ideal person', 'youth', 'adult', and 'old person'. *Educational Gerontology*, 19, 607–621.

Öberg, P. & Tornstam, L. (1999) Body images among men and women of different ages. *Ageing and Society*, 19, 629–644.

Ogilvie, D.M. (1987) The undesired self: A neglected variable in personality research. *Journal of Personality and Social Psychology*, 52, 379–385.

Partridge, C.J. & Johnston, M. (1989) Perceived control and recovery from stroke. *British Journal of Clinical Psychology*, 28, 53–60.

Peterson, C., Seligman, M.E.P., Yurko, K.H., Martin, L.R. & Friedman, H.S. (1998) Catastrophizing and untimely death. *Psychological Science*, 9, 127–130.

Pridal, C.G. (2001) Male gender role issues in the treatment of sexual dysfunction. In *The New Handbook of Psychotherapy and Counselling with Men: A Comprehensive Guide to Settings, Problems and Treatment Approaches*, vols. 1 and 2 (pp.309–334). San Fransisco: Jossey-Bass Inc, Publishers.

Reboussin, B.A., Rejeski, W.J., Martin, K.A., Callahan, K., Dunn, A.L., King, A.C. & Sallis, J.F. (2000) Correlates of body satisfaction with body function and body appearance in middle- and older-aged adults: The Activity Counseling Trial (ACT). *Psychology and Health*, 15, 239–254.

Rockwood, K., Stadnyk, K., MacKnight, C., McDowell, I., Hebert, R., and Hogan, D.B. (1999) A brief clinical instrument to classify frailty in elderly people. *Lancet*, 353, 205–206.

Rotter, J.B. (1966) Generalized expectancies for internal versus external control of reinforcement. *Psychological Monographs*, 80 (1, Whole No. 609).

Ryan, W. (1971) *Blaming the Victim*. London: Orbach and Chambers Ltd.

Ryynänen, O., Kivelä, S., Honkanen, R., Laippala, P. & Soini, P. (1991) Incidence of falling injuries leading to medical treatment in the elderly. *Public Health*, 105, 373–386.

Schiavi, R.C. (1999) *Aging and Male Sexuality*. Cambridge: Cambridge University Press.

Simons, J.S. & Carey, M.P. (2001) Prevalence of sexual dysfunctions: Results from a decade of research. *Archives of Sexual Behavior*, 30 (2), 177–219.

Slater, R. (1995) *The Psychology of Growing Old*. Buckingham: Open University Press.

Steinke, E.E. (1994) Knowledge and attitudes of older adults about sexuality in ageing: A comparison of two studies. *Journal of Advanced Nursing*, 19, 477–485.

Tangney, J.P. & Miller, R.S. (1996) Are shame, guilt and embarrassment distinct emotions? *Journal of Personality and Social Psychology*, 70, 1256–1269.

Tinetti, M.E. (1990) Falls. In C.K. Cassel, D.E. Riesenberg, L.B. Sorensen & J.R. Walsh (eds) *Geriatric Medicine* (2nd edn.) (pp.528–534). New York: Springer-Verlag.

Turner, B.S. (1995) Ageing and identity: Some reflections on the somatization of the self. In M. Featherstone & A. Wernick (eds) *Images of Ageing: Cultural Representations of Later Life* (pp.245–262). London: Routledge.

Turnquist, D.C., Harvey, J.H., Anderson, B. (1988) Attributions and adjustment to life threatening illness. *British Journal of Clinical Psychology*, 27, 55–65.

Unsworth, K., McKee, K.J. & Mulligan, C. (2001) When does old age begin? The role of attitudes in age parameter placement. *Social Psychological Review*, 3, 5–15.

Vincent, C., Riddell, J. & Shmueli, A. (2000) *Sexuality and the Older Woman: A Literature Review*. London: The Pennell Initiative for Women's Health.

Weinberg, L.E. and Strain, L.A. (1995) Community-dwelling older adults' attributions about falls. *Archives of Physical and Medical Rehabilitation*, 76, 955–960.

Williamson, J.D. & Fried, L.P. (1996) Characterization of older adults who attribute functional decrements to 'old age'. *Journal of the American Geriatrics Society*, 44, 1429–1434.

Winton, M.A. (2000) The medicalization of male sexual dysfunctions: An analysis of sex therapy journals. *Journal of Sex Education and Therapy*, 25(4), 231–239.

Woodhouse, K.W., Wynne, H., Baillie, S., James, O.F.W. & Rawlins, M.D. (1988) Who are the frail elderly? *Quarterly Journal of Medicine*, 68, 505–506.

Yardley, L. (in press) Influence of perceived consequences of falling on activity restriction in later life. *Proceedings of the British Psychological Society*.

Chapter 4

Body shame
Issues of assessment and measurement

Anthony T. Carr

Introduction

At first sight the assessment of body shame raises a fundamental question, in that approaches to the measurement of attitudes to and feelings about the way one's body looks do not explicitly address the concept of shame. Rather, they have been concerned with body image distortion (Slade & Russell, 1973), body image avoidance (Rosen et al., 1991), dysmorphophobia (Rosen, Reiter & Orosan, 1995), appearance schemas (Cash & Labarge, 1996) and self-consciousness of appearance (Carr, Harris & James, 2000). However, the conceptual elaboration of shame by Gilbert (Chapter 1, this volume) clearly reveals a commonality of meaning with the constructs underlying assessment scales for appearance-related difficulties. There is also a clear and extensive overlap in the scales' attention to associated emotions, behaviour and cognitions with the multiple dimensions of shame as delineated by Gilbert (op. cit.), for example, external social, internal self-evaluative, emotional and behavioural dimensions.

The majority of appearance-related assessment scales emphasise only a subset of the shame dimensions identified by Gilbert, for example, external body image, camouflage and social avoidance or appearance-related cognitions and, in so doing, can contribute to the assessment of body-shame only within their domains of interest. Even some specific scales in other fields of assessment can be seen by their item contents to coincide with specific dimensions of body-shame, for example, social anxiety and the fear of negative evaluation (FNE) (Watson & Friend, 1969) with social/external cognitive aspects and the behavioural component of body shame (Gilbert, op. cit.). However, the majority of non-specific scales lack adequate content validity (Carr, 1997a) and can contribute little to the assessment of body shame.

In having items based directly upon the statements of patients and non-patients with appearance difficulties, the Derriford Appearance Scale (DAS59) Carr, Harris and James (2000) appear to achieve the closest correspondence with body shame conceptually and in terms of content. Indeed, factor analyses of the DAS(59) revealed a stable underlying dimension, which the authors called 'self-consciousness of appearance' and which appears almost indistinguishable from body shame as proposed earlier in this volume (Gilbert, op. cit.). Also, Gilbert, Pehl and Allan (1994) concluded that the shame experience and FNE were conceptually and psychometrically very similar and Carr, Harris and James (2000) report a positive correlation (0.63) between self-consciousness of appearance, as measured by the DAS(59), and Fear of Negative Evaluation (FNE) (Watson & Friend, 1969).

Effective approaches to the assessment of body shame, self-consciousness of appearance, body image distortion and so on are fundamental to improving our better understanding of a range of clinical problems such as anorexia and bulimia nervosa, core developmental issues such as body-schema and self-esteem, and to the evolution and refinement of more effective physical and psychological therapies in appearance-related disorders. Andrews (1995, see Chapter 13, this volume), for example, developed a shame interview that focuses on shame of character, shame of behaviour and body shame. She found that body shame mediated the link between sexual abuse and chronic depression. However, despite an apparent plethora of relevant scales (Cash & Pruzinsky, 1990; Thompson et al., 1999) the majority have not been developed beyond an initial small-scale study. There is a dearth of adequate psychometric refinement and, even where it is present, standardisation all too often has been based predominantly on white, female, non-clinical samples (Carr, 1997a, 1997b; Carr, Harris & James, 2000).

The assessment of general, non-appearance-specific, shame and its relationship with a range of psychological problems such as depression, suicidality, violence and social anxiety, has been explored and developed by a number of authors, for example, Cook (1991), Gilbert, Pehl and Allan (1994) and Allan, Gilbert and Goss (1995). There are no empirical studies of the relationship between the resulting scales and those measuring appearance-related affect, behaviour and cognition, but inspection of the item contents of the scales suggests, interestingly, that body shame probably subsumes general shame but is also more extensively represented in related behaviour and cognition. That is, shame about the body or body parts includes the same core experiences as general shame but it prompts a wider range of specific, related behaviours and cognitions. Also, the centrality of concern about appearance in body shame provides a distinctive 'flavour' that permeates most aspects of the shame experience.

In reviewing approaches to the assessment of body shame, we must recognise their original purposes as concerned with specific or wider aspects of problems of appearance that 'map on' to body shame to a greater or lesser extent and, thereby, make different contributions to its assessment. In recent years, approaches to the assessment of various aspects of appearance and body image have proliferated. Initially, measurement focused on just two aspects of physical appearance. Firstly, a perceptual cognitive dimension, reflected in constructs of body size, body concept and body boundaries (Fisher, 1986), commonly referred to as *body image* (e.g., Thompson & Psaltis, 1988; Thompson & Spana, 1988). Secondly, an affective dimension, reflected in emotional responses and attitudes to overall appearance or to specific body parts and sites (e.g., Berscheid, Walster & Bohrnstedt, 1973; Pasman & Thompson, 1988). In subsequent approaches to measurement (e.g., Cash & Pruzinsky, 1990) this distinction became less clear and the concept of body image included subjective attitudinal and perceptual experiences of one's own body, particularly its appearance. The concept of body image was further developed to include more cognitive schematic dimensions, building on the work of Markus (1977) who examined how information concerning the self is processed. This gave rise to an interest in body schemata as a cognitive dimension of body image (Cash & Labarge, 1996).

Currently, it appears that body image comprises perceptual, affective and cognitive dimensions of body awareness. It is also clear that there are extensive behavioural concomitants of negative body images, such as body-checking, social comparison and camouflage, for example, Harris and Carr (2001) and Rosen and Ramirez (1998). Although these may be seen as sequelae of body-related cognitions and affects, the interaction between behaviour and the evolution of related schemata and emotion (Young, 1990) argues for the inclusion of behaviour in the concept and measurement of body image. Accordingly, body image, in its perceptual, affective, cognitive and behavioural dimensions is central to our understanding of body shame and a range of related clinical problems such as dysfunctional levels of associated distress and behaviour, relationship and sexual problems, anxiety, depression, anorexia, bulimia and body dysmorphic disorder.

Interest in 'distortion' of the perceptual dimension of body image and in the development of techniques to measure this 'distortion' followed from the work of Slade and Russell (1973). They identified a greater overestimation of body size in anorexic patients than in controls by using a perceptual matching technique. This technique, which used lights and calipers that participants adjusted to reflect their perception of body size or body part, gave rise to a plethora of similar, physically based approaches such as the body image detection device (Ruff & Barrios, 1986) and the adjustable light beam apparatus (Thompson & Spana, 1988). Subsequently, approaches to assessing the perceptual dimension of body image have used computer-generated images that participants manipulate to match their own perceived body image or body site (e.g., Dickson-Parnell, Jones & Braddy, 1987). More recently, Rosen (1996) described the use of figure drawings to assess body size and body part distortion. With the exception of the adjustable light beam apparatus (Thompson & Spana, 1988), the majority of the perceptual measures have not been psychometrically developed. Also, on the few occasions that convergence between the measures has been investigated, the results have been poor with low inter-test correlations (e.g., Keeton, Cash & Brown, 1990).

It seems likely that size and shape estimation procedures, far from being straightforward perceptual measures, are strongly influenced by affective dimensions of body image and by emotional responses to the stimuli presented for comparison. The varying stimulus materials between procedures, as well as large procedural variations, provide very different opportunities for affect, motivation and demand characteristics to influence the outcome.

Disturbances of the affective, cognitive and behavioural aspects of body image are core components of body dysmorphic disorder (BDD) and eating disorders (Veale, Chapter 14, this volume). These disorders, in turn, have a significant overlap with a number of other clinical problems which, themselves, do not involve disturbances of body image, for example, obsessive-compulsive disorder (checking and ritual) and social anxiety (social avoidance and FNE). A number of relevant assessment methods have evolved from the need to assess these clinical conditions and from existing measures in overlapping conditions. The assessment of eating disorders provides several scales that, despite emphasising weight and eating concerns, include items tapping into aspects of body image. The body dissatisfaction scale of the Eating Disorders Inventory (Garner, Olmsted & Polivy, 1983) is a useful measure of satisfaction with a range of body parts and the Body Shape Questionnaire (Cooper et al., 1987) measures negative attitudes towards and preoccupation with physical appearance. Additionally, Cooper and Fairburn (1987) developed the Eating Disorders Examination interview to assess the degree of importance respondents place on shape and weight in their evaluations of self – or self-schema. A limited number of eating disorders scales have been validated on child and adolescent populations (e.g., Mendelson & White, 1985; Peterson et al., 1984; Williams et al., 1986). These are particularly useful since the direct assessment of body image appears to be concerned almost exclusively with adult populations.

The formal assessment of body dysmorphic disorder (BDD), while attending to the essential criteria for its identification, offers several useful measures of various aspects of body image. BDD is defined as a preoccupation with some imagined defect in physical appearance or a gross exaggeration of a slight physical anomaly (see Veale, Chapter 14, this volume). This preoccupation with appearance is excessively time-consuming and causes significant distress and dysfunction. *DSM-IV* allows for an intensity of dysmorphic belief of delusional intensity, beyond that of an overvalued idea, and which may be classified as a delusional disorder, somatic subtype. Dissatisfaction with body shape and size associated with an eating disorder excludes a classification of BDD. The overlap with some aspects of obsessive-compulsive disorders prompted the development of a BDD variant of the well-known Yale–Brown Obsessive Compulsive Scale (BDD-YBOCS; Phillips et al., 1997). This is a clinician-administered, semistructured scale that taps into intrusive thinking about the physical defect, consequent thought interference and time spent in related behaviours. It is psychometrically robust and clearly samples some of the cognitive and behavioural aspects of body image but is inevitably limited in scope by the focus on obsessive-compulsive symptomatology.

The Body Dysmorphic Disorder Examination (BDDE; Rosen & Reiter, 1996; Rosen & Ramirez, 1998) is a well-developed instrument explicitly providing a diagnosis of BDD according to *DSM-IV* criteria and useful assessments in six areas defined by item content: preoccupation with appearance, self-consciousness and embarrassment, the importance given to appearance, social avoidance, camouflage activities and body-checking and social comparison. In its original, structured interview format (Rosen & Reiter, 1996), it also allows for a rating of insight and the possibility of a conviction about the supposed physical defect being held with delusional intensity. As a clinical assessment, the interview is thorough and psychometrically sound. The authors report two-week test-retest reliabilities with the same interviewer of 0.87 (clinical) and 0.94 (undergraduate), inter-rater reliability of 0.99, good internal consistency and reasonable concurrent validities (.2 – .77). The BDDE differentiates well between BDD and non-BDD patients and between patients and non-patients. Agreement with clinician diagnoses of BDD is acceptable (k = .82). However, there are no normative data and the interview duration of 1.5 hours makes it impractical in many settings. The authors recognise this difficulty and have developed a self-report version of the BDDE (Rosen & Ramirez, 1998), which has test-retest reliability of .89, good internal consistency (.94), and concurrent validity indices between .69 and .83. Conceptually and clinically, the value of a diagnosis of BDD is open to question. There is no suggestion from therapeutic outcome studies that the treatment options differ according to the presence or absence of the diagnosis (Cororve & Gleaves, 2001) and the criteria for establishing a diagnosis of BDD using the BDDE are explicitly quantitative rather than qualitative. That is, the diagnosis is based upon the *degree* of distress and the *frequency* of avoidance and so on. Clearly, disturbances of body image, in cognitive, affective, perceptual and behavioural domains range from mild to severe and effective assessment is based more appropriately upon this multifaceted, quantitative dimension rather than upon establishing quantitative thresholds for descriptive diagnoses of doubtful utility. A continuum of body image dissatisfaction, ranging from satisfaction, through dissatisfaction and disturbance, to BDD at the upper extreme has been proposed by Sarwer, Wadden, Pertschuk and Whitaker (1998).

In recognition of the unreasonable prominence that has been given to BDD in the field of body image disorders, Oosthuizen, Lambert and Castle (1998) developed a scale to assess over-concern with appearance without attempting to establish a diagnosis. Items in the Dysmorphic Concern Questionnaire (DSQ) sample individuals' judgements about the relative strength of their concern compared with the concerns of other people (non-existent, same as most people, more than most people etc.) As a measure of strength of belief in a perceived defect in appearance, the DSQ is potentially useful but it has, as yet, only very limited psychometric development. Other measures of strength of belief, with adequate psychometric properties, have been developed in the field of mental health, to address delusions (Brown Assessment of Beliefs Scale: BABS; Eisen et al., 1998) and overvalued ideas in obsessional states (Overvalued Ideas Scale: OVIS; Neziroglu et al., 1999). Both of these scales have been used with BDD patients and may be more useful than the DSQ for assessing strength of belief until the psychometric properties of the latter are better established.

The behavioural aspects of body image disturbance were specifically addressed by Rosen et al. (1991) in constructing the Body Image Avoidance Questionnaire (BIAQ). The authors explicitly acknowledge the multi-dimensionality of body image and identify the need to include assessment of related behaviours, in addition to those dimensions covered by existing assessments. The BIAQ is a 19-item self-report scale, based upon the weight and shape concerns of female undergraduates. The psychometric properties of the scale were extensively explored with a further, moderate sample of undergraduates (353) and two small clinical samples of bulimia (20) and extremely disturbed body image in a therapeutic outcome study (37). Overall the psychometric properties of the scale are adequate or good and it effectively discriminates between bulimic patients and normal controls. However, the items reveal a strong representation of weight and eating concerns, which clearly resulted from the questions asked of college-student-participants in generating the original set of items. They were asked if they ever felt dissatisfied with their weight or shape and, if so, how the dissatisfaction affected their behaviour. The resulting emphasis upon weight and eating emerged in the factor analysis as factors of eating restraint and weighing and grooming, and in higher correlations with the shape and weight concern scales of the Eating Disorders Examination than with other criterion tests. Despite the valuable objective of representing the behavioural aspects of body image disturbance, the authors have severely limited the content validity of the scale by generating items from a non-clinical, female, college sample and by biasing their reporting towards weight and eating concerns. Clearly, the BIAQ cannot be used with confidence to measure behavioural aspects of body image disturbance that are unrelated to weight and shape or that might occur frequently mainly in clinical populations.

Assessment of the cognitive aspects of body image was addressed by Cash and Labarge (1996) with the Appearance Schemas Inventory (ASI). From the basic premise of the central role of self-schema in processing information relevant to the self and, in this context, the role of appearance schema in processing physical appearance information relevant to the self, Cash and Labarge derived items to tap beliefs about the importance, meaning and perceived influences of appearance in a person's life. Except to say that the 14 items were 'based on key themes in the body-image literature' (p.39) the process of item generation is unclear. There does not appear to have been a stage of endorsement of the item-set by other judges or key respondents, nor the subsequent refinement of the original item-set. Detailed psychometric evaluation of the ASI was undertaken on a sample of 274 female college students. Although there is no information on temporal stability and there is only adequate internal consistency (.84), correlations with other measures of body image satisfaction are acceptable (.38–.64) and the scale effectively discriminated between women with extreme body image dissatisfaction (the 'clinical' group) and the rest of the sample. It is interesting to note that the strongest correlation was between the ASI and body image dysphoria, reflecting a positive relationship between body image schema and negative body image affect.

While clearly needing further standardisation and psychometric development, data on males and a range of clinical samples, the ASI has potential as a scale for research. Indeed, it is already proving useful in explorations of information processing in appearance-schematic women (Labarge, Cash & Brown, 1998) and in therapeutic outcome studies of cognitive behaviour therapy for body image dissatisfaction (Grant & Cash, 1995). However, there is always the possibility that the item content, and thus the content validity for the relevant participant and patient groups, will be limited by the item generation process. This would have obvious implications for the discriminatory power of the scale and its sensitivity to change. We must await further research to answer these questions.

It is a characteristic of the field that the development of measures has reflected the development of the concept of body image, in seeking to capture the defining attributes of the construct as it has become more conceptually elaborated, that is, its perceptual, cognitive, affective and behavioural dimensions. The potential value of these 'dimensional measures' is clear, in that they permit the measurement of specific aspects of body image that may illuminate theoretical models and facilitate the refinement of therapeutic strategies for disorders of body image. We have already looked at some perceptual, behavioural and cognitive measures, but there is a dearth of specific measures of the affective aspect of negative body image. Distress about appearance in general or about specific body sites is largely overlooked and the relevant measures of the affective dimension are more concerned with satisfaction. For example, satisfaction with appearance is addressed by the sub-scales of a number of measures: the Body Dissatisfaction subscale of the Eating Disorder Inventory 2 (Garner, Garner & Van-Egeren, 1992), the Body Areas Satisfaction Scale of the Multidimensional Body Self-relations Questionnaire (Brown, Cash & Mikulka, 1990) and the Physical Appearance sub-scale of the Extended Satisfaction with Life Scale (Alfonso et al., 1996).

While we would expect there to be a relationship between satisfaction/dissatisfaction and distress, it is unlikely that dissatisfaction with appearance equates with distress about appearance. Distress is sampled directly by items in the Body Dysmorphic Disorder Examination (BDDE) (Rosen and Reiter, 1996), for example, 'distress when other people comment about his/her appearance' and 'distress when other people treat him or her differently due to appearance'. Wider aspects of distress are covered in the Derriford Appearance Scale (DAS59) (Carr, Harris & James, 2000). Items in this scale include distress arising from being *unable* to act in certain ways, or to wear certain clothes as a consequence of self-consciousness of appearance, in addition to distress about appearance *per se*, or arising from the behaviour of others, for example, distress when/from '. . . being unable to go swimming', '. . . not able to go to social events', '. . . being unable to answer the front door' and '. . . being unable to wear favourite clothes'.

In addition to dimensional measures of body image disturbance, there is a clear research and clinical need for instruments that assess the totality of body image disturbance by appropriate sampling of all dimensions. The self-report version of the Body Dysmorphic Disorder Examination (BDDE-SR) (Rosen, 1997 in Sarwer, Wadden & Foster, 1998) assesses the respondents' ratings of the body part with which they are most dissatisfied on 7-point Likert scales covering preoccupation with and negative evaluation of appearance, importance of appearance in self-evaluation, avoidance of activities and places and body camouflaging. As well as specifying criteria for the diagnosis of BDD, the measure yields a total score which reflects a sample of the cognitive, affective and behavioural dimensions of body image disturbance. The scale demonstrates concurrent validity with the MBSRQ, internal consistency (.94) and test-retest reliability (.89) but there is a lack of normative data that would significantly increase the utility of the scale.

The Multidimensional Body Self-relations Questionnaire (MBSRQ) (Brown, Cash & Mikulka, 1990) is a general body image disturbance measure which comprises 11 short scales including measures of appearance orientation, that is, cognitive-behavioural investment in appearance, appearance evaluation and appearance satisfaction. However, as a measure of body image disturbance it is over-inclusive, in that there are a number of scales of much less relevance to appearance *per se*, such as attitudes to health and fitness. Essentially, the MBSRQ is a broad measure of interest in and satisfaction with one's body, including appearance. However, the items do not sample the concerns of clinical populations and the important dimensions of social and behavioural dysfunction are not covered. Although it is a widely used scale (Sarwer, Wadden & Foster, 1998), it is perhaps most useful for its dimensional sub-scales, such as the Body Areas Satisfaction Scale discussed earlier. However, more work is needed on the psychometric properties of these sub-scales.

The Derriford Appearance Scale (DAS59) is the most fully psychometrically developed general scale currently available (Carr, Harris & James, 2000). The distribution of items fully represents the affective and behavioural dimensions of body image disturbance and, as discussed earlier in this chapter, the overall item content provides the closest correspondence with the dimensions of body shame as outlined by Gilbert (Chapter 1, this volume). A large number of items were generated originally from the verbatim reports of patients suffering with the full range and types of body image disturbance (Harris, 1982) and in a series of studies (Carr, Harris & James, 2000) these were refined to a scale of 59 items with excellent psychometric properties and good utility with clinical and non-clinical respondents and with professional users. A stable factorial structure emerged through successive factor analyses and the DAS(59) yields a total score, together with scores on five sub-scales corresponding to the five factors identified in these analyses. The scale shows high internal consistency (.98), good three-month test-retest reliability with patients (.86) and non-patients (.76) and good construct, convergent and divergent validities. Psychometric characteristics of the three main sub-scales are similarly robust, for example, internal consistency .98–.89 and test-retest reliability .79–.70. The scale is standardised on large, representative clinical and general population samples (1740 and 1001, respectively) and normative data are provided.

Through the factor analyses, the authors identified the principal underlying construct as self-consciousness of appearance. Conceptually, this is wider than the experience of being self-conscious, in that it includes strong elements of active and avoidant behavioural coping as well as a wide range of sources and types of distress. The total score provides the best measure of overall body shame, while the factorial sub-scale scores differentiate this into general self-consciousness of appearance (non-site and non-situation specific) and self-consciousness of appearance associated with specific body sites, activities or situations, for example, social and sexual situations and activities. There is also a sub-scale measure of the impact of self-consciousness of appearance upon the self-concept. The scale is sensitive to therapeutic change and allows for the identification of the body sites about which respondents are sensitive, self-conscious or ashamed. This latter facility has been used to identify the range of appearance concerns that are found in the general population (Harris & Carr, 2001). For briefer use and for the routine aggregation of data for research and audit purposes, a 24-item version of the DAS has been developed and standardised (DAS24; Carr, Moss & Harris, 2002).

Clinical issues

Throughout this brief chapter, we have considered a range of measures of body image disturbance and body shame, with sufficient validity and reliability to provide useful data for clinical and research purposes. The vast majority of these have been self-report scales whose item contents inevitably determine their range of applicability and most are too restricted in this range of applicability to be effective clinical measures. Also psychometrically sound self-report scales, by definition, are relatively inflexible and cannot be designed to accommodate the full spectrum of patient styles, sensitivities and presentations. However, the very nature of shame is such that some things may be easier to disclose and describe in a self-report format rather than in a face-to-face interview. Also a scale with well-developed and inclusive item content, with high content validity for these clinical populations, whose common experience is that of being frequently misunderstood, is reassuring and encouraging. Many patients with traumatic, congenital and iatrogenic disfigurements, as well as those with less overtly obvious causes for body image disturbance, suffer greatly in terms of their dysfunctional interpersonal, social and sexual relationships. Their work and leisure lives are severely affected, their self-esteem is reduced and they experience high levels of distress (Harris, 1982). The complexity and severity of their psychological disturbance argue for well-developed assessment strategies that can effectively inform appropriate therapeutic interventions.

Clearly, the ideal strategy for clinical assessment is a flexible interview supplemented by an appropriate general, inclusive measure. Useful interview formats need to engage and reassure patients as well as providing some structured evaluation of relevant domains of body image disturbance. Such formats are described by Carr (1997a) and by Rosen and Reiter (1996) in the BDDE, and these may be supplemented by the DAS(59) as a well standardised, reliable and valid measure of both general and specific dimensions of body shame for adults. In eating disorders a useful scale could be the Eating Disorders Inventory (Garner, Olmstedt & Polivy, 1983) and for adolescents there is the Self Image Questionnaire for Young Adolescents (Peterson et al., 1984) and the Body Esteem Scale (Mendelson, Mendelson & White, 2001).

Conclusion

Our review of measures and their conceptual bases has shown that the concept of body shame has the potential to bring together different literatures and has real promise for theoretical, empirical and clinical work in this area. It is interesting, for example, that not only may body image concepts benefit from studies and conceptualisations of shame (e.g., by more clearly distinguishing self-evaluation from fear of evaluation by others) but, so too, shame researchers have rarely explored the body image literature. An examination of this literature reveals a progressive elaboration of the concept of body image to include cognitive, affective and behavioural domains that have been reflected in the development of specific and general scales of measurement. Current shame scales have not yet been able to develop in the same way.

Hence, as this chapter has shown, to take body shame further, there are a number of key questions about conceptualisation and measurement that need to be addressed. Whether we call the psychological problems people experience with their bodies 'body image disturbance', 'self-consciousness of appearance' or 'body shame', it is clear that these are multifaceted experiences stretching across cognitive, behavioural and affective domains. Each of these requires careful assessment for further research and clinical intervention, and there is no guarantee that in any one person they will be highly correlated. Although there are no specific measures for body shame (although see Andrews, Chapter 13, this volume), a number of measures have been developed to explore the various aspects of body image disturbance which, as we saw at the beginning of this chapter, map onto the construct of body shame. Currently, the DAS(59) shows promise in this respect and may capture some of the key elements of body shame.

References

Alfonso, V.C., Allinson, D.B., Rader, D.E. & Gorman, B.S. (1996) The extended satisfaction with life scale: Development and psychometric properties. *Social Indicators Research*, 38, 275–301.

Allan, S., Gilbert, P. & Goss, K. (1995) An exploration of shame measures: II: Psychopathology. *Personality and Individual Differences*, 17, 719–722.

Andrews, B. (1995). Bodily shame as a mediator between abusive experiences and depression. *Journal of Abnormal Psychology*, 104, 277–285.

Berscheid, E., Walster, E. & Bohrnstedt, G. (1973) The happy American body: A survey report. *Psychology Today*, 11, 119–131.

Brown, T.A., Cash, T.F. & Mikulka, P.J. (1990) Attitudinal body-image assessment: Factor analysis of the Body Self-relations Questionnaire. *Journal of Personality Assessment*, 55, 135–144.

Carr, A.T. (1997a) Assessment and measurement in clinical practice. In R. Lansdown, N. Rumsey, E. Bradbury, T. Carr & J. Partridge (eds) *Visibly Different: Coping with Disfigurement* (pp.131–146). Oxford: Butterworth-Heinemann.

Carr, A.T. (1997b) *Physical and Psychological Therapies in Disfigurement: A Selective Overview*. Paper presented at the Annual Conference of the Disfigurement Interest Group, King's Fund, London.

Carr, A.T., Harris, D. & James, C. (2000) The Derriford Appearance Scale: A new scale to measure individual responses to living with problems of appearance. *British Journal of Health Psychology*, 5, 201–215.

Carr, A.T., Moss, T. & Harris, D.L. (2002) Psychometric development of the DAS (24): A short version of the Derriford Appearance Scale (DAS59) for the assessment of individual responses to living with problems of appearance. *British Journal of Health Psychology*, submitted.

Cash T.F. & Labarge, A.S. (1996) Development of the Appearance Schemas Inventory: A new cognitive body-image assessment. *Cognitive Therapy and Research*, 20, 37–50.

Cash T.F. & Pruzinsky, T. (1990) *Body Images: Development, Deviance and Change*. New York: Guilford Press.

Cook, D.R. (1991) Shame attachment and addictions: Implications for family therapists. *Contemporary Family Therapy*, 13, 405–419.

Cooper, P.J., Taylor, M.J., Cooper, Z. & Fairburn, C.G. (1987) The development and validation of the Body Shape Questionnaire. *International Journal of Eating Disorders*. 6, 485–494.

Cooper, Z. & Fairburn, C.G. (1987) The Eating Disorder Examination: A semi-structured interview for the assessment of the specific psychopathology of eating disorders. *International Journal of Eating Disorders*, 6, 1–8.

Cororve, M.B. & Gleaves, D.H. (2001) Body dysmorphic disorder: A review of conceptualisations, assessment and treatment strategies. *Clinical Psychology Review*, 21, 949–970.

Dickson-Parnell, B., Jones, M. & Braddy, D. (1987) Assessment of body image perceptions using a computer program. *Behavior Research Methods, Instruments and Computers*, 19, 353–354.

Eisen, J.L., Phillips, K.A., Baer, L., Beer, D.A., Atala, K.D. & Rasmussen, S.A. (1998) The Brown assessment of Beliefs Scale: Reliability and validity. *American Journal of Psychiatry*, 155, 102–108.

Fisher, S. (1986) *Development and Structure of the Body Image*. Hillsdale, NJ: Lawrence Erlbaum Associates Inc.

Garner, D.M., Garner, M.V. & Van-Egeren, L.F. (1992) Body dissatisfaction adjusted for weight: The body illusion index. *International Journal of Eating Disorders*, 12, 263–272.

Garner, D.M., Olmstedt, M.P. & Polivy, J. (1983) Development and validation of a multidimensional eating disorder inventory for anorexia nervosa and bulimia. *International Journal of Eating Disorders*, 2, 15–34.

Gilbert, P., Pehl, J. & Allan, S. (1994) The phenomenology of shame and guilt: An empirical investigation. *British Journal of Medical Psychology*, 67, 23–36.

Grant, J. & Cash, T.F. (1995) Cognitive behavioral body-image therapy: Comparative efficacy of group and modest-contact treatments. *Behavior Therapy*, 26, 69–84.

Harris, D.L. (1982) The symptomatology of abnormal appearance: An anecdotal survey. *British Journal of Plastic Surgery*, 35, 312–323.

Harris, D.L. & Carr, A.T. (2001) Prevalence of concern about physical appearance in the general population. *British Journal of Plastic Surgery*, 54, 223–226.

Keeton, W.P., Cash, T.F. & Brown, T.A. (1990) Body image or body images? Comparative, multidimensional assessment among college students. *Journal of Personality Assessment*, 54, 213–230.

Labarge, A.S., Cash, T.F. & Brown, T.A. (1998) Use of a modified stroop task to examine appearance schematic information processing in college women. *Cognitive Therapy and Research*, 22, 179–190.

Markus, H. (1977) Self-schemata and processing information about the self. *Journal of Personality and Social Psychology*, 17, 60–71.

Mendelson, B.K. & White, D.R. (1985) Development of self-body-esteem in overweight youngsters. *Developmental Psychology*, 21, 90–96.

Mendelson, B.K., Mendelson, M.J. & White, D.R. (2001) Body-esteem Scale for Adolescents and Adults. *Journal of Personality Assessment*, 76, 90–106

Neziroglu, F., McKay, D., Yaryura-Tobias, J.A., K.P. & Todaro, J. (1999) The over-valued ideas scale: Development, reliability, and validity in obsessive-compulsive disorder. *Behaviour Research and Therapy*, 37, 881–902.

Oosthuizen, P., Lambert, T. & Castle, D.J. (1998) Dysmorphic concern: Prevalence and associations with clinical variables. *Australian and New Zealand Journal of Psychiatry*, 32, 129–132.

Pasman, L. & Thompson, J. K. (1988) Body image and eating disturbance in obligatory runners, obligatory weightlifters and sedentary individuals. *International Journal of Eating Disorders*, 7, 759–769.

Peterson, A.C., Schulenberg, J.E., Abramowitz, R.H., Offer, D. & Jarcho, H.D. (1984) The Self-image Questionnaire for Young Adolescents (SIQYA): Reliability and validity studies. *Journal of Youth and Adolescence*, 13, 93–110.

Phillips, K.A., Hollander, E., Rasmussen, S.A., Aronowitz, B.R., DeCaria, C. & Goodman, W.K. (1997) A severity rating for body dysmorphic disorder: Development, reliability, and validity of a modified version of the Yale–Brown Obsessive Compulsive Scale. *Psychopharmacology Bulletin*, 33, 17–22.

Rosen, J.C. & Ramirez, E. (1998) A comparison of eating disorders and body dysmorphic disorder on body image and psychological adjustment. *Journal of Psychosomatic Research*, 44, 441–449.

Rosen, J.C. & Reiter, J. (1996) Development of the body dysmorphic disorder examination. *Behaviour Research and Therapy*, 34, 755–766.

Rosen, J.C., Reiter, J. & Orosan, P. (1995) Assessment of body image in eating disorders with the body dysmorphic disorder examination. *Behaviour Research and Therapy*, 33, 77–84.

Rosen, J.C., Srebnik, D., Saltzburg, E. & Wendt, S. (1991) Development of a body image avoidance questionnaire. *Psychological Assessment: Journal of Consulting and Clinical Psychology*, 3, 32–37.

Ruff, G.A. & Barrios, B.A. (1986) Realistic assessment of body image. *Behavioral Assessment*, 8, 237–252.

Sarwer, D.B., Wadden, T.A. & Foster, G.D. (1998) Assessment of body image dissatisfaction in obese women: Specificity, severity and clinical significance. *Journal of Consulting and Clinical Psychology*, 66, 651–654.

Sarwer, D.B., Wadden, T.A. Pertschuk, M.J. & Whitaker, L.A. (1998) The psychology of cosmetic surgery: A review and reconceptualisation. *Clinical Psychology Review*, 18, 1–22.

Slade, P.D. & Russell, G.F.M. (1973) Awareness of body dimensions in anorexia nervosa: Cross-sectional and longitudinal studies. *Psychological Medicine*, 3, 188–199.

Thompson, J.K. & Psaltis, K. (1988) Multiple aspects and correlates of body figure ratings: A replication and extension of Fallon and Rozin (1985). *International Journal of Eating Disorders*, 7, 813–818.

Thompson, J.K. & Spana, R.E. (1988) The adjustable light beam method for the assessment of size estimation accuracy: Description, psychometrics and normative data. *International Journal of Eating Disorders*, 7, 521–526.

Thompson, J.K., Heinberg, L.J., Altabe, M. & Tantleff-Dunn, S. (1999) *Exacting Beauty: Theory, Assessment and Treatment of Body-Image Disturbance*. Washington DC: American Psychological Association.

Watson, D. & Friend, R. (1969) Measurement of social evaluative anxiety. *Journal of Consulting and Clinical Psychology*, 33, 448–457.

Williams, R.L., Schaeffer, C.A., Shisslak, C.M., Gronwaldt, V.H. & Comerci, G.D. (1986) Eating attitudes and behaviors in adolescent women: Discrimination of normals, dieters and suspected bulimics using Eating Attitudes Test and Eating Disorder Inventory. *International Journal of Eating Disorders*, 5, 879–894.

Young, J.E. (1990) *Cognitive Therapy for Personality Disorders: A Schema Focused Approach* (revised edn.). Sarasota, FL: Professional Resource Exchange.

Chapter 5

The development and maintenance of shame in disfigurement

Implications for treatment

Gerry Kent and Andrew R. Thompson

Introduction

> The role of shame in encounters between the disfigured and the nondisfigured is one that has been greatly neglected by psychologists. Yet the research reveals that it is a predominant feeling associated with facial deviance and is central to the problem (MacGregor, 1990, p.252).

MacGregor (1990) was correct in noting that psychologists have been slow in examining the role of shame in the experience of living with a disfigurement. This chapter provides an overview of the research on disfigurement and makes links with concepts originating from work in the area of shame. It intends to show how making such links can assist in understanding the impact and experience of living with an altered appearance and suggests successful avenues for intervention. This chapter does not consider concerns about appearance that are illusory, such as in the case of Body Dysmorphic Disorder.

Disfigurements are defined here as potentially noticeable differences in appearance that are not culturally sanctioned, as is the case with tattoos or foot-binding. There are three broad causes of such disfigurement: congenital malformations (e.g., port-wine stains and cleft palate/lip), traumatic events (e.g., fires and road traffic accidents) and disease (Harris, 1997). Many diseases can cause disfigurement directly (e.g., acne), but disfigurement can also result from treatment as in radical surgery for head and neck cancer. Perhaps 10% of the population has a scar, blemish or other visible difference that affects their lives (Rumsey, 1998). If other appearance-related difficulties such as Parkinson's Disease or strokes are included, the proportion of affected people could be considered to be much higher. Despite this high prevalence, until recently there has been a dearth of psychological research generally in disfigurement. The majority of the work in the area of appearance has either explored the advantages of being highly attractive or examined 'body image' dissatisfaction, within the normally appearing population.

The first section of the chapter provides a summary of the research on the consequences of being visibly different. Research has tended to fall within one of two overlapping perspectives (Thompson & Kent, 2001). The first of these has been concerned with how disfigurement influences social interactions. The second perspective has been concerned with the impact of disfigurement on individual well-being. The second section of the chapter explores ways that these social and psychological difficulties might be prevented and ameliorated. People with visible differences can be helped to deal with negative views about themselves (internal shame) and negative views of how others perceive them (external shame). Further, they can be helped to develop strategies to minimise the likelihood of, and to reduce the impact of, objective discrimination and prejudice.

Understanding the experience of being visibly different

As demonstrated by several reviewers (Bull & Rumsey, 1988; Papadopoulos & Bor, 1999; Papadopoulos, Bor & Legg, 1999a; Rumsey, 1998; Thompson & Kent, 2001), the field is characterised by three main findings. Firstly, affected individuals often report instances of discrimination or what has been termed 'enacted stigma' (Scambler & Hopkins, 1986). For example, 26% of people with psoriasis reported an instance when 'people made a conscious effort not to touch them' within the previous month (Gupta, Gupta & Watteel, 1998). Such reports are not simply due to oversensitivity. In several experimental studies, where confederates have worn cosmetic creams to look as if they had some form of facial blemish, people were observed to offer less help and to try to avoid the confederate (Bull & Rumsey, 1988; Rumsey, Bull & Gahagan, 1982). Such reactions to disfigurements are often culturally sanctioned and can be seen in many children's stories: 'Out popped the troll's ugly head. He was so ugly that the youngest billy-goat Gruff nearly fell down with fright' (*The Three Billy Goats Gruff*).

The second main finding is that such reactions can have significant effects on well-being. Many studies have indicated that, as a group, people with visible differences show lower levels of self-esteem and higher levels of depression, anxiety and social disability (Thompson & Kent, 2001). Concealment and various subtle avoidance strategies may also occur, even with intimate friends. Lanigan and Cotterill (1989) found that 9% of the women in their sample concealed their port-wine stain from their partners and 89% of Ginsburg and Link's (1989) sample of psoriasis patients reported shame and embarrassment about their condition. Such findings testify to the depth of feeling that many people experience.

Thirdly, there is a considerable variation in well-being between individuals living with a disfigurement. Although some individuals seem to have great difficulty in coping with their appearance, many others do not (Thompson & Kent, 2001). For example, Kalick, Goldwyn and Noe (1981) studied 82 people with port-wine stains who were attending hospital for laser treatment. Using a range of standardised measures, they found that their sample did not demonstrate any emotional disturbance in comparison to the normative population. Importantly, the clinical severity of the disfigurement seems to have relatively little impact on adjustment. Even a small area can be of great concern; in a prospective study of burns' patients, Isaacs (1996) found that even those who had injuries covering less than 1% of their bodies could experience clinically significant levels of psychological difficulty. Conversely, MacGregor (1990), basing his observations on clinical experience, argues that adapting to a major disfigurement can be more straightforward than adapting to relatively minor blemishes.

The development and maintenance of shame in disfigurement

It is clear that the experience of stigmatisation, particularly when it occurs repeatedly, when the sufferer is young and when there is little validating social support, can lead to the development of body shame and social anxiety. In theoretical terms, it is suggested here that such experiences of stigmatisation can result in the development of 'self-schema' associated with increased anxiety about social encounters, sensitivity to further rejections and concealment. Figure 5.1 provides a model of the origins and maintenance of shame-proneness in individuals distressed by disfigurement.

There are some indications that children with congenital disfigurements can be at risk of developing anxious attachments to their parents (Barden et al., 1989). Langlois and Sawin (1989) have found that at two days old less attractive babies are held less close and given less contact than infants seen as attractive. Storry (in Lansdown et al., 1997) has written about his own experiences as a child living with a facial disfigurement and the effect of this on his sense of self:

> I will always remember the look on his [father's] face. It is a mixture of bewilderment and derision. He cannot equate deformity with intelligence. He is unable to accept my deformity. I feel that he is ashamed of me (Lansdown et al., 1997, p.31).

Although there are discrepancies in findings (Blakeney et al., 1988) and some children and families show remarkable resiliency (Walters, 1997), the possibility that variations in distress associated with disfigurement may be related to early parent–child interactions is consistent with many theories, and particularly attachment theory, regarding the development of psychopathology.

However, people who acquire a disfigurement later in life are also at risk of suffering with associated psychological distress. This could be because of the confirmation of existing underlying negative self-beliefs, or because of the

Early experiences and cultural stereotypes
Predisposing factors for shame-proneness
• Receiving signals (*enacted stigma*) from society and/or family that one's appearance
marks one out as unattractive, defective and in some way at risk of exclusion or rejection

Emotionally charged beliefs
Self (shamed)-other (shaming)
• **Self:** Self is inadequate as appearance is unattractive *(i.e., internal shame schema)*
• **Others:** Others will reject, be disgusted or discriminate *(i.e., external shame schema)*

Feelings of Shame and Anxiety

Cognitive distortions and associated automatic negative thoughts
(i.e., discounting positives, selective abstraction, jumping to conclusions)

Coping strategies
• Avoidance of social contact involving perceived exposure of disfigurement
• Concealment and various subtle avoidance strategies
• Escape from perceived exposing social situations
• Overcompensatory behaviours (i.e., overly familiar or putting oneself down first)

Ongoing critical incidents
• Prejudice
• Discrimination
• Rejection
• Reduced social opportunities

Figure 5.1 A model of the origins and maintenance of shame-proneness in individuals
distressed by disfigurement

disconfirmation of existing positive self-beliefs. Following the acquirement of
a disfigurement, individuals may encounter incidents of enacted stigma,
which may be internalised and lead to the experience of shame in previously
unaffected individuals. Most studies of adjustment to disfigurement have
measured adjustment at one point and few have described the process of
adjustment. One exception to this is a qualitative study conducted by

Thompson, Kent and Smith (2002) that describes how a sample of people living with vitiligo are engaged in a continuous process of adjustment over a long time period. Perhaps ongoing experiences of enacted stigma leads to fluctuating feelings of shame.

An evolutionary explanation is helpful in understanding the above processes. It has been argued that inclusion in the social group is crucial for physical survival (Baumeister & Leary, 1995; Gilbert, 1997; Greenwald & Harder, 1998; Leary, 1990). Consequently, people have evolved strategies to maximise their chances of being included and approved of (see Gilbert, Chapter 1, this volume). Greenwald and Harder (1998) argue that shame can be seen as a signal that inclusion in the group is threatened, while Leary et al. (1995) contend that self-esteem acts as a gauge of the degree to which a person feels accepted by others. It seems that the emotive experiences of shame and low self-esteem are a direct result of perceiving oneself to be vulnerable to exclusion or rejection. Where there is an expectation that others will be rejecting on the basis of one's appearance, feelings of external shame will develop. Internal shame will only be experienced if an individual has internalised (or agrees with) this sense of being inadequate. As already mentioned, individuals with a disfigurement do not necessarily have low self-esteem and many adjust well to living with the reactions of others (Thompson, Kent & Smith, 2002). In such situations individuals may experience humiliation at the 'put-downs' of others and react in such a way as to defend themselves from further attack as is illustrated by the following description of how a vitiligo sufferer deals with intrusive staring:

> I mean it does get you sometimes, if you see them actually staring at you, it's not very nice and you say stop staring, and they say 'I wasn't looking'. 'Yes you were', then they just change. 'Oh, OK I'm sorry'. 'There's nothing to be sorry about it's one of those things, it's part of my life' (Thompson, 1998, p.118).

Dion, Dion & Keelan (1990) have used the term 'appearance anxiety' to denote the particular form of social evaluative anxiety that can develop after the experience of disparaging remarks about appearance. In fact, there is evidence to indicate that appearance anxiety operates in much the same way as does social anxiety. Newell and Marks (2000) have recently shown that people with disfiguring conditions score in a similar fashion to those with a social phobia on the Fear Questionnaire. Appearance anxiety and social anxiety involve similar beliefs and cognitive distortions. Cognitive distortions such as jumping to conclusions, dichotomous thinking, emotional reasoning, personalisation, magnification and minimisation have long been indicated by cognitive therapists as being involved in the maintenance of psychopathology (Beck et al., 1979). For example, individuals feeling shame in association with disfigurement may jump to conclusions that others will reject them, they may minimise compliments and personalise others' staring. Kellett (Chapter 7, this volume) discusses examples of how cognitive distortions may operate to maintain, compensate or avoid body shame schema.

Similar coping strategies are also used in both appearance and social anxiety. Avoidance, concealment, escape and the use of subtle body movements (e.g., turning one's head to present the perceived 'better' side during social encounters) are all common as already mentioned. An example of avoidance and concealment is illustrated by the following description of how vitiligo affects the life of one woman:

> [I have been] making excuses for not wanting a physical/sexual relationship with a male friend who I have known for two years. I would like to be more closely involved but don't feel that I can tell him about my vitiligo. He sees me as being attractive (part of this is because I have learnt how to dress well) and I don't want to disappoint him. I don't want to take the risk of being rejected. Part of this could be because my vitiligo has been my greatest secret for years. Few people are aware of it, even less have seen it! (Kent, 2000, p.124).

Thus, there is a tendency to avoid situations where a discrepancy between the actual and socially acceptable selves may be apparent to others. Such events act as triggers (Cash & Grant, 1996) which activate appearance-related schemas. Further, the concealment strategies themselves can be a potential source of embarrassment and shame:

> I have vitiligo on my hands which is very difficult to cover. I feel self-conscious about leaving make-up marks on everything I touch. Patches are developing around my mouth which makes me think twice about eating in public or getting involved (as a single person) in a kiss. The anxiety is always at the back of your mind, as is the anxiety of being rejected for it (Kent, 2000, p.125).

Implications for treatment

Individuals with disfigurements face two different and difficult tasks if they are to avoid becoming ashamed. Firstly, they have to deal with others negative reactions and secondly, they have to develop a healthy sense of self not 'saturated' by their disfigurement (Thompson, 1998). Interventions that may assist individuals with these two tasks can be grouped under four headings: medical, community, social skills development and cognitive behavioural.

Medical interventions

Reducing the severity of visible differences can have substantial beneficial effects. Medical interventions can include medication (as in the reduction of skin disorders such as acne, psoriasis and eczema), plastic and reconstructive surgery, gastroplasty for major obesity, dental interventions, steroid injections for tortocollis and laser treatment for port-wine stains (Thompson & Kent, 2001). There can be positive effects even when the visible difference is relatively minor to an outside observer (Cole et al., 1994; Kent, 2002; Sarwer et al., 1998).

However, it is also clear that medical interventions can be insufficient in themselves. Often, total removal of a blemish or complete reconstruction is not possible and therefore significant psychosocial issues may remain (Pertchuk & Whitaker, 1988). It could also be argued that medical interventions may help in a rather superficial way, not addressing underlying precipitating and predisposing psychosocial factors. It is also possible that difficulties persist because of pre-existing psychological difficulties related to underlying schema. Further, in a survey of plastic surgeons, Borah, Rankin and Wey (1999) found that psychological complications were reported as more common than physical problems and most surgeons had encountered patients who were distressed after surgery.

Community interventions

Given the critical role that experiences of stigmatisation appear to have on the development of shame and social anxiety, it is surprising that there are very few reports of preventive interventions at a societal and family level. The aim of such interventions would be to ensure that people with a visible difference do not become self-conscious and shamed by others. Several charities have recently emerged, such as Changing Faces (Clarke, 2001), which have taken as one of their aims fighting the prejudice that surrounds disfigurement. Such organisations have begun to raise the profile of disfigurement through the production of literature for the public and professionals.

Because stigmatisation is related to the types of attributions made about the condition (Smart & Wegner, 1999), it seems possible that an educational approach might be effective in some instances. Cline et al. (1998) developed an information pack that aimed to increase awareness and understanding of facial disfigurement, with the larger goal of encouraging the 9–11-year-old children in their schools to accept those with facial disfigurements and to combat discrimination. The children were interviewed before the study commenced and then four months later. The results showed some success, with the children in the study showing greater knowledge about disfigurement than those in the control group.

A related area concerns familial reactions. Lefebvre and Arndt (1988) argue that prevention of psychopathology in children with cranio-facial disfigurements requires interventions that focus upon increasing competence. They suggest that realistic information about the effects of possible surgical interventions should be provided. Further interventions with the family need to be aimed at promoting communication with the medical team, helping parents to find and develop solutions to difficulties, modelling suitable attachment behaviours and open communication between the parents. They also argue that the child needs to be helped to develop assertive strategies for dealing with others' questions and staring.

Brazelton, Koslowski and Main (1974) have helped mothers to interact with their infants in a responsive way by emphasising their infants' competence and by promoting affectionate handling of the child. These interventions were effective in increasing shared eye contact, physical contact and the number of vocal exchanges. Although such interventions have not as yet been evaluated with disfigured children and their families, the aim of helping parents to appreciate their children's competencies, rather than concentrating on their disfigurement, may be central in preventing disfigured children from becoming shame prone.

Cognitive behavioural interventions

Given the conceptual and empirical overlap between social anxiety and appearance anxiety, it seems likely that the cognitive-behavioural therapies (CBT) that have proved effective for social anxiety and social phobia (Heimberg, 1994) would also be effective for appearance anxiety and shame in disfigurement. CBT approaches for social anxiety include systematic exposure to the feared situations, relaxation procedures, video-taped feedback and cognitive restructuring.

Cash (Cash, 1977; Cash & Grant, 1996) has concentrated his work with people whose appearance falls within the normal range but who are nevertheless disturbed by their appearance. However, he has shown that similar principles apply for people who have undergone surgery, such as a mastectomy. For his eight-step programme, he recommends a comprehensive body image assessment, to include a range of standardised assessments as well as more informal information gathering. As cited in Cash and Grant (1996), there are a wide range of such instruments available, including the Multidimensional Body-self Relations Questionnaire, which assesses attitudes about body image, the Body Image Automatic Thoughts Questionnaire to give information about the kinds of self-statements used by the client, and the Appearance Schemas Inventory, which measures the degree of importance given to appearance. Step two involves diary-keeping to help both the therapist and the client to identify problem areas. The third step aims to help clients become desensitised to areas of the body and to situations that provoke distress. He uses a systematic desentisation approach; relaxation paired with items on a hierarchy. The identification and challenge of appearance-related assumptions constitute steps four and five. Here, Cash draws on techniques used by Beck and Ellis to identify and alter maladaptive cognitive errors.

These cognitive interventions are supplemented by behavioural techniques during steps six and seven. He asks clients to indicate their confidence that they would be able to avoid safety behaviours, such as repeated checking in the mirror, and to engage in positive behaviours, such as swimming and trying on clothes in the shops. In order to develop a positive body image, Cash also encourages clients to undertake positive activities, such as playing sports, wearing attractive clothes, riding a bicycle and so on. Finally, in step eight, strategies are developed to maintain positive body-image changes.

Cash's therapeutic steps are outlined in a client-friendly manner in his self-help workbook (Cash, 1977). Although the effects of this treatment format have not been systematically analysed, a study by Newell and Clarke (2000) suggests that even a minimal self-help intervention can be beneficial. They gave half of a group with a facial disfigurement a self-help leaflet that offered cognitive-behavioural guidance. Compared to the non-intervention group, the intervention group reported lower anxiety and depressed mood and were engaging in more social leisure activities afterwards.

In a series of case studies, Bradbury (1996) has described the uses of CBT in this area. For example, she describes her work with 'Maria', who was having difficulty in coping with social encounters. As a result of surgery, Maria was left with a pronounced droop on the left side of her face. She had become preoccupied with and shamed by her appearance. As a result, she was uncertain in social encounters, especially with new acquaintances. Bradbury first asked Maria to keep a diary of what social encounters were difficult, when and where they happened, what other people said or did, what Maria said or did, and her thoughts and feelings about the encounter. This diary indicated that one situation that Maria found particularly difficult was interacting with other mothers when she took her children to school. Once the particular setting had been identified, Maria and the therapist discussed how she might handle it, and a strategy was rehearsed through role play before being put into action. Relaxation exercises were also taught. The actual encounter was very difficult for her, but Maria reported a greater sense of control and achievement after using these strategies. After this initial success, Maria and the therapist began to address other situations by exploring ways in which they could be dealt with.

There are few formal evaluations of CBT in this area. In an analogue study, Butters and Cash (1987) offered a six-session individualised intervention to undergraduate psychology students. Compared to the waiting list controls, the 16 students reported improvements on a wide range of assessments, including appearance evaluation, appearance satisfaction and self-esteem. There were also significant reductions in cognitive errors.

Rosen, Reiter and Orosan (1995) compared 16 hours of CBT with a no-treatment group for clients with Body Dysmorphic Disorder (BDD). The treatment group showed evidence of a reduction of symptoms, the disorder being eliminated in 82% of participants at the end of treatment and in 77% at the follow-up four to five months afterwards. There was also a significant reduction in psychological symptoms and an increase in self-esteem. Similar results were reported by Papadopoulos, Bor and Legg (1999b), who also found improvements after a seven-session CBT intervention for clients with vitiligo. The clients reported improvements on self-esteem, quality of life, body image distress and the Body Image Automatic Thoughts Questionnaire.

While structured interventions such as those outlined above are useful, there is a need to balance these with the opportunity to share experiences. For example, Nixon and Singer (1993), in reporting their study on the effects of group CBT for excessive self-blame and guilt in parents of severely disabled children, described how important peer support was for the parents involved. It seemed that Nixon and Singer had some difficulty in delivering their planned intervention because the parents were so keen to share their experiences with each other. Perhaps it was this sharing that was important for outcome, rather than the planned therapy. In this context Schwartz (1999) found that although teaching social skills to patients with multiple sclerosis was more effective than peer support overall, peer support was especially helpful for those with emotional difficulties. Social support may be particularly pertinent where issues of shame are concerned.

Social skills training

As described above, helping clients to develop strategies to cope with difficult events and situations forms an important component of the CBT approach. As outlined by Coughlan and Clarke (Chapter 8, this volume), social skills training (SST) has received attention in its own right. Several studies have indicated that people with disfiguring conditions can interact in ways that are not conducive to competent interactions and the development of supportive relationships (Kapp-Simon & McGuire, 1997).

It is clear that having behavioural strategies to deal with instances of enacted stigma is of benefit. Robinson, Rumsey and Partridge (1996) and Partridge (1994) take the position that a person with a disfigurement needs to be able to learn how to be socially 'proactive'. On a first meeting, a non-disfigured person will be naturally hesitant and almost certainly curious. Thus, in social settings it is important that the disfigured person be able to shift the others attention away from the disfigurement and towards their personality and abilities. Since there is a relationship between the presence of good social skills and social support (Cohen, Sherrod & Clark, 1986), assistance in these respects could potentially have additional psychological benefits. Through the use of instruction, modelling, role play and open discussion, the aim is to help participants learn more about the nature of social interactions, engender a sense of empowerment rather than shame, and provide practical skills that help them to influence the views of others. Robinson, Rumsey and Partridge (1996) have demonstrated that such a package can lead to reductions of social anxiety and distress and increase confidence, changes that were maintained at a six-month follow-up.

Interventions at this level might also be informed by the work on bullying, particularly in schools. Since many people with visible disfigurements report teasing and bullying in school associated with their appearance, the successful approaches reported by Smith (1994) might be appropriate. He reports that giving children the skills needed to deal with bullies appropriately, enlisting peer counsellors and the use of peer advocates are inexpensive and effective methods for dealing with this type of problem.

Conclusion

Despite the fact that psychologists have neglected the social and psychological issues associated with disfiguring conditions until relatively recently, great strides have been made in both understanding the experiences of those affected by disfigurement and designing interventions aimed at alleviating distress. At the same time, however, there is much to be done.

Most of the above research on interventions operates on an individual level. CBT, for example, concentrates on the cognitions and behaviour of the individual. However, much distress is due to the reactions of others (Chang & Herzog, 1976). There may be a parallel with the literature on disability where, until recently, problems related to social mobility and discrimination have been located within the disabled person. Concentrating on the effects of disfigurement on the individual runs the risk of the wider societal issues being ignored. Clearly, a greater understanding of the causes and consequences of stigmatisation as well as the assessment of interventions at a social level are needed.

However, individuals living with either a congenital or acquired disfigurement are at risk of experiencing feelings of both internal and external shame and may therefore benefit from individually tailored interventions that are able to consider underlying schema. Although exposure to feared situations is an important component of CBT in other areas where the emotions of shame are present, it may be damaging if used alone in this population. As illustrated above, enacted stigma does occur and people may well encounter negative reactions, to which they will need to manage through the use of appropriate social skills. Clearly, CBT seems extremely promising as an intervention for ashamed and shamed people living with a disfigurement. However, further research is needed to develop clarity with regard to the most useful components of such interventions.

Note

Correspondence should be addressed to: Gerry Kent, Department of Clinical Psychology, University Of Sheffield, Western Bank, Sheffield, S10 2TP, UK; Andrew R. Thompson, Department of Psychological Health Care, Barnsley Community & Priority Services NHS Trust, Keresforth Centre, Barnsley, S70 6RS, UK.

References

Barden, R.C., Ford, M., Jensen, A.G., Rogers-Salyer, M. & Salyer, K. (1989) Effects of craniofacial deformity in infancy on the quality of mother–infant interactions. *Child Development*, 60, 819–824.

Baumeister, R. & Leary, M. (1995) The need to belong: Desire for interpersonal attachments as a fundamental human motivation. *Psychological Bulletin*, 117, 497–529.

Beck, A., Rush, A., Shaw, B. & Emery, G. (1979) *Cognitive Therapy of Depression*. New York: Guilford Press.

Blakeney, P., Herndon, D., Desai, M., Beard, S. & Wales-Seale, P. (1988) Long-term psychological adjustment following burn injury. *Journal of Burn Care and Rehabilitation*, 9, 661–665.

Borah, G., Rankin, M. & Wey, P. (1999) Psychological complications in 281 plastic surgery practices. *Plastic and Reconstructive Surgery*, 104, 1241–1246.

Bradbury, E. (1996) *Counselling People with Disfigurement*. Leicester: British Psychological Society.

Brazelton, T., Koslowski, B. & Main, M. (1974) The origins of reciprocity. In M. Lewis & L. Rosenbum (eds) *The Effect of the Infant on its Caregiver*. Chichester: John Wiley & Sons.

Bull, R. & Rumsey, N. (1988) *The Social Psychology of Facial Appearance*. New York: Springer-Verlag.

Butters, J. & Cash, T.F. (1987) Cognitive-behavioral treatment of women's body-image dissatisfaction. *Journal of Consulting and Clinical Psychology*, 55, 889–897.

Cash, T.F. (1977) *The Body Image Workbook*. Oakland: New Harbinger Publications.

Cash, T.F. & Grant, J. (1996) Cognitive-behavioral treatment of body-image disturbances. In V. van Hasselt & M. Hersen (eds) *Sourcebook of Psychological Treatment Manuals for Adult Disorders* (pp.567–614). New York: Plenum Press.

Chang, F. & Herzog, B. (1976) Burn morbidity: A follow-up study of physical and psychological disability. *Annals of Surgery*, 183, 34–37.

Cline, T., Proto, A., Raval, P. & Di Paolo, T. (1998) The effects of brief exposure and of classroom teaching on attitudes children express towards facial disfigurement in peers. *Educational Research*, 40, 55–68.

Cohen, S., Sherrod, D. & Clark, M. (1986) Social skills and the stress-protective role of social support. *Journal of Personality and Social Psychology*, 50, 963–973.

Cole, R., Shakespeare, V., Shakespeare, P. & Hobby, J. (1994) Measuring outcome in low-priority plastic surgery patients using Quality of Life indices. *British Journal of Plastic Surgery*, 47, 117–121.

Dion, K.L., Dion, K.K. & Keelan, J.P. (1990) Appearance anxiety as a dimension of social-evaluative anxiety: Exploring the ugly duckling syndrome. *Contemporary Social Psychology*, 14, 220–224.

Gilbert, P. (1997) The evolution of social attractiveness and its role in shame, humiliation, guilt and therapy. *British Journal of Medical Psychology*, 70, 113–147.

Ginsburg, I. & Link, B. (1989) Feelings of stigmatization in patients with psoriasis. *Journal of the American Academy of Dermatology*, 20, 53–63.

Greenwald, D. & Harder, D. (1998) Domains of shame. In P. Gilbert & B. Andrews (eds) *Shame: Interpersonal Behaviour, Psychopathology and Culture* (pp.225–245). Oxford: Oxford University Press.

Gupta, M., Gupta, A. & Watteel, G. (1998) Perceived deprivation of social touch in psoriasis is associated with greater psychological morbidity: An index of the stigma experienced in dermatological disorders. *Cutis*, 61, 339–342.

Harris, D. (1997) Types, causes and physical treatment of visible differences. In R. Lansdown, N. Rumsey, E. Bradbury, T. Carr & J. Partridge (eds) *Visibly Different: Coping with Disfigurement* (pp. 79–90). Oxford: Butterworth-Heinemann.

Heimberg, R. (1994) Cognitive assessment strategies and the measurement of outcome of treatment for social phobia. *Behaviour Research and Therapy*, 32, 269–280.

Isaacs, J. (1996) *An investigation of predictive factors of psychological morbidity in burn injured patients three months post burn*. Unpublished thesis, University of Manchester.

Kalick, S., Goldwyn, R. & Noe, J. (1981) Social issues and body image concerns of port-wine stain patients undergoing laser therapy. *Lasers in Surgery and Medicine*, 1, 205–213.

Kapp-Simon, K. & McGuire, D. (1997) Observed social interaction patterns in adolescents with and without craniofacial conditions. *Cleft Palate – Craniofacial Journal*, 34, 380–384.

Kent, G. (2000) Understanding the experiences of people with disfigurements: An integration of four models of social and psychological functioning. *Psychology, Health and Medicine*, 5, 117–129.

Kent, G. (2002) Testing a model of disfigurement: Effects of a skin camouflage service on well-being and appearance anxiety. *Psychology and Health*, 17, 377–386.

Langlois, J. and Sawin, D. (1981) Infant physical attractiveness as an elicitor of differential parenting behaviours. Paper presented at the Society for Research in Child Development, Boston. Cited in: Walters, E. (1997) Problems faced by children and families living with visible differences. In: R. Lansdown, N. Rumsey, E. Bradbury, T. Carr & J. Partridge (eds) *Visibly Different: Coping with Disfigurement*. Oxford: Butterworth-Heinemann.

Lanigan, S. & Cotterill, J. (1989) Psychological disabilities amongst patients with port wine stains. *British Journal of Dermatology*, 121, 209–215.

Lansdown, R., Rumsey, N., Bradbury, E., Carr, T. & Partridge, J. (eds) (1997) *Visibly Different: Coping with Disfigurement*. Oxford: Butterworth Heinemann.

Leary, M. (1990) Responses to social exclusion: Social anxiety, jealousy, loneliness, depression, and low self-esteem. *Journal of Social and Clinical Psychology*, 9, 221–229.

Leary, M., Tambor, E., Terdal, S. & Downs, D. (1995) Self-esteem as an interpersonal monitor: The sociometer hypothesis. *Journal of Personality and Social Psychology*, 68, 518–530.

Lefebvre, A. & Arndt, E. (1988) Working with facially disfigured children: A challenge in prevention. *Canadian Journal of Psychiatry*, 33, 453–458.

MacGregor, F. (1990) Facial disfigurement: Problems and management of social interaction and implications for mental health. *Aesthetic Plastic Surgery*, 14, 249–257.

Newell, R. & Clarke, M. (2000) Evaluation of a self-help leaflet in treatment of social difficulties following facial disfigurement. *International Journal of Nursing Studies*, 37, 381–388.

Newell, R. & Marks, I. (2000) Phobic nature of social difficulty in facially disfigured people. *British Journal of Psychiatry*, 176, 177–181.

Nixon, C. & Singer, G. (1993) Group cognitive-behavioral treatment for excessive parental self-blame and guilt. *American Journal of Mental Retardation*, 97, 665–672.

Papadopoulos, L. & Bor, R. (1999) *Psychological Approaches to Dermatology*. Leicester: British Psychological Society.

Papadopoulos, L., Bor, R. & Legg, C. (1999a) Psychological factors in cutaneous disease: An overview of research. *Psychology, Health and Medicine*, 4, 107–128.

Papadopoulos, L., Bor, R. & Legg, C. (1999b) Coping with the disfiguring effects of vitiligo: A preliminary investigation into the effects of Cognitive Behavioural Therapy. *British Journal of Medical Psychology*, 10, 11–12.

Partridge, J. (1994) *Changing Faces: The Challenge of Facial Disfigurement*. London: Changing Faces.

Pertchuk, M. & Whitaker, L. (1988) Psychosocial outcome of craniofacial surgery in children. *Plastic and Reconstructive Surgery*, 82, 741–746.

Robinson, E., Rumsey, N. & Partridge, J. (1996) An evaluation of the impact of social interaction skills training for facially disfigured people. *British Journal of Plastic Surgery*, 49, 281–289.

Rosen, J., Reiter, J. & Orosan, P. (1995) Cognitive-behavioural body image therapy for Body Dysmorphic Disorder. *Journal of Consulting and Clinical Psychology*, 63, 263–269.

Rumsey, N. (1998) Visible disfigurement. In M. Johnston & D. Johnston (eds) *Comprehensive Clinical Psychology*, Vol. 8 (pp.575–593). Amsterdam: Elsevier.

Rumsey, N., Bull, R. & Gahagan, D. (1982) The effect of facial disfigurement on the proxemic behaviour of the general public. *Journal of Applied Social Psychology*, 12, 137–150.

Sarwer, D., Wadden, T., Pertchuk, M. & Whitaker, L. (1998) The psychology of cosmetic surgery: A review and reconceptualization. *Clinical Psychology Review*, 18, 1–22.

Scambler, G. & Hopkins, A. (1986) Being epileptic: Coming to terms with stigma. *Sociology of Health and Illness*, 8, 26–43.

Schwartz, C. (1999) Teaching coping skills enhances quality of life more than peer support: Results of a randomised trial with multiple sclerosis patients. *Health Psychology*, 18, 211–220.

Smart, L. & Wegner, D. (1999) Covering up what can't be seen: Concealable stigma and mental control. *Journal of Personality and Social Psychology*, 77, 474–486.

Thompson, A. (1988) Exploring the process of adjustment to disfigurement with particular reference to vitiligo. Unpublished D. Clin. Psy. thesis, Department of Psychology, University of Sheffield.

Thompson, A. & Kent, G. (2001) Adjusting to disfigurement: Processes involved in dealing with being visibly different. *Clinical Psychology Review*, 21, 663–682.

Thompson, A., Kent, G. & Smith, J. (2002) Living with vitiligo: Dealing with difference. *British Journal of Health Psychology*, 7, 213–225.

Walters, E. (1997) Problems faced by children and families living with visible differences. In R. Lansdown, N. Rumsey, E. Bradbury, T. Carr & J. Partridge (eds) *Visibly Different: Coping with Disfigurement*. Oxford: Butterworth-Heinemann.

Part II

Body shame and disfigurement

Chapter 6

Psoriasis

The role of shame on quality of life

Jeremy Miles

Introduction

A large body of research examining the psychological impact of psoriasis has shown that this skin disorder can seriously affect an individual's quality of life and psychological functioning. However, there is also good evidence that, as with other disfiguring conditions, the degree of disfigurement is not a good guide to psychological adjustment (Kent & Thompson, Chapter 5, this volume). This chapter argues that research into factors affecting adjustment can be advanced by integrating findings with concepts in the wider formulations of body shame (Gilbert, Chapter 1, this volume).

Psoriasis

Psoriasis is a common skin disease, affecting 1–2% of the white British and American population (Camisa, 1994), and a similar proportion of most white Western European and Western populations. There are considerable variations among ethnic groups in the incidence of psoriasis. Leder and Farber (1997) found that the condition is more common in people who originate in eastern Africa than western Africa, and it is less common in people who originate in tropical areas than people who originate in northern regions (Farber & Nall, 1994).

While the underlying causes of psoriasis are unknown, the immediate cause of psoriasis is the rate of growth and differentiation of the epidermis (the outer layer of the skin). In unaffected skin, the epidermis is renewed approximately every 28 days – the outer layer of the skin separates from the lower layers, and is sloughed off. In psoriasis, the epidermis is renewed every 4 days – a process referred to as hyperproliferation. This hyperproliferation leads to the four main indicators of psoriasis.

1 The skin thickens to form psoriatic plaques – a process of lichenification.
2 The capillaries in the plaques become dilated, causing the plaques to redden (erythema).

3   Silvery scales of skin are shed from the plaques (scaling).
4   The plaques itch (pruritus) leading to scratching, which can cause bleeding from pinpoint punctures in the skin.

The plaques are usually oval in shape and can vary in size from less than a centimetre in diameter to very large. The amount of the body affected can vary from almost none to total coverage. For some sufferers the condition may manifest as a few pinpoint spots, for others it may cover much larger areas. Although a number of subtypes of psoriasis have been identified, there is not total agreement about the level at which psoriasis should be differentiated into separate conditions. Plaque psoriasis (the most common kind) may affect the whole body, while in other sufferers the condition is much more localised. Psoriasis may affect only the nails (it causes them to thicken and yellow), only the elbows and knees, only the scalp area, or it may affect all of those areas and others. Thus, it is unclear whether, for example, 'scalp psoriasis' should be treated as a separate condition from 'fingernail psoriasis'. This chapter follows Camisa (1994), who proposes to 'consider psoriasis as a single disease with several morphological variants' (Camisa, 1994, p.7)

Psoriasis is a skin condition with both genetic and environmental components, which interact in a complex fashion, best formulated with biopsychosocial approaches (Gilbert, Chapter 1, this volume). The condition is approximately ten times more common in first-degree relatives than in other members of the population – 30% of sufferers have a first-degree relative with the condition. Duffy, Spelman and Martin (1993) found that the concordance rate among monozygotic (identical) twins was approximately 35%, and that among dizygotic (fraternal, or non-identical) twins was approximately 12%. Potential environmental factors in the aetiology include stress, infection and injury.

As noted, psoriasis can affect almost any part of the body. In most sufferers it tends to recur in the same places – the scalp, elbows and knees, ears or fingers, and in some sufferers it only affects particular parts of the body. The most common sites for psoriatic plaques are the elbows, knees, scalp, sacrum (base of the spine), nails and sometimes the hands and feet. In addition to the skin disease, psoriasis sufferers are likely to suffer from psoriatic arthropathy, a form of arthritis, in later life.

Psoriasis can appear at any age although it is rare under the age of three, and in approximately two-thirds of cases, the psoriasis emerges first before the age of 30 (Fry, 1988). The long-term prognosis of psoriasis was studied by Romanus (1945), who carried out a longitudinal study of 1417 patients over 20 years. He found that during that time, only 10% of the patients were completely disease-free, 16% had intermittent flare-ups and 71% had continuous psoriasis.

Until the eighteenth century, psoriasis was not distinguished from leprosy, and sufferers from psoriasis sometimes suffered the same fate as those with leprosy (including being burnt at the stake during the fourteenth century). In 1809 Willan described psoriasis, but did not distinguish it from leprosy, and it was not until 1841 that Hebra made the final definite distinction (Fry, 1988).

Management and treatment

As with other disfiguring conditions, management should attend to both the physical aspects of the disorder as well as the psychosocial. Moreover, physical treatments themselves may have psychosocial consequences. Although currently psoriasis is not curable, a range of treatments that attempt to control the condition are available. None are without drawbacks and many patients choose to go without treatment (Williams, 1991). Topical coal tar is a common treatment for mild psoriasis as it is very safe and available in a range of preparations that can be selected to suit the patient. The obvious main disadvantage of coal tar is that it is unpleasant to handle and messy when used in anything but very weak concentrations. There are also suggestions that coal tar treatments may be carcinogenic, although this is currently disputed. (Currently there is a lawsuit pending in the Superior Court in California which will, if the plaintiff is successful, require manufacturers to reduce the concentration of coal tar in their products and/or print warnings on the labels.)

Dithranol (known under the generic term anthralin in America) is a topical treatment applied directly to psoriasis plaques. It can be damaging to non-psoriatic skin, and so is only suitable to be applied to large plaques. It is usually applied once every 24 hours in 'short contact mode' in which the preparation is left on the skin for 15 to 45 minutes and then washed off. This mode of treatment can cause a considerable disruption of the sufferer's daily routine. In addition, Dithranol is a very messy substance to use – it is brown, stains clothes, furniture, bedding and so on, and is difficult to remove (one psoriasis support web page includes a small section containing advice on how to clean Dithranol from different household items).

Topical corticosteroids are an effective topical treatment, but their use is accompanied by a risk of side-effects and therefore they are used rarely, and not for long periods.

The above three treatments are usually administered by the family doctor – general practitioner (GP) in Britain. If these treatments do not manage to control the disease successfully, the sufferer may be referred to a dermatologist for more specialised treatments. It is necessary for these treatments to be prescribed by a specialist because of the need for careful control and risk of side-effects.

A useful short-term treatment for psoriasis is phototherapy where the sufferer is exposed to UVB light. This carries an associated risk of short-term erythema, and if used for longer terms, cutaneous malignancy. Treatment length is therefore usually limited to eight to ten weeks. Similar to phototherapy is photochemotherapy, or PUVA. This involves the patient taking the drug Psoralens, which increases the sensitivity of the skin to light, and then the patient being exposed to UVA light (Psoralens + UVA). PUVA treatment carries with it an increased risk of cataract formation – patients should wear sunglasses for 24 hours after taking Psoralens. In addition, it is thought that the total lifetime dose of PUVA should be limited, not just to avoid the risk of cataracts, but also to avoid the risk of malignancy (Williams, 1991). As well as the side-effects associated with UVB and PUVA treatment, the necessity for such a large number of hospital appointments as are necessary for a treatment regimen can be disruptive to the patient's lifestyle.

For more severe psoriasis, or to control serious short-term outbreaks, a range of systemic drugs are available, for example Methotrexate, retinoids and cyclosporin. Each of these has a range of potentially dangerous side-effects and can interact with other common drugs and foods with fatal effects, and so these tend to be used sparingly.

Current approaches to psychological adjustment

A number of the problems are encountered when studying the psychological impact of psoriasis. It is difficult to find and recruit a representative sample of sufferers – most studies are carried out using hospital samples (comprising either outpatients, inpatients or a mixture of both). These people tend to represent either severe cases of psoriasis, or newly diagnosed cases of psoriasis. As most sufferers do not regularly consult a dermatologist, or even their family doctor, about their condition, this sampling technique excludes those sufferers who have less severe psoriasis, or who have been living with the condition for some time – the vast majority of sufferers.

In one of the earliest studies to examine the psychological impact of psoriasis, Jobling (1976) carried out a survey using two branches of members of the British Psoriasis Association, a total of 186 respondents. Participants were asked, in an open response format, what they felt was the worst thing about having psoriasis. Most of the 180 respondents gave more than one response, and it was not therefore possible to establish the single most important difficulty each one suffered. The most commonly mentioned complaint was the difficulty of establishing social contacts and forming relationships, mentioned by 84% of respondents. Indeed, most research suggests that social behaviour can be significantly affected by the disorder, typically via social avoidance. Also mentioned were embarrassment and self-consciousness (by 25% of respondents), having to wear clothes that concealed the psoriasis (21%), irritation or soreness (35%) and the unpleasantness of the treatment regimes (13%). Some of these difficulties seem clearly related to various forms of shame, such as fear of negative evaluations and stigmatisation (external shame) and negative self-evaluations. The survey also asked respondents how the way in which they were treated could be improved. Here a 'great many' (the author was not more specific; p.235) patients commented on the treatment that they had received from the medical profession. They said that doctors showed little empathy for the condition 'routinely recommending marginally effective treatments and regimes which were often impractical or unpleasant' (p.286).

McHenry and Doherty (1992) carried out a similar investigation to examine the effect of psoriasis on patients' lifestyles; including the effect of attendance at an outpatient clinic. Forty-five dermatology outpatients were surveyed at the time of their first referral to the clinic and again three months later when they had been to three appointments. The results of the study demonstrate the wide-ranging impact of psoriasis. At the first attendance, 67% felt that their lifestyle was affected by their psoriasis, although this had dropped to 37% after the three-month period. When patients were asked at their first assessment what aspect of their lifestyle had been affected, 20% said that they had lost time from work or education, 49% said that they had stopped sports or hobbies and 28% said that their social life had been limited. Patients were also asked to select what they felt was the one 'worst thing' about their psoriasis. The results of this are shown as Figure 6.1. On the first visit the 'worst things' are considered to be cosmetic and physical symptoms. On the second visit, more of the patients were indicating physical symptoms and embarrassment as their 'worst thing', whereas the proportion choosing cosmetic aspects drops. It should be noted that the three-month sample consisted of only 25 sufferers, so only tentative conclusions may be drawn.

Gupta and Gupta (1995; see also Gupta et al., 1990) carried out a survey on the impact of psoriasis on the quality of life, using 138 patients at a hospital dermatology department. Patients were given a list of potentially

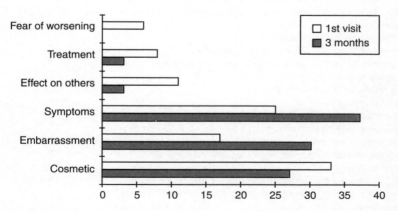

Figure 6.1 Patients' selection of the 'worst thing' about their psoriasis at first visit and three months later (from McHenry and Doherty, 1992)

stressful events, and asked if they had experienced them in the last month. The results are shown as Table 6.1.

These different impacts are associated with both internal and external shame. Because the researchers did not clearly separate out fear of negative evaluations and stigmatisation (external shame) from negative self-evaluations and self-focused feelings, it is difficult to be know the relative extent of each of these. It is possible that internal shame may be reflected in themes such as *'Patient feeling inconvenienced by shedding of skin'*. However, for nearly all the other events, there is a strong focus on external shame and stigmatisation. Moreover, this study shows the variety of contexts in which such can appear. Within a biopsychosocial context, it is worth noting that 14% of sufferers thought that family members were embarrassed by their condition, suggesting that it is not just individual sufferers who can feel the impact of disfiguring conditions. It is likely that the reaction of family will impact on adjustment, although there are few studies of these factors.

Stigma and shame

Ginsburg and Link (1989) investigated feelings of stigmatisation in psoriasis. They defined stigma as 'a biologic or social mark that sets a person off from others, is discrediting, and disrupts interactions with others' (p.53). They did

Table 6.1 Impact of psoriasis on quality of life (Gupta et al., 1990)

Psoriasis-related event	% Experienced 1 month prior to survey
Patient feeling inconvenienced by shedding of skin	72
Patient avoiding a public place such as a restaurant	64
Having to wear unattractive or uncomfortable clothes to cover affected regions	55
Avoiding a social situation	40
Worried about side-effects of treatment	40
Being treated as though psoriasis were contagious	37
Strangers making rude remarks	35
Being made to feel like an outcast	29
Loss of income	26
People making an effort not to touch the patient	26
People implying the psoriasis may be due to AIDS or leprosy	20
Major arguments with partner	20
Hairdresser/barber appearing reluctant to cut hair	19
Fear of losing job	17
Going out of the house after dark so as not to be seen	15
Being criticised for taking too much time off work for appointments	15
Family members appearing embarrassed regarding condition	14

not treat stigma as a single unidimensional construct but attempted to examine the underlying structure and causes of feelings of stigmatisation using sophisticated statistical techniques. They developed an instrument based on interviews with psoriasis patients, and relevant items taken from similar scales for work with other conditions. The 38-item scale was administered to 100 patients at a dermatology department (approximately half were inpatients, and half were outpatients). In the first stage, exploratory factor analysis was applied to the data. Factor analysis is a multivariate technique that attempts to find clusters of items that covary, and therefore in a sense could be said to be measuring the same, or similar, underlying psychological constructs. Two questions were removed from the analysis because, according to the authors, 'They correlated with most of the stigma items' (p.57). These two items were summed to create a variable called 'psoriasis related despair'. Their factor analysis resulted in a six-factor solution (plus the additional category, labelled 'psoriasis related despair'). The factors were labelled by the authors, and are shown in Table 6.2.

Using the concepts of internal and external shame, it can be seen that their factors may map onto these concepts. For example, factors 1 (anticipation of rejection), 2 (feeling flawed) and 4 (guilt and shame) all address self-focused and internal shame concerns. Factor 3 (sensitivity to the opinions of others) appears directly related to concerns with others views of the self (and to some extent so does factor 5). Factor 6 (secretiveness) appears to be a coping and shame-avoidant factor related to forms of safety behaviour (Gilbert, Chapter 1, this volume).

Multiple regression was then used to examine predictors of the different dimensions of stigmatisation. Twelve predictors were used (listed in Table 6.3), and a regression equation was calculated for each of the dimensions of stigmatisation that had been identified.

Overall the most important predictors were age at onset, extent of bleeding, employment status and duration. No direct measure of coverage or severity was used as a predictor of feelings of stigmatisation.

Visibility

Body shame processes may be significantly affected by the visibility of the condition. Kent and Keohane (2001) examined the fear of negative evaluation as a predictor of quality of life, and as a moderator of the relationship between disease visibility and quality of life. To examine degree of visibility, they divided their participants into sufferers who had no psoriasis on either hands or face (the areas which are almost always on public display), those who had psoriasis on either the hands, or the face, and those who had psoriasis on the hands and the face. Fear of negative evaluation had a main effect on quality of life, and also interacted with visibility in predicting quality of

Table 6.2 Labels and two example items for each factor extracted by Ginsburg and Link (1989)

Number	Label	Example items
1	Anticipation of rejection	When my psoriasis improves after intensive treatment, I feel much better about myself. I feel physically and sexually undesirable when the psoriasis is bad.
2	Feelings of being flawed	Many people assume that having psoriasis is a sign of personal weakness. There are times when I feel dirty, as though there is something deeply the matter with me, beyond the fact of my psoriasis.
3	Sensitivity to the opinions of others	Some people act as though having psoriasis were my fault somehow. Most people believe that a person with psoriasis is just as emotionally stable as the average person.
4	Guilt and shame	Having psoriasis makes me feel different from other people. I never feel embarrassed or ashamed because I have psoriasis.
5	Positive attitudes	If my child developed psoriasis, I feel he or she could have just as good a life as if he or she did not have it. Psoriasis patients are treated like lepers. [Reverse scored item]
6	Secretiveness	I do my best to keep family members that I do not live with from knowing that I have psoriasis. If someone were to notice a psoriasis plaque and ask what it was, I do not say that it is psoriasis.

life. When post-hoc tests were carried out, it transpired that a greater fear of negative evaluation had a small effect on quality of life for sufferers with low levels of visibility, but very large effects for sufferers with higher levels of visibility.

Mood and emotional consequences

Fried et al. (1995) examined the psychosocial impact of psoriasis on 64 hospital patients and ex-patients. They found a range of self-reported problems that resulted from psoriasis: 83% of sufferers experienced at least some anxiety during flare-ups; 80% experienced discomfort; 65% experienced anger; and 75% reported that they experienced at least slight depression during flare-ups. It should be noted that patients were not rated for degree of

Table 6.3 Predictors of stigmatisation, as used by
Ginsburg and Link

Extent of bleeding
Work status
Marital status
Sampled from
Rejection experience
Age at onset
Duration
Methotrexate treatment
Years of education
Parent or sibling with psoriasis
Child with psoriasis
Sex

depression or anger during flare-ups, but were asked if they did experience these during flare-ups.

Gupta et al. (1994) studied 77 psoriasis sufferers (along with 143 dermatitis and 32 urticaria sufferers). They measured depression using the Carroll Self Rating for Depression Scale (CSRD), and used a Likert scale to obtain a subjective measure of itching. The Likert scale had 10 points, ranging from 'not at all' (point 1) to very severe (point 10). Overall they found a correlation of $r = 0.34$ ($p < 0.001$), between severity of itching and depression. Gupta et al. suggest that this demonstrates either that depression is a factor that causes or exacerbates psoriasis, or that depression alters the sufferer's perception of itching. Curiously, they did not consider that severity of disease may be a factor in depression, nor do they consider the alternative model, that depression may result because of the itching. They do provide one piece of evidence in favour of their hypothesis: that antidepressant drugs have been shown to reduce the subjective perception of itching, but this may be because of the antihistamine properties of some antidepressants.

Gupta and Gupta (1997) investigated the effects of psoriasis on sexual activities of 120 sufferers of moderate to severe psoriasis. In their study, 40% of sufferers said that their sexual activity had declined as a result of their psoriasis. The sufferers who said that their sex lives had been affected had significantly higher depression scores than non-affected sufferers, and these scores were in the range for clinical depression. Only a minority of the sufferers (15%) who said that their sexual activities had been affected attributed this to a reduced desire for sexual activity in their partner.

The studies described thus far have established that psoriasis has the potential to have an adverse psychological impact (effects on quality of life, feelings of stigmatisation), and that it also realises that potential (depression, psychological symptoms). The studies that are examined in the following section examine some of variables that can moderate the psychological influences of psoriasis.

Gupta, Gupta and Watteel (1996) compared people who had early onset psoriasis (defined as the condition appearing prior to 40 years of age) with those sufferers who had late onset psoriasis. They found that, when controlling for age, there were significant negative correlations between age of onset and interpersonal sensitivity ($r = -0.23$) and age of onset and anger-in ($r = -0.21$), indicating that those sufferers who first suffered psoriasis later in life scored lower on these two psychological measures. Although it may be tempting to conclude that this result shows that age at which psoriasis first appeared alters the psychological impact of the condition, there are problems with this conclusion. First, as the authors point out, there are some differences between sufferers with early and late onset psoriasis, and it may be that these represent two separate conditions. Second, there are three different chronological measures that may relate to the psychological impact of psoriasis, and be worthy of study. Age of the sufferer may relate to the impact of the condition, because older people tend to be less concerned about the impact of their looks on others, and are less highly motivated to form sexual relationships (Porter & Beuf, 1988). The length of time for which the sufferer has had the condition may affect the psychological impact of the condition, because the sufferer may have had longer to learn appropriate coping strategies. Finally, the age of onset may influence the effect of the condition – psoriasis first appearing at puberty is likely to have a much greater psychological impact than psoriasis that first appears at age 50. Unfortunately, it is not possible to isolate the effects of any one of these measures while controlling for the other two – if this is done there will be complete collinearity, and the analysis will not be possible (Miles & Shevlin, 2001).

Miles (1999) examined the effects of psoriasis severity in emotionally charged areas (hands, face, neck, scalp, groin), and non-emotionally charged areas (legs, arms, trunk). They found that severity of psoriasis in the emotionally charged areas is a significant predictor of levels of anxiety and depression, but that severity of non-emotional areas is a much less powerful predictor of these psychological measures. In addition, they did not find any moderating effects for either age or sex.

In two studies, Wahl and her colleagues examined different variables that moderated the effects of psoriasis on quality of life (Wahl et al., 1999a; Wahl et al., 1999b). The first study looked at the relationship between demographic and clinical variables and quality of life in psoriasis sufferers. They assessed a wide range of demographic variables (including age, gender, housing situation, education) and clinical variables (duration, symptoms, severity in emotionally charged areas), and looked at the effect of these measures on physical health, disability, mental health and quality of life. The effect sizes found were in the large to very large range (by Cohen's criteria, 1988), R^2 ranged from 0.2 to 0.5 for the different dependent variables. Symptom severity was a significant predictor of most of the dependent variables (although it only had a small effect on quality of life). The most important predictors of quality of life were living status (alone or otherwise) and age. (Interestingly, the lowest R^2 was quality of life, in which $R^2 = 0.20$.)

In the second study, Wahl et al. (1999b) measured the use of different coping strategies in psoriasis sufferers, and also investigated their quality of life, psoriasis-related disability, mental health and physical health. They found that the coping strategies had an effect on psoriasis related disability, mental health and quality of life. The major finding was that the sufferers who used emotive coping strategies reported higher levels of disability, lower mental health scores and a reduced quality of life (statistically controlling for a range of other variables, including symptoms and duration of disease).

Body shame and psoriasis

Theories of shame differentiate shame into internal and external cognitive domains. Internal shame relates to the self-evaluation and self-feelings of the individual, while external shame relates to beliefs and feelings about the reactions of others. As Gilbert (1998) states, these two manifestations are likely to be correlated, but it is not necessary that they will be. Keeping these two domains conceptually distinct, it can be suggested that different as well as similar processes may be involved in each. Hence, internal and external body shame can arise as a result of psoriasis from two separate, but related, processes – through the appearance effects of psoriasis and the symptoms and treatment effects of psoriasis. This is shown in Figure 6.2.

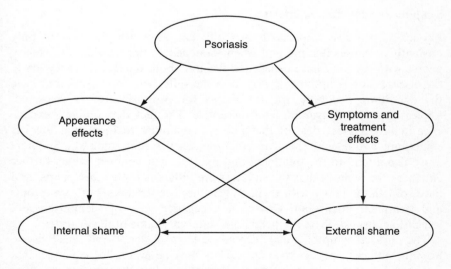

Figure 6.2 Possible routes from psoriasis to body shame

Appearance effects

The greatest impact of psoriasis is on the appearance of the sufferer. Individuals can be acutely aware of how they appear to others. When individuals focus on how they exist in the minds of others but do not have a negative view of themselves as a result of their psoriasis, then their shame can stay at the level of being external. They may be aware of stigmatisation by others and distressed by the possibility of social rejection. They may engage in a variety of safety behaviours to cover their disorder from exposure, and reduce the chance of the discovery of their disorder. There may also be significant levels of social anxiety (Kent & Thompson, Chapter 5, this volume) related to both being seen and where concealment works, being discovered. Nonetheless, as suggested by other authors in this volume, learning to manage the external world's reaction to the disorder can bring enormous relief.

While it is possible to have high levels of external shame without internal shame, the reverse is unlikely. When people with psoriasis focus on their appearance as a source of self-disgust or self-dislike, or if they engage in avoidance behaviour, for example, mirror avoidance because they do not want to see their own bodies, there can be a sense of internal shame. Many authors in this book have addressed the way in which disfiguring conditions can lead to serious problems with internal shame, which, in turn, affect quality of life, depression and anxiety. As noted by Gilbert (Chapter 1, this volume) and Veale (Chapter 14, this volume) internalised shame over disfiguring conditions can be associated with more severe psychological difficulties, and can be more difficult to treat and resistant to change.

Symptoms and treatment effects

Physically, psoriasis impacts in two different ways. Psoriasis is not only unsightly, it causes itching, and when scratched, it may cause pain. Hence, people with psoriasis have beliefs and feelings about the fact that they 'have' the disease. The symptoms do not allow the sufferer to forget that they have the condition. Secondly, the treatments for psoriasis are, as discussed, unpleasant, time-consuming and disruptive. The fact that sufferers experience itching a great deal of the time is a reminder to them that there is something 'wrong' with them, and that they are flawed in some way. Sufferers must also attend to the treatment and management regimen, which further enhances the feelings that the sufferers are different from other people and have something wrong with them. When these experiences, both symptoms and treatment, focus individuals on a negative view of themselves, and self-dislike/disgust, there is a heightened internal shame of the disorder.

The physical symptoms may also cause external shame and sensitivity to how the sufferer appears to others. They may be aware, for example, that frequent scratching or rubbing, in an attempt to reduce the constant irritation of itching will worsen their appearance. Symptoms such as shedding skin can increase sensitivity and awareness that they are 'objects for others'. A person with psoriasis may feel anxious about staying in hotels, or as guests at other people's houses, because they know that the rapid turnover of the epidermis is likely to cause a large number of flakes of skin to be left behind. Further enhancing the external shame of the individual with psoriasis is the management and treatment of the condition.

Treatment for psoriasis can be a source of external shame, in that sufferers have to be exposed to observation (e.g., in the medical consultations) with doctors they feel are not always sympathetic. People may need to take time away from work or studies to attend for regular treatment sessions. This may need to be explained to colleagues who will question the reason for the regular absences. Finally, a person who has psoriasis also feels that they look different to other people and negative social comparison is highly correlated with shame (Gilbert, 2000) and may be a source of both internal and external shame.

As noted in recent theories of social anxiety and shame (see Gilbert, Chapter 1, this volume for a review), some forms of coping behaviour that involve avoidance and concealment can compound problems. The effect of psoriasis on internal shame via this route is shown in Figure 6.2. A person who suffers from psoriasis can keep this fact disguised from others. It is frequently possible to keep the affected areas covered – using long-sleeveed clothes, long trousers/skirts, socks and hairstyles. A sufferer in this way can avoid exposing their psoriasis – and therefore the source of their shame – to others. However, by covering their psoriasis and not allowing people close to them to know about the condition, the sufferer may inadvertently ensure that a potential source of social support is removed. Their own shame about their body may not be reflected in the reactions of others, if only they were to give others the chance.

Although various disfigurements can produce social avoidance, psoriasis has the added problem in that the symptoms (e.g., flaking skin) are frequently taken to be contagious – sufferers have borne the humiliation of being asked to leave swimming pools or hairdressers in order to avoid the potential risk of infecting others (as already discussed, psoriasis was not distinguished from leprosy at some points in history). A further source of external shame is the reactions of others, and sometimes the medical profession, to the psoriasis. A reaction of 'it's just dry skin' is likely to make the individual feel as if their concerns are not legitimate.

Conclusion

The studies reviewed are admirable in their aim of documenting and disseminating to researchers the psychological impact of psoriasis – a much needed task. However, the studies do not link together clearly, and do not

build upon each other as much as they might. In addition, they do not expli-
cate the psychological mechanism that underlies the relationship between
psoriasis and psychological symptoms – it is an implicit assumption throughout the research that psoriasis will have some form of adverse psychological
impact, but the mechanism of the impact is not discussed.

The theory and research that is described elsewhere in this volume provide
mechanisms that describe the impact of psoriasis. The use of shame provides
a theoretical mechanism that can tie together disparate areas of research, and
unite findings. Findings relating to the effects of demographic variables (such
as age, marital status), disease variables (severity, visibility) and psychological
variables (coping style, anger) cannot be easily linked to one another. They
simply exist as a list of findings. The use of shame as a theoretical construct
links these findings, and provides a coherent framework in which they can be
considered.

In addition, the area of shame research provides a rich vein of psychological theory, methods and measuring instruments that can be mined by
researchers investigating the psychological impact of psoriasis. These will
enable studies of the impact of skin disease to 'mature' (in Schmidt's terms,
1996) and become more sophisticated. Psychological research can then begin
to untangle the complex relationship between the skin and the mind,
and these results can be used to inform both psychological and medical
interventions to help people suffering from psoriasis.

This chapter has indicated that psoriasis can have a negative impact on
people's social relationships. Moreover, there are various emotional reactions to psoriasis. It can be suggested that we need to more carefully study
the impact of psoriasis on internal shame (people's self-evaluations) and
external shame (people's fears and concerns about other's reactions).
Clearly, psychological interventions will need to be different according to
which focus they are aimed at. Also important is the increasing awareness
of the role of defensive and safety behaviours. Gilbert (Chapter 1, this
volume) outlines how studies of social anxiety have highlighted the fact that
some coping behaviours such as avoidance can exacerbate problems leading
to dysfunctional cycles of shame and more psychological distress. Indeed, it
is possible that social withdrawal is a key variable in people's emotional
reactions. That is, the more they withdraw, the more socially isolated and
cut-off they feel, the more anxious and depressed they become and the
more they withdraw. It is anticipated that psychological interventions to
help people learn to cope with their psoriasis could benefit from a range of
cognitive-behavioural approaches outlined in other chapters of this book.
Although psoriasis comes with its own special problems (such as itching,
types of treatment used), there is considerable overlap with other disorders
(e.g., acne, see Kellett, Chapter 7, this volume). It is hoped that as we
develop our understanding of body shame and the way in which people
cope with body disfigurements, we will be able to develop better therapeutic

interventions to help them cope and adjust with these distressing conditions.

References

Camisa, C. (1994) *Psoriasis*. Oxford: Blackwell Scientific Publications.

Cohen, J. (1988) *Power Analysis for the Behavioural Sciences* (2nd edn). Hillsdale, NJ: Lawrence Erlbaum Inc.

Duffy, D.L., Spelman, L.S. & Martin, N.G. (1993) Psoriasis in Australian twins. *Journal of the American Academy of Dermatology*, 29, 428–434.

Farber, E.M. & Nall, L. (1994) Psoriasis in the tropics: Epidemiologic, genetic, clinical, and therapeutic aspects. *Dermatologic Clinics*, 12, 805–816.

Fried, R.G., Friedman, S., Paradis, C., Hatch, M., Lynfield, Y., Duncanson, C. & Shalita, A. (1995) Trivial or terrible? The psychosocial impact of psoriasis. *International Journal of Dermatology*, 34 (2), 101–105.

Fry, L. (1988) Psoriasis: Centenary review. *British Journal of Dermatology*, 119, 445–446

Gilbert, P. (1998) Shame and humiliation in the treatment of complex cases. In N. Tarrier, A. Wells & G. Haddock (eds) *Treating Complex Cases: The Cognitive Behavioural Therapy Approach* (pp. 241–271). Chichester: John Wiley & Sons.

Gilbert, P. (2000) The relationship of shame, social anxiety and depression: The role of the evaluation of social rank. *Clinical Psychology and Psychotherapy*, 7, 174–189.

Ginsburg, I.H. & Link, B.G. (1989) Feelings of stigmatisation in patients with psoriasis. *Journal of the American Academy of Dermatology*, 20 (1), 53–63.

Gupta, M.A. & Gupta, A.K. (1995) The psoriasis life stress inventory: A preliminary index of psoriasis related stress. *Acta Dermato-Venereologica*, 75, 240–243.

Gupta, M.A. & Gupta, A.K. (1997) Psoriasis and sex: A study of moderately to severely affected patients. *International Journal of Dermatology*, 36, 359–262.

Gupta, M.A., Gupta, A.K., Ellis, C.N. & Voorhees, J.J. (1990) Some psychiatric aspects of psoriasis. *Archives of Dermatology*, 5, 21–32.

Gupta, M.A., Gupta, A.K., Schork, N.J. & Ellis, C.N. (1994) Depression modulates pruritus perception: A study of pruritus, atopic dermatitis and chronic idiopathic urticarion. *Psychosomatic Medicine*, 56, 36–40.

Gupta, M.A., Gupta, A.K. & Watteel, G.N. (1996) Early onset (<40 years age) psoriasis is comorbid with greater psychopathology than late onset psoriasis: A study of 137 patients. *Acta Dermato-Veneorologica (Stockh)*, 76, 464–466.

Jobling, R.G. (1976) Psoriasis – a preliminary questionnaire study of sufferers' subjective experience. *Clinical and Experimental Dermatology*, 1, 233–236.

Kent, G. & Keohane, S. (2001) Social anxiety and disfigurement: The moderating effects of fear of negative evaluation and past experience. *British Journal of Clinical Psychology*, 40, 23–34.

Leder, R.O. & Farber, E.M. (1997) The variable incidence of psoriasis in sub-Saharan Africa. *International Journal of Dermatology*, 36, 911–919.

McHenry, P.M. & Doherty, V.R. (1992) Psoriasis: An audit of patients views on the disease and it treatment. *British Journal of Dermatology*, 127, 13–17.

Miles, J.N.V. (1999) Psychological aspects of psoriasis. Unpublished PhD dissertation, Derby University, UK.

Miles, J. & Shevlin, M. (2001) *Applying Regression and Correlation*. London: Sage.

Porter, J.R. & Beuf, A.H. (1988) Response of older people to impaired appearance: The effect of age on disturbance by vitiligo. *Journal of Ageing Studies*, 2(2), 167–181.

Romanus (1945) Cited in Fry (1988) Psoriasis: Centenary review. *British Journal of Dermatology*, 119, 445–446.

Schmidt, F. (1996) Statistical significance testing and cumulative knowledge in psychology. *Psychological Methods*, 1, 115–129.

Wahl, A., Moum, T., Hanestad, B.R. & Wiklund, I. (1999a) The relationship between demographic and clinical variables and quality of life in patients with psoriasis. *Quality of Life Research*, 8, 319–326.

Wahl, A., Wiklund, I., Hanestad, B.R. & Moum, T. (1999) Coping and quality of life in patients with psoriasis. *Quality of Life Research*, 8, 427–433.

Williams, R.E.A. (1991) Guidelines for the management of patients with psoriasis. *British Medical Journal*, 303, 829–835.

Chapter 7

Shame-fused acne

A biopsychosocial conceptualisation and treatment rationale

Stephen Kellett

Introduction

Acne is a polymorphic skin disease that tends to be evident on the face (99%) and to a lesser degree the back (60%) and chest (15%). Biological models of acne point to the increased metabolism of androgens in the dermis, in combination with sebaceous gland sensitivity to androgens creating varying degrees of comedones, papules and pustules ('spots'; Cunliffe & Simpson, 1998). The most common form of acne is that of *acne vulgaris*. This form of acne usually starts in adolescence and frequently resolves by the mid-twenties (Burton, Cunliffe & Stafford, 1971). Epidemiological research indicates that some degree of acne affects 95% and 83% of 16-year-old girls and boys, respectively (Burton, Cunliffe & Stafford, 1971). In about 20% of cases, the disease necessitates contact with health services (Munroe-Ashman, 1963). Research indicates an increase in the number of people suffering from acne in the adult years. Cunliffe and Gould (1997) illustrated that 25% of patients attending a dermatology clinic with acne had an average age of 34 years. There are a number of less common but more severe variants of acne: acne conglobata, acne fulminans and gram-negative folliculitis. These forms of acne are associated with gross disruption of the skin and risk of extensive scarring (Cunliffe & Simpson, 1998).

Kellett and Gilbert (2001) reviewed the many theories concerning the onset and maintenance of acne and suggested a biopsychosocial model that integrated genetic sensitivities with psychological and social factors. This is depicted in figure 7.1.

It was suggested that the psychological and social responses to acne interact, via various stress mechanisms, with the physiological mediators of acne to affect both skin pathology and psychological adjustment (e.g., depression and social anxiety). In this model, stigma and shame are seen as central to coping and psychological adjustment. The model is an attempt to synthesise the dermatological and psychological models of acne development and maintenance. The skin disease of acne is developed through the process of genetic susceptibility being acted upon by psychological stress to produce observable

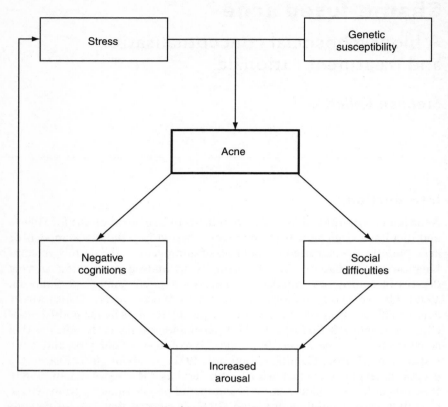

Figure 7.1 The biopsychosocial model of acne development and maintenance

skin disturbance. However, once acne is active for the individual, this requires an appraisal by the individual of what the disease means to them and how they will cope in social situations. If the individual interprets the presence of acne as meaning that they are unacceptable and receive little social support, then a shame response is likely (termed 'increased arousal' in the model). This can be called *shame-fused acne*. The propensity for shame and social anxiety to influence physiological systems has been outlined by Gilbert (2000a). In acne this linkage is indexed by the mental confusion, blushing, perspiration and social anxiety observed at the point of exposure (Crozier, 1979). Indeed, Teshima et al. (1982) illustrated the mechanism via which emotional distress can affect skin presentation; the efficacy of skin health related to immuno-logical functioning was compromised in the context of heightened stress. In the model, the physiological arousal created by shame is hypothesised to increase levels of stress in sufferers, thus maintaining the acne process. Shame is reconceptualised in the biopsychosocial model as not merely a troubling by-product of acne, but rather a key mechanism in the maintenance of the dermatological pathology.

The biopsychosocial model has received support via studies that have attempted to treat acne through the application of psychological therapy. Hughes et al. (1983) found that relaxation, cognitive imagery and physical treatment produced significantly greater reductions in facial acne compared to a matched physical treatment alone. Furthermore, patients who failed to continue with these learnt techniques tended to suffer from dermatological relapse. The investigation of shame-focused psychological treatments of acne is an obvious avenue for empirical examination.

Stigma

As noted by Gilbert (Chapter 1, this volume), stigma refers to the social devaluing of traits and attitudes. The reason for stigmatising are many (Gilbert, 2000b) and include fear of contamination, rejection of those seen as having poor health, and clear skin has evolved as one of the key indicators of sexual attractiveness (Buss, 1999). The stigmatisation of acne can be noted in the speculations by the general public concerning its development, management and amelioration. Many 'folk theories' have emerged over the years concerning these mechanisms, with most centring on either an excess or absence of particular behaviours in the sufferer. These include personality factors (e.g., too much repressed anger), lifestyle factors (e.g., too many late nights), habit factors (e.g., too much masturbation), dietary factors (e.g., too much fried food and chocolate, greedy and poor impulse control) and general hygiene factors (e.g., too little attention to cleaning, washing and cleansing, i.e., dirty). All these factors have been collated under the collective banner of 'acne myths' (Alderman, 1989), as they have little connection with the clinical course of acne development and maintenance (Cunliffe & Simpson, 1998). Nonetheless, sufferers may occupy juxtaposition between the sympathy offered to more esoteric skin disorders and the widespread disparagement and ostracisation that people with skin disorders report (Bach & Bach, 1993). Indeed, acne has its own unique vocabulary of disparagement and stigma such as the labels 'pizza-face' and 'crater-face.'

Shame

Gilbert (Chapter 1, this volume) has outlined the linkage between stigma and shame. Shame is an internal set of cognitions and feelings about the self as a social object ('How I appear to others') and personal self-evaluations. Shame is closely linked to social anxiety and the defensive behaviours of submissiveness, social avoidance and concealment (Gilbert, 1998). Acne sufferers tend to be highly aware of being different from their peers (Krowchuk, Stancin, Keskinen, Wslker, Bass & Anglin, 1991) and often experience difficulties seeking mutual support from similarly suffering peers and tend to prefer isolation (Motley & Finlay, 1989). Such defensive behaviours are likely to enhance and compound the shame response by means of a 'vicious circle' of avoidance (Ryle, 1993) similar to that for social anxiety (Clark & Wells, 1995). We do not need to rehearse the arguments in regard to internal and external shame here (see Gilbert, Chapter 1, this volume), suffice it to say that external shame relates to perceptions that others will look down on or reject the self for having acne. Internal shame relates to devaluing oneself. When shame is internalised, the person adopts the attitudes to the self that are socially represented for the trait or attribute (i.e., 'Acne is something bad about me. I am globally unattractive, and undesirable due to basic flaws in my skin').

Although self-blame is not necessary for shame (Gilbert, 1998), Kaufman (1993) noted that if the antecedents of a problem are construed as some form of personal failure or deficit, then a shame response is likely through a process of self-blame. Thus, the acne sufferer who believes their skin disease is active due to their personal habits (e.g., 'It's my fault, I should not eat chocolate, or masturbate') is likely to excessively self-blame. Be it with or without self-blame, when shame is internalised the person will commonly be highly judgemental, punitive and even persecutory towards the self. These responses centre on the damage that is being done to the self by having these attributes (e.g., 'Because I have acne I will not find a sexual partner') and determining fault rather than mobilising coping, possible treatment and general management strategies.

Dermatological shame

Although there are a number of differing conceptions and definitions emerging from the general shame literature about the generic characteristics of the shame response (Gilbert & Andrews, 1998; Tangney & Fisher, 1995), there is agreement that shame often involves dysfunctional self-evaluations and dysfunctional self-other relationships. This chapter suggests that there can be a specific form of body shame that is *dermatological shame*, which is specifically concerned with the presentation of the skin and its relative attractiveness. Shame-fused acne is a specific form of dermatological shame.

There are two reasons for focusing on dermatological shame. The first is that disturbances of the body (including appearance, bodily processes and excretions) are commonly associated with the affect of disgust, an affect related to avoidance of contamination (Miller, 1998). Self-disgust and self repugnance are seen as central to some shame responses (Kaufman, 1993) and although disgust is probably not related to all forms of shame (Gilbert, 1998) there are obvious reasons for believing it may be central to skin problems (Lazare, 1986). Not only may an individual fear inducing a disgust response in others, but may internalise such to the self.

Secondly, we can distinguish between a specific and generalised shame response and their relation to self-schema. A *specific* dermatological shame reaction may occur, with all its attendant cognitive and behavioural manifestations, but the person may have other aspects of the self that remain unaffected and function relatively effectively (e.g., 'My skin may be poor, but I am good at sports, a kind person and my friends keep calling round showing me that I am liked'). Indeed, this may be the manner in which many acne sufferers cope with the skin disease. In other words their shame is domain-specific.

However, dermatological shame may in some sufferers connect to and merge with other shame schemas that further disable psychological and social functioning. For example, people who carried a sense of inferiority to others and were prone to social anxiety before the onset of acne may experience the onset of acne as another major source of inferiority and reason for social rejection. In this sense acne is fused with a global sense of a shamed self, and in such cases the psychological adjustment will be more complex and difficult because people see themselves as having less personal resources to fall back on.

Hence, we can define dermatological shame as:

> the inner emotional experience of the self as fundamentally unattractive to the self and others, vulnerable to rejection and put-down because of the state of the skin. The dermatological shame sufferer comes to see themselves as different, flawed, defective, ugly and rejectable because of the difference between their skin presentation and that of clear-skinned peers. A state of self-disgust is created by the skin disturbance and shaped by unfavourable social comparison, social stigma and negative attitudes towards the self.

The development of dermatological shame

It is evident that acne, like other skin diseases, tends to develop (and resolve) slowly and that the changes in the presentation and appearance of the skin do not occur overnight (Cunliffe & Simpson, 1998). Unlike the shamed burns victim, there is not a traumatic incident that shatters and therefore impairs people's conception of themselves. Rather, acne can be conceptualised as a potential shaming agent through the development and associated chronicity of the skin disease slowly changing the manner in which sufferers relate to themselves and others. This can be seen as shame by stealth rather than immediate impact. This is not to suggest that particular events (e.g., intense teasing or rejection by peers) are not traumatic events that punctuate the development of shame schema. Rather, it is to highlight that the genesis of the shamed response may be traced back to the *early feelings* of unattractiveness, negative social comparisons and differences that were evident in the early stages of the disease's development. Similarly, if people have pre-morbid unattractive issues then the onset of acne in the adolescent years is a major risk factor for the more global and general shame-problems.

As with all life stressors, such as changes in health status, there is wide individual variation in efficacy of coping response. For some individuals with severe cystic acne, there may be little evidence of serious shame, while a person with very mild papular acne may experience a crushing sense of shame regarding the state of their skin. Indeed, it is known that the extent of skin pathology is a poor predictor of psychological outcome (Fried & Shalita, 1992). Such variability of psychological response highlights the need to understand how the onset of acne is integrated into the sufferer's psychological make-up. The relatively slow development of acne may also mask the initial behavioural changes that the sufferer instigates in order to compensate for and avoid shame. Such changes may be out of the consciousness of the sufferer at the time. Thus, the sufferer in the early stages of the disease may be relatively unaware of the subtle cognitive and behavioural shifts that may be occurring. As shame develops, however, the acne sufferer may become increasingly shame-prone. For example, the shame-prone acne patient may react with shame to a delayed return phone call due to the delicate overtures of rejection.

Although there is individual variation in the development and maintenance of acne, for most it is a skin disease that occurs during the adolescent years (Cunliffe & Simpson, 1998). Many theorists and commentators have noted the primacy of the adolescent years in terms of development of identity, peer relationships, social aspects of self and increasing awareness of sexual attractiveness (Gardner, 1982). Adolescence is one of a number of crucial stages in human development during which physical and psychological developments and transformations occur. However, the overlap between adolescence and acne, created by hormonal and biochemical shifts, results in the skin disease developing during a critical phase of psychological, emotional and sexual development. The shame of acne for the adolescent may lie in the acknowledgement (and perhaps over-emphasis) of disruption to group membership processes (Powers, 1957) and problems it can create in attracting sexual partners (Kellett & Gilbert, 2001). The disruption to the presentation of the skin demarcates the sufferer as different from the rest of the group (in terms of their skin), and the shame of acne may lie in the individual's acknowledgement of this difference. The motivation to be a member of a peer group and associated peer acceptance and validation processes appears ubiquitous between cultures (Gardner, 1982). Thus, the potential for acne to create a shamed response appears to be due to the disruption that difference creates between peers and the acne sufferers associated downward and negative social comparison cognitions.

Some forms of acne (especially the cystic acnes) create such disruption to skin structures that the appearance of the skin is permanently altered and scar tissue is formed (Cunliffe & Simpson, 1998). Thus, even when acne may no longer be active for the individual, the skin surface may be pitted and pockmarked as a result of the disease. Thus shame may be evident regarding body image that outlasts the presence of 'active' acne. Adult acne is on the increase (Cunliffe & Simpson, 1998) which presents a major challenge to the sufferer. For the adult acne sufferer, the number of similar sufferers is less than for adolescent acne sufferers. Thus, the perceptions of difference from the group and the associated feelings of shame may be particularly acute for the adult acne sufferer. Similarly, there may be a loss of hope in the individual that they will 'grow out' of the disease and effective adjustment to acne may entail an active and ongoing coping response across the life cycle (Thompson, Kent & Smith, 2002). There is a general societal belief that acne is somewhat 'normal' during adolescence and 'abnormal' during adulthood.

Across all the stages of development from adolescence to adult noted above, there appears a differential affect of gender in terms of the potential shame of acne. Although the 'typecasting' of gender roles in Western society is extensive, there does appear to be specific stereotyping concerning effective means of controlling others' attention. There appears to be stereotyping for males around themes of performance (i.e., intellectual, sporty, matey etc.) whereas for women the themes appear to converge around appearance (i.e., thin, clear-skinned, physically attractive, Buss, 1999). For females there may be higher risks of shame-fused acne than for male counterparts due to social stereotypes. In consideration of the earlier point concerning age, heightened shame reactions in adult female acne sufferers may be an under-recognised issue.

Past, present and future

Like other forms of shame, dermatological shame can be experienced in relation to past, present and future events and across each of the time frames, self-exposure represents the major activating event (Levin, 1967). Self-exposure represents a complex set of perceptual processes. Acne sufferers' appearance is not simply perceived by others; they perceive that they are being perceived (self as social object, Gilbert, 1998). Further, the perceptual processes likely to promote a shame response involve further evaluations. Acne sufferers not only perceive that they have been perceived, but sufferers become aware that the people perceiving them are having a negative reaction to them. The reaction typically reported is one of rejection (Motley & Finlay, 1989).

When the acne sufferer re-experiences the affect of shame (e.g., by recalling being rejected by a person they were sexually attracted to at a party), the element of self-exposure pertains to the past. When the acne sufferer experiences shame while undergoing a rejecting experience (e.g., a new sexual partner finding 'spot cream' in the bathroom cabinet), the element of self-exposure pertains to the present. When the acne sufferer experiences shame through anticipating a rejection experience (e.g., taking off their blouse before playing hockey), the element of self-exposure pertains to the future.

A cognitive-behavioural model of dermatological shame

Modern cognitive theories of psychopathology tend to emphasise that the early environment of the infant/child has a major effect on personality development and associated stress vulnerability (Young & Lindeman, 1992; Gilbert, 2000c). Developmental aspects of the cognitive model illustrate that the manner in which others behave towards the infant/child have a major effect on the infant's model of the world, self and others (Lewis, 1992). Experience is internalised in the infant/child to form stable psychological rules (schematic rules and social roles) for a future relating both towards others and towards the self. When an adolescent is faced with the development of acne, the outer dermatological changes may create the conditions for transformations at an inner schematic level. In order to account for the wide variability in psychological response to acne observed in the literature (Papadopoulos, Bor & Legg, 1999), three types of schematic change are suggested and described below:

Schema reinforcement

In the pre-morbid acne phase, sufferers may have been in an environment that is characterised by non-nurturance with abolition of emotional development responsibilities by carers. Such an early emotional environment leaves individuals vulnerable to developing poor models of self-care and coping due to learning to see themselves as unlovable, unlikeable and generally socially unattractive to others. The onset of the skin disease of acne will serve to reinforce and underline already maladaptive schema to create the psychological conditions for shame.

Schema attrition

In the pre-morbid acne phase, nurturance is ready, competent and available. However, the affect of the development of the skin disease is to slowly erode the person's sense of self-confidence via the development of maladaptive coping strategies such as avoidance. The longevity of the skin disease may predict the establishment of shame schemas via the erosion of previously healthy modes of relating and self-schema.

Schema vulnerability

In the pre-morbid acne phase, nurturance can be conditional, varied or random. The effect of such an environment is the establishment of schemas that are relatively self-caring but unstable and fragile in difficult environments. As within the teenage years, social comparison and competition are enhanced (Buss, 1999); such an environment may create the conditions within which shame schemas can develop or be activated when the sufferer develops or becomes aware of a sense of difference from peers and possible rejection by them.

The maintenance of dermatological shame

There are, of course, many other possible sources for the origins of dermatological shame schema, such as personality dispositions (e.g., neuroticism, dispositional shyness) and cultural attitudes and stigma that become internalised. However, as negative schema of the self develop, they can undergo either transformation such that the person is able to disconfirm the more catastrophic implications, or the defensive and safety behaviours (e.g., avoidance) used to cope with shame lead to a intensification of shame. Young's (1990) cognitive schema theory can be used to highlight the manner in which dermatological shame schemas may be maintained, avoided or compensated for by the acne sufferer.

Shame maintenance

Shame schema maintenance is accompanied by the acne sufferer cognitively highlighting information that confirms the dermatological shame schema and by cognitively minimising the information that contradicts the shame schema. An example of this may be by what cognitive therapists have called selective abstraction (Beck, 1976); focusing on specific negative details of interactions. For example, while talking to another person, the acne sufferer may exaggerate the amount of time the person looks at their face and minimise the amount of eye contact, glancing and friendly signals. Such an attentional bias maintains and reinforces the acne shame schema.

Thus, a (now) clear-skinned adult may continue to display the shame maintaining cognitive and behavioural manifestations that were developed and evident during the development of the skin disorder (most likely adolescence). Such individuals may present to adult mental health services with social anxiety or social phobia type presentations. This pattern of long-range difficulties could be characterised as the *internal scarring process* of shame-fused acne. The key for recovery for such an 'ex-acne sufferer' would be to challenge the basis or generalisability of the shame schema and to develop and reinforce new schemas regarding the acceptability of self.

Shame avoidance

Young (1990) noted that *avoidance* can occur in behavioural, cognitive and affect domains and Gilbert (1992) noted that avoidance of painful feelings and cognitions can be unconscious. At a behavioural level, an individual with dermatological shame may select social activities that do not rely on exposure of the skin for fear of negative evaluation. The behavioural patterns that evolve out of the dermatological shame schema may outlast the presence of the skin disorder due to social learning processes (Young, 1990). Indeed, the most frequent shame-avoidance strategies employed by acne patients are behavioural avoidance (Motley & Finlay, 1989).

The development of shame-based avoidance has implications on long-term psychosocial maturation processes through the narrowing of choices available for development. An example of behavioural avoidance are sufferers who presume a priori that social contact will involve exposure of the skin and elicit disgust in others. Based on this assumption, sufferers avoid social contact such as playing basketball with their friends because of the need to expose their skin in the shower after the game. By not engaging in the game of basketball, sufferers do, in fact, avoid the anticipated, and in their mind inevitable, shame of exposure. However, through the avoidance process, sufferers also maintain the damaging self-image problems of seeing themselves as different and flawed (Clark & Wells, 1995).

Young (1990) noted that when negative schemas are activated, it is usual for the individual to suffer high levels of associated affect. Because the experience of shame is particularly emotionally distressing and aversive (Kaufman, 1993), the sufferer may develop volitional and automatic responses to avoid triggering shame-based schema and affect. The avoidance of the affects associated with shame can result in both pubic (going out) and private avoidance such as to avoid looking in mirrors due to the anticipation of the intense shame affect (e.g., 'I just can't stand to look at myself in the mirror'). Behavioural and affect avoidance similarly create a 'vicious circle' scenario whereby short-term avoidance strategies create longer-term and more diffuse psychological and social problems.

Cognitive avoidance involves not attending to or thinking about the problem. Such strategies may disable help seeking behaviour (e.g., going to the GP) due to the person simply blocking out considering the state of their skin or suppressing skin related affect. For some individuals, denial and cognitive avoidance may be useful although the person is always at risk of this coping strategy breaking down and becoming flooded with shame affect.

Concealment

Although Young (1990) does not focus on concealment specifically, it is a key aspect of shame and related closely to avoidance. Indeed, one of the primary characteristics of shame is that the aspect of self the person is ashamed of will be concealed and hidden from others (Wurmser, 1981). As acne is typically carried on the face, sufferers cannot hide the source of their shame; however, they can hide themselves. This has marked implications for help-seeking behaviours. Acne sufferers may acknowledge that the state of their skin requires medical attention, but may avoid seeking help appropriately for fear of the anticipated shame of exposure in the medical encounter (Lazare, 1986). Thus, attendance at general practice, the first port of call for medical attention, may be avoided for fear of exposure. Indeed, if the acne sufferer requires a referral to a specialist dermatology clinic, then the actual process of assessment may in itself be a shaming experience. The assessment process for acne requires the removal of clothes and the close inspection of the skin by the dermatologist, typically under bright examination lights. If such procedures are not handled with sensitivity for the potential to elicit shame affect, then the person may be traumatised by the help-seeking process and thus remove themselves from a possible source of help (Lazare, 1986).

Shame compensation

Shame compensation occurs when the acne sufferer may overcompensate for the potential to experience shame. The shame-prone acne sufferer may attempt to compensate for the presence of the skin disorder by signalling competitiveness and attractiveness in other areas of life that are not reliant on skin clarity. For example, the shame-prone acne sufferer may place huge emphasis on intellectual or physical prowess as a compensation mechanism for the sense of difference they carry regarding their skin. However, the competitiveness, because it is driven by shame-compensation mechanisms, may either lead to a further narrowing of options or rejection by peers due to the over-emphasising process. Young (1990) notes that schema compensation represents essentially partially successful attempts by people to challenge their schemas. However, in the case of dermatological shame it typically involves a failure to recognise their hidden and underlying susceptibility to shame. Therefore, if schema compensation mechanisms fail (e.g., not getting an 'A' grade in the physics exam or not being picked for the netball team), then the sufferer is typically unprepared for coping with the emotion of shame if or when the schema is triggered. Psychological intervention would focus on the attempt to produce a more balanced compensation process that acknowledges the sense of shame concerning the skin that may have been previously warded off by the sufferer.

In Table 7.1 potential acne-fused shame schemas are detailed with examples of behavioural artefacts and also an example of an adaptive response.

Dilemmas, traps and snags

In terms of the 'here-and-now' difficulties experienced by the person with shame-fused acne, skin disturbance and dysfunctional coping styles create what have been called *dilemmas, traps and snags*. The section draws on Ryle's (1979, 1993) cognitive analytic conceptions of these processes and their linkage to mental health problems.

Table 7.1 Examples of possible shame schemas and associated behaviours

Schema	Maintenance	Compensation	Avoidance	Adaptation
Alienation	Stays on the periphery of group activities	Rejects others in group	Does not engage in group activities	Develop and maintain group memberships
Undesirability	Does not seek sexual partner	Demands constant admiration for other efforts	Not engaging in close physical relationships	Develop close physical relationship
Embarrassment	Inability to discuss difficult feelings with others	Overconfidence in social abilities	Failure to reveal any aspects of self to others	Discuss feelings and difficulties in an open and adult manner

Dilemmas

Dilemmas in the context of acne can be characterised as two similar mechanisms. In the first, the acne sufferer's perception of others or themselves can be organised on an 'either/or' basis (which cognitive therapists called 'dichotomised thinking', Beck, 1976). For example: (a) 'Either I stay at home and do not expose my skin but feel lonely *or* I go out and will be the focus of people's negative attention and be overwhelmed my own sense of shame'; (b) 'I'm either covered in spots and therefore totally different *or* I'm totally clean-skinned and the same'; (c) 'I'm either a victim to the variable course of acne *or* I'm in total control of my skin and my life'. Such dichotomies narrow options concerning potential choices and constrict the range of anxiety-free behaviour available to the person. Not uncommonly, both options in a dilemma of this type have negative outcomes of some kind and the person is left with choosing the lesser of the 'two evils'.

In the second type of dilemma, acne-related perceptions and beliefs are organised on an 'if/then' basis (which cognitive therapists view as 'basic assumptions', Clark & Wells, 1995). For example: (a) 'If I got to the party *then* others will see my face *then* they will reject me'; (b) 'If I am sexually interested in somebody *then* when we have sex they will reject and ridicule me when they see the spots on my chest I have previously been able to hide'; (c) 'If I have acne as an adult *then* nobody will be interested in me sexually'.

Such 'if/then' thinking is crucial to ascertain in shame-fused acne and is the basis of inference chains (Gilbert, 2000b). Such pairing of limited dichotomies combine to limit the range of feelings, thoughts and behaviours that are in the sufferer's repertoire of responding and relating. The acne sufferer will tend to experience the psychological dichotomies in everyday life as being caught in a number of predicaments. Psychological intervention would focus on the identification of the if/then and either/or assumptions with the sufferer and the experimentation via behavioural techniques of adopting new and more adaptive positions between the dichotomies.

Traps

Traps in the context of acne are patterns of relating that the acne sufferer feels they cannot escape from. The acne sufferer may think or act in a certain way that results in a vicious circle that, despite the obvious efforts of the sufferer, maintains the shame schemas of being different, defective and flawed. In essence, the shame-prone acne sufferer may try to deal with the feelings of shame, only to act or think in ways that tend to confirm and compound their sense of shame. Examples of possible acne traps include:

Avoidance: 'I feel anxious and shamed in social situations because my skin is unsightly in comparison to other peoples. I try to force myself to go out and to stay in social situations, but feel overwhelmed by shame when I do. Not going out so much has made me feel better, so I've ceased trying to stop the shame getting the better of me. However, by constantly avoiding social situations, my life is becoming limiting and boring and I feel increasingly ineffective and shame-prone as a result.'

Depression: 'I feel depressed because my skin is covered in these spots. Being depressed makes me certain that each situation or challenge I face will not go successfully. This makes me feel more depressed about the state of my skin and about my effectiveness as a person.'

Unattractiveness: 'I feel unacceptable and unattractive in social situations because the spots on my face are on show. When I am in such situations, I am sensitive to people looking at my skin, so I try not to engage in conversations and find it hard to respond to people's approaches. People can see me as unfriendly and stand-offish and tend to back away convincing me of my unacceptability and unattractiveness.'

Fear of rejection: 'I feel uncertain of myself because I am visibly different from most people I meet because of my acne. When I do meet people I try to win their affection by trying to please them by doing what they want. As this process goes on I tend to be taken advantage of by people (which can make me angry) and my uncertainty of myself never gets tested out.'

Many of these behaviours can be seen as defensive or safety behaviours as depicted by social anxiety theorists (e.g., Clark & Wells, 1995). They are traps to the extent they fail to produce adaptive change and actually intensify problems.

Snags

A possible obstacle to challenging shame schemas and adjusting to the presence of acne (or seeking treatment for the acne itself) may be the perceived negative consequences anticipated as a result of such a change. These consequences may be the behaviour elicited from others as a result of the change or the mere expectation of their response. Examples of possible acne snags: (a) 'If I begin to challenge my shame problem and begin to interact with people to a greater extent, they will find out that I am actually an unlikeable person and a fraud'; (b) 'If I try to engage in a sexual relationship, my partner will find out that I am actually worried about my sexual performance and not (just) the state of my skin'. Such snags can be illuminated with a patient by exploring the advantages and disadvantages of doing the things necessary for change (e.g., reducing safety and avoidance behaviours, Gilbert, 2000c).

Shame-prone reciprocal roles

The previous section has illustrated that acne sufferers who experience shame regarding the condition of their skin can experience a sense of inner restriction mediated through dilemmas, traps and snags. As such the shame-prone acne sufferer will perceive and interpret many social situations as dangerous and navigate their social worlds in such a way that there is often a confirmation of the inner sense of inferiority, difference and rejectability. The choices shame-prone acne sufferers make may be arbitrary or narrowly selected from a wide variety of possible alternatives. These processes may leave sufferers lacking in the self-trust and self-confidence to explore possible alternatives to the shame position (e.g., valuing non-affected aspects of self). Sufferers' rules for living therefore remain oriented around the themes of safety and intense fear of the expected shame of exposure.

As noted above, shame-fused acne sufferers will tend to see the interpersonal world as a source of anxiety and threat and tend to be acutely aware of the reactions and behaviour of others (Powers, 1957). Ryle (1993) noted that to anticipate the consequences of our own role behaviour (e.g., shamed, rejected, ignored), we must first predict the reciprocal role behaviour of others (e.g., shaming, rejecting, ignoring), and in perceiving the consequences of our own role behaviour (e.g., less attractive, less able of commanding others' attention), we must evaluate the responding role of others (more attractive, more able of commanding others' attention). Self-esteem is based on the integration of a range of discrete experiences of peers and authority figures providing messages that the self is valued, accepted and appreciated. Through this process, the individual begins to appreciate and experience two roles; one played by the other (e.g., encouraging and valuing) and one played by the self (e.g., encouraged and valued). This learning process is the foundation of schemas regarding the safety and style of relationships with others and basis of models of self-care.

Although the establishment of a sound sense of self-esteem is an example of a positive reciprocal role, the consideration of shame in the context of acne obviously entails the delineation of negative reciprocal roles and associated limiting procedures of coping. The establishment of shame-fused acne reciprocal roles is most likely to occur where there is a pre-existing template of authority figures and/or peers behaving in ways in which sufferers experience others as stigmatising and shunning and themselves as unacceptable as a result. In the case of the safety of social relationships, shame-prone acne sufferers will tend to see social contact as possible sources of exposure, rejection, ridicule and being less 'chosen' than clear-skinned peers. Through the internalisation process, shame-prone acne sufferers will begin to relate to themselves in a non-nurturing and non-soothing manner, thus disabling effective self-care. Such internal mechanisms may contain internal put-downs, self-attack, bullying and negation of positive attributes and aspects of appearance.

Therapy

An awareness of dematological shame issues in acne should pervade all areas of support-giving and treatment including the GP's surgery through to specialist skin clinics. Clinicians could routinely ask the sufferer how they feel about their acne (e.g., give opportunity to mention shame) and if shame is acknowledged would be followed by an empathic response such as, 'I can see how that must make you feel.' Or 'It is understandable how you might feel that.' This is not to suggest that such feelings and beliefs are inevitable, and indeed psychological help would be aimed to change such feelings. However, an early empathetic response to people's emotional reactions to the skin condition can help create a 'safe' bond with the clinician and that the clinician is not looking down on them but is understanding of the pain and shame they feel. A hurried or dismissive clinician can do much to enhance shame. When a sufferer is engaged in treatment, it is important to recognise that the central issue may well be shame and therefore the therapist needs to be aware of the potential for unwittingly shaming the client during the process of treatment (Lazare, 1986).

For psychological treatment, the development of a sound therapeutic relationship can make the difference between engagement in treatment and avoidance. To achieve this, the therapist would go into more detail about the feelings and concerns the person has about their skin as well as those about their treatment. It is useful to take a full history including understanding the context of shame and whether this is a specific dermatogical shame problem or whether shame of the skin disorder is fused with more global shame issues and negative self-schema.

The therapist will then seek to identity key cognitions, beliefs and coping behaviours that are part of the shame experience and consider these as possible sources for intervention (Gilbert, 2000b). All the aspects discussed above, such as how self-schema are formed, maintained, the processes of avoidance and the complication of dilemmas, traps and snags can be delineated. Ideally, therapist and patient will then have some agreed formulation that outlines the origins of their shame experiences, and shame schema (including key beliefs, 'I am ugly; everybody will reject me'), how these are maintained (e.g., safety and defensive behaviours) and the steps towards their modification.

It is useful to identify the shame experience being discussed as either being past shame, present shame or future shame. The 'tense' of the shame can indicate the style of intervention that will be useful. Present and future shame could be more amenable to cognitive and behavioural intervention and modification. If behavioural experiments that seek to reduce safety and defensive behaviours (e.g., going out without make-up or not totally covering up in summer) are not carefully negotiated and agreed, then clients may feel overexposed and shamed and re-engage with their previous patterns of avoidance or even drop out of therapy. Further, one may need to acknowledge with the client that the mere process of talking about the state of the skin may itself be elicit shame affect and be a shame-provoking experience. One can usually detect this by the non-verbal communication (e.g., eye gaze) of patients, their speech flow and the way they articulate their concerns about their skin.

Clients need to be fully involved in understanding the formulation that will act as the basis of the treatment (i.e., it is collaborative) and in designing their own hierarchies of exposure that strike a balance between safety and challenge. It may also be crucial to discuss the nature of shame, the typical defensive behaviours it promotes and how these often make things worse. The use of diagrams in the formulation can be helpful (Gilbert, 2000b; Ryle, 1993) as they provide clients with visual maps of difficulties promoting insight.

Figure 7.2 contains an example formulation diagram for shame-prone acne. Within the diagram 'shaming' can constitute the behaviours of others towards the person, but also crucially through an internalised stigma process the manner in which the client behaves and relates towards themselves. In the formulation 'shamed' is the affective reaction that is the end result of the shaming process.

In the diagrammatic formulation, two loops are identified that form the chains of cognitions and behaviours that create a vicious circle of shame. The avoidance loop provides an example that once shame is anticipated or activated then avoidance of shame can result in self-limitation in relation to social activities. Such limitations are likely to have a negative effect on mental

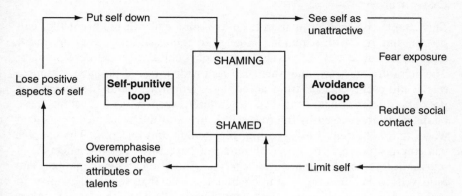

Figure 7.2 Example formulation of shame-prone acne

health. The self-punitive loop illustrates that cognitive distortions relating to the skin can result in clients engaging in internal cognitive attacks that constitute an internal shaming process. The use of diagrammatic formulations empowers clients to choose at which point they wish to break the vicious circles. Again, due to the sensitivity of the subject, therapists should be aware that diagrams may be unintentionally shaming and should be aware of this possibility. Clients can be requested to state and rate their affective responses to the development of the diagrammatic formulation in order to be sensitive to shame exposure issues.

Acne suffers, like those with other facial unattractive traits, coming for psychological help will often have either social anxiety and/or depression as part of their shame (see Kent & Thompson, Chapter 5, this volume). If social anxiety dominates the clinical picture then the clinician may be guided by the current work on social anxiety that focuses on meta-cognitions and safety behaviours (e.g., Clark & Wells, 1995) and in some cases groups may be useful (Bates & Clark, 1998). If depression dominates the clinical picture then again therapies developed for depression (Beck et al., 1979; Blackburn & Twaddle, 1996; Gilbert, 2000c) may be useful. In some cases, people may have very self-critical and self-hating feelings towards themselves and their skin disorder. Recently, Gilbert (2000b) has suggested ways that the cognitive approach to working with such negative self-evaluations can be modified to help develop a more compassionate self-structure. To date these interventions, borrowed from work with depressed and anxious people and modified for work on acne, have not been subjected to clinical trials. However, there is good reason to believe that they will aid in the development of therapies for those who have serious psychological problems associated with their acne.

Conclusions

This chapter has conceptualised acne as a major health life event that can present sufferers with a major challenge to their self-image and group-fit, often at a crucial time of psychological, physical and sexual development. The literature illustrates that there can be a wide range of possible responses to the life event of acne from acceptance, adjustment and the seeking of possible sources of help to that of the sufferer experiencing a crushing sense of shame characterised by internal self-dislike and the avoidance of a social world that is perceived as exposing, threatening and rejecting. The chapter has emphasised that the onset of acne can have three possible effects at a schematic level for the sufferer; reinforcement, attrition and vulnerability. The biopsychosocial orientation emphasised the role that shame may play in maintaining observable skin pathology. Once schematic change has taken place in the sufferer, possible shame maintaining mechanisms were described in terms of dilemmas traps and snags. The expansion from that of schematic changes to the establishment of reciprocal roles using Ryle's (1993) theory has underlined that dermatological shame can confirm and reinforce already negative models of self-care or erode and replace positive models of self-care. The shame-prone acne sufferer may well suffer in silence due to the crippling effect of the shame on coping strategies and help-seeking behaviour.

Although shame has been previously recognised as the psychological kernel of dysfunctional reactions to dermatological problems (Bach & Bach, 1994), definition and delineation of the shamed response has been absent from the literature. The central challenge to psychodermatological research is to attempt to operationalise dermatological shame and begin to test hypotheses regarding its relationship to psychopathology and adjustment. Finally, it was noted that there are a number of therapies developed in the mental health field that can be easily adapted for working with acne and the psychological reactions to it. The cross-fertilisation of ideas in health psychology and clinical psychology, conceptualised in a biopsychosocial framework, may do much to advance our treatments for this distressing skin condition.

References

Alderman, C. (1989) Not just skin deep. *Nursing Standard*, 37 (3), 22–24.

Bach, M. & Bach, D. (1993) Psychiatric and psychometric issues in acne excoriee. *Psychotherapy and Psychosomatics*, 60, 207–210.

Bates, A. & Clark, M. (1998) A new cognitive treatment for social phobia: A single case study. *Journal of Cognitive Psychotherapy: An International Quarterly*, 12, 289–302.

Beck, A.T. (1976) *Cognitive Therapy and the Emotional Disorders*. New York: International Universities Press.

Beck, A.T., Rush, A.J., Shaw, B.F. & Emery, G. (1979) *Cognitive Therapy of Depression*. New York: Guilford Press.

Blackburn, I.M. & Twaddle, V. (1996) *Cognitive Therapy in Action: A Practitioner's Casebook*. London: Souvenir Press.

Burton, J.L. Cunliffe, W.J. & Stafford, L. (1971) The prevalence of acne vulgaris in adolescence. *British Journal of Dermatology*, 85, 119–26.

Buss, D.M (1999) *Evolutionary Psychology: The New Science of Mind*. Boston, MA: Allyn and Bacon.

Clark, D.M. & Wells, A. (1995) A cognitive model of social phobia. In R.G. Heimberg, M.R. Liebowitz, D.A. Hope & R.R. Schneier (eds) *Social Phobia: Diagnosis, Assessment and Treatment* (pp.69–93). New York: Guilford Press.

Crozier, W.R. (1979) Shyness as a dimension of personality. *British Journal of Social and Clinical Psychology*, 18, 121–128.

Cunliffe, W.J. & Gould, D.J. (1979) Prevalence of facial acne vulgaris in late adolescence and in adults. *British Medical Journal*, 138, 1109–1110.

Cunliffe, W.J. & Simpson, N.B. (1998) Disorders of the sebaceous gland. In R.H. Champion, J.L. Burton, D.A. Burns & S.M. Breathnach (eds) *Textbook of Dermatology* (vol. 2) (pp.1927–1984). Oxford: Blackwell Scientific.

Fried, R.G. & Shalita, A.R. (1992) The reciprocal interaction between acne and the psyche. *Focus on Cutis and the Psyche*, 2, 28–33.

Gardner, G. (1982) *Developmental Psychology*. Canada: Little, Brown & Co.

Gilbert, P. (1992) *Depression: The Evolution of Powerlessness*. Hove, UK: Lawrence Erlbaum Associates Ltd and New York: Guilford Press.

Gilbert, P. (1998) What is shame? Some core issues and controversies. In P. Gilbert & B. Andrews (eds) *Shame: Interpersonal Behavior, Psychopathology and Culture* (pp.3–38). New York: Oxford University Press.

Gilbert, P. (2000a) Social mentalities: Internal 'social' conflicts and the role of inner warmth and compassion in cognitive therapy. In P. Gilbert & K.G. Bailey (eds) *Genes on the Couch: Explorations in Evolutionary Psychotherapy* (pp.118–150). Hove: Psychology Press.

Gilbert, P. (2000b) The origins of stigmatisation: Stigmatisation as a survival strategy. In A.H. Crisp (ed.) *Every Family in the Land: Tackling Prejudice and Discrimination Against People with Mental Illness*. www.stigma.org

Gilbert P. (2000c) *Counselling for Depression: Second Edition*. London: Sage.

Gilbert, P. (2001) Evolution and social anxiety: The role of social competition and social hierarchies. In F. Schnieder (ed.) *Social Anxiety: Psychiatric Clinics of North America*, 24, 723–751.

Gilbert, P. & Andrews, B. (1998) (eds) *Shame: Interpersonal Behavior, Psychopathology and Culture*. New York: Oxford University Press.

Hughes, H., Brown, B.W., Lawlis, G.F. & Fulton, J.E. (1983) The treatment of acne vulgaris by biofeedback, relaxation and cognitive imagery. *Journal of Psychosomatic Research*, 27 (3), 185–191.

Kaufman, G. (1993) *The Psychology of Shame*. London: Routledge.

Kellett, S. & Gilbert, P. (2001) Acne: A biopsychosocial and evolutionary perspective with a focus on shame. *British Journal of Health Psychology*, 6, 1–24.

Krowchuk, D.P., Stancin, T., Keskinen, R., Walker, R., Bass, J. & Anglin, T.M. (1991) The psychological effect of acne on adolescents. *Paediatric Dermatology*, 8, 332–338.

Lazare, A. (1986) Shame and humiliation in the medical encounter. *Archives of General Medicine*, 147, 1653–1658.

Levin, S. (1967) Some metapsychological considerations on the differentiation of guilt and shame. *International Journal of Psychoanalysis*, 48, 267–276.

Lewis, M. (1992) *Shame: The Exposed Self*. New York: The Free Press.

Miller, W.I. (1998) *The Anatomy of Disgust*. Cambridge, MA: Harvard University Press.

Motley, R.J. & Finlay, A.Y. (1989) How much disability is caused by acne? *Clinical and Experimental Dermatology*, 14, 194–198.

Munroe-Ashman, D. (1963) Acne vulgaris in a public school. *Transcripts of St John's Hospital Dermatological Society*, 49, 144–148.

Papadoupoulos, L., Bor, R. & Legg, C. (1999) Psychological factors in cutaneous disease. An overview of research. *Psychology, Health and Medicine*, 4 (2), 107–126.

Powers, D. (1957) Emotional implications of acne. *NY State Journal of Medicine*, 57, 751–753.

Ryle, A. (1979) The focus in brief interpretive psychotherapy: Dilemmas, traps and snags as target problems. *British Journal of Psychiatry*, 134, 46–64.

Ryle, A. (1993) *Cognitive Analytic Therapy: Active Participation in Change*. Chichester: John Wiley & Sons.

Tangney, J.P. & Fischer, K.W. (1995) *The Self-conscious Emotions: The Psychology of Shame, Guilt, Embarrassment and Pride*. New York: Guilford Press.

Teshima, H., Kubo, C., Kohara, H., Imada, Y., Ago, Y. & Ikemi, Y. (1982) Psychosomatic aspects of skin disease from the standpoint of immunology. *Psychotherapy and Psychosomatics*, 37 (3), 165–175.

Thompson, A.R., Kent, G. & Smith (2002) Living with vitiligo: Dealing with difference. *British Journal of Health Psychology*, 7, 213–225.

Wurmser, L. (1981) *The Mask of Shame*. Baltimore, MD: The John Hopkins University Press.

Young, G.E. (1990) *Schema-focussed Cognitive Therapy for Personality Disorders*. Sarasota, FL: Professional Resource Exchange.

Young, G.E. & Lindeman, M.D. (1992) An integrative schema-focussed model of personality disorders. *Journal of Cognitive Psychotherapy: An International Quarterly*, 1 (6), 11–23.

Chapter 8

Shame and burns

Geraldine Coughlan and Alex Clarke

Burns and disfigurement

In Britain, 250 000 people per year are injured as a result of thermal, electrical and chemical burns. The majority of burns are thermal, the biggest subgroup being scalding, particularly of children. Thirteen thousand people per year are hospitalised and approximately 1000 require fluid resuscitation; about half of this latter group are children under 16 (National Burn Care Review Committee Report, 2001). Treatment may be provided in a regional burns centre containing a burns unit linked to a department of plastic surgery, or in a local non-specialist hospital where plastic surgeons collaborate with the intensive care team.

Burn injuries disfigure by causing long-term scarring as well as changes in skin colour and body contour. Some burns survivors have lost digits, ears or hair. Single or multiple areas of the body may be affected, and donor tissue for reconstructive surgery may be harvested from a non-burnt part of the body. Surgical repair and reconstruction can take months or years, and involves rehabilitation challenges such as uncertainty of aesthetic outcome, wearing of pressure garments, pain and severe itching.

Disfigurement following a burn injury may be highly visible in social situations or concealed by clothing or skin camouflage (specialist make-up). Medical treatment, plastic surgery and skin camouflage can help to make the changes in appearance less noticeable but they are not always convenient, particularly for children, and often they will improve, but not remove, the disfigurement.

Psychological reactions to disfigurement following burns

Burns injuries are always unexpected. The circumstances in which a person is burnt can be life-threatening. Some burns injuries are the result of deliberate assault, or a suicide attempt. Patients admitted to burns units have a higher level of psychiatric or personality disorders pre-injury than community samples. Hospitalisation, pain, repeated medical procedures and disruption of life narrative constitute a crisis for the injured person and those who are close to them. In the early stages, the physical impact of a severe injury, and its treatment, can have a profound impact on psychological processes.

Follow-up studies of burns patients 6–24 months following discharge have reported that 30–50% of patients report sufficient psychological disturbance to warrant specialist referral (Kleve & Robinson, 1999; Tarrier, 1995; Wallace & Lees, 1988). Post-traumatic reactions, distressing hospital procedures, disability and rehabilitation are common challenges for burns patients and their families, schools and employers. However, this chapter focuses only on the issues of psychological adjustment to a burns disfigurement. In clinical practice, appearance-related issues should be understood within the context of a broad psychological assessment and formulation that includes many developmental, psychological and social processes, including stress reactions to the disfiguring event.

Research studies are consistent in describing the problems people with a disfigurement encounter. The predominant difficulties are in the areas of personal meanings of a disfigurement and impact on social interaction. Macgregor (1974) highlighted these issues.

> in their attempts to go about their daily lives, people are subjected to visual and verbal assaults, and a level of familiarity from strangers . . . (including) naked stares, startled reactions, 'double takes', whispering, remarks, furtive looks, curiosity, personal questions, advice, manifestations of pity or aversion, laughter, ridicule and outright avoidance (p.250).

Other studies report high levels of social anxiety (Newell & Marks, 2000), and evidence that this group of people may have very low self-esteem and expectations about future opportunities. For example, individuals with a disfigurement may believe that they need to make compromises in terms of relationships or believe that they have low employment prospects: 'you have to take what you can get' (Bradbury, 1996; Noar 1991; Partridge, 1994; Rubinow et al., 1987).

In *The Social Psychology of Facial Appearance* Bull and Rumsey (1988) reviewed experimental evidence of the effects of disfigurement on the behaviour, attributions and attentional processes of people with disfigurements, and of people around them. Rumsey, Bull and Gahagen (1982) used actors made up to appear disfigured, either with scars, birthmarks or bruising, to demonstrate the subtle, non-verbal ways in which people without disfigurements convey their discomfort in the presence of facial differences. Comparison with a control group found that members of the public avoided looking at the facial anomaly and attempted to ignore the presence of the person with a disfigurement. The public stood significantly further from them in an everyday situation (waiting to cross the road) and moved to stand on the non-affected side when they had the opportunity (Rumsey, Bull & Gahagen, 1982).

Not only do people behave differently towards someone with a disfigurement, but also having a disfigurement can change the perception of social interactions. Strenta and Kleck (1985) examined the impact of beliefs about disfigurement on social perception. Actors were made up to look disfigured, but under the guise of having fixative added, and unknown to them, the experimental group had the make-up removed before being exposed to the experimental situation. Subjects who believed themselves to be scarred reported stronger reactions from other people than the control group. This finding could be due to cognitive distortions in the form of misinterpretation of events, or to subtle alterations in the subject's behaviour – poor posture, eye contact and so on – producing genuinely stronger reactions from the onlooker.

The social behaviour of someone with a disfigurement is more important than the disfigurement itself in predicting the outcome of social interactions. Rumsey, Bull & Gagahen et al. (1986) reported the effects of co-varying social skill and disfigurement in an interview task. Not only did subjects report feeling more comfortable in the presence of an actor with good social skills, whether or not the actor was disfigured, but their own social skills were better when rated by an independent observer.

Positive self-beliefs, type and amount of social support, and communication skills are more important than physical factors in predicting levels of shame and social avoidance among people with disfigurements. Those who cope well and report fewer problems tend to use 'positive' coping strategies; they have good social skills, are assertive and take the initiative in new settings; 'negative' coping strategies include aggression, use of alcohol, unrealistic pursuit of surgical solutions, and above all, avoidance and withdrawal from difficult situations. (Robinson, Rumsey & Partridge, 1996; Partridge, 1994; Macgregor, 1974). The number and range of effective coping strategies used by an individual is a better predictor of good outcome than a particular kind of strategy *per se*; in other words, those who manage their disfigurement most effectively and report fewer problems, are those who have developed a variety of alternative responses (Partridge, Rumsey & Robinson, 1997).

The relationship between burn severity and psychological adjustment

Given the impact and prevalence of the medical model in generating treatment options, it can be argued that severity is one of the most important variables in studying the psychological impact of any disfigurement. Severity of burn injury is routinely measured in terms of total burn surface area (TBSA). This has been criticised for its lack of acknowledgement of complexity of the injury, and there is no relationship between this measure and psychological distress (National Burn Care Review Committee Report, 2001).

In most studies of disfigurement across other conditions, judgements of severity based on size, location and visibility all contribute to what is usually a highly subjective measurement standardised by inter-rater agreement across very simple categories. Even where these additional factors are included, a simple medical model does not predict psychological distress. Indeed the predictive value of site and severity of disfiguring medical conditions and their psychosocial effects is weak (Kent, 2000; see Kent & Thompson, Chapter 5, this volume). A more useful interpretation of the evidence from studies of disfigurement is that it is the extent to which the social/communication process is interrupted, which is more closely associated with adjustment and that severity of the lesion is only one of the factors that will have an impact in this process. We explore this below.

Bull and Rumsey (1988) proposed the hypothesis that the breakdown in the reciprocal behaviour of social encounters accounted for much of the distress both on the part of the disfigured individual and the observer (Table 8.1). Repeated failures to achieve desired levels of social interaction, or smooth-running social interactions, threaten psychological adjustment. Initial social encounters tend to be a particular challenge for people with disfigurements because the other person is often disconcerted by their unusual appearance. Meeting new people is essential to achieving common goals such as starting a new school, shopping, finding employment and forming a social network.

Table 8.1 Breakdowns in social interaction due to disfigurement encoded as an acronym (Partridge, 1994)

Person with a disfigurement feels		Other people feel
Self-conscious	S	Sorry, shocked
Conspicuous	C	Curious, confused
Angry, anxious	A	Anxious
Rejected	R	Repelled
Embarrassed	E	Embarrassed
'Different'	D	Distressed

Person with a disfigurement behaves		Other people behave
Shy	S	Staring, speechless
Cowardly	C	Clumsy
Aggressive	A	Awkward, asking
Retreating	R	Rude, recoiling
Evasive	E	Evasive
Defensive	D	Distracted

Disfigurement and body shame

The experience of negative social interactions due to disfigurement depicted in Table 8.1 shows considerable overlap with the features of shame listed by Gilbert, Pehl and Allan (1994; see Gilbert, Chapter 1, this volume). There is often an evaluation of how self is seen and evaluated by more powerful others for something one is and cannot change; the outcome of which is a negative image of self in the eyes of potential evaluators (e.g., external shame, see Gilbert, Chapter 1, this volume). There can also be unease at an unfavourable comparison between self and others that persists when one is alone, with avoidance of wanting to see one's own appearance (internal shame). There can be a range of defensive emotions and behaviours to such shame experiences including fear, avoidance, inhibition, compliance versus aggression and attack, with submissive behaviours commonly prominent. One noticeable effect of a burns disfigurement is that both self and other share some aspects of social unease due to disfigurement. Both parties are often uncertain of how to relate to each other or proceed and can be anxious not to embarrass themselves or the other person.

The relative rarity of people with disfigurements fosters negative stereotypes (stigma) connecting disfigurement with incompetence, failure and sometimes tainted biology or morality. Disfigurement is a socially devalued characteristic, encountered most often in the villain of a fairy-tale or horror movie. The relatively low incidence of burn injury in the general population (15 hospital admissions/100 000 whole population) has obvious implications for finding successful role models.

Body shame in burns has three possible origins, that may exist singly or in combination:

1 Believing oneself to be unattractive and worthless due to having a disfigurement (internal shame).
2 Believing other people see oneself as unattractive and worthless due to disfigurement (external shame). How one expects to be perceived is not necessarily related to actual experiences.
3 Experiencing scorn, contempt, disgust, ridicule, rejection or discrimination during social interactions (enacted stigma).

The adverse effects of disfigurement on human interaction are a serious social disadvantage, reinforcing a cycle of internal and external body shame (Figure 8.1).

Concerns about social acceptance and appearance (felt stigma) may be triggered when:

• the disfigurement is highly visible;
• its discovery by others is anticipated, for example, during sports activities where fewer clothes are worn;

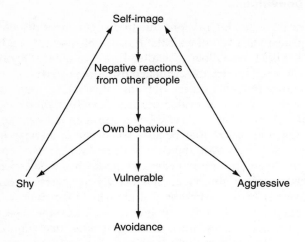

Figure 8.1 The negative feedback loop (Partridge, 1994)

- there is ambiguity about the visibility of the disfigurement to others, and therefore of how to proceed during conversation;
- as relationships develop, greater physical intimacy or personal information is sought.

Parental behaviours

Since 90% of burn injuries are estimated to be avoidable, and since most *childhood* burns occur in the home, parents commonly experience shame. For example, they often expect others to infer parental inadequacy on seeing a child with a disfigurement. In efforts to defend against their own shame and stigma they may seek to shift the blame on to the child (externalising), or to hide the disfigurement from others (concealment), or try to pretend that there is nothing to notice (denial), or may even 'distance' themselves from their 'damaged child'. Clearly, these coping behaviours will impact on the child and give clear messages about the social meaning of 'burn disfigurement'. On the other hand, when parents have internalised a sense of responsibility for the child coming to harm, they may experience profound guilt, which will also impact on the child–parent relationship in various complex ways (e.g., over protection). For children with burns, it is important then to explore parental behaviours, and if working with people who acquired their burns in childhood, to reflect on how parents may have responded to the burn and how this might have affected the children's interpretation of their own disfigurement.

Re-establishing one's appearance

Feeling pressure to re-establish a 'normal' appearance in order to re-establish oneself in the opinions of others is an understandable response to body shame. However, lack of awareness of the limitations of plastic surgery contributes to unrealistic requests for surgery by patients (and parents) and unsolicited advice from others who wonder, sometimes aloud, how someone with a disfigurement dares to be seen in public before the disfigurement is 'fixed'.

Anticipation of negative social evaluation due to burns scars produces a variety of affects and cognitions whose consequences range from reduced participation in social encounters to mild verbal aggression. Feelings of self-consciousness, powerlessness, inferiority and anger are communicated orally and via non-verbal behaviour to other people whose response complements, and maintains, the low-status demeanour and self-image. The outcome of restricted social, educational and employment opportunities confirms negative stereotypes of people with disfigurements and magnifies internal devaluing of self.

In the absence of preparation via overt rehearsal of a range of proactive coping strategies, partial or complete social avoidance are regularly used to avoid rejection and ridicule from people of unremarkable appearance. Health professionals and support groups can facilitate the development of enhanced social skills and positive self-beliefs as an alternative protective measure; one that leads to personal renewal and self-acceptance (Cochrane & Slade, 1999).

Prevention and treatment of body shame to burn disfigurement

Burns survivors often need new or enhanced skills for managing both the intrapsychic and social difficulties posed by looking 'different'. We discuss internal and external body shame in separate sections for the purposes of clarity, although in practice these are highly overlapping features of intervention. For example, it is not therapeutic to give up social avoidance as a coping strategy without simultaneously learning how to put oneself, and other people, more at ease with an unusual or altered appearance.

Managing external shame

As noted earlier (Gilbert, Chapter 1, this volume), external shame relates to the feelings and beliefs that others look down on the self and see the self as unattractive and undesirable, with the expectation that others will not wish to engage in positive relationships (e.g., close friendships or sexual relations). Drawing on his own experience of severe facial burns, Partridge (1994) emphasises the role of the disfigured individual in managing the success or failure of social situations. Effective intervention for this aspect of burns survival includes, but is not limited to, offering a range of coping skills to use in a range of social settings with people of all ages and different levels of familiarity and physical intimacy (Table 8.2).

As a first step, social skills should be assessed, and where necessary a social skills package focusing on body language, posture, eye contact and so on implemented. Conversation skills are often weak and perceived to be weak by this population, adding to the need for training in participating in and initiating conversation, with a particular emphasis on dealing with questions and comments about appearance, with alternative responses being generated and tested. The REACH OUT acronym assists recall of a 'tool box' of eight principles or 'tools', which the individuals use to shape their behaviour. Self-monitoring via written diaries and practice with therapist should precede graded practice of target situations.

REACH OUT represents a social cognition model that helps the individual to understand the general problems of disfigurement in a social context and to identify inaccurate beliefs while devising new coping behaviours that reduce feelings of helplessness. It also places the disfigured person in the role of expert, whose enhanced communication skills allow others to see beyond disfigurement and weaken expectations of social rejection. Research confirms increases in self-esteem and social confidence among adults with a range of disfigurements after learning this model via brief individual therapy or in group workshops. (Partridge, Rumsey & Robinson, 1997; Robinson, Rumsey & Partridge, 1996). Elements of therapies developed for social anxiety and

Table 8.2 Eight principles, or tools, encoded as an acronym REACH OUT, which help individuals to develop different coping strategies in social interactions (Partridge, 1994)

R	REASSURANCE involves getting in first, letting the other person know that you are human with a brief remark, a nod or a smile
E	EFFORT, ENERGY and ENTHUSIASM are needed to tell the other person that you are worth spending time with
A	ASSERTIVENESS means being quite clear about what you want, and saying it effectively
C	COURAGE means tackling the future, taking one step at a time to face the situations you find difficult and focusing on your positive achievements
H	HUMOUR is one of your most effective tools. Making a situation more light-hearted helps other people to approach you
O	OVER THERE! – means changing the subject, and shifting the attention away from your appearance onto something that interests everybody
U	UNDERSTANDING other people and find it difficult to deal with anything that is new to them. If people seem uncertain, don't assume that they are hostile. They may be wondering how to approach you
T	TRY AGAIN – sometimes situations don't go well. Don't give up. Try to understand how you could have managed things differently and have another go

anger can be used to enhance mental control, making it easier to apply the new coping plan (examples in Tables 8.3 and 8.4).

The power of the skills represented by the acronym REACH OUT lies in their ability to elicit a positive response from others, without first increasing other people's knowledge or understanding. Social models of disability would stress the role of the non-disfigured majority in changing *their* behaviour to accommodate those who do not necessarily fit a standard or norm. Historically, this has been an issue for psychologists and anyone working with people who have a disfigurement needs to be quite clear about their objectives. Perhaps the strongest argument for individual change is the high social anxiety in a significant percentage of this population. It can also be argued that the two approaches are not incompatible, and it is through the ability of people, who have an unusual appearance to succeed in social situations, that there will be an eventual shift towards increased tolerance from a population that currently discriminates against them.

Identifying the reactions of others as *uncertain* rather than *hostile* allows people to develop strategies for taking the initiative and putting people at their ease. Negative or unhelpful beliefs are often concerned with the perception of others. Examples include employment: 'no one will be prepared to employ someone who is visibly different'. This can be challenged with 'my qualifications and experience are the things that will influence my employer the most'. Similarly, there may be a strong belief that intimate relationships will be impossible: 'no one is going to want a relationship with someone who

Table 8.3 Reducing physical tension in social situations

Cued muscle relaxation fosters open, confident posture and calm voice
Slow, steady breathing
Mental images associated with calmness and positive achievements
Lifestyle changes such as yoga, tai chi, regular exercise
Reduce alcohol intake in situations where you tend to feel vulnerable
or aggressive
Choose whether to express anger constructively with its target or talk to someone supportive later on

Table 8.4 Coping with negative thoughts in social situations

Focusing on the task (i.e., 'Remind myself of what I want to achieve here')
Self-calming statements (e.g., 'Don't take it personally, once you get to know me, you'll like me, it's normal for people to notice my scars when they first see me')
Coping self-statements
Distraction via neutral mental activity
Distraction via planning use of the REACH OUT toolkit
Self-praise (e.g., for remaining in control of negative feelings)
Remembering rewards of resisting safety behaviours

looks like me' can be challenged with the alternative statement 'close relationships are based on personality and not on face values'. Cognitive-behavioural therapy (e.g., challenging negative cognitions and defensive behaviours) can be particularly useful for those individuals with high levels of external shame with little experience of enacted stigma.

Reducing internal shame

Internal shame relates to one's own feelings and beliefs about a burn disfigurement, or the attitudes of the self to the disfigurement. These can range from self-acceptance to self-hatred for the disfigurement. Like external shame, these experiences will be reflected in mood states including anxiety and depression. Positive beliefs about one's future prospects, which include the presence of disfigurement, and positive beliefs of family and significant others in society about the future prospects of someone with a burns injury, reduce the likelihood of seeing oneself as unattractive and worthy of self-criticism and self-loathing. Therapeutic techniques developed for managing social anxiety, body image disturbance and anger can be used to help individuals to:

- analyse and feel compassion towards their own distress;
- value themselves more positively;
- tolerate being visible to others;
- manage disappointments and setbacks;
- empathise with non-disfigured others instead of appeasing, seeking revenge, entering into power struggles or anxious avoidance.

Identifying and challenging beliefs about disfigurement is an important step in psychological intervention. Patients and their relatives will not usually have encountered disfigurement until it has happened to them or someone close to them. Prevailing individual and collective beliefs about appearance help to determine how the individual thinks about their future. Parents, teachers or health professionals may share common beliefs concerning the importance of looking good that it is useful to re-examine following injury.

Aspects of internal shame to review with client following a burn injury are listed below.

1 Identify feelings about the disfigurement.
2 Explore possible reasons behind those feelings (personal and cultural values, enacted stigma, absence of successful role models, safety behaviours, external pressure to seek more surgery, stigmatising remarks, magnification of disfigurement, minimisation of uninjured body, adverts for beauty treatments and cosmetic surgery).
3 Evaluate positive and negative impact of those feelings on quality of life (to enhance motivation to develop a different approach).

4 Challenge general beliefs about disfigurement.
5 Distinguish beliefs about physical appearance from personal worth.
6 Understand how disfigurement affects social interaction.
7 Understand what makes physical appearance psychologically important.
8 Practise self-talk that is more self-enhancing and powerful, and therefore less helpless, self-blaming, self-attacking.
9 Learn about practical tools for putting client and other people at ease with a disfigurement.

Timing and level of psychosocial interventions

Many psychological interventions will be psycho-educational, concentrating on changing automatic thoughts and skills development. Modification of negative beliefs soon follows the appearance of disconfirming evidence. Further brief interventions may be sought to support developmental transitions, for example, starting school, job interviews, entering employment, forming sexual relationships, establishing new social networks. Brief self-help materials can produce significant decreases in social anxiety and depression without any direct therapeutic contact (Newell & Clarke, 2000). Any stigma attached to referral for psychological therapy can be minimised by the provision of care in a multidisciplinary setting, and by emphasising the skills component of intervention, for example, 'growing your self-confidence', 'learning how people who look "different" get a positive response from people'.

Some clients will have so little confidence in new, more adaptive schemas that they will question the relevance and similarity of role models with disfigurements, discount evidence that contradicts negative self-schema, and feel no motivation to achieve goals of which they might otherwise be capable due to a strong expectation of failure. Therapy in such cases produces stronger negative affects and a greater amount and proportion of time is needed to target conditional and core beliefs and establish a therapeutic alliance.

Disfigurement-focused intervention may not take place until some time after injury because a newly disfigured person may be in a state of shock and looking for support. An associated issue is that disfigurement may be experienced as a permanent symbol or reminder of a traumatic event (injury, surgery, dressings) or associated feelings of grief, helplessness, anger or degradation. Although post-traumatic stress disorder (PTSD) is a recognised complication of recovery from burn injury, its relationship with disfigurement is unclear. Baur, Hardy and Van Dorsten (1998), reviewing the literature on PTSD following burn injury, conclude that there is no relationship between total burn surface area and PTSD. Patients' appraisals of their coping resources, both in terms of individual factors and social support, are better predictors of good outcome.

The disfigurement may be usefully understood as one of several post-trauma factors that are subject to appraisal and reappraisal of personal meaning and its impact such as anxiety, anger, flashbacks. Balanced, informed discussion of the importance of physical appearance helps patients to make realistic plans for coping. Use of the REACH OUT toolkit can assist clients to 'ground' themselves in the present, carry out meaningful daily activities and terminate episodes of rumination. Effective intervention for body shame can assist with the containment, re-exposure and re-framing components of intervention for post-traumatic stress disorder. Working with internal body shame is thus focused on developing self-acceptance, compassion to the self and reducing in self-devaluations.

Making psychosocial rehabilitation after burns injuries part of hospital care

Health professionals can facilitate self-management of appearance-related issues as part of routine inpatient and outpatient care. Some professionals will be able to offer comprehensive psychological intervention themselves throughout the patient's medical care. At a minimum, the professional team needs to know how to:

- Sensitively initiate discussion of appearance-related issues.
- Equip patients with information about their condition, its treatments and the range of outcomes.
- Assist patients with developing a long and a short answer to questions about their disfigurement that is consistent with the patient's unique interpersonal style.
- Suggest three effective strategies for dealing with other people's staring.
- Identify a source of additional psychosocial support, for example, NHS counsellor, Changing Faces Client Service.

Finding out more about the cause of disfigurement, and the scope and limitations of medical treatment, as well as differing treatment goals, can facilitate self-acceptance and an ability to put medical interventions in perspective. A forum for exploring and sharing feelings of fear, anger and grief for lost looks is an essential prerequisite for skills-based interventions. Contact with role models is also useful, whether via personal contact with a former patient, or in groups or a video library.

Professionals should be reactive in matching the kind of support offered to client need. Since medical variables do not predict the psychosocial impact of disfigurement, it is more effective to use a few routine questions of obvious relevance to daily life that allow the patient to take the lead in discussing the emotional sequelae of disfigurement. A brief method of raising appearance-related issues in a routine outpatient consultation starts towards the end of assessment with recognising the change in appearance and asking how this in particular has affected everyday life. If the patient, or their family, identifies no impact they can be asked to confirm that there is nothing they feel less comfortable about doing because of how they look now, and what advice they would offer others with regard to intrusive staring from others. The most effective way of exploring social interaction difficulties is to ask for examples in relevant settings, for example, work/school/in public places. Where restrictions and difficulties in lifestyle are reported, staff can make clear their attention is on the common social aspects of living with disfigurement, not on a few patients' pathological failure to cope.

Pre-school children are not generally troubled by variations in appearance, especially if their natural curiosity brings an assured, informative response. References to a child's disfigurement should be accompanied by reference to all their physical characteristics. Bringing their attention to other people around them, noticing the ways in which they are not like each other, for example, height, build, hair colour, eye colour, freckles and birthmarks, is a method of sharing and enjoying diversity. Time spent with any child provides positive attention and feedback, and enables parents to get to know the child who 'looks so different now'. Children do pick up on adults' uncertainty and anxiety so teachers, playworkers and extended family members all make important contributions to learning how to deal with comments, staring and intrusive personal questions (Frances, 2000).

Routine discussion of appearance-related issues lets patients know that staff offer interest and expertise in this aspect of disfigurement, and normalises feelings of body shame. With children it is useful to say to the family, 'sometimes children we see here tell us they are being teased or bullied at school so I ask everyone if that is happening to them. If it does I think it is important for everyone concerned that you tell us or contact . . . . . ., their address is in . . . . . .'

Skin camouflage is one of many ways in which people with a disfigurement influence the impression they make on others. Camouflage alone cannot increase self-confidence, particularly if it is used to avoid the need to develop a coping repertoire or supports the belief that social acceptance is dependent on concealment. Indeed, concealment as a coping strategy may reinforce internal body shame by magnifying preoccupation with the perceived flaw (Smart & Wegner, 1999).

All health professionals will be better able to support someone when they see their scars for the first time if they can refer to a range of options for managing disfigurement at this early stage. Keeping appearance-related issues on the agenda supports the patient's own coping response of introspection, emotional ventilation and trying out new behaviours. To do this professionals need to develop tools for discussing disfigurement in a realistic, constructive manner. Sensitive use of language sets the scene for viewing disfigurement as a challenge which no one would choose but which does not have to put an end to all hopes and ambitions for the future. The emotional atmosphere and patterns of communication created in the hospital setting have specific implications for people facing a major disruption to self-confidence and social poise. Medical terms such as 'deformity', and 'defect', or value-judgements such as 'unattractive' or 'ugly', are less suitable than phrases such as 'the change in your appearance', 'facial difference', 'unusual/distinctive appearance' and 'the scars on your arm'. Children and parents/carers/teachers should be encouraged to agree on a consistent and non-evaluative descriptor that allows them to discuss appearance-related concerns openly.

Health professionals can facilitate the development of enhanced social skills by helping patients to monitor social interaction post-injury and asking 'feed-forward' questions. These offer the opportunity to troubleshoot, sketch out potential strategies and to synthesise observations of changes in social interaction post-injury. These are not the sole prerogative of psychosocial specialists or formal interviews. Nurses can use episodes of personal care or wound care to ask questions such as: 'Have you thought what you might say if someone asks you what's happened to your face?'

Professionals, like patients, need to feel they can be optimistic about successful psychosocial management in order to avoid therapeutic nihilism, over-reliance on physical solutions or victim-blaming. Recognising our own reactions and beliefs about appearance helps us to support patients and relatives better. While professionals will not have all the answers, they can offer support, encouragement and suggestions in a relationship based on respect and concern for the patient.

Cues from staff are also important for family members when they first see their loved one's disfigurement. Burns survivors start practising self-presentation to laypeople with their friends and family. Children, in particular, look to their adult carers to model use of social skills. Quality of social support is an important predictor of the emotional outcome of disfigurement, so many people in the patient's social network, for example, teachers, grandparents and friends should be involved.

Conclusion

Body disfigurements due to burns can set the stage for major problems in body shame that will affect mental state, coping behaviours and social relationships. Moreover, it may be the shame experiences that influences adjustment, as it is now known that adjustment is not predicted from the degree of disfigurement alone. Recognising and understanding the mechanisms of body shame is therefore important in assessing and helping people adjust to these traumas. Treatment approaches based on enhancing social skills and cognitive-behavioural therapy for appearance-related distress have demonstrated their potential benefit to those who feel ashamed of a disfigurement. There is evidence to challenge professionals' beliefs that 'it is only a minor disfigurement' or 'there is nothing to be done once surgery is finished'.

Specific reductions in social anxiety, depression and social avoidance have been reported. There have not yet been enough trials of treatments, or treatment components, to say whom this self-management approach works best or least for.

Lay-led organisations can develop a framework that includes roles for health professionals and people drawn from the client group. This integrated approach is less stigmatising for patients and highly applicable to health care settings that promote behaviour change via coping skills training. The underlying philosophy of this approach is that managing the problems of enacted stigma described by Macgregor (1974) will impact on internal shame.

Disfigurement is primarily an attitudinal disability, one that is only just beginning to be included in Disability Awareness training. The Changing Faces approach described in this chapter is heavily influenced by a cultural context in which assertiveness is valued, disfigurement is medicalised and legislation is set up to create equal opportunities.

Note

In addition to direct work with individuals with any disfiguring medical condition (via self-help booklets, small groupwork and telephone counselling), Changing Faces works to promote better health care and to raise public awareness. The authors can be contacted at 1–2 Junction Mews, London, W2 1PN. E-mail: info@changingfaces.co.uk

References

Baur, K.M., Hardy, P.E. & Van Dorsten, B. (1998) Post-traumatic stress disorders in burn populations: A critical review of the literature. *Journal of Burn Care and Rehabilitation*, 19 (3), 230–240.

Bradbury, E. (1996) *Counselling People with Disfigurement*. Leicester: British Psychological Society Books.

Bull, R. & Rumsey, N. (1988) *The Social Psychology of Facial Appearance*. New York: Springer Verlag.

Cochrane, V.M. & Slade, P. (1999) Appraisal and coping in adults with cleft lip: Associations with well-being and anxiety. *British Journal of Medical Psychology*, 72, 485–503.

Frances, J. (2000) Supporting a child who has a disfigurement. *Practical Pre-school*, 24.

Gilbert, P., Pehl, J. & Allan, S. (1994) The phenomenology of shame and guilt: An empirical investigation. *British Journal of Medical Psychology*, 67, 23–36.

Kent, G. (2000) Understanding the experiences of people with disfigurements: An integration of four models of social and psychological functioning. *Psychology Health and Medicine*, 5 (2), 117–129.

Kleve, L. & Robinson, E. (1999) A survey of psychological need amongst adult burn-injured patients. *Burns*, 25, 575–579.

Macgregor, F. (1974) *Transformation and Identity: The Face and Plastic Surgery*. New York: Quadrangle/The New York Times Book Company.

National Burn Care Review Committee Report (2001) Standards and strategy for burns care: A review of burns care in the British Isles.

Newell, R. & Clarke, M. (2000) Evaluation of a self-help leaflet in treatment of social difficulties following facial disfigurement. *International Journal of Nursing Studies*, 37, 381–388.

Newell, R. & Marks, I. (2000) Phobic nature of social difficulty in facially disfigured people. *British Journal of Psychiatry*, 176, 176–181.

Noar, J. (1991) Questionnaire survey of attitudes and concerns of patients with cleft lip and palate and their parents. *Cleft Palate–Craniofacial Journal*, 28 (3), 279–284.

Partridge J. (1994) *Changing Faces: The Challenge of Facial Disfigurement*. London: Penguin Books.

Partridge, J., Rumsey, N. & Robinson, E. (1997) An evaluation of a pilot disfigurement support unit. Report for the Nuffield Provincial Hospitals Trust.

Robinson, E., Rumsey, N. & Partridge J. (1996) An evaluation of the impact of social interaction skills training for facially disfigured people. *British Journal of Plastic Surgery*, 1 (49), 281–289.

Rubinow, D., Peck, G., Squillace, B. & Gnatt, R. (1987) Reduced anxiety and depression in cystic acne patients after successful treatment with oral isotretinoin. *Journal of the American Academy of Dermatology*, 17, 25–32.

Rumsey, N., Bull, R. & Gahagen, D. (1982) The effect of facial disfigurement on the proxemic behaviour of the general public. *Journal of Applied Social Psychology*, 12 (2), 137–150.

Rumsey, N., Bull, R. & Gahagen, D. (1986) A preliminary study of the effects of social skills training for improving the quality of social interaction for the facially disfigured. *Social Behaviour*, 1, 143–145.

Smart, L. & Wegner, D.M. (1999) Covering up what can't be seen: Concealable stigma and mental control. *Journal of Personality and Social Psychology*, 77 (3), 474–486.

Strenta, F. & Kleck, R. (1985) Physical disability and the attribution dilemma: Perceiving the causes of social behaviour. *Journal of Social and Clinical Psychology*, 3, 129–142.

Tarrier, N. (1995) Psychological morbidity in adult burns patients: Prevalence and treatment. *Journal of Mental Health*, 1, 51–62.

Wallace, L. & Lees, J. (1988) A psychological follow-up study of adult patients discharged from a British burn unit. *Burns*, 14 (1), 39–45.

Chapter 9

Body shame in children who have bowel disorders

Ann-Sophie Ekströmer

Introduction

As discussed by many authors in this volume, body shame can have major impacts on the development of self-esteem, social behaviour and vulnerability to psychological problems (Gilbert, Chapter 1, this volume). This chapter explores the special problems associated with bowel diseases in children and adolescents and some of psychological interventions for helping children adjust to their condition.

In my work as an art therapist and cognitive psychotherapist at The Astrid Lindgren Children's Hospital in Stockholm, I work with children with different intestinal diseases. Living with such a disease is accompanied by purely practical as well as psychological difficulties. Patients may have to plan their day around visits to the toilet and always be aware of where the nearest toilet is. This limits their spontaneity and freedom. A colostomy bag might break in the middle of a wild and wonderful game – a catastrophic event for a child.

Some have an irritable bowel or are born with a malformation of the intestine (atresia, for example). When born with a malformation it causes problems when the patient must empty the bowel. It may also lead to problems with leaking or makes it necessary to have a stoma. However, all do not need a colostomy performed. To avoid constipation, you can have a Malone operation; an opening is made in the appendix so that the colon can be irrigated with top-water in an antigrade fashion.

Not only may a child fear the discovery of their 'disfigurement' and fear some unplanned event (e.g., not being able to reach the toilet or a bag breaking) but diseases associated with a colostomy can present special problems in self-consciousness of how one *smells* and desires to hide the smell. Indeed, the fear of the smell being detected is a common reason for social anxiety and social avoidance. As Lazare (1987) has pointed out, diseases that involve loss of control of body functions and bodily discharges are associated with the emotion of disgust. Disgust is an affect intimately linked to avoidance and fear of contamination in observers and thus it is understandable that if one sees oneself as a source of disgust then this would be a powerful source for the experience of shame (Miller, 1997). In children, this can focus on fear of being seen as smelly, dirty or disgusting resulting in social exclusion/ostracism by peers and playmates. In older adolescents the fear can be especially focused on 'self as sexually undesirable'.

There are various techniques for helping young people cope with shame associated with bowel disorders. Some of these overlap with other therapies designed to help people with body shame and social anxiety as depicted by other authors to this volume. These may involve eliciting and changing key negative cognitions (e.g., 'I will be rejected'; 'I am unlovable'; 'I am worthless'), working through distress and feelings of loss, working with feelings of being different to others and being ostracised, and reducing safety and defensive behaviours where they exacerbate problems. However, young children may be unable to articulate clearly their feelings and thoughts about themselves, or how they think others see them. For these children, communication of their feelings can be aided with painting and play therapies. Sharing experiences with other sufferers can also help children feel less isolated and find ways to cope with shame.

Developmental stages

Clinicians should be aware that children and adolescents will be at different stages of the cognitive-emotional developmental (Piaget, 1951) and this will impact on how they experience their colostomy or disorder and hence any therapy chosen and conducted. For example, small children trust their mothers to be always on hand with nappies, care and attention. If their bowel is not hurting, children may not see themselves as different from others. If children understand that they have an illness, they may believe that mummy, daddy or the doctor is going to help them become well one day.

Gradually, children develop increasing awareness of 'self as a social object' (Lewis, 1992). When children understand that they have a problem, which others do not have (e.g., is different from mum, dad or siblings), their ability to handle this may depend on their basic sense of attachment security and the way their parents are able to support them. Indeed, how the parents cope with the problem (e.g., with openness and care, or with their own shame or disgust difficulties) can impact on their children's adjustment. Children are likely to subtly internalise the attitudes of their parents to their disorder, especially in the transition to increasing self-management. For this reason, when working with younger children, it can be important to involve the whole family who may need support and help in coping with their own feelings and cognitions, and in how they interact with their children and teach them to self-manage. Clinicians will be sensitive to potential shaming signals in family discourses and problems of neglect, overprotection or unrealistic expectations.

The family remain a key source of support as children make the transition into increasing peer group interactions. They will help their children cope with these interactions and the increasing awareness of difference to other children and the possible rejecting behaviours of other children. Such comparisons and experiences can be a source of sadness, anxiety and anger. Unlike within the family, the relationships with peers can be marked by having 'a secret'; that is a concealable stigma (see Gilbert, Chapter 1, this volume) with increasing concerns of something happening (e.g., smell detected or bag leaking) that can lead to detection. Such fears are common as, for example, voiced by one of my six-year-old patients who whispers, 'If Carl knew that I have a bag on my stomach he would not like me.' As she says this, her body collapses in a shame-like posture.

Internal and external shame

As noted by Gilbert (Chapter 1, this volume), shame can be external or internal according to the different types of self-other evaluations and different types of defensive or safety behaviours. External shame is focused on thoughts about what others may think about the self, and feelings are related to felt stigma and social rejection. Anything to do with the functioning of the bowel is usually private (especially in Western societies). Hence, although visits to the toilet are normal and mark the activity as a private one, they should not be heard or noticed and not too often. Hence, the intrusion into the public domain of this aspect of one's functioning via sounds, smell and needs to use the toilet at a moment's notice can ignite strong fears of what others will think about the self. The child may fear that others will: 'laugh at me'; 'they are not going to want someone like me joining in their game'; or 'you can't play with someone like me who has a bag'. There may be focused attention on what they think others can hear or smell and see themselves as the focus of others' attention and become preoccupied with their attention: 'They are all looking every time I go to the toilet'; 'Everyone can hear when my guts are rumbling and they can smell my bag'; 'I'll never get a boy/girlfriend with a bowel like mine'; or 'They all think I'm disgusting'.

Thoughts and preoccupation with what others perceive about the self, fear of negative evaluations and how this affects safety and defensive behaviours has been well described for social anxiety (Clark & Wells, 1995) and other forms of disfigurement (Kent & Thompson, Chapter 5, this volume). The same processes are prominent for these children and can lead to a host of defensive and safety behaviours such as social avoidance and disengagement, and efforts to hide their disorder, leading children to isolate themselves and other shame-avoidant behaviours. Such fears may have a significant impact on the ability of the child to feel free to play or engage in other peer interactions with knock-on effects on social development.

While some children's main difficulties are in dealing with and avoiding external shame (or being shamed), for others the problems is more internalised. In these cases children have internalised highly negative beliefs and feelings about themselves in response to the colostomy or bowel disease. Internal shame may manifest as feelings of being flawed and abnormal. Internal shame can manifest as a complete degrading of self. This makes it difficult to like one's own body and especially one's 'tummy'. Internal shame can be focused (e.g., on the colostomy) and it may become a 'hated' part of the self, a part that contaminates 'the self'. This is especially so if children feels powerless when unable to control their bowels. In some cases children are more focused on how to 'get rid' of the problem than on self-management.

Internal shame can become globalised. In this case children may come to feel bad about themselves in general with low self-esteem and various beliefs that they are (globally) unlovable, inferior or disgusting. In severe cases children may be unable to see anything good about themselves and feel it would be better if they did not exist. Globalised internal shame is likely to be associated with depression.

Hence, clinicians should assess carefully: (1) what children think others think about them; (2) how they evaluate themselves; and (3) whether their focus is specific, and on the colostomy or disorder, or more globalised and on the sense of 'whole self'. According to the nature of these evaluations, clinicians can then explore safety and defensive behaviours; those behaviours used to avoid episodes of potential shame. In this context, avoidance may be on avoiding social encounters where others may be shaming and rejecting and/or avoiding feelings of shame.

Strategies to avoid shame

As other authors to this volume note, various forms of body disfigurements are linked to psychological distress and psychopathology via the special meanings the person gives to their body difficulty. The level of dysfunction is not always a good guide to the level of distress and different children adjust in different ways. Personal meanings also affect coping behaviours. Robin, who is seven years old, loves to play football with the boys in the neighbourhood. Then, in the middle of the football game, when he least wants it, he gets an urgent need to empty his bowels. He has come up with a solution: he tells his friends that he has to run home and ask his mum when food will be ready. While at home he goes to the toilet, and he can then run back and say that the food was not ready, his friends hopefully being none the wiser about his real reason for leaving the game.

Sixteen-year-old Cecilia frequently left school during the day with the excuse that she had a bad headache. When she got home, she slumped on the settee and allowed herself to be absorbed by TV soaps in an attempt to get away from her painful reality. In the security of her home, it did not matter if her bowels made a noise or created a smell. She found it easier to mix with people she did not know very well. Brief and superficial encounters reduced the risk of exposure. Cecilia used the strategy of 'better safe than sorry', and this was manifest in both her thinking and behaviour (Gilbert, 1998a).

Many children put a lot of extra effort into their appearance and clothes. No one must be allowed to discover that they are different or the nature of the problems (i.e., it must remain a *concealable* stigma). When they are unable to fully control their bowels, they may become preoccupied with those aspects of their lives over which they are able to exercise control, such as cleanliness and clothes. They may wash excessively and be always checking that they do not smell. Indeed, in some children checking behaviour can become excessive and have obsessional-like qualities.

There are also those children who lack the energy or will to care that they are leaking or smell. This is a form of self-neglect that can have serious consequences on their social relationships. For these children, it is important to ascertain if this self-neglect is due to feeling too depressed or hopeless to bother or because they are immature. Yet other children may deal with shame by denial. These children may need help to sensitively confront the problems and learn how to self-manage.

For some children, a colostomy or bowel disorder is weaved into the dynamics of child–parent interaction. For example, there may be conflict between the child and parent on changing clothes. Such behaviours can become a focus for conflicts within the relationship. A 13-year-old boy managed to create contact with his mother in this negative way. He felt he deserved more sympathy and pity because of his bowel disease and often acted to try to elicit this behaviour from her. For example, he would ask her to tie his shoelaces for him even though he was perfectly capable of tying his own. If she did not make sure he changed his clothes, he felt that it was her fault if he was smelly and evidence of not caring enough.

Anger at having the disease can be played out in complex family dynamics that affect attachment behaviour. High levels of anger and blaming others (i.e., acting from a sense of humiliation; Gilbert, Chapter 1, this volume) may protect the child from shame to some extent but have serious effects on family and social relationships.

The identification of shame

Before children can be helped to handle their feelings of shame, they will often need to learn to identify the shame affect. When children notice that they are different from other children, they may become withdrawn and start to feel unsure of the feelings of others and such uncertainty may continue throughout childhood. Teenagers may find it helpful to give the shame affect its proper name to make it possible to talk about it. Both young children and teenagers may perceive themselves to be 'all wrong', flawed, embarrassing, unsuccessful and unattractive. There are many ways that clinicians can begin the process of helping children recognise and learn to cope with their complex feelings and fears about their disease. Art therapy can play a key role.

Art therapy

Children find it perfectly natural to express themselves in images. There are two different kinds of image creation: the outer, descriptive picture, the diagrammatic image, which may be an aid to communication. The inner picture contains subconscious material that the person creating the picture may not be aware of but is implicit in the picture. This is called the embodied image (Schawarien, 1992). Embodiment represents authentic emotions expressed through pictures. Embodiment occurs when an emotion and an image are united. Thus, one does not make an image of an emotion, one inhabits an emotion. The therapist often does not ask directly about these images. The art therapist is there, sharing the experience. The subconscious material that is important to the patient will usually keep turning up in the descriptive pictures until its meaning becomes clear and can be talked about. Hence, the art therapist can use pictures as a form of journey and self-discovery.

The materials used in art therapy are important. The use of creative media provides opportunities for a variety of sensual experiences. Visual, auditory and emotional impressions are mixed or succeed each other in the patients' use of the art materials. The materials can be experienced as attractive or repulsive, ordered or chaotic. They may flow freely or be firmly controlled. There is the sensuality and unpredictability of water colours, the strength of the oil pastels and the transience of the chalk pastels. It can be heard and felt in the body when the crayon is pulled across the paper. Water colours give way to the fat in the oil pastels. The stars can sparkle in the deep-blue sky by painting with water colour over the crayon.

Clay may be black, yellow or white. It can be soft and pliable or firm and resistant. It can be hit or cut. It can be held against the cheek, as a soft, beautiful, smooth surface. How the art media are handled and experienced gives rise to feelings. There may be strong feelings of joy, or anger, which to start with were rather vague, but may break through with full force and the session continues. The affects and emotions which surface in connection with the creation of images feed information to the cognitive system to be processed and integrated in the self-system. Interaction between the affects and the cognitive mechanisms influence the child's awareness, perception of and ability to work through these experiences. By exploring how thoughts and emotions influence each other and actions, it becomes possible to exchange dysfunctional patterns for more functional ones.

When engaged in this kind of therapy (like other therapies), tuning in to the affect is important (Stern, 1985). The ability to 'tune in' to the feelings in their children makes it possible for mothers and children to mutually share affects. If mothers identify wrongly with their children's emotional state, the children may find it difficult to comprehend or trust their own feelings. Similarly, this tuning in to the children's feelings, and an ability to match the rhythm, intensity and duration of the way in which these feelings are expressed, must be present in the patient–therapist relationship (Stern, 1985). For the art therapist, this requires a sensitivity to the changing flow of feelings and thoughts as the art and creative work unfolds.

Little Philippa who is seven years old and has recently undergone a bowel operation. She enters the art therapy room quietly but with dogged determination. She whispers that she wants to work with clay. The clay has first to be hit or bashed in order to remove any air bubbles. Philippa bashes the lump of clay softly on to the table. 'I think you have to do that a bit harder,' I say and pick up another lump. I bash it on to the table following Philippa's rhythm. Philippa hits the clay steadily, harder and harder with increasing rage, until she furiously exclaims: 'I get so angry when everyone always asks about my tummy!' In this way, she is able to verbalise her feelings and thus become more aware of them.

The 'tuning in' is a link to the verbal self (Stern, 1985). After a few Socratic questions, such as, 'Why do you think they ask these questions? Or 'Why do you think they have this interest in your tummy?' Philippa is able to consider that those asking the questions might be motivated by concern for her and not mere curiosity. She is thus enabled to reply in a way that helps her to feel less exposed or vulnerable.

Creative activities can be a powerful way to bring out shame affect, to get behind the concealing efforts of the child. For example as the child draws, the figure taking shape on the paper is often alone. It can be an animal, a plant or a human being. The figure may even have the 'collapsed body' so typical of the shame affect's body language. If this becomes an embodied image, the child may simultaneously be showing this affect. Through creative media work, one can enable different affects to appear and this makes it possible to talk about what is happening at that moment in the room. In art therapy, it is generally more common that one discusses something which has already happened in a way, which resembles the cognitive therapy *in vivo* technique. The child can, within the secure relationship of the art therapy room, expose herself to emotions, memories and experiences. The creative media work can result in the child having to confront issues head on (Reynolds, 1999). The child might think: 'I am no good at drawing'; 'I must paint nicely'; 'I ought not to be sad, I'd better paint something cheerful'. These ideas can, with the help of cognitive intervention, be expressed in words and transformed into more functional patterns.

By allowing children to work freely and to choose their own materials, one can gain information about his/her moods, feelings and fears. Sad and shy children will often choose coloured pencils or lead pencils rather than paints that flow freely over the paper. It is not possible to fully control runny paint. It therefore feels much safer using coloured pencils that stay in their place. Nor do pencils awaken as many emotions and by using them the child can keep the affect at bay. A child with intestinal disease and a core belief that 'no one will ever like anyone who has a strange bowel', will not produce a picture that gives a very self-confident impression.

When working with children and young people, humour and playfulness is of great importance. It sets an atmosphere that can help the child to find the courage to confront their shame and release it in a playful way. But, as noted above, before this can be done, the shame must be recognised and acknowledged.

It is natural for children to want to draw and paint. Silence, which can sometimes be experienced as painful or embarrassing in verbal-based therapies, can in art therapy be instead filled with creativity. Indeed, at times the pictures are best produced in relative silence, making it possible for the child to sense and become aware of their feelings, affects and thoughts through the picture-making. After that the verbal discussion can begin. With the support of the pictures, the patients can give shape to their negative thoughts and perceptions about themselves and see what these look like. This practice is often calming. Hence, art therapy also gives an opportunity for externalisation as a way to approach internal feelings. For example, it may be much easier to talk about the feelings of the lonely little figure demonstrated in the picture before one can find the courage to talk about oneself. Shame affect and avoidance of painful feelings can be very strong, even for small children. They can look at the picture, which is now outside themselves, and challenge what they see and their negative thoughts about it. This gives them the opportunity to change their schemata or beliefs to more functional ones.

Thus, if art therapy is included in psychotherapy, one can work with emotions and affects through the artistic material. By this means, and at that moment, a strong emotional component is added to the process. A fruitful dialogue can develop between these two forms of therapy (art and cognitive) with their different emphases on emotion and thought, verbal and non-verbal expression.

Separating the self from one's stomach

So then art can offer a medium for exploration and reflection as well as challenge. In regard to helping children change their feelings and thoughts about their disorder, Cognitive and Rational Emotive Therapists have emphasised the importance of distinguishing evaluations about behaviours and aspects of the self from global self-evaluations (Gilbert, Chapter 1, this volume), and this is especially important for shame-based difficulties (Gilbert, 1998b). Some of the children I work with are unable to see themselves as separate from their stomach. When they are playing with friends, they almost feel that other children are playing with a bowel rather than with them as a person and friend. It is important to help these children distinguish themselves as complex, multi-varied persons from their stomachs and to realise that no one is defined purely by their stomach. Children need, for example, to realise that 'I am a girl who likes music' or 'a boy who enjoys ball sports', and that although they have a problem, namely an irritable or deformed bowel, this is only one part of them. Once children have accepted this, and can focus on the positive aspects of themselves, they often start to feel better, although there may still be feelings of anger and injustice and much sadness, which must be allowed to take shape and be shared.

Little Sara, seven years old, was born with an intestine malformation. She often had a stomach ache and was leaking. She had to wear nappies to school. In therapy, Sara wanted to draw an animal that she felt like. It turned out to be a fine little monkey. The monkey liked climbing trees. Sara liked that too. She was pleased with the monkey's face, but the body got rubbed out and redrawn over and over again. However hard she tried, she was not satisfied. The body was too big or too small and the legs were not right. She became more and more unhappy. Finally, we agreed that the monkey did not want to be seen, so it was allowed to sit behind a bush. The monkey's biggest fear was that someone would laugh at it. The monkey looked pleased as it peered cheekily out from behind its bush, and Sara at last looked at it with tenderness.

It is hard to depict a body one cannot really trust. Talking about the monkey enabled us to talk about how Sara felt ashamed of her body and her operation scars. She did not feel certain that she was an appreciated playmate. Sara's belief of herself as 'girl with a strange body' was changed to an understanding of herself as a normal schoolgirl who enjoys drawing and likes dogs. However, she has this problem (her bowel) that other children do not have, and because of it she has operation scars.

Sara demonstrated another important aspect of body shame, that is one can also feel ashamed of the more negative feelings one has to others, especially when others do not appear diseased as one does oneself. It is not surprising that she felt envious of those children who manage their visits to the toilet in two minutes, while she has to start each day spending 45 minutes on the toilet. Nonetheless, she was ashamed of her envious feelings (found them difficult to talk about or admit to) for the girls who had nice, smooth tummies. Hence, therapy can also help children explore their understandable envy and anger with others and come to accept these feelings as normal and not further evidence of an unlovable person. Indeed, helping children process, understand and cope with the negative (especially envy) feelings to others can be an important part of the therapy. These feelings may also emerge in pictures.

On a more practical note, it is beneficial for children if they can be encouraged to find ways to make boring toilet sessions more interesting. Some children like to listen to music. Others enjoy reading: these children often develop notably advanced language skills because they get through so many books. One boy happily played board games in the toilet with his cousins until he was about seven. Another child had their dog for patient and steadfast company.

Helping children challenge their shame-based thinking

For children who expect rejection, rather than focus on evidence for and evidence against such a belief, as in standard cognitive therapy, it may be useful to focus first on using their own thoughts about someone in their position. One might ask children: 'If you had a friend with a problem like yours, would you play with him?' and 'what would you say to that friend?' Children usually answer that they would like to comfort the friend; and that of course one can play with him or her. Sometimes children are surprised at how easily they can understand other children, since they imagine that others have such difficulties in understanding them. From here it may be possible to help the child consider that others might think about them in the same way. Of course children can be very insensitive and cruel to each other so it is important for children to also learn how to think about and cope with rejection.

A not uncommon problem for children who have a sense of shame about the self is fantasies about wanting to be someone else. Jenny, a six-year-old girl was very sad one day and told me that she wanted to be a different girl. Instead of Jenny, she wanted her name to be Sophie. Sophie would not have a bag on her tummy.

THERAPIST: So this evening when mummy and daddy are eating dinner it will be Sophie sitting there instead?
JENNY: Yes. Then they'd get rid of everything. Bags and things like that.
THERAPIST: I wonder what they would think of that?
JENNY: Great to have a girl who is not ill.
THERAPIST: Would they think about Jenny?
JENNY: Perhaps a little [*said sadly and a little hesitantly*].
THERAPIST: I think mummy and daddy would miss their Jenny. I don't think they want any other girl. I'm sure they want their own Jenny, bags and all. Let's ask mummy.

Mummy was fetched from the waiting room and asked. With tears in her eyes she explained to Jenny that she could not possibly think of having a different girl. If parents are successful in giving their children a safe base, and a sense of very secure attachment to the 'child as they are', the children will be better able to cope with their bowel problems. It can also be noted that for Jenny and her mother, this sharing of a sadness and grief was a powerful emotional experience for both of them. Such emotional explorations and experiences that can be facilitated by therapy can have profound effects on shame and the acceptance of oneself.

Sharing experiences with someone else with similar difficulties

Sharing experiences with others who have similar experiences and health problems can be very helpful, although not always (Buunk & Gibbons, 1997) and thus needs careful consideration. However, one way it can help is to break through feelings of isolation. Jenny believed, just like Emma, another girl with a colostomy, that she was alone in the world with her problem. I asked the girls if they would like to meet each other, which they did.

When Emma and Jenny met for the first time, they observed each other with both curiosity and shyness. After a little warm-up chat, they started to compare their experiences of the hospital. Both had undergone several operations. Both of them were used to injections and anaesthetics. Then they were able to talk about their bags.

JENNY: I've had a bag for hundreds of years [*said with a sigh*].
EMMA: Me too [*identifying with this sentiment immediately*].

They were able to talk about how boring it is always to have to spend so much time looking after one's bowel instead of playing. At last! Someone who really understood. I asked if any of their friends knew that they had these bags. At playschool the other children knew about it, but now, in primary school, it was much harder to say anything. Especially to the boys. Some friends who they really trusted could be told. Both of them had friends who knew about their problem and who often played with them. But the anxiety that they might be teased and laughed at was still there. *Together* they formulated what they might say to another child with a colostomy bag. They decided on: 'It doesn't matter if you have a bag, let's just play as usual.' After an hour of talking, the girls could not really concentrate on their paintings. They were so excited at having met each other that they had to go out and jump about in the corridor for a while: when one is little one cannot talk about problems the whole time. When they were playing ordinary games with each other, they agreed that they were just like any other girls. While the girls were talking, the two mothers also had the opportunity to share their experiences over a cup of coffee. Their excitement was no less than the girls.

Advising the school

It is important that the school is informed about these problems, especially where younger children are concerned, so that teachers can look out for any signs of them being bullied or emotional problems emerging. If the other children are given clear and careful explanations of the problems faced by those with intestinal disease, they can more readily understand how important it is to be kind and considerate. It is, however, never certain that teasing will not occur. The patients' self-esteem must be strengthened to help them cope if these situations arise, have learnt social skills to cope and if possible have someone at school to confide in.

Psychosomatic bowel problems: A case example

Pychosocial factors, especially when they constitute 'stresses', can interact with a number of bowel diseases. When dealing with more psychosomatic bowel problems, as for example 'irritable colon', it is useful to examine in which situations the bowel reacts. Patients suffering from psychosomatic illnesses often find it difficult to create symbols for their emotions or to describe them in words, and they may have little ability to work through their experiences in an imaginative way. They may find it hard to distinguish and name emotions such as joy, sadness, fear or anger. They may find it easier to describe how they act in practical ways, rather than how they feel. It is easier to describe the external rather than the internal world. The creation of pictures or clay models provides opportunities for patients to talk about their feelings through the art. This is easier to do for a person with a psychosomatic bowel disorder, who may easily get bogged down trying to explain where in the body or bowel the pain is located. Below I outline various interventions used to help a 16-year old (Cecilia noted above) who was suffering from an irritable colon.

In addition to her bowel disease, Cecilia had a generalised inferiority complex and strong feelings of shame. She coped by withdrawing to the television. She felt that her problem was worse than anyone else's as 'it had to do with poo'. She was also ashamed at having to go to a therapist. To tell anyone about her bowel problems felt impossible. Her problem had started two years earlier when her parents got divorced. At the beginning of therapy, she was often in pain and had to go to the toilet five to seven times a day. She was not able to find ways to express her sadness, anger and disappointment and as a result she reacted in a psychosomatic way, with bowel problems.

Her automatic thoughts were: 'Everyone knows when I'm going to the toilet. No one wants to be friends with someone who smells. God, what am I going to do now, everyone can hear my tummy', and 'I'll end up as a psychiatric case!' Core beliefs included: 'If they know that I have this kind of tummy, they won't like me. You can't get married and have children with a stomach like this'; and 'the only reason I exist is for my parents.' Her conditional belief was: 'I must make my parents happy, otherwise I'm not a good daughter.'

Cecilia chose to work with clay. She was not very used to thinking symbolically; this was obvious from the figures she made. They turned out to be pretty and pleasant, just like herself. As she produced these pastel-coloured little figures, she described how she spent whole days figuring out how to manage so that others don't notice when she goes to the toilet. There was a lot of sadness and anger hidden in her anxious talk.

After some discussion of the advantages and disadvantages, one of Cecilia's early homeworks was to challenge some of her defensive and safety behaviours by telling her best friend about her problems. The friend was very sympathetic and understanding. The worst of Cecilia's fears that a catastrophe would follow such a disclosure reduced when she realised that her friends liked her and that they were not put off by her bowel problem. The personalisation also diminished when she recognised that her friends had other things to think about other than how often she goes to the toilet.

In terms of the family dynamics, Cecilia often became the messenger in the conflicts between her parents. She had difficulties separating her own problems from theirs. This affected her stomach and she immediately developed symptoms. Through the therapy, she learnt to recognise these situations and found alternative ways of dealing with them. She learnt to speak up and made it clear to her parents that she did not want them to talk to her about each other; they respected this. By handing over to her parents the responsibility for solving their own conflicts, she protected herself and her stomach calmed down.

Cecilia was also taught relaxation and imagery exercises through which she could find her own 'safe place' to conjure up whenever she wanted to. Her 'safe place' was a rock by the sea where she could sit and watch the waves and listen to the wind. She also learnt to calm herself down through 'imagination exercises', which she worked out herself.

Gilbert (2000) has noted that when people have very negative and self-attacking thoughts and feelings to the self or aspects of the self, it can be useful to help people replace anger with compassionate feelings. Just as relaxation can act as a counter-affect for anxiety, compassion can act as an alternative and counter-affect to (self-)hostility. Cecilia achieved this through imagery. At first her bowel was seen as a hated part of the self that caused so many problems. However, she gradually changed this imagery and imagined her bowel as a little pink piglet in need of lullabies. She made paintings of it and eventually felt tenderness for her bowel instead of disgust. In this way her belief was altered from 'hated bowel, which causes me so much shame' to 'poor little bowel, I need to take care of it'. It is thus useful to teach people how to challenge their negative shaming thoughts with warmth (Gilbert, 2000).

So Cecilia learnt to use the relaxation exercises and pictures whenever there was a possibility that her bowel would play up. She became more and more accomplished at doing this and both she and her bowel calmed down. After a time she patted her stomach tenderly and declared that she now liked it. Thus, it is possible, through imagery and play, albeit of a serious nature, to change the fantasy that embodies the shame into something outside and separate from the body. This allows the patient to tackle the problems of self-management and acceptance in a different way.

Eventually, Cecilia's little clay animals began to have eyes. They had not had them before 'as they were ashamed and didn't want to see anything that was troublesome'. Gradually, her pictures became more symbolic and mature. They contained less loneliness and more social relations. Cecilia started to reflect upon how she thought and acted in different situations. Ordinary life with friends, school and dance lessons became more and more important and her bowel problems diminished until they finally disappeared.

Conclusion

Bowel disorders in childhood and adolescence can be associated with significant problems in adjustment; one of the most serious being in the form of body shame. This chapter has explored how external shame (fear of what others think and controlling one's social behaviour) and internal shame (relating to self-evaluations and self-directed feelings) can arise. The chapter has also explored the importance of considering the family contexts of shame and various art-based ways of working with shame material in this patient group. As for all therapies, the therapeutic relationship can be key to a successful outcome and this is especially true for body-shame associated with these difficulties. For children, the art medium itself engages them and they can also tolerate and contain distress. It can also offer ways to explore feelings and, in a playful atmosphere with the therapist, the children can consider new coping behaviours. Helping children become more able to face and tolerate shame, reduce unhelpful avoidance and safety behaviours, learn how to deal with rejecting behaviour, and develop more compassionate feelings for the self and the problematic bodily process can all be used to advantage with these children. With help and support, many of these child show remarkable abilities for adjustment and courage.

References

Buunk, B.P. & Gibbons, F.X. (1997) *Health Coping and Well Being*. Mahwah, NJ: Lawrence Erlbaum Associates Inc.

Clark, D.M. & Wells, A. (1995) A cognitive model of social phobia. In R.G. Heimberg, M.R. Liebowitz, D.A. Hope & R.R. Schneier (eds) *Social Phobia: Diagnosis, Assessment and Treatment* (pp.69–93). New York: Guilford Press.

Gilbert, P. (1998a) The evolved basis and adaptive functions of cognitive distortions. *British Journal of Medical Psychology*, 71, 447–463.

Gilbert, P. (1998b) Shame and humiliation in complex cases. In N. Tarrier, G. Haddock & A. Wells (eds) *Treating Complex Cases: The Cognitive Behavioural Approach* (pp.241–271). Chichester: John Wiley & Sons.

Gilbert, P. (2000) Social mentalities: Internal 'social' conflicts and the role of inner warmth and compassion in cognitive therapy. In P. Gilbert & K.G. Bailey (eds) *Genes on the Couch: Explorations in Evolutionary Psychotherapy* (pp.118–150). Hove: Psychology Press.

Lazare, A. (1987) Shame and humiliation in the medical encounter. *Archives of Internal Medicine*, 147, 1653–1658.

Lewis, M. (1992) *Shame: The Exposed Self*. New York: The Free Press.

Miller, W.I. (1997) *The Anatomy of Disgust*. Cambridge, MA: Harvard University Press.

Piaget, J. (1951) *The Origins of Intelligence in Children*. New York: International Universities Press.

Reynolds, F. (1999) Cognitive behavioural counselling of unresolved grief through therapeutic adjustment of tapestry-making. *The Arts of Psychotherapy*, 26 (3), 165–171.

Schawarien, J. (1992) *The Revealing Image*. London: Routledge.

Stern, D. (1985) *The Interpersonal World of the Infant: A View from Psychoanalysis and Developmental Psychology*. New York: Basic Books.

Chapter 10

Prostate cancer and body shame with special regard to sexual functioning

Gabrielle Lodnert

Introduction

Many people can experience a diagnosis of cancer as a stigmatisation in itself (Lazare, 1986). For men with prostate cancer, there is not only fear and anxiety about the disorder, but feelings of stigmatisation and shame can be compounded by the location of the cancer in areas associated with 'lower or dirtier' parts of the body, the loss of sexual functioning and the loss of capacity to regulate basic body functions (e.g., urination). Moreover, treatment for prostate cancer can lead to sexual dysfunction (Paterson, 2000; Schover, 1993) that can be experienced as a form of body shame (see also McKee & Gott, Chapter 3, this volume).

Body shame becomes especially obvious in sexual relationships and during sexual intercourse. Nathanson (1994) suggests that there is no part of adult life that is so linked to shame and pride as our relationship to sexuality. Indeed, for many animals the ability to attract mates and reproduce is a central life task. For many people sexual activity can be an important aspect of intimate relating and self-esteem. To be sexually attractive to others and to be able to function well can create positive feelings in both self and partner (see Gilbert, Chapter 1, this volume) and play a key role in bonding. Feeling sexually undesirable and inadequate in functioning courts negative affects in self and others (Etcoff, 1999). Loss of sexual function as people age can be a source of shame and disrupt relationships (McKee & Gott, Chapter 3, this volume). Moreover, accusations of sexual inadequacy (e.g., being impotent or 'can't get it up') are common shaming taunts in male groups. Hence, sexual difficulties can be seen as threats to the self *and* to intimate relationships. Such threats can activate a number of defences such as anger and social withdrawal (Gilbert, Chapter 1, this volume). When treating prostate cancer, it is therefore important to address the psychological reactions to the disorder and its treatment, especially problems of both external and internal sexual shame.

Prostate cancer

The prostate is a gland, about the size of a walnut, which surrounds the upper part of the urethra immediately below the bladder. It produces a fluid which carries sperm cells in ejaculation. The growth and function of the prostate is dependent on the male sex hormone testosterone, which is produced mostly in the testicles. About 50% of men over the age of 60 have an enlarged prostate gland. This enlargement is usually benign, but can sometimes be a malignant cancer tumour. In Western society prostate cancer is the most common form of cancer in males (Boyle et al., 2001). About one in ten men run the risk of contracting prostate cancer. It is, however, rare before the age of 50. Most cases of prostate cancer are discovered because urinating becomes difficult – the urine flows at a low pressure, it is difficult to begin to urinate and the need to urinate becomes more frequent. The cause of prostate cancer remains unclear, but testosterone is a prerequisite for its occurrence and heredity plays some part. There is no evidence that the illness is infectious or that it can be sexually transmitted.

Methods of discovering and treating prostate cancer have improved during the last few years. Those afflicted by this type of cancer can often be cured and many others can live a good life for many years in spite of their illness, even without treatment but with regular check-ups (Adolfsson, Steineck & Hedlund, 1999). Taking into account the stage of the illness, the age and general state of health of the patient, one tries to find the most suitable treatment for each individual patient. However, many men who are treated for prostate cancer lose, partially or totally, their sexual ability (Fitzpatrick et al., 1998; Helgason et al., 1996). It is therefore important that the man, and preferably also his partner, take part in a discussion as to which treatment he will undergo, as different treatments have different side-effects and these, in turn, can affect their quality of life (Schover, 1993).

There are various ways of treating prostate cancer. One is radiation, the aim of which is to kill the cancer cells. Another is radical prostatectomy, which is an operation where the entire prostate gland and the seminal vesicles are removed, in order to remove all the tumour tissue. Both of these methods frequently result in the loss of capacity to have an erection, as adjacent nerves are very liable to be damaged. Another risk is that they can result in the leakage of urine and excrement, a condition which can be permanent. Another method of treating prostate cancer is hormone treatment. This means that one prevents the production or the effects of testosterone. Unfortunately, a reduction of testosterone also affects sexual desire, which in most cases ceases. This treatment can also cause hot flushes, sweating and a certain degree of breast development. The choice of treatment is, of course, a difficult decision to make at the same time as one is trying to cope with the information that one is suffering from cancer, which has such a strong association with death. This means that the various consequences of treatment are not always taken into account although they may, in the long run, be very tangible (Singer et al., 1991).

Psychological reactions to prostate cancer

In consultations, as well as in psychotherapy sessions, with men who have prostate cancer and with their partners, certain central shame-related themes recur. Some of these are discussed below and elucidated by relevant quotations.

Self-schema and masculinity

Most men who contract prostate cancer change in various ways, including their attitudes towards their bodies, as well as their ideas about, and their conception of, themselves. A common feature is their perception of their physical and mental vulnerability, a subject which they deal with in different ways. While some do not discuss or reflect on their illness, either alone or in the presence of others, others integrate their illness into every part of their lives. For example, patients have said: 'It's only me, my wife and the kids that know about this' (concealment); 'I don't really want to know about my body . . . it's not like it used to be' (avoidance); 'Everybody knows about it, absolutely everything . . . it's best that way' (openness); 'Sure, I talk a lot about it, but never about the side-effects . . .' (selectivity).

Men's experience and conception of their masculinity are commonly affected and some share the idea of feeling crushed, shamed or inadequate. 'Yes, one is a fallen hero, it's as simple as that . . .' 'Maybe one hasn't been enough of a man as one got cancer in the most sacred of places.' 'I'm not that much use these days, you have to make way for the young guys.'

Sometimes men who have prostate cancer admit, more or less openly, to seeing their illness as a punishment. 'You wonder what you have done to deserve this.' 'Hasn't my family had enough problems?' 'I don't know why things have turned out like this. I've always taken care of myself.' 'Do you think this has affected me sexually because I've fooled around a few times?' The theme of punishment for past behaviours can be closely linked to shame in some of these men but as yet this is not a well-researched area.

Relationships

Cancers, like other serious illnesses, have a major impact on relationships and such an impact needs to be considered when treating those with prostate cancer. Thus, it is not only the *personal* meaning and effects of the cancer but also the partner's and couple's meanings that can affect coping. Relationships change, in varying degrees and in different ways, in areas such as role-taking, conflict management and taboos. 'My little wife has to be the strong one now . . .' 'Sure things have changed, now it is me that's the old lady.' 'No, I don't want to fight . . . maybe then she won't want me at all.' 'Neither my wife nor I want to talk about how this is really affecting us.' Shame can be an important reason why the subjects of both the cancer and its effects on the relationship are avoided. Women can be aware of the feelings of shame and pain in their partners and avoid discussion in order not to be hurtful to them or to ignite conflicts.

The couple's sexuality (including sexual initiative, sexual urge, orgasm, fondling, caressing, fantasies and masturbation) is affected, generally for the worse, even in cases where the capacity for erection remains intact. In many cases where men feel impotent and no longer attractive or capable, an explanation for avoidance of intimacy is that they do not want their old image of themselves as lovers and their previous experiences of sexual intercourse to be spoilt. Moreover, having a sexual dysfunction is a harsh reminder that they have cancer. Thus, by avoiding sexual intercourse, they avoid focusing on the cancer and its effects.

There is often some ignorance about this disorder. For some men, it is possible to identify an underlying fear, which seems an unrealistic belief, at a conscious level, that the cancer could be activated and stimulated by sexual intercourse or even that it could be transmitted to the partner via coitus or oral sex.

Partners and wives can be affected in various ways. For example, not only can there be loss or reduction of their own sexual activity but, in men who withdraw, there can be a reduction of physical affection. Some partners can feel 'reflected shame' in that they feel unable to discuss the man's sexual problems, partly from a sense of betrayal (need to keep the secret) but also from a sense of shame. When the partners' experiences are explored, it is sometimes not the loss of the man's sexual function that is perceived as the major problem – it is the consequences of the loss. For example, a partner may believe that prior to the illness, sexual intercourse made the man happier, more active and more benevolent towards his immediate family. They may have seen this as advantageous or as a means of control when they wanted something special for themselves or their children. Some women convey, directly or indirectly, that the result of the cancer is for them *a release* from sexual intercourse. This reaction is, however, closely connected with guilt as they obviously did not want their partners to contract cancer.

Future thinking

Obviously a man's conception of his future is influenced by a diagnosis of prostate cancer, especially when it comes to fears and misgivings, visions, values and hopes. Men can display reduced confidence in themselves and their ability – a feeling that can influence most areas of their lives. While the fear of death can be associated with grief, depression and anxiety, it can also be associated with changing life values. 'Sure one has changed . . . I don't know how long I'll be around.' 'I want to see as much as possible of the grandchildren . . .' Others may put their trust in their doctors and seek to be optimistic. 'The doctors know what they are doing . . . they got rid of my previous problems.' 'There is so much research, so one has to hope . . .' It is not unusual for some men to feel fatalistic, at least from time to time. 'Whatever happens, happens . . .' 'If it's decided, then that's that . . . and you can't change it.' It is possible that fatalism fills the same function as magical thinking in stressful circumstances.

Cognitive sex psychotherapy of shame

Cognitive sex psychotherapy addresses the sexual dysfunctions that can arise in the wake of the cancer and its treatment. It is based on an eclectic foundation and makes use of experience and knowledge from different forms of therapy. This is a consequence of there being no specialised sexual therapy training available for prostate cancer, although special therapeutic interventions are usually required to cope with sexual difficulties however they arise (Bancroft, 1989; O'Donohue & Geer, 1993). The psychotherapy we use is directive, 'here-and-now' oriented, focused on dysfunctional beliefs and behaviours, the inner dialogue and external problems, and seeks possible practical solutions. It is important that the client/couple, at an early stage, are helped to make clear their problems in order to make therapeutic interventions possible. The therapist strives to establish an open, non-confrontational relationship with the client/couple. In general, the treatment process is characterised by co-operation between two 'research workers' (the clients and the therapist) who put forward various hypotheses which, after a practical trial (e.g., homework), are either accepted or rejected. This is a form of collaborative empiricism (Beck et al., 1979).

As this kind of therapy often involves working with a couple, cognitive sex psychotherapy has been considerably influenced by John Bowlby's attachment theory, which is based on the idea of the 'affectionate bond' or 'attachment' (Bowlby, 1969–1980). An important part of this theory is that children are biologically programmed to seek and strive for closeness from their attachment person and that attachment behaviour is a lifelong process. The attachment pattern, which one finds in children, can also be seen in adults, as our attitude to close relationships seems to be relatively stable. This has been shown by, among others, West and Sheldon-Keller (1994) and Collins and Read (1990). Hazan and Shaver (1987) have shown that there is a concordance between attachment patterns with early, important attachment persons and those one has with one's partner. This is due to the fact that, at an early stage, a child develops internal working models (IWMs) of self and others. The constructive aspect of IWMs is that they work as a dynamic process and are active throughout life. In other words, major life events, like a prostate cancer, can impact on people's IWMs of their attachment relationships.

A recurring clinical observation when working with sexual shame problems is that they involve a fear of being physically and/or psychologically vulnerable. A common theme is being less desirable to partners which disrupts or threatens attachments. This fear can lead people, directly or indirectly, to distance themselves out of shame (forms of safety behaviours or damage limitation behaviours; Gilbert, Chapter 1, this volume). This can occur even when it seems possible to establish a sexual and emotional relationship with a deeper dimension. A prerequisite for developing a sexual and emotional relationship in the wake of prostate cancer is a certain degree of emotional availability which, in itself, involves an element of examination of negative thoughts and feelings. However, this can also expose people to possible shame feelings.

When individuals or couples have a problem of this kind it is important to identify the inner dialogue (people's automatic thoughts about themselves and their relationships), which can make a strong contribution to the reasons why difficulties exist. Sometimes problems relate to past experiences, for example, that one of the partners has been emotionally taken advantage of or rejected. Even before a cancer a person may have had an anxious or avoidant attachment style. The problems of prostate cancer can accentuate these styles of relating leading to attachment anxiety and/or avoidance of intimacy. The therapist's role is then to make the problem clear and to ventilate and clarify what it is that the client thinks will happen (e.g., 'my partner won't love me any more') and also to make a realistic test, which shows that the expected result is seldom the case, especially in the present circumstances. Even when the different components of the problem are relevant one tries, as far as possible, to put into practice various solutions that might aid adjustment to the current sexual situation. It is important to make clear that strategies, which have been useful in the past (e.g., that sexual closeness is dependent on erections), may no longer be relevant in the present circumstances, and that it is these previous beliefs and strategies that may now stand in the way of, or make it more difficult to achieve, a style of sexual relating that can be worth while and enriching. Linking pre-existing fears and beliefs to an understanding of attachment styles means that the therapist can use the individuals'/ couples' history in both formulation and intervention (Murray-Parkes, Stevenson-Hinde & Marris, 1991).

The following case study shows clearly the linkage between shame themes and pre-existing attachment schemata of relationships. An outline of Sven and Elsa's backgrounds is followed by extracts from a recording of a therapy session.

A case study: Sven and Elsa

Sven and Elsa have been a couple for eight years. They took the initiative to contact me for cognitive sex psychotherapy as they had experienced a gradual deterioration in their personal and sexual relationship after Sven was diagnosed, just over two years ago, as having prostate cancer. Sven was immediately given radiotherapy, which worked well, and his cancer is now considered to be under control. The radiation treatment did, however, cause Sven to develop a slight leakage of excrement and also difficulties in achieving an erection strong enough for penetration. The second side-effect was treated successfully, without complications, with Viagra.

Background: Sven, who is 59, started his working life as a dispensing chemist. He now works as a developer of new medicinal products for a successful private company that specialises in skin pharmacology. Sven took his doctoral degree in natural science when he was 25 years old and had intended to take up a career as a research worker at a university. This, however, did not materialise as his problem with accepting authority became unmanageable. In spite of this, Sven has a good reputation as a researcher although he has never, much to his annoyance, been made a professor.

Sven describes his father, who worked in a bank, as a stable and responsible family father with probably only 'the best' intentions. However, Sven experienced him as almost completely unreasonable, with a marked inability to see things in any other way than from his own point of view. This obviously led to a certain insensitivity towards Sven, who learnt at an early age that confronting his father was impossible and therefore always adopted a passive, polite, slightly evasive and submissive attitude towards him, in order to avoid his father subjecting him to his 'idiocy'. Sven doesn't believe his father was conscious of the effect he had on him or that he intended to make him feel such deep shame. When Sven was older their relationship became 'extremely formal'.

Sven has always seen his mother, who was a nurse, as correct and respectful but cool. He says that he got the impression that emotionally his mother was a very private person that you couldn't get close to. Sven doesn't think his parents had an unhappy marriage but not a happy one either. There were never any open conflicts as such, but when they had a disagreement they could go up to four days without saying a word to each other. Sven says that you could 'cut the air with a knife'.

Sven has a sister who is five years younger than he is, and is, according to him, very emotional. He has always felt that she was his father's favourite and that 'she could wrap him round her little finger'. Today, Sven can admit that he has felt, without doubt, both jealousy and envy towards his sister. He says that they had relatively little contact when they were young but that there has been more since she married a Mexican industrialist, to whom family relationships are very important.

In many areas things came easily to Sven and he has always been considered clever, something his father was very proud of. Sven says that he has never put much special value on personal relationships, although he has always had friends when he wanted them. Moreover, since he was young, Sven has had a recurring shame problem – he has never been able to cope with being made fun of or being subjected to irony. Luckily, he feels that few people have taken advantage of this sensitivity and Sven thinks that he has always been seen as somebody with a high status.

It would seem that, in his early attachments, Sven experienced his parents as somewhat inaccessible and having critical and negative attitudes towards him. This has contributed to the fact that he has, as a consequence and to a certain extent, developed an insecure-evasive and avoidant attachment style, with a trace of compulsive self-reliance. Sven has developed IWMs and beliefs that are very shame-focused, such as: 'To be vulnerable is to be weak' and 'My vulnerability will be misused.' These IWMs manifest themselves in Sven's defensive, rather disdainful and arrogant attitude.

When Sven was 26, he got married to a 'kind, pleasant doctor's secretary'. They had two children together, a daughter, who is now 31, and a son, who is 29. Their daughter has two children, 5 and 3. Sven describes his marriage as being, on the whole, satisfactory. However, he took comparatively little part in family life as he spent most of his time working. He does not believe that this was a cause of conflict as his wife considered that he had 'done his duty', since she had got two children, 'one of each sort', and he provided a high standard of living for the family. However, after 23 years of marriage, his wife divorced him. She had got back in contact with an old flame, who, according to Sven, had never done anything except inferior scientific work. The divorce threw Sven severely off balance as it brought to the fore his, for many years hidden, shame-based assumptions about his insignificance and inferiority. In order to control this he took antidepressants from time to time until he met Elsa two years later. Elsa became for him the sun, which 'brought light into the tunnel'.

Backgound: Elsa is 58 and works as a costume-maker and seamstress at a theatre, a job which she really enjoys. Her parents were farmers and she is the second of four temperamental sisters. She describes her childhood as safe and predictable. She had a very close relationship with her father. Elsa says that she learnt at an early age to mediate in various relationships and conflicts and to 'pour oil on troubled waters'. Elsa has often been credited with social competence, as she has always been flexible and easy to get on with. She thinks that she developed early IWMs and beliefs such as 'I can influence every relationship in the right direction.' and 'Too much emotional stress isn't healthy.'

Elsa married a vet when she was 24, shortly after she had qualified as a teacher of textile handicraft. Unfortunately, it turned out that she was infertile. She would have liked to adopt but her husband refused. Not being able to have children is Elsa's greatest sorrow, even if she has taken comfort from her almost daily contact with her sisters' children. When Elsa was 49 her husband died suddenly of a stroke. She feels that she coped with that fairly well. After this she lived alone for a year before she started a relationship with Sven.

Elsa feels that to a great extent she and Sven have a good life together. She says that she has had plenty of practice at mixing with and managing self-willed and eccentric people, which has been a great help in her relationship with Sven. She believes that the fact that she has 'no prestige' and can 'forgive and forget' are of vital importance to the functioning of their relationship.

Elsa appreciates very much that Sven is 'internationally at ease', as travel and experiencing different scenery and different cultures gives her more pleasure than anything else. The fact that Sven's brother-in-law has been stationed in various places all over the world has meant that they have been to quite a few interesting places.

The psychotherapy process

The psychotherapy lasted just over six months, with a total of 17 sessions. It was evident at the very first meeting that the relationship was very strong and important to both of them. This means that their motivation was good and, at an early stage, we generated a feeling of security and assurance that therapy could be useful to them. This led to the development of a strong therapeutic alliance.

After discussion of their difficulties and exploring their history, our conversations were conducted at a hypothetical generative level, based on collaborative empiricism. It proved favourable to start from various theoretical lines of reasoning and explanatory models around shame. This applies especially to Sven as he finds things like this easy to take in and thus feels competent and consequently less 'psychopathologised'. Sven also found it valuable to read specialised literature about shame. It became clear that it was constructive to discuss things in the third person or to refer to other people's relationships in order to elucidate the couple's interpersonal attitudes. On several occasions, parallels were drawn with other psychotherapies where shame was a central theme. This increased Elsa's understanding considerably. Below are extracts from the fifth session where shame themes come through strongly.

Extract from therapy session number 5

ELSA: It seems as though there has been less and less closeness, even though we sometimes have sex, yes especially since we began with Viagra.
THERAPIST: In what way less closeness?

ELSA: Well, sort of ordinary everyday closeness.

THERAPIST: How does this show itself?

ELSA: It can be that I go into the bathroom just when he comes out of the shower.

THERAPIST: What happens then?

ELSA: He covers himself quickly with his towel or turns away so that I won't see.

THERAPIST Is that what it's like Sven?

SVEN: Perhaps . . .

THERAPIST: Why isn't she allowed to see?

SVEN: Well, I suppose she can . . .

THERAPIST: What is it then?

SVEN: I feel as though I'm being examined . . .

THERAPIST: Why examined?

SVEN: Well, that's just what it is!

It can be noted here that taking a specific event (being seen naked in the bathroom) has revealed a particular shame experience of being 'examined' or scrutinised. Sven becomes acutely sensitive to his body as seen by the other (Elsa), which is a key aspect of external shame (Gilbert, Chapter 1, this volume). At this point I, the therapist, do not focus on whether this is 'true or not' for this could induce more shame-defensive responses but instead explore further Sven's thoughts about the outcome of this scrutiny, that is, the assumptions of negative evaluations.

THERAPIST: If that's what it is, what is the result of this examination?

SVEN: It's difficult to say . . .

THERAPIST: Is it on the positive or the negative side?

SVEN: Probably more the latter.

THERAPIST: And what do you think then?

SVEN: Well, that Elsa probably doesn't think I'm attractive.

This clarifies that it is not so much the sense of being examined or not, but the experience of being seen as 'unattractive' that is the key here. In other words, this is clearly a shame issue. Elsa seems to respond to this as a criticism and feels the blame (shame) has been put on her, to which she reacts defensively.

ELSA: Have I indicated that in some way?!

SVEN: Yes . . . no . . . perhaps not . . .

THERAPIST: If Elsa hasn't indicated this to you, then who has?

SVEN: I don't know!

THERAPIST: Who is it who usually looks on you as unattractive?

SVEN: Well . . . I suppose it's me . . .

THERAPIST: [*smiling and gently*] Exactly.

The couple are then silent for a while reflecting on this. In this short section, the idea that Elsa looks down on Sven is challenged (she says clearly 'Have I indicated that in some way?!') and from this Sven is able to offer the insight that it is actually he who is seeing himself as unattractive. It might have been possible to test whether Sven believes that Elsa does not look down on him. In other words, even if she has never said anything of this nature he might believe that she thinks it. However, he seems to accept that there is no evidence of her having negative views of him and then to see that it is internal shame – what he thinks about himself, that is important. Elsa then breaks the silence by introducing a more general issue about their ability to be intimate with each other.

ELSA: There's another problem I'd like to take up today, I guess the two things hang together . . .
THERAPIST: What's that Elsa?
ELSA: Well, it's that we hardly ever kiss and caress each other all over, like we used to.
THERAPIST: How is it now?
ELSA: There's no problem as long as we keep to around the face and neck and . . .
THERAPIST: But . . .
ELSA: Well, Sven is so tense.
THERAPIST: Tense?
ELSA: Yes, he is tense as soon as it's a more intimate caress like . . .
THERAPIST: Like . . .
ELSA Like when I touch his penis or caress his testicles.
THERAPIST: What happens then?
ELSA: Sven takes my hand to divert it . . . hoping that I won't notice . . .
THERAPIST: Anything else?
ELSA: Yes, then he retreats like . . .
THERAPIST: Yes . . .
ELSA: I know the times when I kiss him all over his chest, down towards his stomach and tried to go even further down, but then it was stop.
THERAPIST: Stop?
ELSA: Yes, then he lifts up my face or pushes my head away.
THERAPIST: Is this right, Sven?
SVEN: Yes, I suppose so.

In this section Elsa draws attention to other aspects of Sven's shame-avoidant and safety behaviours and how these are interfering with their physical affectionate relationships. I invite Sven to reflect on why he might be using these kinds of defensive behaviours. It soon becomes evident that Sven is using the defensive behaviours to ward off very painful feelings. Although I use questions to aid guided discovery, the tone is gentle not interrogatory.

THERAPIST: Why do you think you do that?

SVEN: Don't know . . . but it's too much or too near in some way.

THERAPIST: What is it you feel then?

SVEN: I just can't stand it any longer.

THERAPIST: What is it that you can't stand then, Sven?

SVEN: Well, that I'm really not so fine.

ELSA: How do you mean not fine?

SVEN: I don't know . . . it just feels like that.

ELSA: But I think I really try to show you how much I like you and how fine I think you are. Don't you notice that?

SVEN: Yes, it's just that . . .

ELSA: What?

SVEN: It's too much in some way . . .

ELSA: What?

SVEN: Can't really explain . . .

THERAPIST: Mmm . . .

SVEN: I don't know but . . . first those kind, gentle hands and then . . . all that fine talk . . .

THERAPIST: Yes . . .

SVEN: It doesn't make sense . . .

THERAPIST: What doesn't make sense?

ELSA: Are you saying I lie to you, Sven?

SVEN: No, but . . . but I'm not so bloody fine . . . [cries]

THERAPIST: Why aren't you fine, Sven?

SVEN: No, it's all so shitty . . . I'm bloody well corroded . . .

ELSA: Sven . . .

SVEN: It's simply that I don't like her saying that I'm fine . . . That's just the way it is!

In this section, we can see an important aspect of their interaction is Elsa's efforts to be reassuring and affectionate (to get close), which ignite more shame in Sven. At the very time she is trying to be loving and sending positive signals of Sven's attractiveness to her, she is activating in Sven a greater sense of his own unattractiveness and feelings of self-disgust. It compounds his own internal shame feelings that 'I'm bloody well corroded.' It is not uncommon for couples to be confused by this – of how shame can increase when a person is trying to be caring.

ELSA: Yes, but you used to like oral sex . . .!

SVEN: Yes, yes of course!

THERAPIST: What is it that's different now, Sven?

SVEN: Don't know . . . but I feel I'm not clean like . . . even though I know that in some way I am . . .

THERAPIST: But in another way?

SVEN: There's a mass of rotten stuff down there . . . That's where it all comes
from . . .
THERAPIST: Mmm . . .
SVEN: That's the way it is . . .
THERAPIST: What's it like when Elsa tries to stimulate you orally?
SVEN: Well, it's all so obvious!
THERAPIST: What is it that is obvious?
SVEN: It's clear that it (genitals) exists and then it's also obvious that the
cancer exists, because that, as we know, is where it is. . . .

It became clear that part of their problem was that Elsa had begun to 'tread
very warily' around Sven since he became evasive, introverted and moody. It
will be recalled that Elsa has a belief (developed in childhood) that she should
reduce relationship conflicts, but her efforts with Sven are failing. This
may be a source of shame for her. She is hurt by this but her behaviour is
also based on respect for Sven and a desire to protect him from feeling
exposed and vulnerable. Elsa's attitude has led her to being somewhat on her
guard and as a result of this has been slightly distant towards Sven, who
interprets this as a sign that he has lost his power of attraction. In order to
be able to cope with this 'inadequacy and shame', he falls back on his old
defensive strategies of bad temper (anger) and rejection (avoidance). In this
way a negative shame-distancing, interpersonal spiral has developed between
them.

Therapeutic interventions

There are, of course, many aspects to intervention, so here I will only focus on
those relevant to working with shame. In order to understand the shame
elements in their interaction, they were encouraged to try some 'homework'.
Elsa was told to try to behave in a different way and to gather evidence of
what might be useful; to dare to be more forthright towards Sven even if he is
having 'a tough time'. Elsa was also advised to be a little more willing to give
sexual directives and to be the driving force, in order to break into Sven's
shame polarisation. As well as this, she was encouraged not to react too
defensively and back off, as she had done previously, when Sven tried to push
her away with his 'affliction and corrosion' feelings. It was also suggested that
Elsa should be careful not to give Sven too much *verbal* confirmation about
his body but instead to intensify her caresses and other expressions of physical warmth, for example, a kiss on his cheek, holding hands, walking arm in
arm and sitting close to him. This is because it had been established that Sven
could not accept more than 'one kindness at a time'. Otherwise the discrepancy between Sven's inner world (what he thought about himself) and outer
world (what Elsa was saying and doing) seemed to be too great. As this work
was conducted with them as a couple, Sven was able to listen and agree to the

homework and monitor and challenge some of his own thoughts. The idea is for them to form a bond/alliance against the 'sexual shame difficulties' with the aim of regaining their closeness.

Another problem was that is had become difficult for Sven to relax and let go, and he therefore had a problem with ejaculation. This happened after he, on two occasions, had an excrement leakage in connection with ejaculation during intercourse. The only way to cope with this was to say that, when it happens, there is nothing else to do but 'stop and clean things up'. Here I also empathised with this difficulty and explained that there are very few people who would be able to face loss of control for such a basic bodily function without some shame and embarrassment; that is, his reaction is perfectly understandable. To help people with body shame-based problems, it is often useful to note that their feelings of shame and avoidance behaviours are not 'wrong' or 'abnormal' but understandable and protective. People can become ashamed of their own shame and defensive behaviours (i.e., with beliefs such as 'I should cope with this better; therefore I am coping inadequately').

As noted by Gilbert (Chapter 1, this volume), in order not to 'shame' defensive behaviours it can be useful to explore how shame-based problems can also have advantages (e.g., of self-protection or inspiring achievements). Hence, on some occasions we talked about the fact that Sven's shame has also had a positive side. He had compensated by being driven by a desire to be successful in order to triumph over and convince those around him of his capacity. His shame had, in a way, been the source of inspiration for his creative and intellectual achievements and hard work. Positive framing in this way (seeing the advantages) enabled Sven to think about how his shame sensitivity was, however, undesirable (see the disadvantages) in his intimate relationship.

Sensuality training

One of the cornerstones of a satisfactory sex life is good sexual communication. This can only be possible once one has identified the cognitive components that steer and characterise the present sexual relationship. Many couples find it difficult to tell each other what sort of caresses they prefer and their physical contact is therefore unsatisfactory. Fear of expressing these needs often emanates from the fear of being brushed aside, rebuffed or shamed. Sexual communications are specific for each individual. It is, therefore, important to be sensitive to one's partner's signals. In this way, a foundation for sexual communication is developed. The therapist seeks to convey information to couples about this and many other sexual norms, so that they can be integrated into their sex lives. This is one of the reasons why great emphasis is put on *sensuality training* during the treatment.

Sensuality training is a method that has proved very successful in cases of sexual shame and anxiety (Kaplan, 1974, 1983). It is partly a matter of practising, or possibly reviving, the ability to give and accept caresses, and partly a matter of practising the capacity of the whole body to receive sensations, at the same time as reducing the necessity for achievement. This happens gradually and is not a preparation for intercourse. At the start of sensitivity training intercourse is avoided. Before the next therapy session, the couple should have completed the exercise two or three times and then be able to recount, in detail, how it had worked. These exercises can often have a major effect on the couple. A couple, who have been tense and avoidant of physical closeness at the previous session, can have become more hopeful. If the exercises work well, the caresses go on to include the breasts and genitals, but intercourse is still not allowed.

If these efforts and exercises do not work, the couple often come with various excuses and evasive answers. It is important to focus on this resistance immediately. It often then transpires that there is a shame script hidden behind their difficulties. Some couples do the exercises but complain that they find them boring. In this case, it is very often one of the partners who is dissatisfied while the other has found it enjoyable. It is a rule that one does not proceed with the next stage of the treatment before the current part of the programme has been satisfactorily completed. Sensitivity training contributes to putting sexuality in context, something that cannot be isolated from other forms of contact and other everyday activities.

With the help of sensuality training, Sven came to feel more physically comfortable with himself and can 'see his own potentials'. The couple were also encouraged to discover the value of sexual caresses and petting, which means that their sexual activities were no longer so performance- and penetration-oriented. As a result of these therapeutic interventions a clearer and more straightforward non-verbal, verbal and sexual communication developed. New, more functional relationship-centred beliefs and IWMs also developed. For Sven they included: 'One can be loved in spite of one's faults' and 'I need affection and closeness just as much as anybody else', and for Elsa they included: 'Conflicts can lead to both development and enrichment' and 'It is not possible to influence everything in a relationship.'

The therapeutic relationship

In shame-prone clients, the therapeutic relationship can be crucial to a successful outcome. Throughout the psychotherapy, we talked about the transferences within the room, so that Sven could feel secure and know where he stood with me. Bit by bit, he was able to mention his fear of being made a fool of, or that I, in some way, might criticise him or take advantage of his vulnerability. At the same time, he could see how illogical it would be for a therapist to heckle or deride a client or to do anything out of spite, as this would hardly lead the therapy in the right direction. Nonetheless, it is important for a therapist to address these issues openly and to expect them.

With shame-prone clients, it is very easy for there to be therapeutic ruptures where a client can feel misunderstood or belittled. On such occasions with Sven and Elsa, I would acknowledge the rupture and take some responsibility for it. This relieved the pressure on Sven, offered emphatic awareness of his sensitivity and modelled ways of coping with relationship ruptures without feeling intense shame and acting defensively. At other times, the use of humour and emphasising the comic side of things in various situations during our work together proved to be very positive in developing our working relationship. His own ability to accept some responsibility changed slowly when he could see more clearly, understand and, above all, *put into words* his shame reactions.

Follow-up sessions showed that the couple's relationship was functioning just as well as it had at the end of the main course of therapy. Deeper dimensions of closeness, tenderness and trust had also developed and these contributed to Sven's and Elsa's feeling that they had been given a new chance.

Conclusion

It is generally known that the side-effects of the curative treatment that men receive for prostate cancer are frequently sex-related. They can often lead to feelings of inadequacy and vulnerability that can generate body shame. The result of this can be that men avoid sexual contact, which probably leads to relationship problems (Schover, 1993). Understanding that body shame is psychologically a leading factor in a sex psychotherapy can contribute to an increased understanding of various attitudes and reactions between the man and his partner. It is important for the therapeutic process that the nature of the shame is made understandable and also how the shame is expressed (Gilbert, Chapter 1, this volume; Kaufman, 1989). One should therefore work together to reduce dysfunctional, defensive and safety behaviours (e.g., avoidance or hostile-distancing) and develop and practise concrete strategies that can improve the clients' ability to cope with shame and shame reactions. These interventions help to increase interpersonal competence which is the basis for creating more fulfilling relationships and improving self-esteem.

All in all, this knowledge gives a more profound and nuanced picture of men, their partners and their sexuality and, in the long run, it can also influence the quality of the care and treatment given to men with prostate cancer.

Acknowledgement

Special thanks to Brenda Bennett, without her patience and help this chapter would not have been written.

References

Adolfsson, J., Steineck, G. & Hedlund, P.O. (1999) Deferred treatment of locally advanced nonmetastatic prostate cancer: A long term follow-up. *Journal of Urology*, 161, 505–508.

Bancroft, J. (1989) *Human Sexuality and Its Problems* (2nd edn.) Edinburgh: Churchill Livingstone.

Beck, A.T., Rush, A.J., Shaw, B.F. & Emery, G. (1979) Cognitive Therapy of Depression. New York: John Wiley & Sons.

Bowlby, J. (1969–1980) *Attachment and Loss*. London: Hogarth Press.

Boyle, P., Gandini, S., Baglietto, L., Severi, G. & Robertson C. (2001) Epidemiology of prostate cancer. *European Urology*, April; 39, Supplement, 4, 2–3.

Collins, N.L. & Read, S.J. (1990) Adult attachment, working models and relationship quality in dating couples. *Journal of Personality and Social Psychology*, 58, 644–666.

Etcoff, N. (1999) *Survival of the Prettiest: The Science of Beauty*. New York: Doubleday.

Fitzpatrick, J., Kirby, R.J., Krane, R.J., Adolfsson, J., Newling, D.W.W. & Goldstein, I. (1998) Sexual dysfunction associated with the management of prostate cancer. *European Urology*, 33, 513–522.

Hazan, S. & Shaver, P. (1987) Romantic love conceptualized as an attachment process. *Journal of Personality and Social Psychology*, 52, 11–24.

Helgason, Å.R., Adolfsson, J., Dickman, P., Arver, S., Fredriksson, M. & Steinbeck, G. (1996) Waning sexual function – the most important disease-specific distress for patients with prostate cancer. *British Journal Cancer*, 73, 1417–1421.

Kaplan, H.S. (1974) *The New Sex Therapy*. New York: Brunner-Mazel, Inc.

Kaplan, H.S. (1983) *The Evaluation of Sexual Disorders*. New York: Brunner-Mazel.

Kaufman, G. (1989) *The Psychology of Shame: The Theory and Treatment of Shame-based Syndromes*. New York: Springer.

Lazare, A. (1986) Shame and humiliation in the medical encounter. *Archives of Internal Medicine*, 147, 1653–1658.

Murray-Parkes, C., Stevenson-Hinde, J. & Marris, P. (1991) *Attachment Across the Life Cycle*. London: Routledge.

Nathanson, D.L. (1994) *Shame and Pride: Affect, Sex and the Birth of the Self*. Norton Paperbacks.

O'Donohue, W. & Geer, J.H. (1993) (eds) *Handbook of Sexual Dysfunction: Assessment and Treatment*. Boston: Allyn and Bacon.

Paterson, J. (2000) Stigma associated with postprostatectomy urinary incontinence. *Journal of Wound, Ostomy and Continence Nurse Sociology*, 27, 168–173.

Schover, L.R. (1993) Sexual rehabilitation after treatment for prostate cancer. *Cancer*, 71, 1024–1030.

Singer, P.A., Tasch, E.S., Stocking, C., Rubin, S., Siegler, M. & Weichelbaum, R. (1991) Sex or survival: Trade-offs between quality and quantity of life. *Journal of Clinical Oncology*, 9, 328–334.

West, M.L. & Sheldon-Keller, A.E. (1994) Classification. *Patterns of Relating: An Adult Attachment Perspective*. New York: Guilford Press.

Part III

Body shame and psychological disorders

Chapter 11

Blushing, shame and social anxiety

W. Ray Crozier

The blush is regarded as a facial expression of the 'self-conscious' emotions – an outward manifestation of shame, embarrassment, shyness and/or modesty. In addition, the blush *itself* can be a source of self-consciousness and shame. Fear of blushing (erythophobia) can be the major presenting problem in social phobia and social anxiety. It creates a problem in several ways. First, unlike body shame associated with disfigurements, skin diseases or body shape, it is experienced as an *involuntary reaction*. Second, awareness that one is blushing can intensify it; indeed, simply being told (correctly or not) that one is blushing can induce a blush. Third, people can regard their blushing in a negative light. Not only may they be anxious of how others evaluate them because they blush (external shame), they may interpret their dispositions to blush as a sign of personal weakness or evidence of social ineptness (internal shame). Both forms of shame can lead those who are susceptible to blush to engage in a variety of defensive or safety behaviours and avoid social situations in which blushing may occur. Such anxieties and defensive behaviours can be heightened by the perceptions that blushing is beyond their conscious control. Furthermore, as a blush begins attention can become more self-focused interfering with efforts at social presentation and producing cognitive overload, which adds to anxiety, especially as other behaviours (e.g., speech flow) are interrupted (Rapee & Heimberg, 1997). As discussed below, these concerns can lead people to seek professional help and there are a range of psychological and medical approaches to intervention.

Nevertheless, blushing is ubiquitous and, presumably, serves positive functions as well as causing problems. The causes and functions of blushing are only now beginning to be understood and systematic research into this phenomenon is in its infancy. This chapter considers what is known about the nature of blushing, how it is linked to 'body shame' and reviews research into current interventions.

The nature of blushing

Psychophysiology of the blush

Blushing results from an increased blood flow through the subcutaneous capillaries that lie close to the skin in the face, ears, neck and upper part of the chest. Variation in blood flow through these capillaries is related to temperature control. A basically hairless species relies on the circulation of blood close to the skin, particularly at the face, hands and feet, in order to adapt to environmental changes in temperature. Centres in the hypothalamus responsible for control of body temperature regulate the flow of blood. When temperature rises, for example, through physical exertion, the capillaries are opened (the process of vasodilation) and there is an increased flow of blood closer to the surface of the skin, allowing cooling of the blood and consequently a reduction in body temperature. Conversely, when body temperature needs to rise, vasoconstriction narrows the capillaries so that there is a smaller blood flow close to the skin. It has long been recognised that certain parts of the body are more susceptible to the blush, notably the face. This may be a prime site because it has a greater density of capillaries below the skin surface and because the skin is thinner than at other sites (Cutlip & Leary, 1993). Also, there is a greater density of beta-adrenergic receptors in the facial veins, and research has suggested their involvement in blushing (Drummond, 1997).

The visible reddening produced by vasodilation is accompanied by a rise in temperature in those areas of the skin affected. This may be an important cue to individuals that they are blushing since the face is not ordinarily visible to the self. It is also a cue for those whose skin colour renders a blush less visible. Simon and Shields (1996) have explored this aspect in a survey of blushing experiences of four ethnic groups, Asian, Black, Hispanic and White. Respondents with a lighter skin complexion were more likely to report both colouring and increased temperature as components of blushing, were more likely to indicate that its visibility was the reason that people noticed they were blushing, and to believe that the visibility of their blush was an important factor in others' responses to their blush. Those with a darker complexion reported that temperature was the important component and that others responded to them on the basis of their acting in an embarrassed fashion.

There is evidence to suggest that the visible change precedes change in skin temperature by a few seconds. Temporal analysis of the sequence of events during a blush-inducing incident reveals that visual cues, as assessed by the ability of observers to detect blushing from a videotape of the blusher's face, coincide with the peak of measured coloration but not with maximum facial temperature; this occurs a few seconds later (Shearn et al., 1990). This sequence implies that observers can detect a blush while it is still forming and this might be a factor in the phenomenon that blushing can lead to fluster if the blusher can see others' reactions before there is time to prepare an appropriate response. It might explain circumstances where people are unaware that they are blushing even though others see that they are. They might be insensitive to feedback from facial temperature or the cues may be masked by environmental factors, for example, the heat of the room or the effects of alcohol.

Of course, it has to be recognised that what constitutes a blush has not been clearly defined by researchers. Changes in skin coloration ('flushes') and body temperature also accompany physical exercise and can be caused by factors such as alcohol consumption. Closer analysis might reveal different patterns of blushing; indeed, many of the problematic issues might be due to failure to take these into account. For example, Leary and Kowalski (1995, p.150) distinguish between the *classic blush* and the *creeping blush*. The latter spreads slowly, over a period of several minutes, and appears 'blotchy' rather than an overall reddening. Little is known about the circumstances that give rise to one type of blush rather than another. Rex et al. (1998, p.25) suggest that the quickly developing blush that accompanies embarrassment may be mediated by the sympathetic nervous system, implying that other types of blush may not.

There is a widespread assumption that the blush is an expression of social anxiety. Nevertheless, research has failed to establish a reliable association between blushing and anxiety. Fear and anxiety are likely to be expressed in the pallor of the face rather than heightened colour, since heightened sympathetic system arousal involves vasoconstriction of facial capillaries. Blushing is not reliably correlated with other measures of sympathetic arousal. It tends to be associated with reduction in heart rate in embarrassing situations (Keltner & Buswell, 1997), implying inhibited sympathetic and increased parasympathetic nervous system activity. On the other hand, substantial numbers of respondents to surveys do claim that increased heart rate, sweating and butterflies in stomach accompany their blushing (e.g., Simon & Shields, 1996). There is evidence too that blushing is mediated to some extent by sympathetic activity via beta-adrenergic receptors in the facial vein (Mellander et al., 1982). Sympathetic arousal of these receptors produces vasodilation, and they have a high density in the facial veins. Drummond (1989) reported that individuals who have a lesion to the sympathetic pathway to the face and who are presented with an embarrassing situation (such as singing a childish song) do not blush in the damaged region of the face but have a discernible blush in the unaffected region. Drummond (1997) examined the effects of blocking beta-adrenergic receptors in the forehead blood vessels on one side of the head by means of the local administration of an antagonistic drug (propranolol). This produced a small but significant reduction of blushing in an embarrassing situation. Furthermore, as we discuss below, surgical disruption of the sympathetic chain prevents facial blushing (e.g., Rex et al., 1998).

One must be careful not to simplify the situation or assume that anxious reactions are solely caused by, or can be identified with, heightened sympathetic nervous system arousal. Sympathetic and parasympathetic systems work in a complementary fashion. Alpha- and beta-adrenergic receptors respond in opposing fashion to norepinephrine, the neurotransmitter in most sympathetic system nerve endings. Alpha sites are associated with excitatory functions and beta sites with inhibitory functions hence heightened sympathetic activity might produce either vasodilation or vasoconstriction. The research goal is to determine what produces these different reactions. Furthermore, whether or not the blush is an anxious *reaction*, the blush can itself produce anxiety, and as discussed later, the situations that elicit blushing can also give rise to anxiety, just as potentially embarrassing situations can elicit anxiety.

Situations that elicit blushing

A literature review by Leary et al. (1992) concluded that four classes of situation elicit blushing: threats to public identity; praise and positive attention; scrutiny; and accusations of blushing. Threats to public identity include violation of norms, inept performances, loss of control and behaving out-of-role, circumstances that also typically give rise to embarrassment. Second, people blush when they are singled out for praise, compliments or thanks. Conspicuousness is a third cause of blushing such that people will colour just because they are the centre of attention, when, for example, they enter the room late at a public meeting. Finally, being told that you are blushing can induce it, and awareness of your blushing can intensify it.

Factor analysis of the Leary and Meadows (1991) blushing propensity scale provides partial support for this classification, yielding three factors (Bögels, Alberts & de Jong 1996). Items with highest loadings on the first factor refer to being the centre of attention and 'looking stupid or incompetent in front of others'. Items in the second factor refer to interacting with an attractive person and conversing about a personal topic. The third factor has items referring to accusation of blushing and thinking of beginning to blush. Additional kinds of empirical evidence confirm that blushing occurs in these kinds of situations. For example, singing before an audience or listening along with other people to a recording of one's own singing performance produces changes in skin colour and temperature (Drummond, 1989, 1997; Shearn et al., 1990; Mulkens, de Jong & Bögels, 1997).

In the situations that are studied most often, people's behaviour draws attention to themselves. This creates a predicament and the blush is a reaction to this unwanted attention. People also blush when they are only indirectly responsible for the social transgression. If the elderly relative with whom you are dining makes loud remarks about other people in the restaurant, your blush shows that you recognise that this behaviour is unacceptable; perhaps you accompany it with some gesture that suggests to those present that she is not in full control of what she says. On the other hand, as I have argued elsewhere (Crozier, 2000), there are occasions when a blush is not the *consequence* of unwanted attention, but its cause; it attracts attention to the self when otherwise you would not be noticed. It 'gives you away' and creates a predicament rather than being a response to one. For example, if you blush at an allusion to something you wish to keep secret, there is a greater risk of the secret being uncovered. Without the blush the conversation would have continued smoothly and without embarrassment. Or the blush can augment any difficulties. The writer Elizabeth Gaskell (1986, p.224), provides the following example:

> I had to bring out all my stammering inquiries before Mr Holdsworth, who would never have attended to them I dare say, if I had not blushed, and blundered, and made such a fool of myself.

People blush when there is no transgression or when there is one but they are not responsible for it. Thus, they blush when praised, congratulated, complimented or thanked. They blush to witness someone else's embarrassment. They blush if a sexually explicit scene appears on television when, for example, they are viewing with their parents or children. Crozier (2000) pointed out that many of these situations have a common pattern. If an event X brings into the open (or threatens to do so) a topic Y, and Y is something that the individual wishes to keep hidden or believes ought to be kept hidden, X will elicit a blush whether or not the individual is responsible for X. The blush is associated with external shame in the sense that it is what others think of the self rather than what the individual knows to be the case that is important. If, for example, I am looking through a wallet that I have picked up, I might blush if someone observes me doing so or if its owner returns and sees me; I will do so even though I know I am not looking for valuables but am trying to discover who owns it.

Blushing as an aversive experience

People can dislike their blushing. They often describe it in negative terms and see it as a sign of weakness or incompetence (internal shame). Some cope with it by restricting their social life, avoiding situations that they know tend to make them blush. They may rely on alcohol or tranquillizers (Edelmann, 1990). They may employ 'safety behaviours' (Clark & Wells, 1995) such as trying to stay in the background, keeping out of artificial light or away from heat, and eschewing open-necked shirts or garments with low necklines; cosmetics can be used to mask redness of the face, for example, applying a green colour corrective cream under a foundation. Many people come to fear their blushing and see it as a personal problem, leading them to seek professional help; pre-intervention assessments of blushing show that it is an intensely unpleasant experience that can have a marked effect on the blusher's life (e.g., Edelmann, 1990; Scholing & Emmelkamp, 1993; Telaranta, 1998). Scales assessing propensity to blush correlate significantly with scales measuring social anxiety (Crozier & Russell, 1992; Edelmann, 1991) and depression (Edelmann, 1991). Accordingly, the literature focuses on the negative dimension of blushing and some research has evaluated interventions to help people cope with their blushing. Psychotherapeutic approaches to social phobia and panic attacks have been applied – relaxation techniques, *in vivo* exposure, thought changing – but this chapter focuses on published evaluation studies targeted at blushing.

Interventions

Cognitive behaviour therapy

DSM-IV (American Psychiatric Association, 1994) includes among the diagnostic criteria for social phobia the individual's fear of being embarrassed about showing anxiety symptoms. The criteria do not specifically mention blushing, however this is reported as a concern of many social phobics (Scholing & Emmelkamp, 1996). Recent literature distinguishes between generalised social phobia and specific social phobia; in the latter the individual is anxious about particular kinds of situations and concerned about specific reactions, for example, blushing, sweating or trembling. There exists a substantial body of evidence on the evaluation of treatments for social phobia; *in vivo* exposure and cognitive behavioural therapy have been the most widely applied psychological (as opposed to pharmacological) interventions.

Here, we review a study by Scholing and Emmelkamp (1993, 1996) that involved combinations of exposure and cognitive therapy. The emphasis in the former was on homework sessions, where the individual attempts to face situations that elicit the symptoms without relying on avoidance strategies (i.e., reducing safety behaviours). The second was based on rational-emotional therapy and focused on irrational thinking about the symptoms. It was explained to participants that the goal was not to reduce the frequency of blushing, sweating or trembling but to diminish fear of these symptoms. Thirty-five patients began the treatment, all diagnosed with social phobia but whose main problems, and reason for seeking treatment, were their specific symptoms.

There were two blocks of eight one-hour sessions over a period of 12 weeks. Pre-treatment and post-treatment measurements were made, with follow-up at three months and at 18 months. There were four self-report composite measures: responses to feared situations; avoidance of social situations; social phobic cognitions; and somatic symptoms. There were significant pre-post changes on all measures and these were maintained at 18 months. There were no differences in the relative effectiveness of the treatments. These results are encouraging, given that the duration of treatment was short. However, results are not presented separately for the three symptoms, so it is not possible to evaluate the success of treatments for those whose primary concern is with blushing. Reductions in self-reported avoidance of feared situations provide indirect evidence of reduction in fear of blushing but there is no direct evidence. Also, the somatic scales, measuring self-reported frequency of symptoms, are themselves composites, so that it is not possible to assess directly changes in blushing. Furthermore, changes in somatic scales, although statistically significant, are smaller than those reported for the other three outcome measures. In the absence of more targeted intervention studies, the conclusion must be that techniques that have been applied with success to generalised social phobia are potentially of value for fear of blushing.

Reducing self-focused attention

Another cognitive approach also draws upon work on social phobia; specifically, research that shows that cognitive-behavioural treatment can reduce the self-focused attention that is associated with social anxiety and impaired social performance (Rapee & Heimberg, 1997). Excessive self-focus impairs performance by using attention resources that ought to be applied to the encounter (Woody, Chambless & Glass, 1997). Bögels, Mulkens and de Jong (1997) argued that encouraging task concentration would reduce fear of blushing by reducing self-focused attention. Their procedure involves two forms of treatment: task concentration as a coping strategy for coping with blushing and cognitive therapy targeting beliefs about blushing. The first treatment has three phases: increasing participants' awareness of the role of attention in their fear of blushing; practice in focusing outwards in non-threatening situations (e.g., concentrating on the content of a news broadcast); and practice in a threatening situation (social situations where the individual participant reports frequent blushing – these are arranged in a hierarchy, from least to most feared). Data are presented for two individual case studies. There were six to eight weekly task concentration practice sessions and this intervention led to changes in beliefs about blushing that were maintained at one-year follow-up. These changes in beliefs preceded the cognitive therapy or any discussion of the participant's beliefs. The study involved only two participants and only limited conclusions can be drawn; nevertheless, it is a promising technique.

Paradoxical intention

Salter (1952) introduced the technique of paradoxical intention, whereby the patient is encouraged to deliberately bring on a blush: 'I want you to deliberately practice blushing. Tell yourself to blush at all times: when you're alone, and when you're with people' (Salter, 1952, p.106, cited by Timms, 1980, p.60). In these circumstances the blush can become rewarding (an achievement), not the aversive event hitherto experienced. Timms (1980) reported positive results from an individual case study; the woman reported an improvement at 22-month follow-up. Mersch et al. (1992) summarise similar positive findings in a review of case studies. Their own intervention study involved three patients diagnosed with social phobia with a predominant fear of bodily symptoms, and paradoxical intervention was combined with a cognitive form of therapy, rational emotive therapy. One man reported erythophobia and took medication (benzodiazepines) to manage his fear. Treatment comprised 14 one-hour weekly sessions; seven of these were devoted to paradoxical intervention, and the patient carried out *in vivo* sessions where he tried to induce blushing. After treatment he reported blushing less frequently and this improvement was maintained at 18-month follow-up. However, although he reported less anxiety in blush-inducing situations immediately following treatment, levels had increased significantly after 18 months. Furthermore, all three patients attributed the reduction in their symptoms to the cognitive therapy. Further research is needed before paradoxical intervention can be established as a reliable technique and before its relationship with other approaches, for example, the exposure involved in homework sessions, can be assessed.

Psychopharmacological intervention

There is now a considerable literature on pharmacological interventions for social phobia (Hood & Nutt, 2001). A range of medications have attracted research: beta-blockers, benzodiazepines, monoamine oxidase inhibitors (MAOIs) and selective serotonin reuptake inhibitors (SSRIs). In some evaluation studies, these are combined with *in vivo* exposure or cognitive-behavioural treatments. Van Ameringen et al. (1999) suggest that the SSRIs are emerging as the 'gold standard' for pharmacological treatment. Nevertheless, additional research is necessary to establish their effectiveness and to understand why they are effective or why they work for some patients and not for others. Studies have been directed at generalised social phobia and outcome measures are frequently self-reports of anxiety. There seems to be no research that deals specifically with applications to blushing.

Surgical intervention

There are reports in the medical literature of large-scale studies that have treated problems of blushing by surgical procedures, specifically using endoscopic techniques to divide the sympathetic chain in the upper thoracic region. This technique was originally applied to problems of excessive perspiration (hyperhidrosis) but it also led to patients reporting reductions in facial blushing (improvement data tend to be based on telephone surveys conducted some months after surgery). A team of researchers at Boras Hospital in Sweden systematically evaluated the procedure with a sample of 244 individuals, mean age 34 years (Drott et al., 1998; Rex et al., 1998). Prior to the operation, patients reported high levels of fear of blushing, describing its marked effects on their social and professional life. They reported widespread use of medication and alcohol for coping with blushing. The operation produced few complications or serious side effects and there were substantial and statistically significant reductions in reported fear of blushing. Telaranta (1998) described similar positive results among a sample of 43 patients meeting diagnostic criteria for social phobia. Self-ratings of severity of blushing on a five-point (0–5) visual analogue scale changed significantly from a preoperative mean of 3.7 to a mean of 1.3 at four-month follow-up.

Despite the apparent success of surgical intervention, the research raises several issues. First, the alteration is permanent and irreversible. Second, there are risks with any surgery performed under general anaesthetic. Third, the side-effects can be unpleasant and potentially as embarrassing as the original blushing. Although the operation reduces sweating in the face, armpit and palms of the hands, it does lead to significant increases in sweating in other parts of the body, including trunk, groin and 'gustatory' sweating associated with tastes and smells (Drott et al., 1998). Fourth, gains in patient satisfaction at the high level reported a matter of months after surgery are not necessarily maintained in the longer term, as patients experience these side-effects (Drummond, 2000).

Furthermore, the technique is addressed at the physiological reaction, not the patient's interpretation of the reaction. Drott et al. (1998, p.643) make this point explicitly: 'Our philosophy of treatment is to abolish an important somatic expression of social phobia and pathological "shyness". Generally the patient's social and professional life was improved by the operation.' They point out that many of the patients were distressed by their blushing and had received little benefit from cognitive-behavioural therapy. The assumption underlying the approach is that blushing is inherently an unpleasant experience and that patients blush more frequently or intensely than others, or at least more than they find acceptable. However, if the problem is fear of blushing rather than blushing per se, then this is the problem that should be addressed, and efforts should be made to improve psychological interventions to reduce anxiety. Indeed, as Drummond (2000) points out, individuals who are anxious about blushing may not in fact blush any more than others but may exaggerate the frequency and social significance of their reaction. This is plausible given the substantial evidence that socially anxious individuals are prone to misperception of their behaviour (Clark, 1999).

There is some empirical support for a dislocation between physiological measurement of blushing and self-reports of experience. Mulkens et al.

(1999) found that individuals high in fear of blushing reported more intense blushing in an embarrassing situation than those with less fear but the groups did not differ on physiological measurements of cheek colour, temperature or skin conductance (these measures were responsive to the degree of social stress, thus findings are not due to insensitivity of measurement). They argue that fear of blushing can give rise to a 'vicious circle' where it produces heightened self-awareness that magnifies awareness of blushing, which intensifies fear of blushing, and so on. Nevertheless blushing has positive features and these should be taken into account when evaluating interventions aimed at reducing its frequency. We now consider that blushing can be a useful social signal, and that 'unblushing' can be synonymous with shamelessness, immodesty or insensitivity.

Positive functions of the blush

One of the problems of focusing on blushing as something to be overcome is that this perspective neglects the positive social functions that a blush can serve. Specifically, the blush can be a means of communication, and several theorists have addressed this property. Castelfranchi and Poggi (1990, p.240) argue that the blush is functional; those who blush 'are somehow saying that they know, care about, and fear others' evaluations and that they share those values deeply. They also communicate their sorrow over any possible faults or inadequacies on their part, thus performing an acknowledgement, a confession, and an apology aimed at inhibiting others' aggression or avoiding social ostracism'. Furthermore, the involuntary nature of the blush augments its effectiveness as an acknowledgement, confession or apology, since it cannot be feigned and hence will be perceived as sincere.

Keltner and Harker (1998) argue that the display of shame (which includes blushing as well as frowning, gaze aversion and downward head movement) is similar to submissive and appeasement-related behaviour. It inhibits others from responding aggressively to the violation of a rule. It has also been claimed that it serves a remediation function, the restoration of social relationships following a social transgression (Halberstadt & Green, 1993).

There is empirical support for the hypothesis that a display of embarrassment can deflect negative evaluation. Semin and Manstead (1982) presented subjects with vignettes describing public incidents (like knocking over a stack of cans in a supermarket) and manipulated the description of the actor responsible for this as embarrassed or not. De Jong (1999) adapted these vignettes to describe the actor as blushing, looking around in a shamefaced way, or leaving without a reaction. The incident was judged as less serious when the actor blushed or appeared shamefaced. The actor who blushed was perceived as less responsible for the transgression, and was evaluated less negatively than those who were shamefaced or left the shop without reacting.

The blusher was perceived as more reliable, sympathetic and likeable than the actor described as shamefaced.

For the blush to work in this way, it has to be perceived by others and interpreted as a blush. The eighteenth-century novelist Henry Fielding was aware of this when he observed that 'when a woman is not seen to blush, she doth not blush at all'. There is empirical support for this observation. Leary, Landel and Patton (1996) report that a blush can serve as a remedial device only if it is noticed by others and interpreted as a blush and not as flushing of the face due, say, to physical exercise or alcohol. There is no doubt that a blush can serve valuable social functions by signalling that the person is appropriately embarrassed. However, it is simplistic to characterise a blush as an apology. Apart from the case of people who blush when they are not responsible for bringing about the predicament (and hence have nothing to apologise for), people blush when they receive positive attention, when they are thanked or complimented or when they announce good news (an engagement or a pregnancy). Nonetheless, a blush adds to these experiences, as evidence of modesty or charm. It is clear that the blush can serve as a socially useful signal in different ways. Conversely, failure to blush in certain circumstances can send an unwanted message, indicating that one is insensitive, rude, aggressive, immodest, shameless or brazen.

Conclusion

Blushing is a ubiquitous feature of social life that is little understood at psychological or physiological levels. It is closely associated with the self-conscious emotions of shame and embarrassment. Being the centre of attention can elicit a blush, a highly visible but involuntary and uncontrollable reaction. However, not all such situations evoke a blush and reddening of the skin and increased skin temperature can also be associated with anger as well as with responses to hot rooms, physical exercise, alcohol consumption and so on. There are also individual differences in the propensity to blush. What features of a social situation are picked up to trigger the blush? Social predicaments, making *faux pas*, facing threats to identity, being seen in a poor light and appearing foolish all regularly appear in lists of blush-inducing situations. All of these are unpleasant experiences that most of us would want to avoid. However, for many the blush is *itself* a reason for shame and is regarded as a visible sign of weakness, immaturity or incompetence. Their blushing *is* the problem, not their anxiety about the situations that induce it; to put it another way, people fear (and avoid) situations because they will blush in them.

Treatments aim at either diminishing the fear of blushing or reducing its frequency. Those that aim for the former draw upon methods that have been developed for anxiety in general and social phobia in particular. However, little research has focused on blushing, presumably because researchers regard it is as a symptom of social phobia that will be manageable once individuals have confronted their fears (*in vivo* exposure) or have learnt to think differently about them (cognitive therapy). No research has developed treatment methods based on the assumption that blushing is a manifestation of shame as opposed to a sign of anxiety.

Although erythophobics are preoccupied with their blushing and wish that they did not do so, treatments that aim to reduce the frequency of blushing (as opposed to fear of it) run several risks. This goal can be achieved surgically but this is a radical approach, a treatment that is irreversible with the likelihood of continuing and unpleasant side-effects. Furthermore, the evidence is not very strong that these individuals blush any more than anyone else, which implies that their problem is not a physical one but lies in their perceptions. Finally, they forego the social advantages of the blush, which may not be conspicuous to them in the context of their fearful preoccupation, but the absence of which may cause them regret in the longer term.

The blush is related to body shame, as an expression of shame and, for many, as a reason for it. The combination of visibility and uncontrollability makes it particularly difficult to cope with fear of blushing. Further research is needed to understand it more fully and to develop interventions to help people cope with the anxieties it creates.

References

American Psychiatric Association (1994) *Diagnostic and Statistical Manual of Mental Disorders* (4th edn.). Washington, DC: American Psychiatric Association.

Bögels, S.M., Alberts, M. & de Jong, P.J. (1996) Self-consciousness, self-focused attention, blushing propensity and fear of blushing. *Personality and Individual Differences*, 21, 573–581.

Bögels, S.M., Mulkens, S. & de Jong, P.J. (1997) Task concentration training and fear of blushing. *Clinical Psychology and Psychotherapy*, 4, 251–258.

Castelfranchi, C. & Poggi, I. (1990) Blushing as a discourse: Was Darwin wrong? In W.R. Crozier (ed.) *Shyness and Embarrassment: Perspectives from Social Psychology* (pp.230–251). New York: Cambridge University Press.

Clark, D.M. (1999) Anxiety disorders: Why they persist and how to treat them. *Behaviour Research and Therapy*, 37, S5–S27.

Clark, D.M. & Wells, A. (1995) A cognitive model of social phobia. In R.G. Heimberg, M. Liebowitz, D. Hope & F. Schneier (eds) *Social Phobia: Diagnosis, Assessment, and Treatment* (pp.69–93). New York: Guilford Press.

Crozier, W.R. (2000) Blushing, social anxiety and exposure. In W.R. Crozier (ed.) *Shyness: Development, Consolidation, and Change* (pp.154–170). London: Routledge.

Crozier, W.R. & Russell, D. (1992) Blushing, embarrassability and self-consciousness. *British Journal of Social Psychology*, 31, 343–349.

Cutlip II, W.D. & Leary, M.R. (1993) Anatomic and physiological bases of social blushing: Speculations from neurology and psychology. *Behavioural Neurology*, 6, 181–185.

De Jong, P.J. (1999) Communicative and remedial effects of social blushing. *Journal of Nonverbal Behavior*, 23, 197–217.

Drott, C., Claes, G., Olsson-Rex, L., Dalman, P., Fahlén, T. & Göthberg, G. (1998) Successful treatment of facial blushing by endoscopic transthoracic sympatheticotomy. *British Journal of Dermatology*, 138, 639–643.

Drummond, P.D. (1989) Mechanism of emotional blushing. In N.W. Bond & D.A.T. Siddle (eds) *Psychobiology: Issues and Applications* (pp.363–370). Amsterdam: North-Holland.

Drummond, P.D. (1997) The effect of adrenergic blockade on blushing and facial flushing. *Psychophysiology*, 34, 163–168.

Drummond, P.D. (2000) A caution about surgical treatment for facial blushing. *British Journal of Dermatology*, 142, 194–195.

Edelmann, R.J. (1990) *Coping with Blushing*. London: Sheldon.

Edelmann, R.J. (1991) Correlates of chronic blushing. *British Journal of Social Psychology*, 30, 177–178.

Gaskell, E. (1986) *Cranford/Cousin Phillis*. London: Penguin (*Cousin Phillis* first published, 1864).

Halberstadt, A.G. & Green, L.R. (1993) Social attention and placation theories of blushing. *Motivation and Emotion*, 17, 53–64.

Hood, S.D. & Nutt, D.J. (2001) Psychopharmacological treatments: An overview. In W.R. Crozier and L.E. Alden (eds) *International Handbook of Social Anxiety* (pp.471–504). Chichester: John Wiley & Sons.

Keltner, D. & Buswell, B.N. (1997) Embarrassment: Its distinct form and appeasement functions. *Psychological Bulletin*, 122, 250–270.

Keltner, D. & L.A. Harker (1998) The forms and functions of the nonverbal signal of shame. In P. Gilbert and B. Andrews (eds) *Shame* (pp.78–98). New York: Oxford University Press.

Leary, M.R., Britt, T.W., Cutlip, W.D. & Templeton, J.L. (1992) Social blushing. *Psychological Bulletin*, 107, 446–460.

Leary, M.R. & Kowalski, R.M. (1995) *Social Anxiety*. New York: Guilford Press.

Leary, M.R., Landel, J.L. & Patton, K.M. (1996) The motivated expression of embarrassment following a self-presentational predicament. *Journal of Personality*, 64, 619–636.

Leary, M.R. & Meadows, S. (1991) Predictors, elicitors, and concomitants of social blushing. *Journal of Personality and Social Psychology*, 60, 254–262.

Mellander, S., Andersson, P.-O., Afzelius, L.-E. & Hellstrand, P. (1982) Neural beta-adrenergic dilation of the facial vein in man: Possible mechanisms in emotional blushing. *Acta Physiologica Scandinavica*, 114, 393–399.

Mersch, P.P.A., Hildebrand, M., Lavy, E.H., Wessel, I. & Hout, W.J.P.J. van (1992) Somatic symptoms in social phobia: A treatment method based on rational emotive therapy and paradoxical interventions. *Journal of Behavior Therapy and Experimental Psychiatry*, 23, 199–211.

Mulkens, S., De Jong, P.J. & Bögels, S.M. (1997) High blushing propensity: Fearful preoccupation or facial coloration? *Personality and Individual Differences*, 22, 817–824.

Mulkens, S., De Jong, P.J., Dobbelaar, A., & Bögels, S.M. (1999) Fear of blushing: Fearful preoccupation irrespective of facial coloration. *Behaviour Research and Therapy*, 37, 1119–1128.

Rapee, R.M. & Heimberg, R.G. (1997) A cognitive behavioral model of anxiety in social phobia. *Behavior Therapy and Research*, 35, 741–756.

Rex, L.O., Drott, C., Claes, G., Göthberg, G. & Dalman, P. (1998) The Boras experience of endoscopic thoracic sympatheticotomy for palmar, axillar, facial hyperhidrosis and facial blushing. *European Journal of Surgery*, Supplement, 580, 23–26.

Salter, A. (1952) *Conditioned Reflex Therapy*. London: Allen and Unwin.

Scholing, A. & Emmelkamp, P.M. (1993) Cognitive and behavioural treatments of fear of blushing, sweating or trembling. *Behaviour Research and Therapy*, 31, 155–170.

Scholing, A. & Emmelkamp, P.M. (1996) Treatment of fear of blushing, sweating or trembling: Results at long-term follow-up. *Behavior Modification*, 20, 338–356.

Semin, G.R. & Manstead, A.S.R. (1982) The social implications of embarrassment displays and restitution behavior. *European Journal of Social Psychology*, 12, 367–377.

Shearn, D., Bergman, E., Hill, K., Abel, A. & Hinds, L. (1990) Facial coloration and temperature responses in blushing. *Psychophysiology*, 27, 687–693.

Simon, A. & Shields, S.A. (1996) Does complexion color affect the experience of blushing? *Journal of Social Behavior and Personality*, 11, 177–188.

Telaranta, T. (1998) Treatment of social phobia by endoscopic thoracic sympatheticotomy. *European Journal of Surgery*, 164, Supplement, 580, 27–32.

Timms, M.W.H. (1980) Treatment of chronic blushing by paradoxical intention. *Behavioural Psychotherapy*, 8, 59–61.

Van Ameringen, M., Mancini, C., Oakman, J.M. & Farvolden, P. (1999) Selective serotonin reuptake inhibitors in the treatment of social phobia: The emerging gold standard. *CNS Drugs*, 11, 307–315.

Woody, S.R., Chambless, D.L. & Glass, C.R. (1997) Self-focused attention in the treatment of social phobia. *Behaviour Research and Therapy*, 35, 117–129.

Chapter 12

Eating disorders, shame and pride

A cognitive-behavioural functional analysis

Kenneth Goss and Paul Gilbert

Introduction

This chapter argues that both shame and pride play important roles in many forms of eating disorder. For some (dietary restrictors), body shame can arise out of a general sense of personal shame and inferiority where changing body shape and controlling desires (such as eating) are seen as solutions. Moreover, they can feel proud of themselves (and at times superior to others) when they control their eating behaviour and weight. The ability to resist their own desires and the influence/control of others can then be built into self-identity. For people who overeat and/or binge, eating behaviour can be used to distract the self from shame affect and negative feelings in general, but such lead, in the long term, to more shame. This sets up a vicious cycle where affect-controlling behaviours (e.g., bingeing) increases shame and thus poor eating control. Indeed, it will be argued that anorexia can involve shame-pride spirals whereas over eating and bingeing involves shame-shame spirals. However, these are not mutually exclusive cycles for they address different difficulties, and an individual may have both.

Eating disorders

Although there is some debate regarding the epidemiology of eating disorders (particularly anorexia nervosa), there is evidence that that the prevalence of all eating disorders has risen over the past 30 years (Russell, 1995). The descriptions of eating disorder symptoms have also developed to the point where there are now four official *DSM-IV* eating disordered criteria: anorexia nervosa; bulimia nervosa; binge eating disorder and eating disorder not otherwise specified (American Psychiatric Association, 1994). Additional diagnostic categories have also been proposed, including multi-impulsive bulimia, to address patients with eating disordered and comorbid borderline personality disorder traits (Lacey & Mourelli, 1986) and machismo nervosa, to address a primarily male preoccupation with weight training and muscle gain (Whitehead, 1994). In turn, many of these categories have been hypothesised to be subdivided by symptom presentation (Hall, Blakey & Hall, 1992; Tobin, Griffing & Griffing, 1997), comorbidity (e.g., with seasonal affective disorder; Ghadirian et al., 1999) or to present differently cross-culturally (Nagi, Lee & Lee, 2000).

Theories of eating disorder

The past 30 years have also seen a dramatic increase in research into the aetiology and maintenance of eating disorders (see Szmukler, Dare & Treasure, 1995 for a review). These have spanned the social and biological sciences and tend to fall into two major categories: aetiology theories and maintenance models. These models tend to polarise into biological, psychological and social theories. Unfortunately, the holy grail of eating disorder theory (a unified definitive casual and maintenance pathway) remains as elusive as ever (Campbell, 1995). Kinder's (1991) analysis that there is no single causative pathway to an eating disorder appears to be hold true 10 years on (see also Jensen, 2001). Moreover, many theorists recognise it is from a better understanding of the *interactions* between biological, psychological and social/cultural factors that clarity on cause and maintenance will come (Gilbert, Chapter 1, this volume).

Part of the problem in developing integrative theories and process models of eating disorders has been the tendency to treat people with eating disorders as a homogeneous group, leading to the oversight of important individual variations that can compromise treatment (Waller, 1993). However, even models that do account for such variations tend to view eating disorders within specific psychiatric diagnostic classifications (e.g., anorexia and bulimia) with over-concern about size and shape and fear of fatness as paramount (Garner & Garfinkel, 1982; Fairburn & Cooper, 1989; Waller, 1993). We suggest that there are a number of processes, such as affect control, pride and shame, which operate differently in different types of eating disorder. Further, we suggest that a functional behavioural analysis helps to illuminate these differences.

Fear of fatness and beyond

Many of the early studies of eating disorders, especially anorexia, saw a fear of fatness as lying at the heart of the problem, thus making it a form of phobia. When fear of fatness is noted as part of an eating disorder, it is usually related to body appearance anxieties rather than health concerns. However, more recently it has been recognised that cross-cultural and historical models, which specifically focus on anorexia and bulimia, do not find these 'core symptoms' to be universal. Studies using Chinese samples report self-starvation associated with both 'fat phobic' and 'non-fat phobic' symptoms (Nagi, Lee & Lee, 2000). Furthermore, these patterns of phobia appear to change over time for some individuals. There are also accounts of ascetic eating disorders historically and cross-culturally, where starvation states are related to religious or ascetic concerns rather than to 'fat phobia' (Szmukler & Patton, 1995). Indeed, there has been recent interest in the relationship between the psychology of the dieting ascetic and those with eating disorders, such as on the special meaning given to the sin (inner badness), self-denial and purifying (Huline-Dickens, 2000). Fear of fatness may not account for disordered eating more generally, particularly in men and in patients who overeat, binge without purging or do not diet.

New research supporting the 'fear of fatness' model has also highlighted the role of shame-type beliefs as a core to the underlying belief system associated with eating disordered psychopathology. Cooper, Todd and Wells' (1998) study of 12 anorexic, 12 bulimic and 12 non-eating disordered controls is indicative of this trend and has extended earlier cognitive-behavioural maintenance models of eating disorders (Fairburn & Cooper, 1989; Garner & Garfinkel, 1982) in an attempt to illuminate aetiological and maintenance factors. They used semi-structured interviews to investigate the negative self-beliefs of these female groups. They concluded that the eating disordered groups differed from normal subjects in two major areas:

1 Higher levels of negative self-belief, which were 'without exception, negative and unconditional', focusing on themes of worthlessness, uselessness, inferiority, being a failure, abandonment and being alone.
2 Greater conditional beliefs about eating and the meaning of size and shape. The focus of these beliefs was on the relationship between weight and shape and self-acceptance.

Cooper, Todd and Wells (1998) hypothesised that dieting was to manage emotional difficulties arising from aversive early experiences and avoid abandonment or rejection. They noted that dieting helped individuals to feel more successful and in control, while bingeing appeared to provide a distraction from unpleasant thoughts, images, negative self-beliefs and emotional states. They hypothesised that eating disorders represent types of schema compensation and cognitive and emotional avoidance. The negative beliefs elicited in Cooper, Todd and Wells' (1998) study are in line with current psychiatric and psychological theories of eating disorders. Primarily, patients were preoccupied with losing fat; anxious about gaining weight and self-attacking if they broke their personal eating rules.

Other theorists have highlighted the important *functional* nature of eating disordered behaviour in at least temporarily improving mood or as dissociative strategies to avoid severe affect shifts (Polivy & Herman, 1993). Some have noted how an eating disorder can become a 'friend' in terms of helping individuals feel protected, special and in control (Serpall et al., 1999). There are also a number of eating disorders where fear of fatness does not seem a central element. These would certainly include binge eating disorder (Striegel-Moore, Silberstein & Rodin, 2000) and many recurrent obese over-eaters (Marcus et al., 1992), particularly those seeking treatment for their obesity (Webb, 2000). The eating styles of these patients are not currently including within the *DSM-IV* criteria (grazing, eating normal size portions more often when distressed, and choosing specific comfort foods). Although exercise is included in anorexia and ENDOS criteria, the usual focus is on weight loss rather than muscle gain and dieting is usually considered to refer to restriction of food intake rather than deliberately ingesting foods, food supplements and drugs (e.g., steroids) to increase muscle mass. Patients who deliberately eat to self-punish or to gain weight to avoid intimacy (Orbach, 1979) are also left out of current eating disorder models. Yet, research suggests that all of these groups of patients experience high levels of comorbid psychopathology, disruption to psychosocial functioning and potentially lethal health risks (Telch & Stice, 1998; Webb, 2000). Preoccupation with size and shape may take second place, or not occur at all for some patients who use bingeing, purging, compulsive eating and exercise as a route to affect management.

It appears that three key themes appear in the literature regarding the role of eating disordered symptoms:

1   To manage key themes of worthlessness, inferiority, failure and abandonment. These pervasive negative self-evaluations are central to shame cognition and affect.
2   To manage more specific 'fear of fatness' beliefs.
3   To regulate more general negative affect states.

In summary, the evidence for the 'fear of fatness' model may hold for many women presenting for treatment for anorexia and bulimia to Western medical services. However, this overlooks historical and cross-cultural variations in disordered eating, may exclude additional or alternate 'core cognitions' underlying similar symptomalogical presentations, give insufficient attention to eating as affect regulation behaviour or be too exclusive in addressing similarities between anorexia and bulimia and other patterns of disordered eating or activity (e.g., binge eating, compulsive eating, and compulsive exercise – to lose or gain weight). One way to move current models forward is to explore a functional nature of disordered eating patterns and, in particular, to examine how pride and shame can operate differently in different types of eating disorder.

A functional analysis of dietary control and weight loss

Because eating disorders are focused on specific behaviours, they are highly appropriate for a functional behavioural analysis. A functional analysis of behaviour requires exploration of the perceived functions of a behaviour. For example, as Ferster (1973) noted long ago, two people may take an overdose but one intended to kill themself, while the other was drunk and simply took too many sleeping tablets. There are many cases where the functional purpose of dietary restraint and weight loss can be positive, for example, to lose weight for sport reasons (a national hunt jockey or athlete), to follow a career (ballet dancer, model), for health reasons (to avoid a heart attack) or try to make oneself more sexually or generally attractive.

Second, a functional analysis suggests that behaviours can be used to stop bad things from happening (e.g., social rejection, getting depressed, punishments) or increase the chances of good things happening (increase social acceptance, feel good, rewards). Behaviours that are punishment-avoidant have been referred to as safety behaviours (Clark, 1999) or defensive behaviours (see Gilbert, Chapter 1, this volume). What therapists may see as dysfunctional beliefs (e.g., 'I must stay thin') are often, in the patient's mind, felt to be highly functional (e,g., 'If I stay thin people will like/want me') and serving positive ends. Hence cognitive-behavioural therapists will often help patients see both the advantages and *dis*advantages of such beliefs and behaviours (i.e., carry out cognitive and behavioural functional analysis with the patient).

Third, functional behaviours can be aimed at changing or controlling external or internal contingencies. Controlling eating behaviour to elicit the positive attention of others or to follow a career (e.g., be this in sport or modelling) is designed to control the self-environment interactions. In sport, while some need to work to keep weight off, others need to put it on (e.g., Sumo wrestlers). When such goals change (e.g., a person retires) such behaviours may be dropped. Internal contingencies, however, relate to behaviours that control one's own moods or emotions or are under self-evaluative control (self-regulation). For example, it has been found that, in students, impulse eating when stressed is common. However, although control over impulse eating (e.g., of sweat and fattening foods) is reduced under condition of emotional distress, this is only so if people believe that eating such foods will help their moods (Tice, Bratslavsky & Baumeister, 2001); that is, seen as functional. Thus, eating behaviour can have multiple functions serving both short- and long-term goals.

Fourth, functional analyses also indicate that functions can change. For example, the drunk person, who took an overdose by accident, discovers that others become highly attentive and concerned and thus the next behaviour of overdosing is to elicit concern from others. People with eating disorders may start by trying to reduce punishments (e.g., criticism and rejection) but then feel good about their control. The feeling good (or as we argue below – pride) in control becomes a new reinforcer of behaviour.

Fifth, disordered eating behaviour, especially when it results in substantial loss of weight, can produce a variety of physiological changes. These changes may play a key role in disorder maintenance. For example, Keys, Broze and Henschel (1950) eloquently documented ways in which starvation can lead to eating disordered behaviours (e.g., bingeing), mood disturbance and pre-occupation with food.

Indeed, perhaps the most easily overlooked comparison between eating disorders and disordered eaters is their shared biology. Garner (1997) argues that normal biological weight regulation systems may serve to maintain or exacerbate eating disordered beliefs, behaviour, cognitive processing and emotional response to periods of 'semi-starvation'. Several consequences of the restriction of food intake may have had some adaptive functions in early mammalian evolution.

One of the yet unanswered questions relating to eating disorders is whether individuals vary in their thresholds for experiencing the physical effects of semi-starvation and how much of this can become a conditioned response. Many patients will 'cross over' between anorexic, bingeing and purging. It is possible that this reflects changes in the body's ability to maintain starvation state. It is also possible, as some patients report, that after one period of restriction initially, they may only need to think about restricting again to experience many of the problems usually associated with semi-starvation states (e.g., preoccupation with food, feelings of gastric bloating or to anticipate feeling elevations in mood and becoming more active).

Sixth, some behaviours may have had adaptive functions in some environments, but become less adaptive in others (Gilbert, 1989). Being motivated to eat high fat and sugar foods may be highly adaptive for early humans for whom food supplies could be sparse, but the same behaviours when such foods are abundant may be less adaptive and associated with various diseases (e.g., heart disease and risk of disordered eating patterns – over 50% of adult Americans are believed to be at health risk due to overweight). In starvation states bingeing, obsessional behaviour around food and eating, preoccupation with eating, emotional lability, hoarding of food and loss of sexual interest would all appear to be adaptive responses to the body's reduced calorific intake. These phenomena have been observed in clinical studies (e.g., Keys, Broze & Henschel, 1950) and anecdotally recounted from survivors of concentration camps and famine. It is only in the latter stages of semi-starvation that depressed mood and retarded activity occur, while emotional lability and psychological disturbance increase.

Seventh, a functional analysis needs to incorporate mediating cognitive variables. This is particularly important in understanding the processes that occur in eating disorders. For example, in the early stages of the disorder individuals may intend to change their body shape and believe that the desired outcome will be gaining greater acceptance from others. In the early phases of anorexia or obsessive weight training this belief is likely to be reinforced by others' positive reactions. However, over time their new body shape may be perceived as indicative of ill health (for low-weight anorexics) or seen to be grotesque (for highly muscled bodybuilders). It appears that cognitive biases (e.g., continuing to see the self as fat), which help individuals to maintain their behaviours, may blind them to these new evaluations by others. In fact, there is much evidence that those with eating disorders have a number of cognitive biases around weight, body shape and eating behaviour (see Vitousek, 1996, for a review). These biases can create 'blind spots' that do not allow individuals to develop self-correcting behaviour strategies. Some biases may arise because people have become proud of their own abilities to control their weight or weight-train and this pride becomes the main reinforcer.

To summarise: a functional analysis suggests a focus on the purpose of eating behaviour and on its outcomes (as perceived by individuals and their wider social network). Much of the literature suggests that disordered eating behaviour functions either as a solution to problems of low self-esteem and/ or as an affect control device. In both of these, we suggest that shame and pride may play key roles. We begin this exploration by first exploring shame in more detail.

The roles of external and internal shame and stigma avoidance

As noted earlier (Gilbert, Chapter 1, this volume) the social rank theory of shame (Gilbert & McGuire, 1998) focuses on involuntary subordination; of seeing oneself in an unwanted, inferior and subordinate position, vulnerable to put-down, rejection and loss of control over social resources. In shame, this outcome is seen to occur due to perceptions of being flawed, inadequate, and in some way carrying undesirable attributes. Indeed, Kaufman (1989) called shame the 'affect of inferiority' – although in social rank theory it is *unwanted or involuntary subordination* that is key (i.e., some people can know they are in subordinate positions but this does not bother them that much, and indeed in some cases may prefer to be lower, or average in rank, rather than in a high(er) rank position; Gilbert, 1989). However, so aversive (both emotionally and to inclusive fitness) can be the outcomes of *involuntary* subordination that people will work hard to avoid feelings of shame and being shamed (Tangney, 1995). Gilbert (2000a) found that shame, depression and social anxiety were all related to feeling inferior to others, thinking that others look down on the self and tendencies to behave submissively. Moreover, subordinate self-evaluation was a powerful predictor of depression and social anxiety. Not surprisingly then, there is good evidence that shame is associated with range of psychopathologies (Gilbert & Andrews, 1998; Tangney, Wagner & Gramzow, 1992a).

However, it is necessary to distinguish what type of shame is involved, for example, internal or external shame. As outlined by Gilbert (Chapter 1, this volume), external shame relates to the affects associated with negative social evaluations. There is much evidence that people with some forms of eating disorder have been teased and criticised for their body shape in the past and these experiences may interact with various personality dispositions. For example, it may be that some people with some types of eating disorders are interpersonally or rejection sensitive and find it hard to tolerate. Davidson et al. (1989) explored *interpersonal sensitivity* and suggest that:

> Interpersonal sensitivity (IPS) is a construct that refers to an individual's hypersensitivity to perceived self-deficiencies in relation to others. It embraces sensitivity to rejection and criticism on the part of others; it also embodies a sense of personal inadequacy, inferiority, and poor morale. Such individuals are quick to take offense, are unduly sensitive to ridicule, feel uncomfortable in the presence of others, and show a negative set of expectations in their dealings with others. A close relationship with social phobia is suggested (p.357).

It is possible that for a variety of reasons (see Szmukler, Dare & Treasure, 1995) some people who go on to develop an eating disorder may start with heightened interpersonal sensitivity (Steiger et al., 1999). For some, weight loss/control seems like a functional behaviour; a solution, for example, 'I will be liked more and less bullied/stigmatised if I am thin'. For others, food becomes a way to manage their negative emotions and sensitivities to rejection. Interpersonal sensitivity, allied to early life events, may account for the high comorbidity in eating disorders. If so, therapies may need to address these elements and direct attention to certain social anxiety aspects of those with eating disorders. It is unclear at this time if one of the reasons the SSRIs (serotonin selective re-uptake inhibitors) can be helpful for some people is that they reduce interpersonal sensitivity and increase social confidence.

Internal shame

Although 'low self-esteem' is usually seen as the common denominator across disordered eating and eating disordered patients (Fairburn et al., 1987), the concept itself has been criticised for being too vague (Robson, 1998) and disorder non-specific. Moreover, there is increasing evidence that people can derive self-esteem from different sources. Validations by others of the intrinsic aspects of self appear to lead to more positive and stable self-esteem than self-esteem rooted in accomplishment and achievements. Achievement rooted self-esteem is dependent on meeting socially approved standards and 'winning approval' but it can be easily lost through failures (Schimel et al., 2001). The concept of internalised shame has been proposed as another way to consider self-evaluation and its association with psychopathology (Cook, 1996).

Internal shame relates to the sense of self as flawed and inadequate, textured with affect (Tangney, 1995). Indeed, one could suggest that some sense of internalised shame may be one of the drivers of efforts to compensate with achievements – but such are unstable. The point is, it is not just having low self-esteem, but having what one could call negative self-esteem that is salient for shame; of seeing oneself as possessing negative attributes that one wants to change, get rid of or hide. We will not discuss the ways a person may come to internalise shame (negative attributes of self) but recognise it to be complex, related to early attachment histories, peer group relationships and cultural processes (Gilbert, Chapter 1, this volume). Through these various forms of social relating, people learn how to judge and feel about themselves (see Gilbert & Thompson, Chapter 2, this volume).

It is clear that many people who are stigmatised for their weight do not necessarily go on to develop low self-esteem or suffer intense personal shame (Crocker & Major, 1989). Perhaps they have more intrinsic stable self-esteem (Schimel et al., 2001). However, as noted above, people with eating disorders seem to be set apart from other forms of eating control behaviours (e.g., losing weight for sports or health reasons) by having high negative (shame-based) cognitions about themselves. These, in turn, may be either a cause or consequence of having high interpersonal or rejection sensitivity.

Internal shame is related to a sense of internal, personal unattractiveness and often associated with intense self-criticism for certain attributes or even self-hatred (Gilbert, Chapter 1, this volume). Jensen (2001) has recently suggested that people with eating disorders may feel *generally* unattractive (ugly) compared to others and the body becomes a vehicle to feeling more generally attractive. It is unclear if some people with eating disorders are more sensitive about body aesthetics than others (e.g., Jensen, 2001; Veale, Chapter 14, this volume). In any event, use of the body by either gaining weight (muscle-building) or losing it, to feel more inwardly or outwardly attractive, links different types of eating disorder behaviours by clarifying their function.

Cognitive bias

At least in Westernised female samples with anorexia and bulimia, there is strong evidence of negative self-evaluation, based upon beliefs about size shape and weight being associated with eating disordered behaviour, distress and impaired psychosocial functioning (Cooper, Todd & Wells, 1998; Vitousek, 1996). These patterns have also been found in binge eating patients (regardless of their weight; Telch & Agras, 1994), patients with chronic obesity seeking treatment (Striegel-Moore et al., 2000; Webb, 2000), and in machismo nervosa (Whitehead, 1994). Thus, it is the meaning of weight/size and shape and the subjective belief that one is overweight that predicts psychological distress and disordered eating behaviour, rather than objective body mass index (BMI) (Cash & Hicks, 1990; Webb, 2000). Such biases then link body shame with meanings of weight/shape.

Personality

In the previous section, we noted the possible role of interpersonal sensitivity as a personality disposition to body shame issues and how eating disorders may represent one way of managing them. Following Bruch's (1973) lead, a number of studies have identified trait narcissism as a core feature across disordered eating and eating disordered populations, both predating and out-lasting eating disordered symptoms (Lehoux, Steiger & Jabalpurlawa, 2000; Steinberg & Shaw 1997), and distinguishes eating disordered patients from psychiatric and normal controls (Steiger et al., 1997). Additional variables that seem to characterise eating disordered and disordered eating individuals are perfectionism (Davis, 1997; Hewitt, Flett & Ediger, 1995), low self-esteem (Fairburn et al., 1987), self-directed hostility and low levels of perceived control (Waller, 1998). Indeed, these are often seen as moderating variables in both the severity and the outcome of eating disorders and disordered eaters.

Affect control

As noted earlier (Gilbert, Chapter 1, this volume) shame-based affects are ones that are constellated around self-presentation, self as a social desirable/ undesirable person and self-esteem. Shame-based affects and emotions can be experienced as blends of (primary) feelings and emotions such as disgust, anger, anxiety, sadness and dejection. It is these negative/unpleasant emotions, centred on the sense of self, that eating behaviours in disordered folk can be used to control. Difficulties in interpersonal functioning have been identified in eating disorders and disordered eaters (Eldredge, Locke & Horowitz, 1998; Kayrooz, 1994; Schmidt, Tiller & Morgan, 1995) with bingeing, purging and compulsive eating problems often hypothesised to be triggered both historically and proximally by emotional problems in inter-personal relationships (Bruch, 1973; Crisp, 1979; Fairburn & Cooper, 1989; Garner & Garfinkel, 1982). The functioning of food as self-soothing and as a method of dissociation from negative affective states has been reported in bulimic, binge-eating subjects (Polivy & Herman 1993), and anorexic patients (Cooper, Todd & Wells, 1998). Even in non-eating disordered people, emotional distress is associated with reduced control over impulse eating if people believe this will help their moods (Tice, Bratslavsky & Baumeister, 2001).

Restricting food intake, bingeing or planning to binge can, in the (very) short term, at least be associated with reduced negative affect and increased positive affect. The direct links with affect are crucial to illuminate however. For example, for some, losing weight for health or for sports' purposes may actually increase negative affect to the extent that people would like to eat more, but perceived positive long-term consequences that maintain the behaviour (e.g., reducing the risk of heart disease or increased sporting prowess).

There is considerable evidence that dietary restrictors feel a sense of achievement from eating control, while binge eaters can feel temporary relief from painful feelings of anxiety depression and shame (Heatherton & Baumeister, 1991). Some anorexic people then may have positive experiences of diet restriction, in that they feel better about themselves (achievement), feel they have more energy and better mood, as well as meeting longer-term goals of meeting societal standards of the attractive body (thin and beautiful). Indirect evidence, drawn from other disciplines (e.g., dietetics and health and sports psychology) may provide clues to the biological mechanisms underlying these behaviours (e.g., the positive impact of exercise on mood, the mood-enhancing properties of some foods and the 'starvation high' effects in the early phases of dieting). Binge eaters, on the other hand, may use food to control negative affects, much as those with other addictions do, but then feel more shame (and negative affect) subsequently.

There can also be various fears in losing control. Some anorexic people believe that if they lose control then their desires for food will run away from them and they will lose *all* control; that is, they see eating as making them feel worse. The fear of loss of control is not only shaming but points to difficulties in regulation in a kind of black and white thinking; for example, 'either I exert strict control or I will lose all control' (Vitousek, 1996).

The temporal nature of shame

Sanftner and Crowther (1998) used a time sampling approach to measure daily fluctuations in shame, guilt and positive and negative affect to compare bingeing and non-bingeing women drawn from a non-eating disordered sample. Their results suggest that women who binge experienced significantly greater fluctuations in self-esteem, negative affect, shame and guilt. However, self-esteem and positive affect *increased*, prior to all eating episodes but shame did not. Sanftner and Crowther (1998) also found that shame and low-state self-esteem significantly differentiated women who binged from those who did not. Interestingly, their methodology measured fluctuations in these (and positive/negative affect) every four hours for seven days. They found that women who binge experience greater daily fluctuations on these measures. Positive self-esteem and affect increased *prior to* binge episodes. This may be consistent with a self-nurturance model (eating to feel better) and the hypothesis that bingeing provides a means to escape from the intense negative affect associated (we would argue) with shame (Heatherton & Baumeister, 1991). This study suggests that shame-related affects are often not permanent affective states, but can vary over time, particularly if strategies are used to manage them.

In a more recent study of 15 bulimics patients, Waters, Hill and Waller (2001) found that bingeing was associated with reduced hedonic tone, higher tensions and *less* hunger. Although, in general, people believe that impulse eating can improve their moods and help them feel better (Tice, Bratslavsky & Baumeister, 2001), in this group of bulimics craving and then bingeing was associated with feeling worse afterwards. In other words, if people were using a binge to ward off negative affect – it didn't work. This might be to do with feeling physically uncomfortable (bloated) or increased shame-based affects. Indeed, craving *but not* bingeing was associated with positive affect. This might be related to pride, having resisted the urge – something more common to anorexia. Waters, Hill and Waller (2001) give a fascinating model (part of which) is based on a conditioning and functional analysis paradigm that outlines how ego threats (we would prefer the concept of shame) give rise to negative affect and craving, plus disinhibition, which are associated with overeating/bingeing.

Eating disorders and shame research

Shame-based clinical descriptions of eating disorders have appeared sporadically in the literature. Bruch's (1973) case description of Karol outlines her patient's feelings of being a failure and her desire not to become a 'horrible person', 'a nothing' and her use of self-starvation to avoid this fate. This fits the idea that eating disorders take root in the context of a *general* sense of an unattractive self (Jensen, 2001). Studies of the relationship between shame and psychopathology have begun in the past 10–15 years. Cook's (1994, 1996) development, the *Internalised Shame Scale* (ISS), represents one approach to the measurement of shame. The ISS views internalised shame as a *global* self-construct. Although the scale was based upon Tomkin's (1963, 1987) and Nathanson's (1992) affect theory of shame, it is a negative self-cognition scale. It requires individuals to rate a series of statements related to how they see themselves (e.g., 'I see myself as inadequate'). Scores are then calculated to give an overall shame score. Cook used the ISS to compare scores of a number of psychiatric groups. He noted that eating disordered patients scored significantly higher on the ISS than all of the other clinical groups tested (Cook, 1994). Other studies measuring shame and guilt have produced similar findings (Garner & Garfinkel, 1985; Sanftner & Crowther, 1998). Indeed, shame cognitions and feelings, especially self-disgust, form part of the differential diagnosis criteria for Binge Eating Disorder (American Psychiatric Association, 1994).

Webb (2000), studying a sample of obese people, found that subjects with disordered eating behaviour were also likely to be highly internally and externally shame-prone and to experience marked psychological distress, at levels consistent with those of patients with an eating disordered diagnosis.

Shame studies using situational scenarios for measuring shame (rather than global measures) have found somewhat lower correlations between shame and eating disordered pathology, but have identified shame about eating to be related to eating disordered pathology (Burney & Irwin, 2000). A recent series of studies by Troop et al. (2001a, 2001b) and Gee and Troop (2001) indicate that shame and low pride (in oneself and behaviour), as measured on a situational scale (the TOSCA; Tangney, Wagner and Gramzow, 1989) and a global external shame scale (the Other as Shamer Scale (OAS); Goss, Gilbert & Allan, 1994) were significantly associated with eating disordered psychopathology for women currently experiencing or having recovered from an eating disorder. This appears to be the case even when depression is controlled for (Gee & Troop, 2001). Of clinical significance are the distribution patterns of shame scores: women with a current eating disorder reported the highest levels of shame. Women who had recovered or were in remission from an eating disorder had an intermediate score, and non-eating disorder controls had the lowest shame scores. Troop et al. (2001b) conclude that 'women who continue to suffer with increased levels of shame that persist even after remission and that these may indicate stable perceptions of the self as being of relatively low social rank' (p.12).

In general then, the data seem to suggest that eating disordered people have elevated rates of both internal shame (negative self-evaluations) and external shame (feeling that others look down on them). Moreover, situational shame measures (e.g., the TOSCA) suggest that given certain imaginal scenarios (e.g., breaking something at work), they are likely to highly endorse shame responses (e.g., using concealment and making negative judgements of themselves).

The focus of shame

Gilbert (1997, 2000b) has suggested that while shame can be seen as a global construct, clinically it can be useful to explore if there is a specific aspect(s) of self that is a main focus for shame.

Body appearance shame

Many (but not all people) with an eating disorder can feel shame of their bodies (see Thompson, 1996 for a review). Fairburn (2001b) has recently highlighted the role that excessive bodily monitoring plays in eating disorders. For example, individuals who engage in excessive mirror-checking, or pinching parts of the skin as a 'fat test' almost invariably report that these tests and checks lead to feelings of shame and self-disgust that promote further attempts to control weight. Alternatively, individuals may take great pains to avoid seeing their body (or having others see it) to avoid body appearance shame. Many obese patients report avoiding mirrors/windows, in case they inadvertently see their reflection. They may also avoid public exposure of their bodies (e.g., in exercise, swimming class, communal changing rooms) for fear of activating shaming interactions from others. There appear to be some overlaps with the safety behaviours of body dysmorphic disorder (see Veale,

Chapter 14, this volume) and those with disfigurements (Kent & Thompson, Chapter 5, this volume).

Body in action and body function shame

Body shame can also relate to how one's body functions (e.g., as in sexual behaviour and shame of impotence). Studies suggest that dancers and athletes who depend on low body weight to power ratio's (e.g., distance runners, gymnasts) are at greater risk of developing eating disorders. Brownell (1995) notes a number of mechanisms that may relate to shame of how the body performs in this group; in particular internal and external pressures to perform. Obese patients often report similar concerns in relation to the shame they feel about not being able to perform everyday activities, such as walking long distances, washing, or playing physical games with their children, as being motivators to restricting their calorific intake.

Bulimic and binge-eating subjects report shame following periods of excessive eating. Indeed, similar processes occur in anorexic patients even when they have eaten objectively small amounts of food. Patients often describe feeling betrayed by their bodies' need to eat and may feel disgusted by the food they are ingesting. Shame can also be activated in individuals who deliberately purge, using diuretics, laxatives or vomiting. Hiding these behaviours is common across these patient groups. Again, this appears to be motivated by fears of shaming responses by other people if they were to be discovered.

Shame of achievement failures

Trying to reach a goal and failing (e.g., failing an examination or an interview) can be a source of shame. In eating disorders and disordered eating, control over eating behaviour and/or body size is often the desired outcome. If these ideals are not reached, this is often perceived as a personal failure, and may be linked to predictions of being shamed by valued others or self-criticism. Individuals who are unable to reach their standards often report feelings of shame, which further motivates attempts to control eating behaviour and body shape. This process has been outlined in the cognitive-behavioural conceptualisation of eating disorders (Fairburn & Cooper, 1989), although shame is not specifically discussed.

However, shame may also be the result of other perceived failures or fear of failure. Adolescence is seen as the peak age of onset for eating disorders. Many eating disordered people report that feelings of failure or fear of failure in educational tasks precipitated their initial period of eating disordered behaviour. It is possible the feelings of failure in one area of one's life will be compensated for, by trying to be successful in another (Jensen, 2001; Vitousek, 1996).

Shame and relationships

Etiologically, studies point to the role of abusive relationships (physical, sexual, emotional) in the development and maintenance of eating disorders (Eisler, 1995). Such early life experiences have been shown to be associated with body shame in chronic depression (see Andrews, Chapter 13, this volume). It is not surprising therefore that individuals with eating disorders and disordered eating often report difficulties in interpersonal relationships. Such people may have an eating disorder superimposed on underlying chronic depression.

Bruch (1973) and Schmidt, Tiller and Morgan (1995) noted that bulimic women appear to have difficulties in establishing intimate relationships with men. A number of studies have reported higher rates of interpersonal difficulties (Eldredge, Locke & Horowitz, 1998), social anxiety (Striegel-Moore, Silberstein & Rodin, 1993) and need for approval and acceptance by others (Friedman & Whisman, 1998; Steins & Remy, 1996,). De Silva (1993) notes that sexual difficulties are common in eating disordered women and in people who are obese; presenting differently dependent on diagnosis, gender and body weight. It is also possible that difficulties in social relationships can persist after the eating disorder has resolved (Norman, Herzog & Chauncey, 1986).

Schmidt, Tiller and Morgan (1995) note that eating disorders impact on a range of relationships, including those with parents, sexual partners, friendships and with their children. Furthermore, they may find it difficult to access social support, and (particularly bulimics) may have greater discrepancies between the social support they desire and what they receive.

Shame about the need to be dependent on others has been anecdotally reported, but has been relatively unexplored in the research literature. Some people may confuse necessary/useful reliance on others for care/support (care receiving) as forms of involuntary submission and that the self will come under the control of the other. This may be particularly so if individuals are being treated against their will, which can be the case in severe anorexia and hunger strikers. If individuals voluntarily submit/comply, they do so by understanding the advantages to them, as in a treatment programme/self-help group. As Serpall et al. (1999) note, trying to get patients to 'submit/comply' to a programme can provoke ambivalence in patients, particularly if they are required to reveal aspects of their eating behaviour that they find shameful. The dependency and power imbalance that is inherent in all therapeutic relationships may also activate shame responses as a defence against intimacy and the threat of rejection.

Shame of feelings/thoughts

Polivy and Herman (1993) and De Silva (1995) note that binge eaters and bulimic binge-eating episodes can be triggered by negative affective states and can be seen as a way of regulating painful thoughts and feelings, of which feelings of shame, and its associated cognitions, may be among the most powerful. These behaviours may appear to be effective, at least in the short term, although in the longer term may lead to weight gain and more shame. As an example of eating and affect control, one of our patients had rage attacks related to jealousy. She would feel so bad about her behaviour that an hour or so later she would go to the fridge and eat all the ice cream she could find. This temporarily distracted her from her feelings and distress. Later she would feel ashamed both of her rage attack and eating the ice cream. Interestingly, she was unclear in her mind if eating was a comfort or self-punishment and even a kind of accusation against her partner, associated with thoughts about her partner: 'Look what you made me do!'

Shame of feelings/thoughts have not been directly explored in people with eating disorders. However, it does appear that anorexic women are more likely to suppress their own emotional needs to protect their interpersonal relationships by not expressing negative emotions (Geller, Cocknell & Goldner, 2000). This is probably a fear of rejection problem, and interestingly it is associated with attempting to present oneself as perfect in some way (Hewitt, Flett & Ediger, 1995). Eating disordered patients also tend not to communicate their feelings, and find it harder to identify them (Troop, Schmidt & Treasure, 1995). In addition, some patients can feel ashamed of just how much they think of eating to the expense of other things such as relationships, work or family.

One can consider these processes in terms of learning theories of affect development and affect discrimination. The relatively traumatic histories of some eating disordered and disordered eating individuals (Schmidt et al., 1997; Welch, Doll & Fairburn, 1997) may mean that they have either not been given the opportunity to learn alternative methods for discriminating between or regulating affective states, or that the expression of negative emotions may have led to actual or perceived physical rejection or attack (Ferster, 1973). This could also be generalised to more 'positive' emotional states, such as sexual feelings. The experiencing/expression of certain feelings may have been particularly dangerous in relationships that were sexually abusive or that run a high risk of rejection (e.g., if one has been labelled or perceives oneself to be sexually unattractive).

Shame of belonging to a stigmatised group

Perhaps the most common experience for clinicians working with people with an eating disorder is the denial/under-reporting of severity that patients respond with, particularly in the early phases of an eating disorder. Patients often say, 'I don't have an eating disorder'. One way of making sense of this is in terms of the stigma and shame associated with having a psychiatric diagnosis.

This difficulty has given rise to a number of approaches to engage people with an eating disorder in treatment (including group psychoeducation; Olmsted & Kaplan, 1995) and motivational interviewing (Blake, Turnball & Treasure, 1997). The idea that shame may be a key reason for denial is not always addressed however, nor the fact that confronting a person with a diagnosis may not only intensify shame but also activate any defences against feeling shame.

The evidence for stigmatisation of mental illness, and for obesity in Western cultures is unequivocal (Falkner et al., 1999). Belonging to these groups is usually perceived to be culturally undesirable. Eating disordered and disordered eating patients may be seen to be trapped by trying to avoid actual discrimination and hostile acts by avoiding being categorised as belonging to one group (the overweight) but engaging in behaviours that may place them in another stigmatised group (the mentally ill). The dilemma is to manage one's group or social identity (e.g., 'I am not going to be seen as one of those fat ladies') but to hide the behaviours that manage it (e.g., purging). Clearly, there is a potential for being shamed, or shaming oneself, for failing to manage this balance. This can seem like a tightrope almost impossible to walk; to avoid being seen to belong to a (stigmatised) group of 'fat people' or a (stigmatised) group of those with a mental health problem.

Coping with shame

Much of the literature exploring the relationship between shame and eating disorders has centred on shame as a relatively stable and global phenomenon. However, in the previous section we noted the importance of: (1) temporal variations in shame affect/cognition; and (2) the individual's focus of shame. These considerations help to identify the complex relationships between shame and eating disorders/disordered eating. In this section we focus on coping with shame.

If shame affects are seen as early warning signs of a potential social rejection or put-down, then individuals will not only need to have rapid ways to detect and cope with these threats, but also work out longer-term strategies. Coping with shame-based problems will be affected by the nature of shame (whether it is internal and/or external) and the focus of shame. Currently, there are no empirical studies exploring how people with eating disorders/disordered eating cope with the different shame as such. The following suggestions are made from clinical observation and based on the various defensive behaviours outlined by Gilbert (Chapter 1, this volume).

Attention

Detection and attention to potential threats is the first element in threat-coping sequences. It is clear from studies on anxiety disorders that attention mechanisms are important for onset and maintenance of disorders (e.g., Clark, 1999). To date, there has been some research on attentional mechanisms in eating disorders, using designs such as the Stroop test. Findings generally support the view that eating disordered people do show attentional and processing biases to food and weight stimuli (Cooper & Todd, 1997), although as Vitousek (1996) notes, it is unclear if such biases are related to other factors such as hunger or chronic deprivation and are picking up on state factors. It is also unclear if some (or which) attentional processes, salient to eating disorders, are unconscious (Gilbert, Chapter 1, this volume).

If an individual sets an ideal self, that is biologically an unachievable pattern of eating behaviour, weight, size and shape, then the inevitable failure to meet this ideal can have negative personal or social consequences. A number of cognitive strategies may be utilised to act as early warning systems of potential failure and to sensitise individuals to specific threats. For eating disordered and disordered eaters, these may include: increased sensitivity to size, shape and food related information; increased attention to external social cues from others regarding size, shape and weight; increased social comparison (particularly for other people's weights); development of catastrophic imaginal scenarios, linked with anxious arousal, related to the negative consequences of failing to live up to the ideal; and increased attention to bodily cues relating to body weight and shape (e.g., increased mirror gazing; Fairburn, 2001a).

Aggression

Aggression is a fundamental defence to threat (Gilbert, Chapter 1, this volume) and people with eating disorders can be hostile of others who criticise their size, shape or eating behaviour. Some may express anger in tantrums if challenged. One of our patients, when challenged by her mother to eat more, would throw herself on the floor, scream, and accuse her mother of not understanding what she was going through. Tangney et al. (1992b) found that shame is associated with increased anger proneness, but guilt is not. Destructive, non-assertive ways of dealing with conflict and anger have also been found to be associated with shame, but these forms of anger tend to increase interpersonal conflicts and shame (Tangney et al., 1996). More passive forms of anger can include resistance, sulking, and non-compliance with therapy programmes aimed at changing eating and activity patterns.

Depressed patients are known to have anger problems, including tendencies for rage attacks, inhibition of anger and fear of anger (Brody et al., 1999). However, anger problems have not been well studied in eating disorders. Aggression is probably best viewed as a rapid onset, short-term, defensive strategy. In this sense it is somewhat different from the often more deliberately planned set of coping strategies outlined below. Indeed, we would suggest that understanding people's immediate responses to a threat (e.g., criticism), their evaluations of their responses, and their longer-term coping behaviours are important in the assessment of eating disorders.

Avoidance and withdrawal

There are a variety of avoidance behaviours that can be recruited to cope with shame and other problematic feelings and thoughts. For example, one may avoid food and food-related stimuli to avoid the triggers for eating; one may withdraw from eating situations particularly in the presence of others. One may avoid size and shape-related information (e.g., avoiding looking in mirrors or being weighed). There can be avoidance of undressing in public changing areas, or going swimming, and avoidance of intimate relationships that involve body observation or contact (e.g., in sexual relationships).

Avoidance may also include non-attendance at therapeutic programmes, or withdrawal from friends and family who remind the individual of their difficulties (e.g., patients often report that they did not want to attend a session because they felt too ashamed to admit a binge). This can be problematic in therapies (e.g., Cognitive Behaviour Therapy (CBT)) that require self-monitoring and diary-keeping. As noted by many cognitive-behavioural therapists, these types of defensive and safety behaviours often set up dysfunctional patterns of behaviour, in part because people assume that negative events and feelings can be warded off by enacting them.

Concealment

The use of concealment to avoid external shame is common. This can involve concealing what is actually eaten (or not), bingeing, vomiting and laxative use. People may conceal hiding and hoarding food (which is common for anorexic people on supervised re-feeding programmes). Body concealment may involve wearing excessively baggy or dark clothes. Many patients report the need to conceal their desire and need to eat from others, and from themselves, and may feel deeply ashamed of their hunger.

Destruction of the object of shame

This strategy appears closely linked to self-disgust and self-directed hostility. For individuals with an eating disorder/disordered eating, it can lead to extreme methods to rid oneself of the undesired object (e.g., body fat) by extreme food restriction, self-mutilation or suicide. Others can be co-opted into this process, for example, the use of potentially hazardous surgical procedures to reduce or change body shape or remove fat (e.g., gastric stapling, jaw wiring), despite the uncertain longer-term outcomes of these procedures. This process is also ripe for commercial exploitation, and the promotion of weight-reducing or muscle-enhancing drugs and compounds, of limited or no clinical efficacy, but with high risks of medical complications (in the instance of steroids and amphetamines) remains both highly profitable and relatively unregulated.

Compensation

There has been much discussion in the literature about what people with eating disorders really want/need. Is it love, acceptance, care? Is it superiority over others or resistance to the authority of others; to stay young and avoid adulthood? None of these are clear. However, there is a view that eating disorders are compensations for other problems. For some, this may be early sexual or physical abuse, or family conflicts. For others, it may be to compensate for a sense of failure in one's peer group. If that child had other ways to win approval, such as sports ability, then maybe these would be the vehicles for success.

The role of pride

As outlined elsewhere (Gilbert, 1989, 1997; Chapter 1, this volume) evolutionary and social psychologists agree that social acceptance and social approval are among the most salient of reinforcers and people will work hard to earn the appreciation and praise of those who are important to them and avoid rejection. There is also a competitive element to this which links success to pride. Pride is the affect associated with social success and feeling approved of or admired by others. Internal pride is feeling the same for one's own attributes and talents (Mascolo & Fischer, 1995). So how does pride relate to eating disorders, given that to date we have focused on its opposite – shame?

It is useful to recognise that there are many domains of restriction, both of foods and other desires/impulses that are culturally encouraged and associated with positive self-esteem and pride in self. For example, in some religious groups, there can be voluntary prohibition of sexual behaviour (celibacy), eating certain foods (meat) or only eating and drinking at certain times of the day. Fasting has long been used in attempts to induce religious experiences, or bring one closer to God. Success at these forms of control can be linked to pride and self-esteem whereas losing control can be associated with shame and guilt (Huline-Dickens, 2000). These examples highlight the vital importance of the functional analysis of behaviour and beliefs; that is, to understand the reasons for dietary controls. Indeed, Szmukler & Patton (1995) suggest widening the criteria for self-starvation caseness to allow greater cross-cultural understanding to include '*subjects who become emaciated through restriction of their dietary intake for whatever reason, this restriction is deliberate, and the subject positively values the resulting state'*.

Using a cognitive-behavioural functional analysis, we suggest that eating disorders can be distinguished between shame-pride spirals (typical of restrictors) and shame-shame spirals (typical of bingers). These, in turn, are related to various forms of external and internal shame and affect control. We see these as prototypical styles and they are likely to overlap over time.

Although there have been many studies linking restriction and control to increased self-esteem (see Vitousek, 1996), an extensive literature search for this chapter found no published studies on the experience of pride that many eating disorder patients report, in either their ability to control their eating, to exercise or to manage their moods more quickly and effectively than 'normal people'. Yet, conversations with eating disordered patients often reflect these themes, and indeed, they were core to some of earliest accounts of eating disorder psychopathology.

Bruch (1973) presents the case of Celia who initially began to lose weight to please her husband but '. . . it now became her own project. There was a sense of glory and pride in the self-denial and feeling hungry' (p.268). McCloed (1981), writing about her own anorexia, comments on the increasing sense of energy and interpersonal power that her eating disorder helped her to achieve. What starts as a way to avoid rejection, win approval (and pride) from others quickly becomes internalised and a source of internal pride with the self. One of our patients started dieting because of teasing at school, but then thought, 'hey this is something I *can do* and I am good at it.' Whenever she lost weight, she felt 'a glow of success, achievement and pride.' The use of weight scales become not a way of feeling shame but of getting a boost of pride and success in herself. Clinicians will recognise the phrase 'I'm only good at being anorexic'. Many individuals with an eating disorder report feeling proud of their ability to limit the amount of food they eat, of their ability to exercise, or (in men) of the muscle bulk they have gained.

Thus, the behaviour that has been designed to reduce shame can become a valued (and often overvalued) ideal. This can result in the denial of any problem with eating, particularly if it requires individuals to give up their behaviour. This can be particularly difficult for individuals who exercise excessively, where the endorphins released can also lead to biological addiction-like behaviour.

Social competition

As noted by Gilbert (1989, 1998a) some forms of pride often involve a social comparison and competitive element, of feeling that one is outperforming others, or winning in some kind of competition. Indeed, social comparison is key to competition via attractiveness (Gilbert, Price & Allan, 1995). Abed

(1998) has suggested that one of the reasons eating disorders have increased in the Western world is because of the intensification of competition among females for certain young-looking and nubile body shapes, fuelled by unrealistic comparisons provided by the media. Gilbert (1989) suggested that when certain attributes (be this aggressive behaviours in street gangs, academic achievements, or body shapes) are highly valued in groups and linked to resources, competition becomes more vigorous, pushing behaviours to extremes as individuals try to outperform each other. This may be a factor in some severe forms of eating disorder.

Wallace (1986), writing about the tragic story of the Gibbens twins, notes how their eating disorders (both anorexia and bulimia) helped them to not only define their own sense of identity (as a couple), but also helped them to feel powerful by competing with each other over who could keep up or go one step further with their eating disordered behaviours. There are many anecdotal reports (though little good research) on how restrictors can feel superior to other women in at least one respect: their ability to rigidly control their food intake.

This form of pride competition can sometimes be observed in in/day patient settings, or complicate the treatment of patients who are related or cohabit with an eating disordered person. It may also work to produce a counter-culture of esteem giving signals by sufferers that can protect individuals against the interventions of others designed to alter their eating behaviours. There are also various anecdotal reports of how some people with anorexia compete with siblings or parents (e.g., mother).

An interesting feature of running group-based treatment programmes for people with eating disorders and disordered eaters is the group process and the social comparisons of who is the fattest or most disturbed. However, this is gradually replaced by a sense of group unity and a reduction in shame, at least if the group works well. Ideally, one helps people move away from individual-competitive and shame-pride focused positions ('I am worse than her but better than him') to a more sharing and mutually helpful orientation to their problems and those in the group; that is, there is a shift from competitive to a cooperative orientation.

It is also possible to observe an in-group/out-group process in other patterns of disordered eating. For example, aesthetics may use starvation to signify their difference from others, or their special holiness, or in the hope of improving relations to God or gain enlightenment. Starvation can also signify protests against other groups and reinforce affiliation with the in-group (e.g., hunger strikers). Research is needed on how people with eating disorders define themselves in terms of group identity where those who are (for example) non-restrictors are defined as out-group. There is not the space to explore this in detail here except to say that who are seen as in-group or out-group (people who do, and people who do not, share the same values or issues) probably affects what messages people attend to. Messages, appeals or instructions from the out-group (e.g., therapists and parents) may be devalued or dismissed (e.g., see Robinson, 1996).

Resistance/rebellion

Although research on the attachment histories of people with eating disorders show mixed results, much depends on the measures used. There is though growing evidence that people with eating disorders have insecure attachment difficulties. Moreover, those with anorexia alone tend to have avoidant patterns of attachment. Such people can be focused on resisting the control of others. (For an excellent review of findings and airing of the issues in this area of research see Ward, Ramsay & Treasure, 2000.) Refusing to 'give in' to external authority and/or change their own behaviour can also be seen as source of pride to some restrictors. The functional nature of these behaviours (the ability to resist both internal impulses and external directives) appears linked to self-esteem and identity – a process clearly outlined by Wallace (1986). It is paradoxical perhaps that although the function of controlled eating behaviour may first have been to elicit self and other approval, subsequently people will become so focused on their own control and ability to resist others' control that now they will risk severe social sanction and even death. 'You can't make me' will be a familiar sentiment to many who work in this area. As Littlewood (1995) notes, the control over the body may represent personal resistance when one experiences a limited degree of personal agency. We suggest that the functional significance of resistance to authority has been seriously under-researched for some eating disorders.

There are other types of self-starvation where resistance to authority has clear political meaning, for example, the 'hunger strikes' of convicted terrorists in Northern Ireland and other political acts. Importantly, while these latter accounts of self-starvation have little to do with a fear of fatness or body shame, they clearly assume that 'authority has a vested interest in trying to make them eat'. Moreover, there is a clear sense that some of the behaviour is aimed to earn prestige in the groups to whom they belong and value. To be seen as a martyr to the cause or be capable of strong defiance of authority may have many prestige-related but also unfortunate consequences.

Clearly, resistance and rebellion are not necessarily unhealthy and dysfunctional. Indeed, they have been regarded as an essential part of child development to enable children to develop an individual identity and sense of self. Nonetheless, it obviously matters greatly what values people adopt in this regard and the vigour, type and tactics of their resistance.

Several systemic therapists have attempted to channel this resistance into a personal and political force to challenge eating disordered beliefs and behaviour. In particular, 'externalising' the eating disorder is seen as providing the individual with a way of 'fighting back' against their difficulties. This may occur at an individual level during therapy (Kayrooz, 2001) or at a more political level (e.g., Madigan's description of the 'Anti-bulimic league' quoted by Kayrooz, 2001).

Shame-pride and shame-shame models for eating disorders

Given the review in the previous section, we are now able to consider two types of process models based on involvement of shame and pride in eating disorders. Like all models of this type they are designed to be illustrative rather than comprehensive. Here we seek to illuminate the differences in shame management in different aspects of eating disorders. Our first model is for anorexia and diet restrictors. Our second model focuses on binge eating and affect control.

Figure 12.1 outlines a process model for shame-pride interactions in restrictors. We can start by noting a number of background factors that set

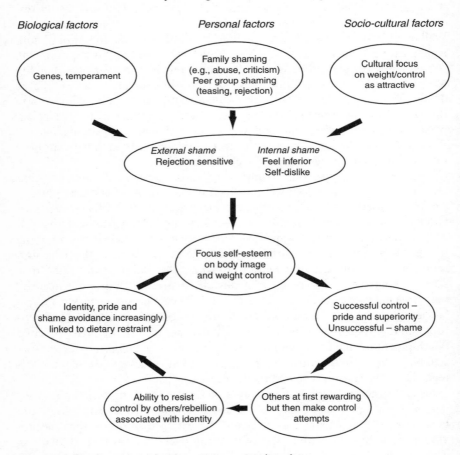

Figure 12.1 Shame-pride cycle in restricting eating disorders

the stage for an eating disorder. These are framed within a biopsychosocial model (Gilbert, Chapter 1, this volume) and as such include background dispositions (such as genetic/temperaments, personal and attachment experiences) and social-cultural values that intensify competition for certain body shapes and appearances (see Stice, Agras & Hammer, 1999; Neumark-Sztainer et al., 2000, for reviews of potential etiological risk factors in eating disorders).

These factors give rise to various forms of external shame cognitions and accentuate interpersonal sensitivities. They also influence internal shame; that is, self-perceptions and identity. Individuals who feel vulnerable to these negative social outcomes (e.g., rejection, or over-control by others) and negative or low self-esteem will seek ways to defend themselves against these threats and self-repair. For the anorexic-to-be, the chosen focus of coping is the body, weight and dietary control. This then sets up a self-perpetuating cycle that takes a life of its own. Successful restriction is associated with pride in achievement, while failure activates shame affects and cognitions. At first significant others (e.g., peers) may be complimentary of their efforts but as weight continues to drop off or parents note the reductions in eating, they become more controlling. However, the anorexic-to-be is feeling better about themselves and superior to others because of their control – it is their project. The ability to resist others and not to give up on their new strategies becomes part of a new (less shame-prone) developing self-identity (Littlewood, 1995). To start eating again not only threatens them with returning to shamed-self (fat, ugly, uncomfortable) but removes a behaviour that gives them pride. Moreover, to start eating again can feel like losing a source of positive social comparison (competition) with other people. This process is similar for those who restrict on religious grounds or to compete with their own gender. Finally, eating again, especially the more it is demanded by others, can feel like involuntary submission and losing – being defeated and externally controlled – which again has very negative implications for one's self-identity. One could build into this model all the various physiological changes that take place in weight loss that will affect energy levels and cognitive and affective processing. These will feed in the processes outlined here, increasing cognitive and affective distortions.

We can see then that the onset factors for an eating disorder may show many overlaps with other disorders, but the coping efforts and focus on weight, size and control focus the person on a specific set of behaviours. We also note that part of the disorder is related to forms of intensified social competition (a key domain in evolutionary approaches to psychopathology; Gilbert, 1989) and a struggle for a self-determined identity of which one can be proud.

In our second model for binge eating, there is a different self-perpetuating cycle. There may be similar factors relating to the background development to external and internal shame as above, although more detailed research will probably reveal subtle but important differences to those for pure anorexia and binge eaters (Ward, Ramsay & Treasure, 2000). Although affect control (pride and avoiding shame) may be important to restrictors, the problem in binge eaters is more coping with unstable and negative affects especially in interpersonal contexts. For these folk, bingeing and purging are associated with various forms of affect control including avoidance of negative affect and disassociation, as noted above (Waters, Hill & Waller, 2001). Moreover, as found by Sanftner & Crowther (1998), planning a binge is associated with positive affect and sense of control. We have also spoken to a few patients who can have a sense of excitement when planning a binge. For example, one our patients would steal food to add to the excitement and also a sense of 'getting one over' on others. Moreover, the very fact that these behaviours are going to be conducted in private ('I can do things others can't know about or stop me') may increase a sense of a separate self-identity outside the gaze of others. There can also be a sense of rebellion; that is, one is doing something one knows others would disapprove of. We wonder if there are many other behaviours (such as smoking behind the bike sheds or visiting prostitutes) where the same kind of psychology applies. In these cases, the ability to deceive others and hide things (and get away with it) seems to strengthen a sense of self-identity and power. Indeed, within the social rank theory of psychopathology (Gilbert, 1992), it is not only necessary to explore how people can feel inferior, subordinated and controlled by others but how they resist. Moreover, as Scott (1990) makes clear, resistance to authority is often concealed, and this concealment (the ability to keep secrets from a disapproving authority or group) can add to the sense of power of the resistance.

Again, the details of these processes need careful research and do not apply the same in all cases. For example, not all patients plan binges – some are spontaneous to feeling bad, and others purge themselves at times when they have had to eat for social reasons (e.g., dinner parties). None of these factors would apply in cultural contexts where binging/purging were part of group-accepted behaviour (e.g., the Roman feasts). Indeed in some contexts (young males) binge eating or drinking can be competitive in a different way – of who can eat/drink the fastest or most. And there has been increasing concern that some find their path into drink and eating problems via this route. In therapy these (mostly men) may speak of their *inability* to resist the cultural pressures to eat or drink heavily and how (as young males) they entered the competition with gusto!

In the longer term, however, people may also feel disgusted by their behaviour, effects on weight, may worry about the harm they are doing to themselves and fearful of discovery and needing to conceal. For those who have become concealing bingers, deceiving others and keeping things (binges) secret can at first feel empowering, but it can also be isolating. The person may come to feel their behaviour is abnormal. This compounds a sense of a shameful self. There is then a kind of catch-22 of 'I can have my secret binges,

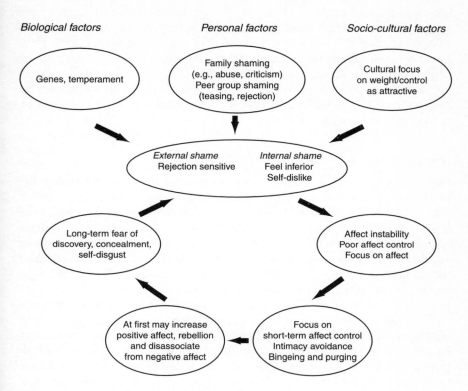

Biological factors

Personal factors

Socio-cultural factors

Genes, temperament

Family shaming
(e.g., abuse, criticism)
Peer group shaming
(teasing, rejection)

Cultural focus
on weight/control
as attractive

External shame
Rejection sensitive

Internal shame
Feel inferior
Self-dislike

Long-term fear of
discovery, concealment,
self-disgust

Affect instability
Poor affect control
Focus on affect

At first may increase
positive affect, rebellion
and disassociate
from negative affect

Focus on
short-term affect control
Intimacy avoidance
Bingeing and purging

Figure 12.2 Shame-shame cycle in binge eating

and this makes me feel special, gives me a way to cope with my feelings, and outside others control – but then this also makes me different from others, alone and more vulnerable to rejection.' Even in the shorter term, for those who are coming forward for therapy at least, craving and then bingeing is associated with more negative affect (Waters, Hill & Waller, 2001). These negative experiences and self-perceptions add to the internal conditions for unstable and negative affects, and do not address the underlying emotional or interpersonal problems. Thus, a self-defeating and self-perpetuating cycle is maintained.

In both cycles we have tried to focus not just on the shame aspects but also pride. We have also drawn attention to the functions of the behaviour in question and, in particular, how some, apparently dysfunctional, behaviours (planning to eat too little or too much) can both be associated with feelings of positive self-identity at least in the short term. However, for both anorexic and bulimic the after-effects of 'giving in' to impulses can be quite negative. Ultimately, eating disorders revolve around giving into impulses to eat or not and in this sense the data emerging from the literature on affect regulation is illuminating. For example, Tice, Bratslavsky and Baumeister (2001) have shown that in non-disordered people, giving in to desires to eat is associated with beliefs that this will improve mood if one is in a negative mood. They found no evidence for lack of control being related to a reduced capacity for control because of stress, or desires for self-punishment. It would be interesting to see if such findings replicate in eating ordered groups, where eating behaviour is likely to be influenced by a multitude of factors that may not be present in non-disordered folk.

Implications for therapy

Despite the range of therapeutic approaches used to work with eating disorders and disordered eaters, and some good early results (Thompson, 1996; Vitousek, 1996), there is still much to do, especially with the more severe forms (Roth & Fogany, 1996). Understanding the complexity of shame-related affects and behaviours, their temporal and focal nature, and the importance of pride and rebellion for self-identity, may help to enhance therapeutic efficacy and improve the take up of potentially effective interventions. Troop et al.'s (2001b) research suggests that women who have recovered from an eating disorder continue to experience levels of shame significantly higher than non-eating disordered controls. However, women currently in treatment experienced the highest levels of shame. It is possible that directly focusing on shame may provide an additional therapeutic approach. With this in mind, the following suggestions to improve services and enhance therapeutic efficacy are outlined below. These are, of course, additional ideas to standard CBT, not alternatives (Vitousek, 1996; see Gilbert, Chapter 1, this volume for therapeutic overview of working with body shame, and Gilbert, 1998b for some key issue in working with shame-based difficulties).

1 Talking about the difficulties experienced due to eating or exercise behaviour is likely to be highly shame-provoking. The more barriers there are to accessing services, the less likely it is that individuals will be able to overcome this challenge. Ideally, services would incorporate self-referral and telephone help lines to enable patients to disclose their difficulties to a service where they are most likely to receive a sympathetic response and treatment.

2 The therapeutic relationship is likely to be key. Therapists need to take an empathic, collaborative and empowering stance. Shame is likely to be triggered relatively easily, and therapeutic ruptures are likely to result, particularly at the beginning of therapy. Restrictors may feel that in changing they will lose the only thing they feel good about (their control) and be thrown back to feeling inferior and more ashamed of themselves. There are probably few other disorders where change means giving up something one has become proud of and supports self-esteem.

Therapists will need to explore this, be empathic to the intense fear of change and painful dilemmas this involves. Motivational interviewing may be helpful here (Blake, Turnball & Treasure, 1997).

3 The above model of eating disorder and disordered eating development and maintenance can be used to help individuals understand their personal evolutionary pattern of their difficulties, and to validate their attempts to cope with events which are likely to have left them feeling helpless, powerless and useless. Group-based psychoeducation can be particularly helpful here, as it normalises the experience as a shared one, without necessarily committing the individual to give up their symptoms at this stage.

4 Therapists will need to be aware of the identity struggles implicit in eating disorders; the need for self-control or deception, that at one level can feel empowering, and the ingroup–outgroup identity issues. This helps therapists understand the incredible resistance people can have to change. Resisting the control of others and not submitting/complying, either to their own impulses to eat or the requests of others, has been important to their identity. Therapists can share the positive and protective functions of the disorder and not inadvertently shame people for suffering from it. Indeed, acknowledging the strength of will to lose weight, or the excitement of a binge help to make the therapist and patient collaborators against the undesirable consequences of the problem.

5 Due to the level of distress experienced by many patients, and the potentially life-threatening consequences of their behaviour, therapists can often feel under external and internal pressure to succeed quickly. For the unwary, this can lead to a battle of wills between patient and therapist, which can reinforce the patient's sense of powerlessness and shame, and may activate intense resistance/rebellion. These behaviours, in turn, may pull on the shame (fear of failure) and power plays of the therapist leading to anger at or rejection of the patient. Also, patients may elicit shaming behaviour from others, for example, bingeing or not eating can lead others to 'police' the person's behaviour by observing them at all times. Hiding food or refusal to comply with eating regimes can lead to hostile interactions from relatives and even therapists.

6 Shame often develops from negative interpersonal interactions. It may be important to work with individuals' wider social network and provide them specific skills for managing interpersonal relationships. This often includes how to view and deal with interpersonal conflicts or even rejection. Some patients have very black-and-white beliefs on conflict: 'You either win or lose!'

7 Indeed, black-and-white thinking, in many domains, is typical of eating disorders (Vitousek, 1996). However, rather than thinking about this as a cognitive error (which at one level it may be), it is preferable to consider

this type of thinking as usually related to a need for certainty which, in turn, is commonly related to stress and threats (Gilbert, 1998c) and/or is a developmental issue. Indeed, black-and-white thinking is common when people feel threatened and this is as true for group-group conflicts as for interpersonal conflicts. Thus, it is useful to see black-and-white thinking not as casual (though it can be) but as a natural defensive orientation. As people understand their black-and-white thinking as a need for certainty, and this, in turn, is related to things that threaten them, they can then address their attention to how to re-evaluate 'the threat' and find alternative ways to cope. Again the message is – 'find the positive functions in the symptom before challenging it'.

8   Eating behaviour is a symptom that does need to be addressed; however, longer-term change and relapse prevention may require additional work on factors which led to vulnerability/triggered the disorder in the first instance. This may be at individual, interpersonal and even cultural levels.

9   When self-dislike and self-attacking are present the therapist may wish to explore with the person the origins, functions and purpose of these. Currently, new ways of working with internalised hostility are being developed but await research evidence on effectiveness (Gilbert, 2000c).

Skilful therapists will orientate themselves to the person as someone who is struggling for their own self-identity, in the context of often problematic personal relationships and strong cultural messages about weight and shape. As Vitousek (1996) notes, sometimes considerable time is given to the discussion of the advantages and disadvantages of beliefs and behaviours in efforts to slowly engage the person. Such approaches help to side-step shame and try to build collaborative relationships rather than re-enacting dominating ones where the person feels under pressure to 'give in' and comply with the therapist. This is often not easy especially when boundaries are at issue. Nonetheless, an understanding of shame can help therapists think through these difficult dilemmas.

Conclusion

We are living at a time where many forms of mental disorder seem to be increasing. One reason may be the intensification of competition in modern societies for prestige and social acceptance. A spin-off of this is that more people seem haunted by negative social comparison and feelings of not matching up. Different people seek different solutions. For some this invigorated competition may lead to excessive working, or use of drugs and alcohol, or steroids to build muscle, while for others it may result in long term problems with diet and efforts at weight control, as they battle to find acceptance in their own eyes and those of others. There is little doubt that social contexts in which social competition takes places, including the role of the media and the way product advertising is targeted (from the latest beauty treatments to the most recent diets), influence people's attitude to their own bodies and eating behaviours. Hence, all models such as ours need to be contextualised in complex social political contexts (Gilbert, Chapter 1, this volume).

This chapter has attempted to illuminate aspects of shame and pride, in part derived from both cultural and more intimate relationships, in the aetiology and maintenance of eating disorders and disordered eating. These offer new foci for investigations that need to be tested empirically. We have outlined some therapeutic implications of working with shame and pride in these populations but there are many others yet to be articulated. We believe that the responses of the patients we have worked with using these principles suggests that they may have clinical validity and utility but again this will need to be tested in further research.

References

Abed, R.T. (1998) The sexual competition hypothesis of eating disorders. *British Journal of Medical Psychology*, 71, 525–547.

American Psychiatric Association (1994) *Diagnostic and Statistical Manual of Mental Disorders* (4th edn.). Washington, DC: American Psychiatric Association.

Blake, W., Turnball, S. & Treasure, J. (1997) Stages and processes of change in eating disorders: Implications for therapy. *Clinical Psychology and Psychotherapy*, 4 (3), 186–191.

Brody, C.L., Haag, D.A.F., Kirk, L. & Solomon, A. (1999) Experiences of anger in people who have recovered from depression and never-depressed people. *Journal of Nervous and Mental Disease*, 187, 400–405.

Brownell, K.D. (1995) Eating disorders in athletes. In K.D. Brownell & C.G. Fairburn (eds) *Eating Disorders and Obesity: A Comprehensive Handbook* (pp.191–198). New York: Guilford Press.

Bruch, H. (1973) *Eating Disorders: Obesity, Anorexia Nervosa and the Person Within*. New York: Basic Books.

Burney, J. & Irwin, H.J. (2000) Shame and guilt in females with eating disordered symptomatology. *Journal of Clinical Psychology*, 56, 51–61.

Campbell, P.G. (1995) What would a causal explanation of the eating disorders look like? In G. Szmukler, C. Dare & J. Treasure (eds) *Handbook of Eating Disorders* (pp.49–64). Chichester: John Wiley & Sons.

Cash, T.F. & Hicks, K.L. (1990) Being fat versus thinking fat: Relationships with body image, eating behaviours, and well-being. *Cognitive Therapy and Research*, 14 (3), 327–341.

Clark D.M. (1999) Anxiety disorders: Why they persist and how to treat them. *Behaviour Research and Therapy*, 37, S5–S27.

Cook, D.R. (1994) *Internalised Shame Scale Professional Manual*. Wisconsin: Channel Press.

Cook, D.R. (1996) Empirical studies of shame and guilt: The Internalized Shame

Scale. In D.L. Nathanson (ed.) *Knowing Feeling: Affect, Script and Psychotherapy* (pp.132–165). New York: Norton.

Cooper, J.M. & Todd, G. (1997) Selective processing of three types of stimuli in eating disorders. *British Journal of Clinical Psychology*, 36, 279–281.

Cooper, J.M., Todd, G. & Wells, A. (1998) Content, origins, and consequences of dysfunctional beliefs in anorexia nervosa and bulimia nervosa. *Journal of Cognitive Psychotherapy*, 12, 213–230.

Cooper, P.J. (1995) Eating disorders and their relationship to mood and anxiety disorders. In K.D. Brownell & C.G. Fairburn (eds) *Eating Disorders and Obesity: A Comprehensive Handbook*. London: Guilford Press.

Crisp, A.H. (1979) *Anorexia Nervosa: Let Me Be*. Hove, UK: Lawrence Erlbaum Associates.

Crocker, J. & Major, B. (1989) Social stigma and self-esteem: The self-protective qualities of stigma. *Psychological Review*, 96, 608–630.

Davidson, J., Zisook, S., Giller, E. & Helms, M. (1989) Symptoms of interpersonal sensitivity in depression. *Comprehensive Psychiatry*, 30, 357–368.

Davis, C. (1997) Normal and neurotic perfectionism in eating disorders: An interactive model. *International Journal of Eating Disorders*, 22, 421–426.

De Silva, P. (1993) Sexual problems in women with eating disorders. In J. Ussher & C. Baker (eds) *Psychological Perspectives on Sexual Problems* (pp.79–109). London: Routledge.

De Silva, P. (1995) Cognitive-behavioural models of eating disorder. In G. Szmukler, C. Dare & J. Treasure (eds) *Handbook of Eating Disorders* (pp.141–154). Chichester: John Wiley & Sons.

Eisler, I. (1995) Family models of eating disorders. In G. Szmukler, C. Dare & J. Treasure (eds) *Handbook of Eating Disorders* (pp.155–174). Chichester: John Wiley & Sons.

Eldredge, K.L., Locke, K.D. & Horowitz, L.M. (1998) Patterns of interpersonal problems associated with binge eating disorder. *International Journal of Eating Disorders*, 23, 383–389.

Fairburn, C.G., Kirk, J., O'Connor, M., Anastansiades, P. & Cooper, P.J. (1987) Prognostic factors in bulimia nervosa. *British Journal of Clinical Psychology*, 26, 223–224.

Fairburn, C.G. & Cooper, P.J. (1989) Eating disorders. In K. Hawton, P.M. Salkovskis, J. Kirk & D.M. Clark (eds) *Cognitive Behaviour Therapy for Psychiatric Problems: A Practical Guide* (pp. 227–314). Oxford: Oxford University Press.

Fairburn, C.G. (2001a) Personal correspondence.

Fairburn, C.G. (2001b) Presentation to the British Association for Behavioural and Cognitive Psychotherapy, Glasgow University, June 2001.

Falkner, N.H., French, S.A., Jeffery, R.W., Neumark-Sztainer, D., Sherwood, N.E. & Morton, N. (1999) Mistreatment due to weight: Prevalence and sources of perceived mistreatment in women and men. *Obesity Research*, 7, 572–576.

Ferster, C.B. (1973). A functional analysis of depression. *American Psychologist*, 28, 857–870.

Friedman, M.A. & Whisman, M.A. (1998) Sociotropy, autonomy, and bulimic symptomatology. *International Journal of Eating Disorders*, 23, 439–442.

Garner, D.M. & Garfinkel, P.E. (1982) *Anorexia Nervosa: A Multidimensional Perspective*. New York: Brunner/Mazel.

Garner, D.M. & Garfinkel, P.E. (1985) *Handbook of Psychotherapy for Anorexia and Bulimia.* New York: Guilford Press.

Garner, D.M. (1997) Psychoeducational principles in treatment. In D.M. Garner & P.E. Garfinkel (eds) *Handbook of Treatment for Eating Disorders* (2nd edn.). New York: Guilford Press.

Gee, A. & Troop, N.N. (2001) Shame, depression and eating disorder symptoms. Submitted for publication.

Geller, J., Cocknell, S.J. & Goldner, E.M. (2000) Inhibited expression of negative emotions and interpersonal orientation in anorexia nervosa. *International Journal of Eating Disorders*, 28, 8–19.

Ghadirian, A.M., Marini, N., Jabalpurwala, S. & Steiger, H. (1999) Seasonal mood patterns in eating disorders. *General Hospital Psychiatry*, 21 (September), 354–359.

Gilbert, P. (1989). *Human Nature and Suffering.* Hove, UK: Lawrence Erlbaum Associates and New York: Guilford Press.

Gilbert, P. (1992) *Depression: The Evolution of Powerlessness.* Hove, UK: Lawrence Erlbaum Associates and New York: Guilford Press.

Gilbert, P. (1997) The evolution of social attractiveness and its role in shame, humiliation, guilt and therapy. *British Journal of Medical Psychology*, 70, 113–147.

Gilbert, P. (1998a) What is shame? Some core issues and controversies. In P. Gilbert & B. Andrews (eds) *Shame: Interpersonal Behaviour, Psychopathology and Culture* (pp.3–38). New York: Oxford University Press.

Gilbert, P. (1998b) Shame and humiliation in the treatment of complex cases. In N. Tarrier, A. Wells & G. Haddock (eds) *Treating Complex Cases: The Cognitive Behavioural Therapy Approach* (pp.241–271). Chichester: John Wiley & Sons.

Gilbert, P. (1998c) The evolved basis and adaptive functions of cognitive distortions. *British Journal of Medical Psychology*, 71, 447–463.

Gilbert, P. (2000a) The relationship of shame, social anxiety and depression: The role of the evaluation of social rank. *Clinical Psychology and Psychotherapy*, 7, 174–189.

Gilbert, P. (2000b) *Overcoming Depression: A Self-guide Using Cognitive Behavioural Techniques* (revised edition). London: Robinsons and New York: Oxford University Press.

Gilbert, P. (2000c) Social Mentalities: Internal 'social' conflicts and the role of inner warmth and compassion in cognitive therapy. In P. Gilbert & K.G. Bailey (eds) *Genes on the Couch: Explorations in Evolutionary Psychotherapy* (pp.118–150). Hove: Psychology Press.

Gilbert, P. & Andrews, B. (1998) (eds) *Shame: Interpersonal Behaviour, Psychopathology and Culture.* New York: Oxford University Press.

Gilbert, P. & McGuire, M. (1998) Shame, social roles and status: The psychobiological continuum from monkey to human. In P. Gilbert & B. Andrews (eds) *Shame: Interpersonal Behaviour, Psychopathology and Culture* (pp. 99–125). New York: Oxford University Press.

Gilbert, P., Price, J.S. & Allan, S. (1995) Social comparison, social attractiveness and evolution: How might they be related? *New Ideas in Psychology*, 13, 149–165.

Goss, K., Gilbert, P. & Allan, S. (1994) An exploration of shame measures. I: The 'other as shamer scale'. *Personality and Individual Differences*, 17, 713–717.

Hall, R.C., Blakey, R.E. & Hall, A.K. (1992) Bulimia Nervosa. Four uncommon subtypes. *Psychosomatics*, 33, 428–346.

Heatherton, T.F. & Baumeister, R.F. (1991) Binge eating as an escape from self-awareness. *Psychological Bulletin*, 110, 86–108.

Hewitt, P.L., Flett, G.L. & Ediger, E. (1995) Perfectionism traits and perfectionistic self-presentation in eating disorder attitudes, characteristics, and symptoms. *International Journal of Eating Disorders*, 18, 317–326.

Huline-Dickens, S. (2000) Anorexia nervosa: Some connections with the religious attitude. *British Journal of Medical Psychology*, 73, 67–76.

Jensen, A. (2001) Towards effective treatments of eating disorders: Nothing is as practical as a good theory. *Behaviour Research and Therapy*, 39, 1007–1021.

Kaufman, G. (1989) *The Psychology of Shame*. New York: Springer.

Kayrooz, C. (1994) A thematic guide to bulimia nervosa. *Australian and New Zealand Journal of Family Therapy*, 16, 64–72.

Kayrooz, C. (2001) *A Systemic Treatment of Bulimia Nervosa: Women in Transition*. London: Jessica Kingsley.

Keys, A., Broze, J. & Henschel, A. (1950) *The Biology of Human Starvation* (vol. 2). Minneapolis, MN: Minnesota University Press.

Kinder, B.N. (1991) Eating disorders (anorexia nervosa and bulimia nervosa). In M. Hershey & S.M. Turner (eds) *Adult Psychopathology and Diagnosis* (2nd edn.). New York: Wiley Interscience.

Lacey, H.J. & Mourelli, E. (1986) Bulimic alcoholics: Some features of a clinical sub-group. *British Journal of Addiction*, 81, 389–393.

Lehoux, P.M., Steiger, H. & Jabalpurlawa, S. (2000) State/trait distinctions in bulimic syndromes. *International Journal of Eating Disorders*, 27 January, 36–42.

Levy, A.B., Dixon, K.N. & Stern, S.L. (1989) How are depression and bulimia related? *American Journal of Psychiatry*, 146, 162–169.

Littlewood, R. (1995) Psychopathology and personal agency: Modernity, culture change and eating disorders in South Asian societies. *British Journal of Medical Psychology*. 68, 45–63.

Marcus, M.D., Smith, D., Santelli, R. & Kaye, W. (1992) Characterization of eating disordered behaviour in obese binge eaters. *International Journal of Eating Disorders*, 12 (3), 249–255.

Marcus, M.D (1993) Binge eating in obesity. In C.G. Fairburn & G.T. Wilson (eds) *Binge Eating: Nature, Assessment and Treatment*. New York: Guilford Press.

Mascolo, M.F. & Fischer, K.W. (1995) Developmental transformations in appraisals of pride, shame and guilt. In J.P. Tangney & K.W. Fischer (eds) *Self-conscious Emotions: The Psychology of Shame, Guilt, Embarrassment and Pride* (pp.64–113). New York: Guilford Press.

McCloed, S. (1981) *The Art of Starvation*. London: Virago.

Nagi, E.S., Lee, S. & Lee, A.M. (2000) The variability of phenomenology in anorexia nervosa. *Acta Psychiatry Scand*, October, 102 (4), 314–317.

Nathanson, D.L. (1992) *Shame and Pride: Affect Sex and the Birth of the Self*. New York: Norton Paperbacks.

Neumark-Sztainer, D., Story, M., Hannan, P.J., Beuhring, T. & Resnick, M.D. (2000) Disordered eating among adolescents: Associations with sexual/physical abuse and other familial/psychosocial factors. *International Journal of Eating Disorders*, 28, 249–258.

Norman, D.K., Herzog, D.B. & Chauncey, S. (1986) A one-year outcome study of bulimia: Psychological and eating symptom changes in a treatment and non-treatment group. *International Journal of Eating Disorders*, 5, 47–48.

Olmsted, M.P. & Kaplan, A.S. (1995) Psychoeducation in the treatment of eating disorders. In K.D. Brownell & C.G. Fairburn (eds) *Eating Disorders and Obesity: A Comprehensive Handbook* (pp.299–305). London: Guilford Press.

Orbach, S. (1979) *Fat is a Feminist Issue*. London: Hamlyn.

Polivy, J. & Herman, C.P. (1993) Etiology of binge eating: Psychological mechanisms. In C.G. Fairburn & G.T. Wilson (eds) *Binge Eating: Nature, Assessment and Treatment* (pp.173–205). New York: Guilford Press.

Robinson, W.P. (1996) (ed) *Social Groups and Identities: Developing the Legacy of Henri Tajfel*. Oxford: Butterworth-Heinmann.

Robson, P.J. (1998) Self-esteem: A psychiatric review. *British Journal of Psychiatry*, 153, 6–15.

Roth, A. & Fogany, P. (1996) *What Works for Whom? A Critical Review of Psychotherapy Research*. New York: Guilford Press.

Russell, G.F.M. (1995) Anorexia through time. In G. Szmukler, C. Dare & J. Treasure (eds) *Handbook of Eating Disorders* (pp.5–18). Chichester: John Wiley & Sons.

Sanftner, J.L. & Crowther, J.H. (1998) Variability in self-esteem, moods, shame and guilt to eating disorder symptomatology. *Journal of Social and Clinical Psychology*, 14, 315–324.

Schimel, J., Arnt, J., Pyszczynski, T. & Greenbergm, J. (2001) Being accepted for who we are: Evidence that social validation of the intrinsic self reduces defensiveness! *Journal of Personality and Social Psychology*, 80, 35–52.

Schmidt, U., Tiller, J. & Morgan, H.G. (1995) The social consequences of eating disorders. In G. Szmukler, C. Dare & J. Treasure (eds) *Handbook of Eating Disorders* (pp.243–258). Chichester: John Wiley & Sons.

Schmidt, U., Tiller, J., Blanchard, M., Andrews, B. & Treasure, J. (1997) Is there a specific trauma precipitating anorexia nervosa? *Psychological Medicine*, 27, 523–530.

Scott, J.C. (1990) *Domination and the Arts of Resistance*. New Haven: Yale University Press.

Serpall, L., Treasure, J., Teasdale, J. & Sullivan, V. (1999) Anorexia nervosa: Friend or foe? *International Journal of Eating Disorders*, March, 25, 177–186.

Steiger, H., Jabalpurlwala, S., Campangne, J. & Stotland, S. (1997) A controlled study of trait narcissism in anorexia and bulimia nervosa. *International Journal of Eating Disorders*, 22 (2), 173–178.

Steiger, H., Gauvin, L., Jabalpurlwala, S., Seguin, J.R. & Stotland, S. (1999) Hypersensitivity to social interactions in bulimic syndromes: Relationship to binge eating. *Journal of Consulting Clinical Psychology*, 67 (5), 765–675.

Steinberg, B.E. & Shaw, R.J. (1997) Bulimia as a disturbance of narcissism: Self-esteem and the capacity to self-soothe. *Addictive Behaviour*, 22, 699–710.

Steins, G. & Remy, C. (1996) Self-concept and need for approval in bulimia patients. *Z Psychol. Z. Angew Psychol.*, 204, 187–198.

Stice, E., Agras, W.S. & Hammer, L.D. (1999) Risk factors for the emergence of childhood eating disturbances: A five-year prospective study. *International Journal of Eating Disorders*, 25, 375–387.

Striegel-Moore, R., Silberstein, L.R. & Rodin, J. (1993) The social self in bulimia nervosa: Public self-consciousness, social anxiety, and perceived fraudulence. *Journal of Abnormal Psychology*, 102, 297–303.

Striegel-Moore, R., Schreiber, G.B., Lo, A., Crawford, P., Obarzanek, E. & Rodin, J. (2000) Eating disorders symptoms in a cohort of 11 to 16-year-old Black and White girls: The NHLBI Growth and Health Study. *International Journal of Eating Disorders*, 27, 49–66.

Szmukler, G., Dare, C. & Treasure, J. (1995) (eds) *Handbook of Eating Disorders*. Chichester: John Wiley & Sons.

Szmukler, G.I. & Patton, G. (1995) Sociocultural models of eating disorders. In G. Szmukler, C. Dare & J. Treasure, J. (eds) *Handbook of Eating Disorders*. Chichester: John Wiley & Sons.

Tangney J.P. (1995) Shame and guilt in interpersonal relationships. In J.P. Tangney & K.W. Fischer (eds) *Self-conscious Emotions: The Psychology of Shame, Guilt, Embarrassment and Pride* (pp.114–139). New York: Guilford Press.

Tangney, J.P. & Fischer, K.W. (1995) (eds) *Self-conscious Emotions: The Psychology of Shame, Guilt, Embarrassment and Pride*. New York: Guilford Press.

Tangney, J.P., Hill-Barlow, D., Wagner, P.E., Marschall, D.E., Borenstein, J.K., Sanftner, J., Mor, T. & Gramzow, R. (1996) Assessing individual differences in constructive versus destructive responses to anger across the lifespan. *Journal of Personality and Social Psychology*, 70, 780–796.

Tangney, J.P., Wagner, P. & Gramzow, R. (1989). *The Test of Self-conscious Affect*. Fairfax, VA: George Mason University.

Tangney, J.P., Wagner, P. & Gramzow, R. (1992a) Proneness to shame, proneness to guilt, and psychopathology. *Journal of Abnormal Psychology*, 101, 469–478.

Tangney, J.P., Wagner, P., Fletcher, C. & Gramzow, R. (1992b) Shamed into anger? The relation of shame and guilt to self-reported aggression. *Journal of Personality and Social Psychology*, 62, 669–675.

Telch, C.F. & Agras, W.S. (1984) Obesity, binge eating and psychopathology: Are they related? *International Journal of Eating Disorders*, 20 (3), 271–279.

Telch, C.F. & Stice, E. (1998) Psychiatric co-morbidity in women with binge eating disorder: Prevalence rates from a non-treatment seeking sample. *Journal of Consulting and Clinical Psychology*, 66, 768–776.

Thompson, J.K. (1996) (ed) *Body Image, Eating Disorders and Obesity: An Integrative Guide for Assessment and Treatment*. Washington, DC: American Psychological Association.

Tice, D.M., Bratslavsky, E. & Baumeister, R.F. (2001) Emotional distress regulation takes precedence over impulse control: If you feel bad do it! *Journal of Personality and Social Psychology*, 80, 53–67.

Tobin, D.L., Griffing, A. & Griffing, S. (1997) An examination of subtype criteria for bulimia nervosa. *International Journal of Eating Disorders*, September, 22, 179–186.

Tomkins (1963) *Affect Imagery Consciousness. Volume 2, Negative Affects*. New York: Springer.

Troop, N.A., Schmidt, U.H. & Treasure, J.L. (1995) Feelings and fantasy in eating disorders: A factor analysis of the Toronto Alexithymia Scale. *International Journal of Eating Disorder*, 18 (2), 151–157.

Troop, N.A., Connan, F., Las Hayas, C. & Treasure, J.L. (2001a) Shame and pride in eating disorders. Submitted for publication.

Troop, N.A., Allan, S., Serpall, L. & Treasure, J.L. (2001b) Shame in women with a history of eating disorders. Submitted for publication.

Vitousek, K.M. (1996) The current status of cognitive-behavioral models of anorexia nervosa and bulimia nervosa. In P.M. Salkovskis (ed.) *Frontiers of Cognitive Therapy* (pp.383–418). New York: Guilford Press.

Wallace, M. (1986) *The Silent Twins*. Suffolk: Penguin.

Waller, G. (1993) Why do we agree different types of eating disorders: Arguments for a change in research and clinical practice. *Eating Disorders Review*, 1, 74–89.

Waller, G. & Meyer, C. (1997) Cognitive avoidance of threat cues: Association with Eating Disorder Inventory scores among a non-eating disordered population. *International Journal of Eating Disorders*, 22, 299–308.

Waller, G. (1998) Perceived control in eating disorders: Relationship with reported sexual abuse. *International Journal of Eating Disorders*, 23, 213–216.

Ward, A., Ramsay, R. & Treasure, J. (2000) Attachment research in eating disorders. *British Journal of Medical Psychology*, 73, 35–51.

Waters, A., Hill, A., & Waller, G. (2001) Bulimics' responses to food cravings: Is binge-eating a product of hunger or emotional state. *Behaviour Research and Therapy*, 29, 877–886.

Webb, C. (2000) Psychological distress in clinical obesity: The role of eating disorder beliefs and behaviours, social comparison and shame. Unpublished Doctoral manuscript. University of Leicester.

Welch, S.L., Doll, H.A. & Fairburn, C.G. (1997) Life events and the onset of bulimia nervosa: A controlled study. *Psychological Medicine*, 27, 515–522.

Whitehead, L. (1994) Machismo nervosa: A new type of eating disorder in men. *International Cognitive Therapy Newsletter*, 8 (1), pp.2–3.

Wilson, G.T. (1995) Eating disorders and addictive disorders. In K.D. Brownell & C.G. Fairburn (eds) *Eating Disorders and Obesity: A Comprehensive Handbook*. New York: Guilford Press.

Chapter 13

Body shame and abuse in childhood

Bernice Andrews

Introduction

Many contributors to this volume address the issue of body shame arising from physical traumas, various diseases and disfigurements. However, body shame can have a variety of psychological causes where there may be no disorder of the body. This chapter explores the relationship of physical and sexual abuse to body shame and disturbances in body schema. There is increasing evidence that body shame, rooted in abusive experiences, is significantly related to vulnerability to psychopathology and chronicity. Abuse not only provides powerful emotional experiences of how one's body is perceived and treated by the other (e.g., as an object of sexual gratification, or a focus for physical harm), but also provides powerful experiences for developing internal schema of one's body (i.e., how one experiences and feels about one's body).

It has been recognised that the degree of any physical disfigurement is not a good predictor of adjustment (e.g., Kent & Thompson, Chapter 5, this volume). Pre-morbid concerns about the body and current coping behaviours significantly contribute to adjustment to disfigurements, be these from skin diseases (e.g., acne or psoriasis), or traumas (e.g., burns and disfiguring surgical procedures). Understanding the potential role of early abusive and neglectful experiences in the development of body shame may not only contribute to understanding the pre-morbid factors involved in various psychopathologies (such as depression and eating disorders) but can contribute to understanding how individuals adjust to injuries and diseases of the body. Clinicians should therefore be (a) mindful of the origins of body shame that may pre-date a disfiguring condition and (b) aware of the role of abusive experiences in body shame, in the absence of any specific disfigurements. This chapter explores recent research on body shame arising from early abusive experiences.

Childhood physical and sexual abuse both involve violations of body boundaries, that is, the body is vulnerable to others' aggressive or sexual behaviour. These traumatic violations can have a profound effect on how abuse survivors subsequently relate to and perceive their bodies. Childhood abuse does not usually leave lasting visual scars, but its emotional impact on how an individual comes to experience their body and body image can be just as devastating as visual disfigurement. At a behavioural level, there is a heightened risk of attacks on the body (Herman, 1994). Attacks may take the form of self-mutilation involving self-disfigurement and disturbed eating patterns involving starvation and binge eating and purging (e.g., Cole & Putnam, 1992; Wonderlich et al., 19997). At a cognitive and emotional level, abuse survivors often report a deep shame and hatred of their bodies that goes far beyond the normative discontent experienced by the majority of women in Western societies (Andrews, 1995, 1997). This chapter first describes how abuse is related to general negative self-perceptions, and how these may be related to feelings of shame. This will be followed by an exploration of the nature of shame in relation to experiences of sexual and physical violation of the body, and the ways in which body shame might mediate the relationship between childhood abuse and later disorders such as depression and bulimia.

The relationship of abuse to negative self-perceptions

An association between negative self-evaluation and abuse has been well described in the clinical literature. However, until fairly recently there was a paucity of research evidence to support clinical observations. Some of the initial research in the area involved extensive interviews with women in the community. These were conducted with a large community sample of women in Islington, an inner-city area of London. The research provided support for clinical observations by showing that women who reported adverse childhoods (including parental antipathy, abuse and neglect) were more likely than other women to be assessed as clinically depressed and to evaluate themselves negatively both in their self-attributions and their performance in personal and work-related roles. Women who reported the very worst abusive childhoods were sometimes very intense in their expression of their negative self-feelings often verging on self-hatred (Andrews & Brown, 1988a, 1993).

The level of reported abuse, both in childhood and adulthood, was high in this sample of inner-city women, and those reporting maritally violent relationships, either currently or in the past, showed double the rate of depression over a three-year period than other women (Andrews & Brown, 1988b). The highest rate by far, however, was among those who had experienced either physical or sexual abuse in both childhood and adulthood (Andrews, 1995). In the subsample of 70 women victims of marital violence, we investigated the reasons for this, considering the women's self-perceptions within an attributional framework (Andrews & Brewin, 1990). Following previous work by Janoff-Bulman (1979), we distinguished behavioural from characterological self-blame for the violence; Janoff-Bulman showed that the latter but not the former type of self-blame was related to depression. She further proposed that in victims of violence, blaming the attack on some modifiable aspect of behaviour (behavioural self-blame) would be a healthy response as survivors would have retained some feeling of control over the risk of future attacks (Janoff-Bulman, 1979). In contrast, those who are repeatedly assaulted or mistreated may be more likely to blame their character; they may feel that there must be something wrong with them if such an event happens more than once (Silver & Wortman, 1980). In relation to this, abused children are often told by their parents that they are bad and unlovable (Herbruck, 1979). If such views are internalised then these become a source for internal shame. Hence, we thought this (internalised attributions of others about the self) would be an additional reason for those abused in childhood to be more likely than others to respond to later abuse by blaming their character. As expected, we found that self-blame for marital violence was common, but women who had experienced either physical or sexual childhood abuse were more likely to blame their character, whereas women without such experiences were more likely to blame their behaviour. We also found that women with characterological self-blame were more likely than the other women survivors to have suffered persistent depression after the violent relationship had ended.

The accounts of three women research participants, all abused in childhood, and again attacked in very violent marriages, are given below. They illustrate the negative pervasive intensity of their self-blame for the violence, and how this was perceived to be due to potentially unalterable aspects of their physical being. One woman said:

> I used to feel maybe it was because I was stupid, unattractive, not doing the right thing.

Another remarked:

> I don't know what it is. I think probably my manner, or the way I speak, something made him react in that way.

And a third said:

> I had this real image of myself as a ball-breaking heavy lady.

These examples offer insight into how people can utilise self-referent explanations for the bad behaviours of others.

Blaming stable negative characteristics of the self for abuse is likely to evoke a sense of helplessness due to the perception that such characteristics are unmodifiable. Feelings of helplessness and an inherent sense of badness have been noted both in the empirical and theoretical literature as central features of the experience of shame (e.g., Lewis, 1987; Tangney et al., 1996; Wicker, Payne & Morgan, 1983). There is also some evidence of an association between questionnaire measures of shame and attributions akin to characterological self-blame in student samples (Tangney, Wagner & Gramzow, 1992; Weiner 1986). Our results, and these additional theoretical insights and evidence, led to further investigations of body shame in the context of childhood abuse and psychological disorder. Characterological self-blame was separately related to both early physical and sexual abuse and, before describing the empirical findings, two broad theoretical perspectives are described that might provide some understanding of the underlying similarities of these abusive experiences and their impact on the self-perceptions of the survivors.

Theoretical accounts of the relation of shame to early abusive experiences and psychopathology

From a social-cognitive perspective, early representations of self and others are the result of experiences with primary attachment figures. According to attachment theory, such representations are assimilated and form the basis of cognitive schema. Mental representations based on negative childhood experiences with primary carers lead to vulnerability in the face of subsequent adversity (Bowlby, 1977, 1980). It has been speculated that the representational model of self, constructed by individuals who have been abused in childhood, is of one who is responsible and deserving of harsh treatment (Egeland, Jacobvitz & Sroufe, 1988). Child sexual abuse may not necessarily be perceived as involving harsh treatment. Nevertheless, one of the earliest theories incorporating a social-cognitive perspective in relation to the impact of abuse was that of Ferenczi (1932/1949). Based on clinical observations of both perpetrators and abuse victims, Ferenczi proposed that experiences of both physical and sexual abuse were damaging to subsequent adult functioning. The experiences were distinct, but the affect or motivation of the actor, which was seen to be so damaging to the recipient, was the same. Both 'passionate loving' and 'passionate punishment' were accompanied by feelings of hatred and guilt towards the recipient, and such feelings were internalised by the innocent child. Ferenczi argued that in the case of sexual abuse, it was the guilt feelings of the adult that made the love object an object of both loving and hating.

A more recent model involving social cognition pertaining to sexual abuse is that of Finkelhor and Browne (1986). According to these authors common patterns of reactions seen among adult victims of childhood sexual abuse are connected with four factors related to the initial experiences: traumatic sexualisation, stigmatisation, betrayal and powerlessness. The factor identified as pertaining to shame is stigmatisation that occurs when the perpetrators of the abuse and others blame the victims and enjoin them with the need for secrecy.

The children grow up with feelings of guilt and shame believing that they are damaged goods. While this model is claimed to be specific to child sexual abuse, stigmatisation, as described, can also be seen as pertinent to early physical abuse.

Gilbert, from an alternative biosocial perspective, specifically addressed the relation of abuse and shame to depression (Gilbert, 1989). Although Gilbert's recent ideas place more emphasis on the relation between shame and attacks on, and loss of, social attractiveness (see Gilbert, 1997), his earlier insights provide a perspective on the common meaning behind different types of abusive experiences. Gilbert cites evidence from ethological studies relating subordinate status, submission and defeat to biochemical changes associated with depressive states. At a cognitive-affective level, it is suggested that in humans, a dominant feeling related to involuntary submissive behaviour and defeat states is shame. Submissive acts can trigger defeat states where submission is evaluated as a mark of inferiority, as in the aftermath of the experience of rape. Or submissive acts may exert an effect over time gradually leading to a state of defeat; so, for example, an autocratic, aggressive husband may gradually succeed in reducing his wife to act like a fearful subordinate, through physical threats and acts. Shame is related to individual concerns about how one is regarded by others and in Gilbert's model it is concerned with issues of defeat, intrusion and ultimately destruction of the self; the perception that one is viewed by the attacker and others as an inferior and subordinate victim presumably involves anticipation of their disdain and rejection.

The experience of abuse, either sexual or physical, particularly where it is prolonged and reduces the victim to subordinate status is thus associated with psychiatric disorder, especially depression, through feelings of submissiveness, a sense of personal inferiority and shame. Gilbert and colleagues have reported an association between questionnaire measures of submissive behaviour and both depression and shame-proneness in a student sample (Gilbert, Pehl & Allan, 1994) and a clinical population (Gilbert, 2000). In essence then, abusive experience can activate submissive behaviours (the child is constantly having to use submissiveness as an automatic defence). This will shape self-schema creating a deep sense of vulnerability to the power of others. The internal representation of self can be of one who is vulnerable because the self is bad, inadequate or flawed.

In drawing together social-cognitive and biosocial explanations of the impact of abuse, a common theme is the view of how one is regarded by the perpetrator of the abusive act. Ferenczi's (1932/1949) premise was that the feelings of guilt and hatred experienced by the perpetrator were introjected by the victim. These insights relate to a phenomenon noted by Finkelhor (1983) that perpetrators use their power to manipulate victims' perceptions of reality, making the victims believe that it is their own fault that the abuse is happening. A psychodynamic interpretation of these observations might be that perpetrators of both physical and sexual abuse project their own shame, guilt and other bad feelings onto their victims, who, in turn, internalise it. In Gilbert's theory, submissive behaviours (observed in both humans and other animal species), such as a strong desire to escape, gaze avoidance, crouch (a tendency to curl up the body and look down), being frozen to the spot and so on, are the same as those seen in severe states of shame in humans. Gilbert (1989) notes 'the central focus is on the negative image of the self that is created in the mind of the other' (p.268). In other words, like Ferenczi, but from a very different perspective, the common meaning of physical and sexual abuse arises from the perception of the (submissive) victims that they are subordinate and of little worth in the eyes of the (dominant) perpetrators.

Research on the role of body shame in the link between abuse and psychopathology

The insights gained from the study of self-blame in the marital violence survivors were incorporated in the design of a subsequent study of a subset of the whole community sample of Islington women who were followed over a further period. Overall these 100 women were investigated over an eight-year period with four contacts, and at the last contact 75 of their daughters, aged between 15 and 25, were also interviewed.

The evidence for an association between characterological self-blame and early abusive experiences, and between such self-blame and general shame-proneness (Tangney, Wagner & Gramzow, 1992; Weiner 1986) prompted this study. Because shame has been consistently noted in the literature to involve self-conscious feelings about the body (e.g., Gilbert, 1989; Mollon, 1984; Sartre, 1956), and because a measure was required that would provide a common and salient real-life focus for all the women, it was decided to measure feelings of bodily shame. Within a lengthy interview covering self-attitudes and past and present life experiences, both the mothers and daughters were asked direct questions about whether they had ever felt ashamed of their body or any part of it and the onset and duration of shame feelings, where they existed. Their accounts were then rated by the investigator, according to the frequency and intensity of the responses. High ratings of bodily shame were associated with early experiences of both sexual and physical abuse in both the older women and their daughters. The relationship held when separate measures of low self-esteem and body dissatisfaction were taken into account, suggesting that it was the specific shame element that was important in the association (Andrews, 1995, 1997).

In the daughters, early abuse was associated with disordered eating and bulimia (Andrews, 1995, 1997). Bodily shame was also strongly related to bulimia (Andrews, 1997). However, it was not clear whether shame was a preceding or concurrent factor in bulimia because the young women were not questioned in detail about the onset of disorders occurring more than

12 months prior to interview. Nevertheless, examination of the transcribed accounts suggested that in all cases of bulimia, onset or exacerbation of symptoms followed abuse and was concurrent with bodily shame. One explanation for the concurrent occurrence of bodily shame with bulimic symptoms may be that the shame measure was tapping directly into a central component of the disorder, that is, undue preoccupation with body shape and dread of getting too fat. However, while much of the focus for shame was on body parts such as breasts, buttocks, stomach and legs, shame of other bodily aspects not directly related to shape, such as body hair, complexion and facial features were also commonly reported. Furthermore, shame *per se* has not been described and defined as a central element of bulimia according to recognised diagnostic criteria. While bodily dissatisfaction is recognised as a bulimic symptom, it could not account for the strong relationship between bodily shame and bulimia.

In the older women, bodily shame mediated the relationship between early abuse and episodes of chronic or recurrent depression in the eight-year period of the study when current level of depression was controlled (Andrews, 1995). In the absence of bodily shame, the relationship between early abuse and chronic or recurrent depression was lost. It was surprising, given the humiliation involved in marital violence and rape, that neither of these abusive adult experiences was related to bodily shame in the absence of childhood experiences. However, it was found that the experience of adult abuse increased the rate of chronic and recurrent depression among those reporting childhood abuse. This might be explained by the propensity of abuse in adulthood to provoke intense shame among women already prone to such feelings on account of their past abusive experiences. In a similar manner, it seems possible that non-physically abusive life events, or chronic problems involving humiliating experiences, such as hostile reactions and rejection in intimate sexual relationships, are more likely than other stressors to provoke or exacerbate bodily shame in already vulnerable individuals.

A further investigation of shame has been carried out in a study of depressed patients (Andrews & Hunter, 1997). The findings confirmed the relation between bodily shame and early abuse in both female and male patients. They showed bodily shame to be more powerfully related to early abuse than non-bodily forms of shame involving character and behaviour. However, shame in all its forms was related to a chronic and recurrent course of the disorder.

Shame of the body was not a fleeting experience for the research partici-pants reporting it in these studies, but a chronic state pervading their adult lives. The two main themes in the content of the accounts involved individual concerns about bodily appearance in the eyes of others, and behaviour involving concealment of the body. One woman recalled that she would not get into the communal shower when she was at school unless she was wearing her underwear. Another reported how she would not go anywhere without a jacket to cover her arms, even in hot weather. Several women spontaneously reported feeling so ashamed of their bodies that they would not let their husbands see them undressed. By way of a further illustration of both concerns about others' evaluations and concealment, one young women said:

> At secondary school I got a complex about my large nose, and that I hadn't got a proper chin. The older you get, the more you discover what other people think you've got wrong with you, so when you get to 18 or 19, you can't walk out the door.

The accounts illustrate how bodily shame may differ from bodily dissatisfaction and low self-esteem. Both these factors involve not living up to one's own standards (which may reflect societal and cultural values), but they do not necessarily involve concealment of supposed deficiencies, and inordinate concern about how one appears to others.

Discussion

It appears that proneness to body shame, as a result of early abuse, has different consequences, depending on the age and life-stage of the women in the research described. In younger women, feelings of shame about the body resulting from abuse may lead to the avoidance of others' scorn through an unrealistic striving for perfection, manifested by restricted intake of food. Research has shown that, psychologically, dieters feel deprived of favourite foods and when 'off' the diet are likely to overeat (Polivy & Herman, 1985). In this way, a disturbed eating pattern of bingeing and dieting ensues. It is possible that on account of her childhood experiences, especially when there has been maternal deprivation, the abused girl feels particularly deprived when she diets and therefore compensates even more than others. She may judge herself more harshly than others when she 'lets herself down' by eating too much. This may lead her to take more severe and punitive action against herself than others might in order to rid herself of unwanted food, in the form of self-induced vomiting and laxative purging.

However, this is only one explanation for why abuse survivors might abuse their own bodies by depriving and then purging themselves of food. An alternative explanation encompasses all forms of body attacks including self-mutilation. Based on clinical observation, theorists such as Herman (1994) have proposed that compulsive attacks on the body by abuse survivors are due to the need to regulate and obliterate unbearably painful emotions. Such attacks are usually followed by a sense of calm, and individuals often report that the discomfort or pain caused to the body is preferable to any emotional pain. However, it is also the case that violent attacks on others are used to alleviate negative feelings (Berkowitz, 1993). As there is a well-documented relationship between being abused in childhood and later violence towards others, this still leaves open the question of why the survivor's own body should sometimes be the target of attack. One resolution to this question involves consideration of chronic feelings of bodily shame. Explanations for bodily attacks involving both self-punishment, and regulation of painful feelings can be mutually compatible; the underlying similarity being the intense self-hatred that is often involved in body shame.

But how might the persistence and severity of depression in older woman who have been abused in childhood be explained by body shame? An explanation has already been mentioned above concerning abuse survivors' particular sensitivity to depressogenic events involving rejection or humiliation by opposite sex relationships. Feelings of bodily shame may be readily elicited in response to real or imagined maltreatment by, or disdain of, others. The ensuing humiliated fury to being put down (Lewis, 1987), and feelings of being 'stuck' with offending physical features may lead to or enhance existing feelings of hopelessness and self-depreciation that are common features in depression.

Unlike the majority of young men who move towards independence as they mature, the majority of women who have children find that their emotional and physical resources are bound up with ensuring the best care for them and there is a greater need for both emotional and material dependence on the male. It is possible that as young women reach the stage of marrying or cohabiting and having children, they become less able to avoid potentially shame-provoking situations because of this dependency and loss of status in the outside world. Women without histories of childhood abuse may cope better in these circumstances than those with such histories. Because of a stronger sense of self-worth, they may feel subjectively equal to their partners, even when this is not the reality in terms of control over objective resources. In situations involving conflict with partners and others, feelings of inferiority, powerlessness and submissiveness that are bound up with shame may not be so readily evoked.

While these speculations appear plausible in terms of the evidence described, it is important to keep in mind that the samples were limited to mainly working-class mothers and their daughters living in a deprived inner-city area. The study of a more heterogeneous group of women or a group with different demographic characteristics might have produced different results. For example, it is possible that in other less deprived samples of women with more objective autonomy, feelings of bodily shame may be less apparent or more readily concealed, because greater material resources may compensate for, or mask, submissive and subordinate feelings. It is possible that in samples of women and men with more objective autonomy, feelings of bodily shame or characterological self-blame resulting from early abuse may be more likely to be repressed and projected onto others – manifested as feelings of scorn and the need to humiliate others (see Miller, 1987). It may be, of course, that both shame and scorn are more easily elicited in those who have been abused and that humiliation of others occurs concurrently with unrepressed shame. The manifestation of feelings and behaviours involving hostility towards others needs further investigation in this context.

Conclusion

The evidence suggests that early abusive experiences may lead to a propensity to feel both bodily shame and characterological self-blame in adulthood. On their own, or in combination, these factors may well lead to feelings of self-hatred and inferiority in relation to others. Body shame is likely to involve the anticipation of rejection and disdain by others for supposed deficiencies, and the potential for self-punishment. These are likely ways in which body shame plays a mediating role in the link between early abuse and disorders such as bulimia and depression. It may act as a vulnerability factor for the onset of disorder such as depression and bulimia in abused individuals as well as being related to a more persistent and chronic course.

References

Andrews, B. (1995) Bodily shame as a mediator between abusive experiences and depression. *Journal of Abnormal Psychology*, 104, 277–285.

Andrews, B. (1997) Bodily shame in relation to abuse in childhood and bulimia. *British Journal of Clinical Psychology*, 36, 41–50.

Andrews, B. & Brewin, C.R. (1990) Attributions for marital violence: A study of antecedents and consequences. *Journal of Marriage and the Family*, 52, 757–767.

Andrews, B. & Brown, G.W. (1988a) Social support, onset of depression and personality: An exploratory analysis. *Social Psychiatry and Psychiatric Epidemiology*, 23, 99–108.

Andrews, B. & Brown, G.W. (1988b) Marital violence in the community: A biographical approach. *British Journal of Psychiatry*, 153, 305–312.

Andrews, B. & Brown, G.W. (1993) Self-esteem and vulnerability to depression: The concurrent validity of interview and questionnaire measures. *Journal of Abnormal Psychology*, 102, 565–572.

Andrews, B. & Hunter, E. (1997) Shame, early abuse and course of depression in a clinical sample: A preliminary study. *Cognition and Emotion*, 11, 373–381.

Berkowitz, L. (1993) *Aggression: Its Causes, Consequences and Control*. New York: McGraw-Hill.

Bowlby, J. (1977) The making and breaking of affectional bonds: 1. Aetiology and psychopathology in the light of attachment theory. *British Journal of Psychiatry*, 130, 201–210.

Bowlby, J. (1980) *Loss: Sadness and Depression. Attachment and Loss* (vol. 3). London: Hogarth Press.

Cole, P.M. & Putnam, F.W. (1992) Effect of incest on self and social functioning: A developmental psychopathology perspective. *Journal of Consulting and Clinical Psychology*, 60, 174–184.

Egeland, B., Jacobvitz, D. & Sroufe, L.A. (1988) Breaking the cycle of abuse. *Child Development*, 59, 1080–1088.

Ferenczi, S. (1932/1949) Confusion of tongues between the adult and the child. *International Journal of Psycho-Analysis*, 30, 225–230.

Finkelhor, D. (1983) Common features of family abuse. In D. Finkelhor, R. Gelles, G. Hotaling & M. Straus (eds) *The Dark Side of Families: Current Family Violence Research* (pp. 17–28). London: Sage.

Finkelhor, D. & Browne, A. (1986) Initial and long-term effects: A conceptual framework. In D. Finkelhor (ed.) *Sourcebook on Child Sexual Abuse* (pp.180–198). Newbury Park, CA: Sage.

Gilbert, P. (1989) *Human Nature and Suffering*. Hove, UK: Lawrence Erlbaum Associates Ltd.

Gilbert, P. (1997) The evolution of social attractiveness and its role in shame, humiliation, guilt and therapy. *British Journal of Medical Psychology*, 70, 113–147.

Gilbert, P. (2000) The relationship of shame, social anxiety and depression: The role of the evaluation of social rank. *Clinical Psychology and Psychotherapy*, 7, 174–189.

Gilbert, P., Pehl, J., & Allan, S. (1994) The phenomenology of shame and guilt: An empirical investigation. *British Journal of Medical Psychology*, 67, 23–36.

Herbruck, C. (1979) *Breaking the Cycle of Child Abuse*. Minneapolis: Winston Press.

Herman, J.L. (1994) *Trauma and Recovery*. London: Pandora.

Janoff-Bulman, R. (1979) Characterological versus behavioral self-blame: Inquiries into depression and rape. *Journal of Personality and Social Psychology*, 37, 1798–1809.

Lewis, H.B. (1987) Shame and depression. In H.B. Lewis (ed.) *The Role of Shame in Symptom Formation* (pp.29–50). Hove, UK: Lawrence Erlbaum Associates Ltd.

Miller, A. (1987) *For Your Own Good: The Roots of Violence in Childrearing*. London: Virago.

Mollon, P. (1984) Shame in relation to narcissistic disturbance. *British Journal of Medical Psychology*, 57, 207–214.

Polivy, J. & Herman, C.P. (1985) Dieting and binging: A causal analysis. *American Psychologist*, 40, 193–201.

Sartre, J.P. (1956) *Being and Nothingness*. New York: Philosophical Library.

Silver, R.L. & Wortman, C.B. (1980) Coping with undesirable life events. In J. Garber & M.E.P. Seligman (eds) *Human Helplessness: Theory and Applications* (pp.279–340). New York: Academic Press.

Tangney, J.P., Miller, R.S., Flicker, L. & Barlow, D.H. (1996) Are shame, guilt, and embarrassment distinct emotions? *Journal of Personality and Social Psychology*, 70, 1256–1269.

Tangney, J.P., Wagner, P. & Gramzow, R. (1992) Proneness to shame, proneness to guilt and psychopathology. *Journal of Abnormal Psychology*, 101, 469–478.

Weiner, B. (1986) *An Attributional Theory of Motivation and Emotion*. New York: Springer.

Wicker, F.W., Payne, G.C. & Morgan, R.D. (1983) Participant descriptions of guilt and shame. *Motivation and Emotion*, 7, 25–39.

Wonderlich, S.A., Brewerton, T.D., Jocic, Z., Dansky, B.S. & Abbott, D.W. (1997) Relationship of childhood sexual abuse and eating disorders. *Journal of American Academy of Child and Adolescent Psychiatry*, 36, 1107–1115.

Chapter 14

Shame in body dysmorphic disorder

David Veale

Introduction

The most extreme form of body shame is found in patients with body dysmorphic disorder (BDD). BDD is perhaps the most puzzling of conditions described in this book. To most observers it is understandable why individuals with disfigurements might experience body shame. However, BDD patients have, *by the defining criteria of the disorder*, a normal appearance, yet believe themselves to be defective or ugly and may think of themselves as the '*Elephant Man*'. Furthermore, of all the conditions characterised by body shame, BDD patients are among the most distressed and handicapped by their appearance with a high rate of depression and suicide.

This chapter first describes the definition of BDD; its general features and psychopathology. It then explores a cognitive-behavioural conceptualisation of BDD. From this, key features in a cognitive-behavioural approach to treatment are described. Many of the areas and themes touched on here have implications and applications for body shame difficulties in general. We do not yet have the evidence whether BDD is best conceptualised as a dimensional problem in other body shame disorders. I would predict that there would be evidence of some aspects of BDD but mainly in the areas of external shame or social anxiety.

Definition and characteristics of BDD

Body dysmorphic disorder (BDD) is defined as a *preoccupation* with an imagined defect in one's appearance. Alternatively, if a slight physical anomaly is present, the person's concern is markedly excessive (American Psychiatric Association, 1994). The preoccupation should last for a minimum of an hour daily (Phillips, 1996). To fulfil the diagnostic criteria for *DSM-IV*, the preoccupation must also cause clinically significant distress or impairment in social, occupational or other important areas of functioning. Lastly, the preoccupation must not be better accounted for by another mental disorder (e.g., the dissatisfaction that occurs in anorexia nervosa). The older term, 'dysmorphophobia' was first introduced by an Italian psychiatrist, Morselli, in 1886 (Jerome, 2001), although it is now falling into disuse probably because ICD-10 (World Health Organization, 1992) has discarded it and subsumed it under that of hypochondriacal disorder.

In *DSM-IV*, if the belief about the defect is regarded as delusional (which is best determined by using a structured interview such as the Brown Assessment of Beliefs Scale) (Eisen et al., 1998), then the patient receives an additional diagnosis of delusional disorder. However, there is no significant difference between the patients or in their response to a selective serotonin reuptake inhibitor (SSRI) with or without the additional diagnosis of delusional disorder other than the severity of the problem (Phillips et al., 1994).

The most common preoccupations in BDD are of the nose, skin, hair, eyes, eyelids, mouth, lips, jaw and chin; however, any part of the body may be involved and the preoccupation is frequently focused on several body parts (Phillips et al., 1993; Veale et al., 1996a). Complaints typically involve perceived or slight flaws on the face, such as a body feature being too small or too big, the hair thinning, acne, wrinkles, scars, vascular markings, paleness or redness of the complexion, asymmetry or lack of proportion. Sometimes the complaint is extremely vague or amounts to no more than that the sufferer is generally ugly.

BDD patients have been found to have a quality of life worse than depressed patients (Phillips, 2000); they are often unemployed or disadvantaged at work, are socially isolated and are at high risk of suicide (Veale et al., 1996a). They often have needless cosmetic surgery or may perform 'DIY' surgery if they cannot afford private surgery or if a surgeon refuses their request (Veale, 2000).

Epidemiology and presentation

BDD has never been included in the large catchment area surveys of psychiatric morbidity. There has been one study which found a one-year prevalence of BDD of 0.7% in Italy (Faravelli et al., 1997). BDD therefore appears relatively common but mental health professionals do not often diagnose and treat patients with BDD. It is a hidden disorder with many patients not seeking help. In this respect, there is a low level of awareness about BDD among the public and health professionals. There tends to be an equal sex incidence and the age of onset of BDD is during adolescence. However, patients are diagnosed on average 10 to 15 years after the onset of the condition (Veale et al., 1996).

When patients do seek help, they are more likely to consult a dermatologist or cosmetic surgeon than a psychiatrist. For example, Sarwer et al. (1998) found that 5% of women presenting at a cosmetic surgery clinic in the USA had BDD. Similarly, Phillips et al. (2000) conducted a survey in a dermatology clinic and found that a staggering 12% of patients were likely to have BDD. The boundaries of BDD are not yet clear as the definition of a 'minor physical anomaly' is subjective and there is a grey area between this and more noticeable 'defects'.

When BDD patients finally seek help from a GP or mental health professional, they are often too ashamed to reveal their main symptoms and present with symptoms of depression, social phobia or obsessive-compulsive disorder (for which there is frequent comorbidity). Patients are especially secretive about symptoms such as mirror gazing, probably because they think they will be viewed as vain or narcissistic. When they are finally diagnosed, they are often treated inappropriately with antipsychotic medication (Phillips, 1998). Alternatively, a therapist may have little experience in treating BDD patients or lack an effective treatment model. There is therefore an unmet need for the diagnosis and effective treatment of BDD. There are however promising results from cognitive-behavioural therapy and the use of serotonin reuptake inhibitors, which will be discussed at the end of this chapter.

Psychopathology of BDD

BDD patients are often dissatisfied with multiple areas of their body. For example, a patient believed that his nose was too big with a hump and that it should be straight and small. He also believed that his facial skin was flawed with spots and wrinkles and that it should be perfectly smooth with no lines. He also had other concerns about his face hair not being symmetrical, his lips being too big, his ears sticking out and veins sticking out on his arms. The nature of the preoccupation may also fluctuate over time and may explain why, after cosmetic surgery, a preoccupation may often shift to another area of the body. Beliefs about defectiveness of appearance have personal meanings. For example, patients might believe that their noses being too big will mean that they will end up alone and unloved or that they look like crooks. For other people, the most disgusting aspect of the flaws in their skin was thinking of it as 'dirty'.

Values are often ignored in our understanding of psychological problems. In BDD, appearance is almost always the dominant and idealised value and the means of defining the self. According to a cognitive-behavioural model, patients implicitly view themselves as 'aesthetic objects'. Other important values in some BDD patients often include perfectionism, symmetry and social acceptance and this may take the form of certain rules, for example, 'I have to be perfect or symmetrical.' Defining the values also assist in differentiating BDD patients from anorexic patients who value the importance of self-control, asceticism or perfectionism (Veale, 2002). Bulimic patients tend to value the importance of social acceptance and being liked. Patients with apotemnophilia who desire amputation of a limb tend to value the importance of being disabled because it feels as if their limb is not part of their self.

Mirror gazing is at the core of BDD and appears to be a complex series of safety behaviours. Why do some BDD patients spend many hours in front of a mirror when invariably it makes them feel more distressed and self-conscious? We recently conducted a study comparing mirror-gazing behaviour in BDD patients and normal controls (Veale & Riley, 2001). The conclusions were that the main motivation for mirror gazing in BDD patients was the hope that they would look different; the desire to know exactly how they look; a desire to camouflage themselves and a belief that they will feel worse if they resist gazing (although they actually felt more distressed after gazing). BDD patients were more likely to focus their attention on an internal impression or feeling (rather than their reflection in the mirror) and on specific parts of their appearance. Although BDD patients and the controls used the mirror to put on make-up, shave, pick their skin, groom their hair or check their appearance, only BDD patients performed 'mental cosmetic surgery' to change their body image and to practise different faces to pull in the mirror. Other reflective surfaces such as the back of CDs or shop window panes may also be used, which further distort their body image. Patients may also check their appearance by measuring their perceived defect; by feeling the contours of the skin with their fingers or repeatedly taking photos or a video of themselves. Other behaviours include asking others to verify the existence of the defect or their camouflage; making comparisons of their appearance with others or old photos of themselves; wearing make-up 24 hours a day; excessive grooming of their hair; excessive cleansing of the skin; use of facial peelers or saunas, facial exercises to improve muscle tone; beauty treatments (e.g., collagen injections to their lips); cosmetic surgery or dermatological treatments. There may also be impulsive behaviours such as skin-picking, which produce a very brief sense of satisfaction or pleasure (similar to trichotillomania), followed by a sense of despair and anger.

Internal and external shame in BDD

The reason for distinguishing internal from external shame (or fear of stigma) has been outlined by Gilbert (Chapter 1, this volume). This is also an important distinction for BDD and directs attention to careful assessment of the focus of people's beliefs and the nature of their fears. Beliefs about being defective and the importance of appearance will be associated with varying degrees of social anxiety and fears of negative evaluation by others (or external shame). Thus, BDD patients will tend to avoid a range of public or social situations or intimate relationships. Alternatively, many patients endure social situations only if they use camouflage or various safety behaviours. These are often idiosyncratic and depend on the perceived defect as well as cultural norms. Behaviours such as avoidance of eye contact, using long hair or excessive make-up for camouflage are obvious, but others are subtler and are difficult to detect unless the patient is asked how they behave in social situations. For example, a BDD patient preoccupied by his nose avoided showing his profile in social situations and only stood face on to an individual. A patient preoccupied by perceived blemishes under her eye wore a pair of glasses to hide the skin under her eyes. Safety behaviours contribute to the inability to disconfirm beliefs and further self-monitoring and intensification of the preoccupation (e.g., by further mirror gazing and other behaviours to determine whether the camouflage is 'working'.)

However, not all BDD patients are preoccupied by external shame and negative evaluation by others. I will illustrate this by two different male patients who both complained about the size and shape of their genitals. The first patient, Dick, complained that the 'flesh' on one side of his penis was flatter than on the other side. He had no avoidance behaviour or concerns about his sexual performance or what his girlfriend would think if she could see it was not symmetrical. Dick was more preoccupied by failing to achieve an internal aesthetic standard. He was extremely distressed because he was aware that the 'problem' could not be rectified and was, as a result, significantly depressed and handicapped. The second patient, called Bill, complained that the size of his penis and his testes was too small. He was aged 30 but had virtually avoided all intimate relationships because of his extreme anxiety and fear of rejection. When Bill once had intercourse, he did not allow his partner to see his genitals. In social situations, he would cross his legs so that his genital area could not be seen. It should be said that both Dick and Bill had 'normal' sized and shaped genitals.

We have explored the role of internal and external body shame with self-discrepancy theory in BDD (Veale et al., in press). Self-discrepancy theory proposes three basic domains of self-beliefs that are important to understanding emotional experience. These three domains may be either from the 'self' or 'other' perspective: (a) *the actual self* – the individual's representation of the attributes that someone (self or significant other) believes the individual actually possesses; (b) *the ideal self* – the individual's representation of the attributes that someone (self or significant other) would ideally hope the individual to possess; (c) *the should or ought self* – the individual's representation of the attributes that someone (self or significant other) believes the individual should as a sense of duty or moral obligation possess. The *ideal* and *should* selves are referred to as self-guides. It is assumed that a discrepancy between the actual self and the self-guides determines the individual's vulnerability to negative emotional states (Higgins, 1987). For example, in an actual self: ideal self-discrepancy, the individual is vulnerable to dejection-related emotions (e.g., sadness), resulting from the appraisal that one's hopes and aspirations are unfulfilled (through the absence of positive reinforcement). In a self-actual: other-should discrepancy, the individual is vulnerable to anxiety resulting from the appraisal that one has been unable to achieve one's responsibilities and is therefore liable for punishment (the anticipated presence of negative outcomes). Patients with social phobia or bulimia have a marked discrepancy between how they perceive themselves and how they think they should appear to others (Strauman, 1989). We recruited 107 BDD patients and 42 healthy controls to complete a questionnaire requiring them to list only their physical characteristics in each of the domains: (a) actual self; (b) ideal self; (c) should self; (d) actual other; and (e) ideal other. BDD patients displayed significant discrepancies between their self-actual and both their self-ideal and self-should. There were no significant discrepancies in BDD patients, however, between their self-actual and other-actual or other-ideal domains. This suggests that BDD patients are predominantly disturbed by a failure to achieve an internal aesthetic standard rather than being punished for not achieving the ideals of others. They are therefore more like depressed patients (who fail to achieve their ideal or experience internal shame) than social phobic, paranoid or bulimic patients, who experience external shame and are more concerned with avoiding punishment by the perceived demands of others. However, the situation is complex as *some* BDD patients, like Dick, are more like social phobic patients, and in my clinical experience easier to treat – a similar situation may exist in eating disorders where patients with bulimia (who seem to have predominantly external shame) may be easier to treat than those with anorexia (who seem to have predominantly internal shame and pride compensations; see Goss & Gilbert, Chapter 12, this volume).

Aesthetic standards in BDD

If BDD patients are more concerned with internal shame and there is a big discrepancy between how they see themselves and how they think they should be, do they have higher aesthetic standards or skills in appreciating art and beauty than others? We hypothesised that BDD patients were more likely to be artists than comparative groups of psychiatric patients (Veale, Ennis & Lambrou, in press). We extracted the data on higher education, training or occupation from the case notes of 100 consecutive patients with BDD and compared them to 100 patients with depression, 100 patients with obsessive compulsive disorder (OCD) and 100 patients with post-traumatic stress disorder (PTSD). We found that 20% of the BDD patients were artists (5 graphic designers, 2 architects, 2 with fine art degrees, 2 with art history degrees, 6 with art and design degrees, 1 artist and 1 art teacher) compared with 4% in the depressed group (1 with fine art degree, 1 with art history degree, 1 artist and 1 art teacher), 3% in the OCD group (1 graphic designer, 1 architect, 1 with fine art degree) and 0% in the PTSD group. These results were highly statistically significant.

The differences between the BDD group and the three comparative groups are relatively large and the frequency of artists in the three comparative groups is similar, which suggests that the association is relatively robust and deserves further investigation. We know of no psychiatric disorder to have such a strong association with a particular education or occupation. We do not have any evidence for a causal relationship between BDD and art and design. The onset of BDD is usually gradual during adolescence and an interest in art and design may be a contributory factor to the development of the disorder. Patients might develop a more critical eye and appreciation of aesthetics, which is then applied to their own appearance. An equally plausible explanation is that subjects have a selection bias for aesthetics.

The association with aesthetics raises an interesting question about the definition of BDD as a preoccupation with an '*imagined* defect or a minor physical anomaly that is grossly excessive' (American Psychiatric Association, 1994). Perhaps BDD patients just have higher aesthetic standards than the mental health professionals who cannot appreciate art and beauty to the same degree? Harris (1982) has proposed that individuals seeking cosmetic surgery are more aesthetically sensitive (an attribute like being musical, which varies in different individuals). However, an objective measure of aesthetic sensitivity is required to test the hypothesis that BDD patients or others seeking cosmetic surgery (or their surgeons) have higher standards in aesthetic perception than the rest of the population. Harris (personal communication) also believes that there is a component of affective sensitivity in aesthetics. He proposes that some individuals react with greater emotional response to beauty or ugliness. Another explanation of our findings of an increased rate of occupation in art and of Harris's observation is that BDD patients have idealised values about the importance of appearance, which have become over-identified with the self (Veale, 2002). Hence, threats to the self are likely to be associated with increased emotional response.

Other predisposing factors to the development of BDD might include a history of teasing about body parts or sexual abuse but this has not been adequately investigated. Genetic factors in BDD have not been investigated and twin studies are awaited with interest. There is virtually no research on biological aspects of BDD. Neuroimaging studies have indicated that self-recognition is associated with the prefrontal cortex and limbic regions, including the insula, which is relevant for the emotion of disgust (Kircher et al., 2000). These findings indicate that similar areas in the brain are important for perception both of emotionally salient information and the self. Abnormalities of self-perception including body shame may therefore be associated with dysfunctional regulation of the prefrontal cortex of activity in brain regions important for emotion and disgust perception.

A cognitive behavioural model of BDD

The model (see Figure 14.1) focuses on the maintaining factors and the experience of BDD patients when they are alone and internal shame (rather than in social situations, that are likely to follow a model similar to that of social phobia or external shame) (Clark & Wells, 1995). These models may

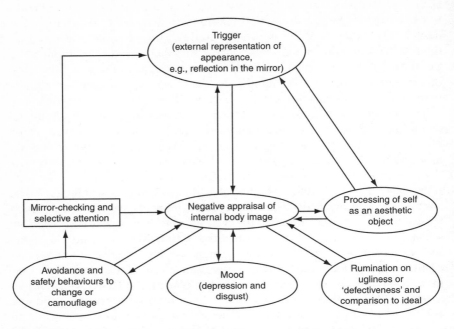

Figure 14.1 A cognitive-behavioural model of body dysmorphic disorder

also be helpful in developing our understanding of other disorders with body shame. The model begins with a trigger that is an external representation of one's body image, typically in front of a mirror. Alternative triggers may include looking at an old photograph taken when the patient was younger. The process of selective attention begins on an external reflection of a mirror by focusing on specific aspects of the appearance leading to a heightened awareness and relative magnification of certain aspects. Mirror gazing activates idealised values about the importance of appearance, and in some patients, values about perfectionism or symmetry and processing of the self as an aesthetic object. This leads to a negative aesthetic appraisal and comparisons of three different images – the external representation (usually in a mirror), the ideal body image and the distorted body image. Not surprisingly, these repeated comparisons result in uncertainty as to how the individual does look and further mirror gazing. The end result is one in which a BDD patient constructs a mental representation of their body image that becomes fused with the external reality (or 'mirror image fusion').

A patient's desire to see exactly how they look is only rewarded while they are actually looking in the mirror. However, the longer a person looks, the worse they feel and the more it reinforces their view of being ugly and defective. (Readers might like to try inducing BDD in themselves for a brief period by focusing their attention on an undesirable body part in a mirror with a demand as to how it should be. They should focus on how they feel for at least half an hour.) When a BDD patient is not looking in a mirror, they may focus attention on their internal body image and ruminate on their ugliness. There is often a marked discrepancy between the actual and ideal body image or how others look which inevitably leads to a depressed mood. The patient may then ruminate on this and other assumptions such as being alone all their life.

Mood and dysmorphic beliefs

Mood changes in BDD are complex. Patients may experience anticipatory anxiety prior to mirror gazing when they hope they may see something different or think they will feel worse if they resist gazing. When they look in a mirror, they may experience a depressed mood as they lose hope that they do not look different. They may feel disgust as they evaluate their body image. During a long session in front of a mirror, some patients may experience a dissociative state (similar to the experience of self-mutilation or bingeing). After mirror gazing, some may become angry or feel guilty for wasting so much time in front of a mirror. This judgement about being ugly appears to be closely linked to mood and is incorporated in the feedback loop of the model. Depressed mood was also noted to be a trigger for looking in a mirror and a further vicious circle. Social avoidance and social isolation will also contribute to a depressed mood.

The drive to change appearance

Negative aesthetic judgement, an internal aversion to the self and social anxiety, will drive patients' demands to change their appearance and their obsession with it. The use of make-up, beauty treatments, cosmetic surgery or the help of a dermatologist may do this physically but does not usually alter their mental state. It may lead to further disappointment and depression at the failure to achieve an ideal or may result in anger directed against self or surgeon for making their appearance worse. Inevitably, the use of camouflage or cosmetic surgery leads to further mirror gazing in an attempt to evaluate its continued efficacy and this feeds the distorted body image in a further vicious circle.

Cognitive behaviour therapy

Two randomised controlled trials have been conducted in BDD for CBT against a waiting list (Rosen, Reiter & Orosan, 1995; Veale et al., 1996b) and several case series (Geremia & Neziroglu, 2001; Gomez Perez, Marks &

Gutierrez Fisac, 1994; Neziroglu & Yaryura Tobias, 1993; Wilhelm et al., 1999). In the first controlled trial, Rosen, Reiter and Orosan (1995) randomly allocated 54 BDD patients to either group-based CBT or a waiting list. CBT was delivered in eight weekly two-hour group sessions. After treatment, 22 out of 27 (82%) of the CBT group were clinically improved and no longer met criteria for BDD, compared to only 2 of the 27 subjects (7%) in the no treatment group. The gains of the CBT group were maintained at follow-up, with 77% remaining well. The subjects were, however, different to those described at other centres; for example, they were all female, 38% were pre-occupied with their weight and shape alone, and they were generally less handicapped and less socially avoidant than in most other clinical series. In our own study (Veale et al., 1996b), we randomly allocated 19 patients with BDD to either CBT over 12 weeks, or a waiting list. We found a 50% reduction in the treated group on the Yale Brown Obsessive Compulsive Scale modified for BDD, and a significant improvement in mood. None of the control group improved in either of these domains. The main weaknesses of this study were the female preponderance (90%); the lack of a non-specific treatment condition; the absence of any validated measurement of the conviction of belief (i.e., delusions); and the lack of follow-up assessment. Further studies will concentrate on establishing that CBT is a specific treatment for BDD and compared against pharmacotherapy.

Thus, much remains to be done in developing and evaluating CBT for BDD. Each of the existing studies have had slightly different emphases in their therapeutic intervention (depending on the emphasis on behavioural or cognitive strategies), and during the next few years, we are likely to see a number of treatment manuals and models developed that can be tested by independent groups.

Engagement

The very nature of BDD means that a therapist will disagree with a patient's description of the problem in terms of the exact beliefs about their appearance. However, both patient and therapist can usually agree upon a description of the problem as a preoccupation with their appearance leading to various self-defeating behaviours. It may be possible to agree initially on goals, such as stopping specific behaviours, for example, skin-picking, or to enter public situations that were previously avoided. Here the implicit message is to help the patient function and do more *despite* their appearance and aesthetic standards. However, patients often have covert goals of wanting to remain excessively camouflaged in public or of changing their appearance. I specifically ask patients not to plan cosmetic surgery or dermatological treatment during therapy and to reconsider their desire for surgery after they have recovered from BDD (or at least finished therapy). In patients who are unable to engage in therapy, it is to best to put the goals to one side and to concentrate on engaging the patient in a cognitive-behavioural model and later negotiate the goals. Not all patients want 'therapy' as they may have been forced to see someone by a relative or cosmetic surgeon. Some are too suicidal or lacking in motivation. Some may accept the offer of medication and this may act as a holding operation while trying to engage the patient in a psychological treatment.

One method of engagement is similar to that described for hypochondriasis (Clark et al., 1998). A patient is presented with two alternative hypotheses to test out. The first hypothesis (that the patient has been following) is that they are defective and ugly and they have therefore tried very hard to know exactly what they look like and to camouflage or change their appearance. The alternative hypothesis to be tested during therapy is that the problem is of excessive worrying about their appearance and making their appearance the most important aspect of their identity. Patients assume a model of 'What You See Is What You Get' in front of a mirror. An alternative model of 'What You See Is What You Have Constructed' is presented as a result of selective attention to an internal representation of their body image. The latter will depend more upon their mood, the meaning that they attach to the importance of appearance and the expectations that they bring to a mirror. This leads to a description of a cognitive-behavioural model for BDD and how a person with BDD becomes excessively aware of their appearance and giving other examples of selective attention in everyday life. Motivational interviewing can be used to focus on the consequences of the preoccupation and the logical consequences of maintaining the values about the importance of appearance to the self. The therapist would then ask the patient to suspend judgement and to test out the alternative hypothesis for the period of therapy. Engagement is usually helped by the credibility of the clinician who has treated other patients and validates their beliefs rather than discounting or trivialising them (Linehan, 1993), for example, 'What you feel about your appearance is very understandable'. The clinician must also search and reflect on the evidence for their beliefs and assumptions.

Patients can also be recommended a book about BDD, which is written for sufferers (Phillips, 1996), or to meet other sufferers in a patient support group or in a workshop at a national conference (OCD Action, London, UK or the OC Foundation in USA). Patients are often extremely relieved and surprised to talk to other BDD patients.

Sometimes, patients are impossible to engage in either CBT or pharmacotherapy and have to go through a long career of unnecessary surgery, beauty therapies, dermatological treatment or suicide attempts before seeking help for the BDD from a mental health professional. There are always cosmetic surgeons, dermatologists and beauty therapists willing to treat them but BDD patients report marked dissatisfaction with cosmetic surgery. Alternatively, even if the patient is somewhat satisfied, the preoccupation moves to a different area of the body so that the handicap remains the same (Veale,

2000). This is in marked contrast to patients without BDD who have good psychological benefits with cosmetic surgery.

Therapeutic strategies

Patients should have an individual formulation based on the model, which emphasises the pattern of thinking and behaviours that maintain the disorder. Therapists should draw upon patients' words to insert into the model their pattern of thinking and behaviours to derive their formulation. Once patients are engaged and willing to test out alternatives, therapists can choose from a variety of strategies. These include: (a) cognitive restructuring and behavioural experiments to test out their assumptions; (b) reverse role play for the rigid beliefs or values; (c) behavioural experiments or exposure to social situations without their safety behaviour; (d) response prevention for compulsive behaviours such as mirror gazing and mirror retraining; and (e) self-monitoring with a tally counter and habit reversal for impulsive behaviours such as skin-picking. Where necessary, others, who are normally involved in the provision of reassurance or verification, are included in a response prevention programme and can be given instructions in how to deal with such requests.

In principle, CBT is probably more effective when it aims to change the assumptions or meaning behind the beliefs about being defective and the importance of appearance to the person's identity rather than the actual beliefs about his or her appearance (e.g., 'My nose is too crooked'). This may include collecting evidence for and against assumptions such as 'If my appearance is defective then I will be unloved and alone all my life.' Values, however, are probably best challenged by questioning the functional costs and by reducing the importance of the value to the self in small degrees on a continuum similar to motivational interviewing of anorexia nervosa (Treasure & Ward, 1997). A fundamental thinking error is overgeneralisation in which a patient identifies their 'self' only through their appearance ('the aesthetic object') and all the other values and selves are diminished. In this regard, a patient may be helped by the concept of 'Big I' and 'Little i' whereby the self or 'Big I' is defined by thousands of 'Little i's' in the form of beliefs, values, and characteristics since birth (Dryden, 1998; Lazarus, 1977). Patients are therefore encouraged to focus on all the other characteristics of themselves to develop a more helpful or flexible view. Reverse role play can be also used to strengthen an alternative belief in which patients can practise arguing the case for their alternative belief while the therapist argues the case for the old beliefs (Newell & Shrubb, 1994).

Mirror gazing is an early target for intervention as it feeds the selective attention on appearance. Some patients try to cover up or take down mirrors (or previous therapists may have encouraged it). However, in our experience, this can lead to a different set of problems of mirror avoidance. In this scenario, a patient is likely to maintain his distorted body image and symptoms of BDD. Furthermore, they will be overwhelmed by a reflection that they accidentally catch when they pass a mirror. We think it is better that patients learn to use mirrors in a healthy way with timed limits depending on the activity (e.g., using a limited amount of make-up). Patients (whether they are gazing or avoiding) may need some guidance on their use of mirrors and often need 'retraining'. In general, patients are encouraged to be aware of their appearance in the external reflection of a mirror but to suspend judgement (similar to 'mindfulness'; Linehan, 1993). They should look at themselves as a whole and focus attention on what they see rather than how they feel. During mirror retraining, patients may describe aloud what they see in a non-judgemental manner.

Pharmacotherapy

The evidence in pharmacotherapy favours serotonin re-uptake inhibitors (SRIs). There has been one randomised controlled trial (RCT) comparing clomipramine (an SRI) and desipramine (a noradrenergic reuptake inhibitor (NRI) (Hollander et al., 1999) and two case series of fluvoxamine (Perugi et al., 1996; Phillips, Dwight & McElroy, 1998), in which there are modest benefits of about 50% reduction in symptoms on the Yale Brown Obsessive Compulsive Scale modified for BDD. There is also likely to be a dose response relationship whereby higher doses obtain a better response. Similar findings occur in obsessive-compulsive disorder with the superiority of a SRI compared to an NRI and a dose response relationship. This is in contrast to depressed patients who respond equally well to an SRI or NRI and in whom there is not usually a dose response relationship.

Deluded patients respond as well as non-deluded patients with an SRI (Phillips, Dwight & McElroy, 1998). Contrary to popular belief, there is no evidence for the efficacy of pimozide or antipsychotics even in 'deluded' patients as the sole treatment of BDD. The old case reports described as responding to pimozide (Riding & Munro, 1975) included cases of delusions of infestation, delusions of body odour and dysmorphic delusions. Although there has never been a randomised controlled trial of an SRI against an antipsychotic, Phillips (1998) reported that an SRI was of benefit in 54% of 113 trials compared with 2% of 83 antipsychotic trials. SRIs are especially indicated when BDD patients have a significantly depressed mood, are a suicide risk, or there is a long waiting list for cognitive-behavioural therapy. Treatment guidelines are the same as for OCD – an SRI in the highest dose for a prolonged period of time. Opinions vary on the treatment of resistant cases. They may require an alternative SRI. Those patients who still remain resistant might be helped by an SRI in combination with a very low dose of a neuroleptic as an adjunct. Like OCD, there is probably a high risk of relapse on discontinuation of an SRI. As yet, there are no controlled trials that compare CBT with an SRI but there is no suggestion that a combined approach is unhelpful. Indeed, maintaining a stable mood and reducing self-consciousness may have a synergistic benefit.

Conclusion

Research into BDD is in its infancy compared with other psychiatric disorders. We have discussed a cognitive-behavioural model and proposed the following:

1   BDD patients may have greater aesthetic emotional sensitivity and perceptual skills and this is manifested in their education or training in art and design.
2   BDD patients have a distorted body image, which is a complex interaction of affective, cognitive and somato-sensory components and selective attention (the self-actual).
3   BDD patients have higher aesthetic standards than the rest of the population (the self-ideal). This is manifested by the marked discrepancy between how patients see themselves and how they would ideally like to be or think they should be. This will contribute to their sense of internal shame.
4   BDD patients have varying degrees of social anxiety and external shame in terms of the degree to which they fear negative evaluation. In therapy, it is important for patients to test out their assumptions.

As yet, there is only limited empirical evidence for these hypotheses and the development of effective therapies but this is likely to increase over the next five years.

References

American Psychiatric Association (1994) *Diagnostic and Statistical Manual of Mental Disorders* (4th edn.). Washington, DC: American Psychiatric Association.

Clark, D.M., Salkovskis, P.M., Hackmann, A., Wells, A., Fennel, M., Ludgate, J., Ahmad, S., Richards, H.C. & Gelder, M. (1998) Two psychological treatments for hypochondriasis: A randomised controlled trial. *British Journal of Psychiatry*, 173, 218–225.

Clark, D.M. & Wells, A. (1995) A cognitive model of social phobia. In R.G. Heimberg, M.R. Liebowitz, D. Hope & F.R. Schneier (eds) *Social Phobia – Diagnosis, Assessment, and Treatment* (pp.69–93). New York: Guilford Press.

Dryden, W. (1998) *Developing Self-acceptance*. Chichester: John Wiley & Sons.

Eisen, J.L., Phillips, K.A., Baer, L., Beer, D.A., Atala, K.D. & Rasmussen, S.A. (1998) The Brown Assessment of Beliefs Scale: Reliability and validity. *American Journal of Psychiatry*, 155, 102–108.

Faravelli, C., Salvatori, S., Galassi, F., Aiazzi, L., Drei, C. & Cabras, P. (1997) Epidemiology of somatoform disorders: A community survey in Florence. *Social Psychiatry and Psychiatric Epidemiology*, 32, 24–29.

Geremia, G. & Neziroglu, F. (2001) Cognitive therapy in the treatment of body dysmorphic disorder. *Clinical Psychology and Psychotherapy*, 8, 243–251.

Gomez Perez, J.C., Marks, I.M. & Gutierrez Fisac, J.L. (1994) Dysmorphophobia: Clinical features and outcome with behaviour therapy. *European Psychiatry*, 9, 229–235.

Harris, D.L. (1982) Cosmetic surgery – where does it begin? *British Journal of Plastic Surgery*, 35, 281–286.

Higgins, E.T. (1987) Self-discrepancy: A theory relating self and affect. *Psychological Review*, 94, 319–340.

Hollander, E., Allen, A., Kwon, J., Aronowitz, B., Schmeidler, J., Wong, C. & Simeon, D. (1999) Clomipramine vs desipramine crossover trial in body dysmorphic disorder: Selective efficacy of a serotonin reuptake inhibitor in imagined ugliness. *Archives of General Psychiatry*, 56, 1033–1042.

Jerome, L. (2001) Dysmorphophobia and taphephobia: Two hitherto undescribed forms of insanity with fixed ideas. A new translation of Enrico Morselli's original article. *History of Psychiatry* 12, 103–114.

Kircher, T., Senior, C., Phillips, M., Benson, P., Bullmore, E., Brammer, M., Simmons, A., Williams, S., Bartels, M. & David, A. (2000) Towards a functional neuroanatomy of self processing: Effects of faces and words. *Brain Research & Cognitive Brain Research*, 10, 133–144.

Lazarus, A. (1977) Towards an egoless state of being. In A. Ellis & R. Grieger (eds) *Handbook of Rational Emotive Therapy* (vol. 1) (pp.113–118). New York: Springer.

Linehan, M.M. (1993). *Skills Training Manual*. New York: Guilford Press.

Newell, R. & Shrubb, S. (1994) Attitude change and behaviour therapy in body dysmorphic disorder: Two case reports. *Behavioural and Cognitive Psychotherapy*, 22, 163–169.

Neziroglu, F. & Yaryura Tobias, J.A. (1993) Exposure, response prevention, and cognitive therapy in the treatment of body dysmorphic disorder. *Behavior Therapy*, 24, 431–438.

Perugi, G., Giannotti, D., Di Vaio, S., Frare, F., Saettoni, M. & Cassano, G.B. (1996) Fluvoxamine in the treatment of body dysmorphic disorder (dysmorphophobia). *International Clinical Psychopharmacology*, 11, 247–254.

Phillips, K. (1996) *The Broken Mirror – Understanding and Treating Body Dysmorphic Disorder*. New York: Oxford University Press.

Phillips, K.A. (1998) Body dysmorphic disorder: Clinical aspects and treatment strategies. *Bulletin of the Menninger Clinic*, 62, A33–A48.

Phillips, K.A. (2000) Quality of life for patients with body dysmorphic disorder. *Journal of Nervous and Mental Disease*, 188, 170–175.

Phillips, K.A., Dufresne, R.G., Jr., Wilkel, C.S. & et al. (2000) Rate of body dysmorphic disorder in dermatology patients. *Journal of the American Academy of Dermatology*, 42, 436–444.

Phillips, K.A., Dwight, M.M. & McElroy, S.L. (1998) Efficacy and safety of fluvoxamine in body dysmorphic disorder. *Journal of Clinical Psychiatry*, 59, 165–171.

Phillips, K.A., McElroy, S.L., Keck, P.E., Jr., Hudson, J.I. & Pope, H.G., Jr. (1994) A comparison of delusional and nondelusional body dysmorphic disorder in 100 cases. *Psychopharmacology Bulletin*, 30, 179–186.

Phillips, K.A., McElroy, S.L., Keck, P.E., Jr., Pope, H.G., Jr. & Hudson, J.I. (1993) Body dysmorphic disorder: 30 cases of imagined ugliness. *American Journal of Psychiatry*, 150, 302–308.

Riding, J. & Munro, A. (1975) Pimozide in the treatment of monosymptomatic hypochondriacal psychosis. *Acta Psychiatrica Scandinavica*, 53, 23–30.

Rosen, J.C., Reiter, J. & Orosan, P. (1995) Cognitive-behavioral body image therapy for body dysmorphic disorder [published erratum appears in *Journal of Consulting and Clinical Psychology* (1995), 63 (3), 437]. *Journal of Consulting and Clinical Psychology*, 63, 263–269.

Sarwer, D.B., Wadden, T.A., Pertschuk, M.J. & Whitaker, L.A. (1998) Body image dissatisfaction and body dysmorphic disorder in 100 cosmetic surgery patients. *Plastic and Reconstructive Surgery*, 101, 1644–1649.

Strauman, T.J. (1989) Self-discrepancies in clinical depression and social phobia: Cognitive structures that underlie emotional disorders? *Journal of Abnormal Psychology*, 98, 14–22.

Treasure, J.L. & Ward, A. (1997) A practical guide to the use of motivational interviewing. *European Eating Disorders Review*, 5, 102–114.

Veale, D. (2000) Outcome of cosmetic surgery and 'D.I.Y.' surgery in patients with body dysmorphic disorder. *Psychiatric Bulletin*, 24, 218–221.

Veale, D. (2002) Overvalued ideas: A conceptual analysis. *Behaviour Research and Therapy*, 40, 383–400.

Veale, D., Boocock, A., Gournay, K., Dryden, W., Shah, F., Willson, R. & Walburn, J. (1996a) Body dysmorphic disorder: A survey of fifty cases. *British Journal of Psychiatry*, 169, 196–201.

Veale, D., Gournay, K., Dryden, W., Boocock, A., Shah, F., Willson, R. & Walburn, J. (1996b) Body dysmorphic disorder: A cognitive behavioural model and pilot randomised controlled trial. *Behaviour Research and Therapy*, 34, 717–729.

Veale, D. & Riley, S. (2001) Mirror mirror on the wall, who is the ugliest of them all? The psychopathology of mirror gazing in body dysmorphic disorder. *Behaviour Research and Therapy*, 39, 1381–1383.

Veale, D., Ennis, M. & Lambrou, C. (in press) Body dysmorphic disorder is associated with an occupation or education in art and design. *American Journal of Psychiatry*.

Veale, D., Kinderman, P., Riley, S. & Lambrou, C. (in press) Self-discrepancy and body dysmorphic disorder. *British Journal of Clinical Psychology*.

Wilhelm, S., Otto, M.W., Lohr, B. & Deckersbach, T. (1999). Cognitive behavior group therapy for body dysmorphic disorder: A case series. *Behaviour Research and Therapy*, 37, 71–75.

World Health Organization (1992) *The ICD-10: Classification of Mental and Behavioural Disorders*. Geneva: World Health Organization.

Index

care 7, 13, 165, 172, 233; hospital 166;
    need for 27; personal 168; self 142,
    149, 168
caresses 196, 200
Carr, A. T. 15, 40, 42, 92, 99
Carroll Self Rating for Depression Scale
    127
Cash, T. F. 42–3, 95–6, 110–11
Castelfranchi, C. 214
Castle, D. J. 94
cataract formation 122
catastrophic imaginal scenarios 236
causality 77; older person's attribution
    of 80
certainty 248
'Chairman Mao' 31
challenges 178, 183; shame based
    thinking 180
Changing Faces (charity) 109, 169
characteristics 278; physical 39, 167, 272;
    socially devalued 159; stable negative
    258; undesirable 39
charm 215
Charmaz, K. 79
chastity 35
checking behaviour 94, 111, 175; mirror
    231
childhood and adolescence 30–2, 55, 105,
    193; abuse 38, 256–66; bowel disorders
    40, 85, 171–85; burns and scalding 155,
    160; criticised for not 'keeping clean'
    or 'being dirty' 37; eating disorders
    scales 93; learning obedience 23;
    pre-school 167; prevention of
    psychopathology 110; self-criticism 40;
    stories 104
China 30, 220
chocolate 137, 138
chronicity 256
civil liberties 37
Clark, D. M. 15, 43, 146, 147
Clark, M. 40
Clarke, A. 21, 33, 43, 44, 42, 112
Clarke, M. 111
cleanliness 28, 30 175; excessive 270
Cloitre, M. 13
clomipramine 279
closeness 194–5, 200; regaining 199;
    sexual 191
clothes 97, 111, 122, 131, 159; children
    and 175; removal of 145
codes 38
coercion 35, 46

cognitions 6, 13, 24, 59, 77, 84, 90, 91,
    137, 161, 234; challenging 44; control
    78; core 222; key 150, 172; negative
    164, 172, 227; painful 143;
    shame-related 63, 222, 243; social
    phobia 210
cognitive behavioural problems 269
cognitive behavioural therapy 20,
    42–4, 83, 96, 110–12, 132, 164, 177,
    210–11, 212, 213, 237, 246; BDD
    273–80
cognitive biases 225, 227
cognitive dissonance 22
cognitive distortions 107, 108, 151,
    157, 243
cognitive errors 111, 247
cognitive restructuring 110, 278
cognitive sex psychotherapy 190–201
Cohen, J. 128
cohesion 46
collaborative empiricism 190, 194
Collins, N. L. 190
colostomy 172, 174, 175, 181
comfort foods 222
communication skills 157, 162
comorbidity 64, 77, 219, 220, 226;
comparison 25; *see also* social
    comparison
compassion 44–5, 183; self 166
compensation 16, 145, 221, 238
competencies 6, 17, 22, 46; self-conscious
    4, 7, 12, 26; unfolding 4
competition 7, 8, 244; enhanced 143;
    intensified 30; social 239–41, 243
competitiveness 145
complexion 206
compliance 23; versus aggression 159
complicity 38
compliments 108, 208
compromises 156
compulsive behaviours 222, 228, 278
concealment 6, 15, 19, 21, 38, 43, 104,
    105, 108, 130, 131, 137, 144–5, 160,
    188, 231, 237, 244, 262–3; as coping
    strategy 167
conditioning 230
confession 214
confidence 8; growing sense of 61; lack
    of 59; low 32; major impact on 45;
    reduced 189; social 162, 226
conflicts 30, 175, 189, 193; destructive,
    non-assertive ways of dealing with
    236; family 238; group-group 248;